FREE Test Taking Tips DVD Offer

To help us better serve you, we have developed a Test Taking Tips DVD that we would like to give you for FREE. **This DVD covers world-class test taking tips that you can use to be even more successful when you are taking your test.**

All that we ask is that you email us your feedback about your study guide. Please let us know what you thought about it – whether that is good, bad or indifferent.

To get your **FREE Test Taking Tips DVD**, email freedvd@studyguideteam.com with "FREE DVD" in the subject line and the following information in the body of the email:

   a. The title of your study guide.

   b. Your product rating on a scale of 1-5, with 5 being the highest rating.

   c. Your feedback about the study guide. What did you think of it?

   d. Your full name and shipping address to send your free DVD.

If you have any questions or concerns, please don't hesitate to contact us at freedvd@studyguideteam.com.

Thanks again!

FSOT Study Guide Review

Test Prep & Practice Test Questions for the
Written Exam & Oral Assessment on the
Foreign Service Officer Test

FSOT Test Prep Team

Table of Contents

Quick Overview

As you draw closer to taking your exam, effective preparation becomes more and more important. Thankfully, you have this study guide to help you get ready. Use this guide to help keep your studying on track and refer to it often.

This study guide contains several key sections that will help you be successful on your exam. The guide contains tips for what you should do the night before and the day of the test. Also included are test-taking tips. Knowing the right information is not always enough. Many well-prepared test takers struggle with exams. These tips will help equip you to accurately read, assess, and answer test questions.

A large part of the guide is devoted to showing you what content to expect on the exam and to helping you better understand that content. Near the end of this guide is a practice test so that you can see how well you have grasped the content. Then, answer explanations are provided so that you can understand why you missed certain questions.

Don't try to cram the night before you take your exam. This is not a wise strategy for a few reasons. First, your retention of the information will be low. Your time would be better used by reviewing information you already know rather than trying to learn a lot of new information. Second, you will likely become stressed as you try to gain a large amount of knowledge in a short amount of time. Third, you will be depriving yourself of sleep. So be sure to go to bed at a reasonable time the night before. Being well-rested helps you focus and remain calm.

Be sure to eat a substantial breakfast the morning of the exam. If you are taking the exam in the afternoon, be sure to have a good lunch as well. Being hungry is distracting and can make it difficult to focus. You have hopefully spent lots of time preparing for the exam. Don't let an empty stomach get in the way of success!

When travelling to the testing center, leave earlier than needed. That way, you have a buffer in case you experience any delays. This will help you remain calm and will keep you from missing your appointment time at the testing center.

Be sure to pace yourself during the exam. Don't try to rush through the exam. There is no need to risk performing poorly on the exam just so you can leave the testing center early. Allow yourself to use all of the allotted time if needed.

Remain positive while taking the exam even if you feel like you are performing poorly. Thinking about the content you should have mastered will not help you perform better on the exam.

Once the exam is complete, take some time to relax. Even if you feel that you need to take the exam again, you will be well served by some down time before you begin studying again. It's often easier to convince yourself to study if you know that it will come with a reward!

Test-Taking Strategies

1. Predicting the Answer

When you feel confident in your preparation for a multiple-choice test, try predicting the answer before reading the answer choices. This is especially useful on questions that test objective factual knowledge or that ask you to fill in a blank. By predicting the answer before reading the available choices, you eliminate the possibility that you will be distracted or led astray by an incorrect answer choice. You will feel more confident in your selection if you read the question, predict the answer, and then find your prediction among the answer choices. After using this strategy, be sure to still read all of the answer choices carefully and completely. If you feel unprepared, you should not attempt to predict the answers. This would be a waste of time and an opportunity for your mind to wander in the wrong direction.

2. Reading the Whole Question

Too often, test takers scan a multiple-choice question, recognize a few familiar words, and immediately jump to the answer choices. Test authors are aware of this common impatience, and they will sometimes prey upon it. For instance, a test author might subtly turn the question into a negative, or he or she might redirect the focus of the question right at the end. The only way to avoid falling into these traps is to read the entirety of the question carefully before reading the answer choices.

3. Looking for Wrong Answers

Long and complicated multiple-choice questions can be intimidating. One way to simplify a difficult multiple-choice question is to eliminate all of the answer choices that are clearly wrong. In most sets of answers, there will be at least one selection that can be dismissed right away. If the test is administered on paper, the test taker could draw a line through it to indicate that it may be ignored; otherwise, the test taker will have to perform this operation mentally or on scratch paper. In either case, once the obviously incorrect answers have been eliminated, the remaining choices may be considered. Sometimes identifying the clearly wrong answers will give the test taker some information about the correct answer. For instance, if one of the remaining answer choices is a direct opposite of one of the eliminated answer choices, it may well be the correct answer. The opposite of obviously wrong is obviously right! Of course, this is not always the case. Some answers are obviously incorrect simply because they are irrelevant to the question being asked. Still, identifying and eliminating some incorrect answer choices is a good way to simplify a multiple-choice question.

4. Don't Overanalyze

Anxious test takers often overanalyze questions. When you are nervous, your brain will often run wild, causing you to make associations and discover clues that don't actually exist. If you feel that this may be a problem for you, do whatever you can to slow down during the test. Try taking a deep breath or counting to ten. As you read and consider the question, restrict yourself to the particular words used by the author. Avoid thought tangents about what the author *really* meant, or what he or she was *trying* to say. The only things that matter on a multiple-choice test are the words that are actually in the question. You must avoid reading too much into a multiple-choice question, or supposing that the writer meant something other than what he or she wrote.

5. No Need for Panic

It is wise to learn as many strategies as possible before taking a multiple-choice test, but it is likely that you will come across a few questions for which you simply don't know the answer. In this situation, avoid panicking. Because most multiple-choice tests include dozens of questions, the relative value of a single wrong answer is small. Moreover, your failure on one question has no effect on your success elsewhere on the test. As much as possible, you should compartmentalize each question on a multiple-choice test. In other words, you should not allow your feelings about one question to affect your success on the others. When you find a question that you either don't understand or don't know how to answer, just take a deep breath and do your best. Read the entire question slowly and carefully. Try rephrasing the question a couple of different ways. Then, read all of the answer choices carefully. After eliminating obviously wrong answers, make a selection and move on to the next question.

6. Confusing Answer Choices

When working on a difficult multiple-choice question, there may be a tendency to focus on the answer choices that are the easiest to understand. Many people, whether consciously or not, gravitate to the answer choices that require the least concentration, knowledge, and memory. This is a mistake. When you come across an answer choice that is confusing, you should give it extra attention. A question might be confusing because you do not know the subject matter to which it refers. If this is the case, don't eliminate the answer before you have affirmatively settled on another. When you come across an answer choice of this type, set it aside as you look at the remaining choices. If you can confidently assert that one of the other choices is correct, you can leave the confusing answer aside. Otherwise, you will need to take a moment to try to better understand the confusing answer choice. Rephrasing is one way to tease out the sense of a confusing answer choice.

7. Your First Instinct

Many people struggle with multiple-choice tests because they overthink the questions. If you have studied sufficiently for the test, you should be prepared to trust your first instinct once you have carefully and completely read the question and all of the answer choices. There is a great deal of research suggesting that the mind can come to the correct conclusion very quickly once it has obtained all of the relevant information. At times, it may seem to you as if your intuition is working faster even than your reasoning mind. This may in fact be true. The knowledge you obtain while studying may be retrieved from your subconscious before you have a chance to work out the associations that support it. Verify your instinct by working out the reasons that it should be trusted.

8. Key Words

Many test takers struggle with multiple-choice questions because they have poor reading comprehension skills. Quickly reading and understanding a multiple-choice question requires a mixture of skill and experience. To help with this, try jotting down a few key words and phrases on a piece of scrap paper. Doing this concentrates the process of reading and forces the mind to weigh the relative importance of the question's parts. In selecting words and phrases to write down, the test taker thinks about the question more deeply and carefully. This is especially true for multiple-choice questions that are preceded by a long prompt.

9. Subtle Negatives

One of the oldest tricks in the multiple-choice test writer's book is to subtly reverse the meaning of a question with a word like *not* or *except*. If you are not paying attention to each word in the question, you can easily be led astray by this trick. For instance, a common question format is, "Which of the following is…?" Obviously, if the question instead is, "Which of the following is not…?," then the answer will be quite different. Even worse, the test makers are aware of the potential for this mistake and will include one answer choice that would be correct if the question were not negated or reversed. A test taker who misses the reversal will find what he or she believes to be a correct answer and will be so confident that he or she will fail to reread the question and discover the original error. The only way to avoid this is to practice a wide variety of multiple-choice questions and to pay close attention to each and every word.

10. Reading Every Answer Choice

It may seem obvious, but you should always read every one of the answer choices! Too many test takers fall into the habit of scanning the question and assuming that they understand the question because they recognize a few key words. From there, they pick the first answer choice that answers the question they believe they have read. Test takers who read all of the answer choices might discover that one of the latter answer choices is actually *more* correct. Moreover, reading all of the answer choices can remind you of facts related to the question that can help you arrive at the correct answer. Sometimes, a misstatement or incorrect detail in one of the latter answer choices will trigger your memory of the subject and will enable you to find the right answer. Failing to read all of the answer choices is like not reading all of the items on a restaurant menu: you might miss out on the perfect choice.

11. Spot the Hedges

One of the keys to success on multiple-choice tests is paying close attention to every word. This is never more true than with words like *almost*, *most*, *some*, and *sometimes*. These words are called "hedges" because they indicate that a statement is not totally true or not true in every place and time. An absolute statement will contain no hedges, but in many subjects, like literature and history, the answers are not always straightforward or absolute. There are always exceptions to the rules in these subjects. For this reason, you should favor those multiple-choice questions that contain hedging language. The presence of qualifying words indicates that the author is taking special care with his or her words, which is certainly important when composing the right answer. After all, there are many ways to be wrong, but there is only one way to be right! For this reason, it is wise to avoid answers that are absolute when taking a multiple-choice test. An absolute answer is one that says things are either all one way or all another. They often include words like *every*, *always*, *best*, and *never*. If you are taking a multiple-choice test in a subject that doesn't lend itself to absolute answers, be on your guard if you see any of these words.

12. Long Answers

In many subject areas, the answers are not simple. As already mentioned, the right answer often requires hedges. Another common feature of the answers to a complex or subjective question are qualifying clauses, which are groups of words that subtly modify the meaning of the sentence. If the question or answer choice describes a rule to which there are exceptions or the subject matter is complicated, ambiguous, or confusing, the correct answer will require many words in order to be expressed clearly and accurately. In essence, you should not be deterred by answer choices that seem excessively long. Oftentimes, the author of the text will not be able to write the correct answer without offering some qualifications and modifications. Your job is to read the answer choices thoroughly and completely and to select the one that most accurately and precisely answers the question.

13. Restating to Understand

Sometimes, a question on a multiple-choice test is difficult not because of what it asks but because of how it is written. If this is the case, restate the question or answer choice in different words. This process serves a couple of important purposes. First, it forces you to concentrate on the core of the question. In order to rephrase the question accurately, you have to understand it well. Rephrasing the question will concentrate your mind on the key words and ideas. Second, it will present the information to your mind in a fresh way. This process may trigger your memory and render some useful scrap of information picked up while studying.

14. True Statements

Sometimes an answer choice will be true in itself, but it does not answer the question. This is one of the main reasons why it is essential to read the question carefully and completely before proceeding to the answer choices. Too often, test takers skip ahead to the answer choices and look for true statements. Having found one of these, they are content to select it without reference to the question above. Obviously, this provides an easy way for test makers to play tricks. The savvy test taker will always read the entire question before turning to the answer choices. Then, having settled on a correct answer choice, he or she will refer to the original question and ensure that the selected answer is relevant. The mistake of choosing a correct-but-irrelevant answer choice is especially common on questions related to specific pieces of objective knowledge, like historical or scientific facts. A prepared test taker will have a wealth of factual knowledge at his or her disposal, and should not be careless in its application.

15. No Patterns

One of the more dangerous ideas that circulates about multiple-choice tests is that the correct answers tend to fall into patterns. These erroneous ideas range from a belief that B and C are the most common right answers, to the idea that an unprepared test-taker should answer "A-B-A-C-A-D-A-B-A." It cannot be emphasized enough that pattern-seeking of this type is exactly the WRONG way to approach a multiple-choice test. To begin with, it is highly unlikely that the test maker will plot the correct answers according to some predetermined pattern. The questions are scrambled and delivered in a random order. Furthermore, even if the test maker was following a pattern in the assignation of correct answers, there is no reason why the test taker would know which pattern he or she was using. Any attempt to discern a pattern in the answer choices is a waste of time and a distraction from the real work of taking the test. A test taker would be much better served by extra preparation before the test than by reliance on a pattern in the answers.

FREE DVD OFFER

Don't forget that doing well on your exam includes both understanding the test content and understanding how to use what you know to do well on the test. We offer a completely FREE Test Taking Tips DVD that covers world class test taking tips that you can use to be even more successful when you are taking your test.

All that we ask is that you email us your feedback about your study guide. To get your **FREE Test Taking Tips DVD**, email freedvd@studyguideteam.com with "FREE DVD" in the subject line and the following information in the body of the email:

- The title of your study guide.
- Your product rating on a scale of 1-5, with 5 being the highest rating.
- Your feedback about the study guide. What did you think of it?
- Your full name and shipping address to send your free DVD.

Introduction to the FSOT

Function of the Test

Taking the Foreign Service Officer Test (FSOT) is one step out of eight to being selected as a Foreign Service Officer (FSO). Those who have a desire to become an FSO must first choose a career track and then register for the FSOT exam. If a candidate passes the FSOT exam, they will move on to the next step in the process of being considered for an FSO.

Although there are no degrees specified in order to become an FSO, the knowledge and skills needed to understand and pass the FSOT are usually comparable to the education on the level of a Bachelor's degree. Additionally, no specific experience is required; however, it is suggested that candidates have strong leadership and negotiation skills and are able to provide sound judgment and analytical ability. Note that those who are considered to be Foreign Service Officers must be US citizens between the ages of 20 and 59. In a given year, approximately 20,000 people take the FSOT, and only 500 to 700 candidates are offered positions in the Foreign Service.

Test Administration

The FSOT is offered three times a year in February, June, and October in both domestic and overseas locations. Each month will have a testing window of eight days. The specific dates displaying when registration opens and closes is listed on the careers.state.gov website. Overseas, the FSOT is offered at Pearson Professional Centers (PPCs) or at some embassies, if available. A list of the FSOT offered in overseas cities is available on the careers.state.gov website. The FSOT will be offered at 130 on base test centers (OBTCs) in US states and territories, Europe, Asia, and the Middle East on US military installations.

Although there is no limit to how many times an individual can take the FSOT, one must wait at least 12 months before taking the test again. Note that those who need to request accommodations for the test can do so through the Pearson VUE website. Accommodations are considered on a case-by-case basis.

Test Format

At the testing center, be sure to bring a current, government or state-issued ID, or a passport, depending on the location. Photos will be taken before the test begins for security purposes, and candidates will be required to sign a Candidate Rules agreement form. The testing period is around 3 hours, so be sure to take care of everything beforehand. Candidates will not be allowed to use their cell phones or leave the testing room for any reason.

The FSOT is a multiple-choice test but also includes a writing section. The multiple-choice sections are Job Knowledge, Situational Judgment, and English Expression. The fourth section is a written essay test. The Job Knowledge section tests your ability on US government, US culture, US and world history, management theory, technology, psychology, world affairs, and economics and finance. The Situational Judgment section presents scenarios that might be potential circumstances of the FSO job, and asks you to choose the best and worse responses to any given situation. The English Expression tests your knowledge of grammar as well as composition. The following table gives an outline of the test:

Section	Questions	Time
Job Knowledge	60 questions	40 minutes
Situational Judgment	28 scenarios	42 minutes
English Expression	65 questions	50 minutes
Written Essay	1 question	30 minutes

Scoring

Although the Department of State does not give information regarding scoring or passing rates on the FSOT, candidates who have taken the test in the past state that the scaled passing score on the multiple-choice portion is 154 points, and a passing score of 6 out of 12 is required on the essay.

Recent Developments

The Situational Judgment section, described above, replaced the Biographic Information Questionnaire beginning in October 2017. The Biographic Information Questionnaire asked personal questions such as work style, communication with others, and one's approach to other cultures. The Situational Judgment section asks how you would react in a given scenario related to an FSO position.

Correct Grammar, Organization, Writing Strategy, Sentence Structure, and Punctuation Required for Writing or Editing Reports

This knowledge area encompasses English expression and language usage skills required for preparing or editing written reports, including correct grammar and good writing at the sentence and paragraph level.

Grammar

Nouns

A noun is a person, place, thing, or idea. All nouns fit into one of two types, common or proper.

A *common noun* is a word that identifies any of a class of people, places, or things. Examples include numbers, objects, animals, feelings, concepts, qualities, and actions. *A, an,* or *the* usually precedes the common noun. These parts of speech are called *articles*. Here are some examples of sentences using nouns preceded by articles.

> *A* building is under construction.
> *The* girl would like to move to *the* city.

A *proper noun* (also called a *proper name*) is used for the specific name of an individual person, place, or organization. The first letter in a proper noun is capitalized. "My name is *Mary*." "I work for *Walmart*."

Nouns sometimes serve as adjectives (which themselves describe nouns), such as "hockey player" and "state government."

An abstract noun is an idea, state, or quality. It is something that can't be touched, such as happiness, courage, evil, or humor.

A concrete noun is something that can be experienced through the senses (touch, taste, hear, smell, see). Examples of concrete nouns are birds, skateboard, pie, and car.

A collective noun refers to a collection of people, places, or things that act as one. Examples of collective nouns are as follows: team, class, jury, family, audience, and flock.

Pronouns

A word used in place of a noun is known as a *pronoun*. Pronouns are words like *I, mine, hers,* and *us.*

Pronouns can be split into different classifications (seen below) which make them easier to learn; however, it's not important to memorize the classifications.

- Personal pronouns: refer to people

- First person: we, I, our, mine

- Second person: you, yours

- Third person: he, them

- Possessive pronouns: demonstrate ownership (mine, my, his, yours)

- Interrogative pronouns: ask questions (what, which, who, whom, whose)

- Relative pronouns: include the five interrogative pronouns and others that are relative (whoever, whomever, that, when, where)

- Demonstrative pronouns: replace something specific (this, that, those, these)

- Reciprocal pronouns: indicate something was done or given in return (each other, one another)

- Indefinite pronouns: have a nonspecific status (anybody, whoever, someone, everybody, somebody)

Indefinite pronouns such as *anybody, whoever, someone, everybody,* and *somebody* command a singular verb form, but others such as *all, none,* and *some* could require a singular or plural verb form.

Antecedents

An *antecedent* is the noun to which a pronoun refers; it needs to be written or spoken before the pronoun is used. For many pronouns, antecedents are imperative for clarity. In particular, many of the personal, possessive, and demonstrative pronouns need antecedents. Otherwise, it would be unclear who or what someone is referring to when they use a pronoun like *he* or *this.*

Pronoun reference means that the pronoun should refer clearly to one, clear, unmistakable noun (the antecedent).

Pronoun-antecedent agreement refers to the need for the antecedent and the corresponding pronoun to agree in gender, person, and number. Here are some examples:

The *kidneys* (plural antecedent) are part of the urinary system. *They* (plural pronoun) serve several roles."

The kidneys are part of the *urinary system* (singular antecedent). *It* (singular pronoun) is also known as the renal system.

Pronoun Cases

The subjective pronouns —*I, you, he/she/it, we, they,* and *who*—are the subjects of the sentence.

Example: *They* have a new house.

The objective pronouns—*me, you* (singular), *him/her, us, them,* and *whom*—are used when something is being done for or given to someone; they are objects of the action.

Example: The teacher has an apple for *us.*

The possessive pronouns—*mine, my, your, yours, his, hers, its, their, theirs, our,* and *ours*—are used to denote that something (or someone) belongs to someone (or something).

Example: It's *their* chocolate cake.
Even Better Example: It's *my* chocolate cake!

One of the greatest challenges and worst abuses of pronouns concerns *who* and *whom*. Just knowing the following rule can eliminate confusion. *Who* is a subjective-case pronoun used only as a subject or subject complement. *Whom* is only objective-case and, therefore, the object of the verb or preposition.

Hint: When using *who* or *whom*, think of whether someone would say *he* or *him*. If the answer is *he*, use *who*. If the answer is *him*, use *whom*. This trick is easy to remember because *he* and *who* both end in vowels, and *him* and *whom* both end in the letter *M*.

<u>Verbs</u>
The *verb* is the part of speech that describes an action, state of being, or occurrence.

A *verb* forms the main part of a predicate of a sentence. This means that the verb explains what the noun (which will be discussed shortly) is doing. A simple example is *time <u>flies</u>*. The verb *flies* explains what the action of the noun, *time*, is doing. This example is a *main* verb.

Helping (auxiliary) verbs are words like *have, do, be, can, may, should, must,* and *will.* "I *should* go to the store." Helping verbs assist main verbs in expressing tense, ability, possibility, permission, or obligation.

Particles are minor function words like *not, in, out, up,* or *down* that become part of the verb itself. "I might *not*."

Participles are words formed from verbs that are often used to modify a noun, noun phrase, verb, or verb phrase.

The *running* teenager collided with the cyclist.

Participles can also create compound verb forms.

He is *speaking*.

Verbs have five basic forms: the *base* form, the *-s* form, the *-ing* form, the *past* form, and the *past participle* form.

The *past* forms are either *regular* (*love/loved; hate/hated*) or *irregular* because they don't end by adding the common past tense suffix "-ed" (*go/went; fall/fell; set/set*).

<u>Verb Forms</u>
Shifting verb forms entails *conjugation*, which is used to indicate *tense, voice,* or *mood*.

Verb tense is used to show when the action in the sentence took place. There are several different verb tenses, and it is important to know how and when to use them. Some verb tenses can be achieved by changing the form of the verb, while others require the use of helping verbs (e.g., *is, was,* or *has*).

- Present tense shows the action is happening currently or is ongoing:

    I walk to work every morning.

    She is stressed about the deadline.

- Past tense shows that the action happened in the past or that the state of being is in the past:

  I walked to work yesterday morning.

  She was stressed about the deadline.

- Future tense shows that the action will happen in the future or is a future state of being:

  I will walk to work tomorrow morning.

  She will be stressed about the deadline.

- Present perfect tense shows action that began in the past, but continues into the present:

  I have walked to work all week.

  She has been stressed about the deadline.

- Past perfect tense shows an action was finished before another took place:

  I had walked all week until I sprained my ankle.

  She had been stressed about the deadline until we talked about it.

- Future perfect tense shows an action that will be completed at some point in the future:

  By the time the bus arrives, I will have walked to work already.

Voice

Verbs can be in the active or passive voice. When the subject completes the action, the verb is in *active voice*. When the subject receives the action of the sentence, the verb is in *passive voice*.

Active: Jamie ate the ice cream.

Passive: The ice cream was eaten by Jamie.

In active voice, the subject (*Jamie*) is the "do-er" of the action (*ate*). In passive voice, the subject *ice cream* receives the action of being eaten.

While passive voice can add variety to writing, active voice is the generally preferred sentence structure.

Mood

Mood is used to show the speaker's feelings about the subject matter. In English, there is *indicative mood, imperative mood,* and *subjective mood.*

Indicative mood is used to state facts, ask questions, or state opinions:

Bob will make the trip next week.

When can Bob make the trip?

Imperative mood is used to state a command or make a request:

Wait in the lobby.

Please call me next week.

Subjunctive mood is used to express a wish, an opinion, or a hope that is contrary to fact:

If I were in charge, none of this would have happened.

Allison wished she could take the exam over again when she saw her score.

Adjectives

Adjectives are words used to modify nouns and pronouns. They can be used alone or in a series and are used to further define or describe the nouns they modify.

Mark made us a delicious, four-course meal.

The words *delicious* and *four-course* are adjectives that describe the kind of meal Mark made.

Articles are also considered adjectives because they help to describe nouns. Articles can be general or specific. The three articles in English are: a, an, and the.

Indefinite articles (a, an) are used to refer to nonspecific nouns. The article *a* proceeds words beginning with consonant sounds, and the article *an* proceeds words beginning with vowel sounds.

A car drove by our house.

An alligator was loose at the zoo.

He has always wanted a ukulele. (The first *u* makes a *y* sound.)

Note that *a* and *an* should only proceed nonspecific nouns that are also singular. If a nonspecific noun is plural, it does not need a preceding article.

Alligators were loose at the zoo.

The *definite article (the)* is used to refer to specific nouns:

The car pulled into our driveway.

Note that *the* should proceed all specific nouns regardless of whether they are singular or plural.

The cars pulled into our driveway.

Comparative adjectives are used to compare nouns. When they are used in this way, they take on positive, comparative, or superlative form.

The positive form is the normal form of the adjective:

Alicia is tall.

The *comparative* form shows a comparison between two things:

Alicia is taller than Maria.

Superlative form shows comparison between more than two things:

Alicia is the tallest girl in her class.

Usually, the comparative and superlative can be made by adding *–er* and *–est* to the positive form, but some verbs call for the helping verbs *more* or *most*. Other exceptions to the rule include adjectives like *bad*, which uses the comparative *worse* and the superlative *worst*.

An adjective phrase is not a bunch of adjectives strung together, but a group of words that describes a noun or pronoun and, thus, functions as an adjective. *Very ugly* is an adjective phrase; so are *way too fat* and *faster than a speeding bullet.*

Adverbs

Adverbs have more functions than adjectives because they modify or qualify verbs, adjectives, or other adverbs as well as word groups that express a relation of place, time, circumstance, or cause. Therefore, adverbs answer any of the following questions: *How, when, where, why, in what way, how often, how much, in what condition,* and/or *to what degree. How good looking is he? He is <u>very</u> handsome.*

Here are some examples of adverbs for different situations:

- how: quickly
- when: daily
- where: there
- in what way: easily
- how often: often
- how much: much
- in what condition: badly
- what degree: hardly

As one can see, for some reason, many adverbs end in *-ly.*

Adverbs do things like emphasize (*really, simply,* and *so*), amplify (*heartily, completely,* and *positively*), and tone down (*almost, somewhat,* and *mildly*).

Adverbs also come in phrases.

The dog ran as <u>though his life depended on it.</u>

Prepositions

Prepositions are connecting words and, while there are only about 150 of them, they are used more often than any other individual groups of words. They describe relationships between other words. They are placed before a noun or pronoun, forming a phrase that modifies another word in the sentence. *Prepositional phrases* begin with a preposition and end with a noun or pronoun, the *object of the preposition. A pristine lake is <u>near the store</u> and <u>behind the bank</u>.*

Some commonly used prepositions are *about, after, anti, around, as, at, behind, beside, by, for, from, in, into, of, off, on, to,* and *with.*

Complex prepositions, which also come before a noun or pronoun, consist of two or three words such as *according to, in regards to,* and *because of.*

Conjunctions

Conjunctions are vital words that connect words, phrases, thoughts, and ideas. Conjunctions show relationships between components. There are two types:

Coordinating conjunctions are the primary class of conjunctions placed between words, phrases, clauses, and sentences that are of equal grammatical rank; the coordinating conjunctions are *or, and, nor, but, or, yes,* and *so.* A useful memorization trick is to remember that the first letter of these conjunctions collectively spell the word *fanboys.*

> I need to go shopping, *but* I must be careful to leave enough money in the bank.
> She wore a black, red, *and* white shirt.

Subordinating conjunctions are the secondary class of conjunctions. They connect two unequal parts, one *main* (or *independent*) and the other *subordinate* (or *dependent*). I must go to the store *even though* I do not have enough money in the bank.

> *Because* I read the review, I do not want to go to the movie.

Notice that the presence of subordinating conjunctions makes clauses dependent. *I read the movie* is an independent clause, but *because* makes the clause dependent. Thus, it needs an independent clause to complete the sentence.

Interjections

Interjections are words used to express emotion. Examples include *wow, ouch,* and *hooray.* Interjections are often separate from sentences; in those cases, the interjection is directly followed by an exclamation point. In other cases, the interjection is included in a sentence and followed by a comma. The punctuation plays a big role in the intensity of the emotion that the interjection is expressing. Using a comma or semicolon indicates less excitement than using an exclamation mark..

Subjects

Every sentence must include a subject and a verb. The *subject* of a sentence is who or what the sentence is about. It's often directly stated and can be determined by asking "Who?" or "What?" did the action:

Most sentences contain a direct subject, in which the subject is mentioned in the sentence.

> *Kelly mowed the lawn.*

> Who mowed the lawn? *Kelly*

> *The air-conditioner ran all night*

> What ran all night? *the air-conditioner*

The subject of imperative sentences is *you,* because imperative subjects are commands. the subject is implied because it is a command:

> *Go home after the meeting.*

> Who should go home after the meeting? *you* (implied)

In *expletive sentences* that start with "there are" or "there is," the subject is found after the predicate. The subject cannot be "there," so it must be another word in the sentence:

> *There is a cup sitting on the coffee table.*

> What is sitting on the coffee table? *a cup*

Simple and Complete Subjects

A *complete subject* includes the simple subject and all the words modifying it, including articles and adjectives. A *simple subject* is the single noun without its modifiers.

> A warm, chocolate-chip cookie sat on the kitchen table.

> Complete subject: *a warm, chocolate-chip cookie*

> Simple subject: *cookie*

The words *a, warm, chocolate,* and *chip* all modify the simple subject *cookie.*

There might also be a *compound subject*, which would be two or more nouns without the modifiers.

> A little girl and her mother walked into the shop.

> Complete subject: *A little girl and her mother*

> Compound subject: *girl, mother*

In this case, *the girl and her mother* are both completing the action of walking into the shop, so this is a *compound subject.*

Predicates

In addition to the subject, a sentence must also have a predicate. The *predicate* contains a verb and tells something about the subject. In addition to the verb, a predicate can also contain a direct or indirect object, object of a preposition, and other phrases.

> The cats napped on the front porch.

In this sentence, *cats* is the subject because they are who or what the sentence is about.

The *complete predicate* is everything else in the sentence: *napped on the front porch.* This phrase is the predicate because it tells us what the cats did.

This sentence can be broken down into a simple subject and predicate:

> Cats napped.

In this sentence, *cats* is the simple subject, and *napped* is the *simple predicate.*

Although the sentence is very short and doesn't offer much information, it's still considered a complete sentence because it contains a subject and predicate.

Like a compound subject, a sentence can also have a **compound predicate**. This is when the subject is or does two or more things in the sentence.

> This easy chair reclines and swivels.

In this sentence, *this easy chair* is the complete subject. *Reclines and swivels* shows two actions of the chair, so this is the compound predicate.

Subject-Verb Agreement

The subject of a sentence and its verb must agree. The cornerstone rule of subject-verb agreement is that subject and verb must agree in number. Whether the subject is singular or plural, the verb must follow suit.

> Incorrect: The houses is new.
> Correct: The houses are new.
> Also Correct: The house is new.

In other words, a singular subject requires a singular verb; a plural subject requires a plural verb. The words or phrases that come between the subject and verb do not alter this rule.

> Incorrect: The houses built of brick is new.
> Correct: The houses built of brick are new.

> Incorrect: The houses with the sturdy porches is new.
> Correct: The houses with the sturdy porches are new.

The subject will always follow the verb when a sentence begins with *here* or *there*. Identify these with care.

> Incorrect: Here *is* the *houses* with sturdy porches.
> Correct: Here *are* the *houses* with sturdy porches.

The subject in the sentences above is not *here*, it is *houses*. Remember, *here* and *there* are never subjects. Be careful that contractions such as *here's* or *there're* do not cause confusion!

Two subjects joined by *and* require a plural verb form, except when the two combine to make one thing:

> Incorrect: Garrett and Jonathan is over there.
> Correct: Garrett and Jonathan are over there.

> Incorrect: Spaghetti and meatballs are a delicious meal!
> Correct: Spaghetti and meatballs is a delicious meal!

In the example above, *spaghetti and meatballs* is a compound noun. However, *Garrett and Jonathan* is not a compound noun.

Two singular subjects joined by *or, either/or,* or *neither/nor* call for a singular verb form.

> Incorrect: Butter or syrup are acceptable.
> Correct: Butter or syrup is acceptable.

Plural subjects joined by *or*, *either/or*, or *neither/nor* are, indeed, plural.

> The chairs or the boxes are being moved next.

If one subject is singular and the other is plural, the verb should agree with the closest noun.

> Correct: The chair or the boxes are being moved next.
> Correct: The chairs or the box is being moved next.

Some plurals of money, distance, and time call for a singular verb.

> Incorrect: Three dollars *are* enough to buy that.
> Correct: Three dollars *is* enough to buy that.

For words declaring degrees of quantity such as *many of, some of,* or *most of,* let the noun that follows *of* be the guide:

> Incorrect: Many of the books is in the shelf.
> Correct: Many of the books are in the shelf.

> Incorrect: Most of the pie *are* on the table.
> Correct: Most of the pie *is* on the table.

For indefinite pronouns like anybody or everybody, use singular verbs.

> Everybody *is* going to the store.

However, the pronouns *few, many, several, all, some,* and *both* have their own rules and use plural forms.

> Some *are* ready.

Some nouns like *crowd* and *congress* are called *collective nouns* and they require a singular verb form.

> Congress *is* in session.
> The news *is* over.

Books and movie titles, though, including plural nouns such as *Great Expectations*, also require a singular verb. Remember that only the subject affects the verb. While writing tricky subject-verb arrangements, say them aloud. Listen to them. Once the rules have been learned, one's ear will become sensitive to them, making it easier to pick out what's right and what's wrong.

Direct Objects
The *direct object* is the part of the sentence that receives the action of the verb. It is a noun and can usually be found after the verb. To find the direct object, first find the verb, and then ask the question *who* or *what* after it.

> The bear climbed the tree.

> What did the bear climb? *the tree*

Indirect Objects

An *indirect object* receives the direct object. It is usually found between the verb and the direct object. A strategy for identifying the indirect object is to find the verb and ask the questions *to whom/for whom* or *to what/ for what*.

> Jane made her daughter a cake.

> For whom did Jane make the cake? *her daughter*

Cake is the direct object because it is what Jane made, and *daughter* is the indirect object because she receives the cake.

Complements

A *complement* completes the meaning of an expression. A complement can be a pronoun, noun, or adjective. A verb complement refers to the direct object or indirect object in the sentence. An object complement gives more information about the direct object:

> The magician got the kids excited.

Kids is the direct object, and *excited* is the object complement.

A *subject complement* comes after a linking verb. It is typically an adjective or noun that gives more information about the subject:

> The king was noble and spared the thief's life.

Noble describes the *king* and follows the linking verb *was*.

Predicate Nouns

A *predicate noun* renames the subject:

> John is a carpenter.

The subject is *John*, and the predicate noun is *carpenter*.

Predicate Adjectives

A *predicate adjective* describes the subject:

> Margaret is beautiful.

The subject is *Margaret*, and the predicate adjective is *beautiful*.

Homonyms

Homonyms are words that sound the same but are spelled differently, and they have different meanings. There are several common homonyms that give writers trouble.

There, They're, and Their
The word *there* can be used as an adverb, adjective, or pronoun:

> *There* are ten children on the swim team this summer.

> I put my book over *there*, but now I can't find it.

The word *they're* is a contraction of the words *they* and *are*:

> *They're* flying in from Texas on Tuesday.

The word *their* is a possessive pronoun:

> I store *their* winter clothes in the attic.

Its and It's
Its is a possessive pronoun:

> The cat licked *its* injured paw.

It's is the contraction for the words *it* and *is*:

> *It's* unbelievable how many people opted not to vote in the last election.

Your and You're
Your is a possessive pronoun:

> Can I borrow *your* lawnmower this weekend?

You're is a contraction for the words *you* and *are*:

> *You're* about to embark on a fantastic journey.

To, Too, and Two
To is an adverb or a preposition used to show direction, relationship, or purpose:

> We are going *to* New York.

> They are going *to* see a show.

Too is an adverb that means more than enough, also, and very:

> You have had *too* much candy.

> We are on vacation that week, *too*.

Two is the written-out form of the numeral 2:

> *Two* of the shirts didn't fit, so I will have to return them.

New and Knew
New is an adjective that means recent:

> There's a *new* customer on the phone.

Knew is the past tense of the verb *know*:

> I *knew* you'd have fun on this ride.

Affect and Effect

Affect and *effect* are complicated because they are used as both nouns and verbs, have similar meanings, and are pronounced the same.

	Affect	**Effect**
Noun Definition	emotional state	result
Noun Example	The patient's affect was flat.	The effects of smoking are well documented.
Verb Definition	to influence	to bring about
Verb Example	The pollen count affects my allergies.	The new candidate hopes to effect change.

Independent and Dependent Clauses

Independent and *dependent* clauses are strings of words that contain both a subject and a verb. An independent clause *can* stand alone as complete thought, but a dependent clause *cannot*. A dependent clause relies on other words to be a complete sentence.

> Independent clause: The keys are on the counter.
> Dependent clause: If the keys are on the counter

Notice that both clauses have a subject (*keys*) and a verb (*are*). The independent clause expresses a complete thought, but the word *if* at the beginning of the dependent clause makes it *dependent* on other words to be a complete thought.

> Independent clause: If the keys are on the counter, please give them to me.

This presents a complete sentence since it includes at least one verb and one subject and is a complete thought. In this case, the independent clause has two subjects (*keys* & an implied *you*) and two verbs (*are* & *give*).

> Independent clause: I went to the store.
> Dependent clause: Because we are out of milk,
>
> Complete Sentence: Because we are out of milk, I went to the store.
> Complete Sentence: I went to the store because we are out of milk.

Phrases

A *phrase* is a group of words that do not make a complete thought or a clause. They are parts of sentences or clauses. Phrases can be used as nouns, adjectives, or adverbs. A phrase does not contain both a subject and a verb.

Prepositional Phrases

A *prepositional phrase* shows the relationship between a word in the sentence and the object of the preposition. The object of the preposition is a noun that follows the preposition.

> The orange pillows are on the couch.

On is the preposition, and *couch* is the object of the preposition.

> She brought her friend with the nice car.

With is the preposition, and *car* is the object of the preposition. Here are some common prepositions:

about	as	at	after
by	for	from	in
of	on	to	with

Verbals and Verbal Phrases

Verbals are forms of verbs that act as other parts of speech. They can be used as nouns, adjectives, or adverbs. Though they are use verb forms, they are not to be used as the verb in the sentence. A word group that is based on a verbal is considered a *verbal phrase*. There are three major types of verbals: *participles, gerunds,* and *infinitives.*

Participles are verbals that act as adjectives. The present participle ends in *–ing*, and the past participle ends in *–d, -ed, -n, or-t*.

Verb	Present Participle	Past Participle
walk	walking	walked
share	sharing	shared

Participial phrases are made up of the participle and modifiers, complements, or objects.

> Crying for most of an hour, the baby didn't seem to want to nap.

> Having already taken this course, the student was bored during class.

> *Crying for most of an hour* and *Having already taken this course* are the participial phrases.

Gerunds are verbals that are used as nouns and end in *–ing*. A gerund can be the subject or object of the sentence like a noun. Note that a present participle can also end in *–ing*, so it is important to distinguish between the two. The gerund is used as a noun, while the participle is used as an adjective.

> Swimming is my favorite sport.

> I wish I were sleeping.

A *gerund phrase* includes the gerund and any modifiers or complements, direct objects, indirect objects, or pronouns.

> Cleaning the house is my least favorite weekend activity.

Cleaning the house is the gerund phrase acting as the subject of the sentence.

> The most important goal this year is raising money for charity.

Raising money for charity is the gerund phrase acting as the direct object.

> The police accused the woman of stealing the car.

The *gerund* phrase *stealing the car* is the object of the preposition in this sentence.

An *infinitive* is a verbal made up of the word to and a verb. Infinitives can be used as nouns, adjectives, or adverbs.

Examples: To eat, to jump, to swim, to lie, to call, to work

An *infinitive phrase* is made up of the infinitive plus any complements or modifiers. The infinitive phrase *to wait* is used as the subject in this sentence:

To wait was not what I had in mind.

The infinitive phrase *to sing* is used as the subject complement in this sentence:

Her dream is to sing.

The infinitive phrase *to grow* is used as an adverb in this sentence:

Children must eat to grow.

Appositive Phrases

An *appositive* is a noun or noun phrase that renames a noun that comes immediately before it in the sentence. An appositive can be a single word or several words. These phrases can be *essential* or *nonessential*. An essential appositive phrase is necessary to the meaning of the sentence and a nonessential appositive phrase is not. It is important to be able to distinguish these for purposes of comma use.

Essential: My sister Christina works at a school.

Naming which sister is essential to the meaning of the sentence, so no commas are needed.

Nonessential: My sister, who is a teacher, is coming over for dinner tonight.

Who is a teacher is not essential to the meaning of the sentence, so commas are required.

Absolute Phrases

An *absolute phrase* modifies a noun without using a conjunction. It is not the subject of the sentence and is not a complete thought on its own. Absolute phrases are set off from the independent clause with a comma.

Arms outstretched, she yelled at the sky.

All things considered, this has been a great day.

Organization

Good writing is not merely a random collection of sentences. No matter how well written, sentences must relate and coordinate appropriately with one another. If not, the writing seems random, haphazard, and disorganized. Therefore, good writing must be organized, where each sentence fits a larger context and relates to the sentences around it.

Transition Words

The writer should act as a guide, showing the reader how all the sentences fit together. Consider the seat belt example again:

> Seat belts save more lives than any other automobile safety feature. Many studies show that airbags save lives as well. Not all cars have airbags. Many older cars don't. Air bags aren't entirely reliable. Studies show that in 15% of accidents, airbags don't deploy as designed. Seat belt malfunctions are extremely rare.

There's nothing wrong with any of these sentences individually, but together they're disjointed and difficult to follow. The best way for the writer to communicate information is through the use of transition words. Here are examples of transition words and phrases that tie sentences together, enabling a more natural flow:

- To show causality: *as a result, therefore,* and *consequently*
- To compare and contrast: *however, but,* and *on the other hand*
- To introduce examples: *for instance, namely,* and *including*
- To show order of importance: *foremost, primarily, secondly,* and *lastly*

NOTE: This is not a complete list of transitions. There are many more that can be used; however, most fit into these or similar categories. The important point is that the words should clearly show the relationship between sentences, supporting information, and the main idea.

Here is an update to the previous example using transition words. These changes make it easier to read and bring clarity to the writer's points:

> Seat belts save more lives than any other automobile safety feature. Many studies show that airbags save lives as well; however, not all cars have airbags. For instance, some older cars don't. Furthermore, air bags aren't entirely reliable. For example, studies show that in 15% of accidents, airbags don't deploy as designed, but, on the other hand, seat belt malfunctions are extremely rare.

Also be prepared to analyze whether the writer is using the best transition word or phrase for the situation. Take this sentence for example: "As a result, seat belt malfunctions are extremely rare." This sentence doesn't make sense in the context above because the writer is trying to show the contrast between seat belts and airbags, not the causality.

Logical Sequence

Even if the writer includes plenty of information to support their point, the writing is only coherent when the information is in a logical order. First, the writer should introduce the main idea, whether for a paragraph, a section, or the entire piece. Then they should present evidence to support the main idea by using transitional language. This shows the reader how the information relates to the main idea and to the sentences around it. The writer should then take time to interpret the information, making sure necessary connections are obvious to the reader. Finally, the writer can summarize the information in a closing section.

Though most writing follows this pattern, it isn't a set rule. Sometimes writers change the order for effect. For example, the writer can begin with a surprising piece of supporting information to grab the reader's attention, and then transition to the main idea. Thus, if a passage doesn't follow the logical order, don't immediately assume it's wrong. However, most writing usually settles into a logical sequence after a nontraditional beginning.

Introductions and Conclusions

Examining the writer's strategies for introductions and conclusions puts the reader in the right mindset to interpret the rest of the text. Look for methods the writer might use for introductions such as:

- Stating the main point immediately, followed by outlining how the rest of the piece supports this claim.

- Establishing important, smaller pieces of the main idea first, and then grouping these points into a case for the main idea.

- Opening with a quotation, anecdote, question, seeming paradox, or other piece of interesting information, and then using it to lead to the main point.

Whatever method the writer chooses, the introduction should make their intention clear, establish their voice as a credible one, and encourage a person to continue reading.

Conclusions tend to follow a similar pattern. In them, the writer restates their main idea a final time, often after summarizing the smaller pieces of that idea. If the introduction uses a quote or anecdote to grab the reader's attention, the conclusion often makes reference to it again. Whatever way the writer chooses to arrange the conclusion, the final restatement of the main idea should be clear and simple for the reader to interpret. Finally, conclusions shouldn't introduce any new information.

Writing Strategy

Distinguishing Between Common Modes of Writing

To distinguish between the common modes of writing, it is important to identify the primary purpose of the work. This can be determined by considering what the author is trying to say to the reader. Although there are countless different styles of writing, all written works tend to fall under four primary categories: argumentative/persuasive, informative expository, descriptive, and narrative.

The below table highlights the purpose, distinct characteristics, and examples of each rhetorical mode.

Writing Mode	Purpose	Distinct Characteristics	Examples
Argumentative	To persuade	Opinions, loaded or subjective language, evidence, suggestions of what the reader should do, calls to action	Critical reviews Political journals Letters of recommendation Cover letters Advertising
Informative	To teach or inform	Objective language, definitions, instructions, factual information	Business and scientific reports Textbooks Instruction manuals News articles Personal letters Wills Informative essays Travel guides Study guides
Descriptive	To deliver sensory details to the reader	Heavy use of adjectives and imagery, language that appeals to any of the five senses	Poetry Journal entries Often used in narrative mode
Narrative	To tell a story, share an experience, entertain	Series of events, plot, characters, dialogue, conflict	Novels Short stories Novellas Anecdotes Biographies Epic poems Autobiographies

Identifying Common Types of Writing
The following steps help to identify examples of common types within the modes of writing:

1. Identifying the audience—to whom or for whom the author is writing
2. Determining the author's purpose—why the author is writing the piece
3. Analyzing the word choices and how they are used

To demonstrate, the following passage has been marked to illustrate *the addressee*, the author's purpose, and word choices:

To Whom It May Concern:

I am extraordinarily excited to be applying to the Master of Environmental Science program at Australian National University. I believe the richness in biological and cultural diversity, as well as Australia's close proximity to the Great Barrier Reef, would provide a deeply fulfilling educational experience. *I am writing to express why I believe I would be an <u>excellent</u> addition to the program.*

While in college, I participated in a three-month public health internship in Ecuador, where I spent time both learning about medicine in a third world country and also about the Ecuadorian environment, including the Amazon Jungle and the Galápagos Islands. <u>My favorite experience</u> through the internship, besides swimming with sea lions in San Cristóbal, was helping to neutralize parasitic potable water and collect samples for analysis in Puyo.

Though my undergraduate studies related primarily to the human body, I took several courses in natural science, including a year of chemistry, biology, and physics as well as a course in a calculus. <u>I am confident</u> that my fundamental knowledge in these fields will prepare me for the science courses integral to the Masters of Environmental Science.

Having identified the *addressee*, it is evident that this selection is a letter of some kind. Further inspection into the author's purpose, seen in *bold*, shows that the author is trying to explain why he or she should be accepted into the environmental science program, which automatically places it into the argumentative mode as the writer is trying to persuade the reader to agree and to incite the reader into action by encouraging the program to accept the writer as a candidate. In addition to revealing the purpose, the use of emotional language—extraordinarily, excellent, deeply fulfilling, favorite experience, confident—illustrates that this is a persuasive piece. It also provides evidence for why this person would be an excellent addition to the program—his/her experience in Ecuador and with scientific curriculum.

The following passage presents an opportunity to solidify this method of analysis and practice the steps above to determine the mode of writing:

> The biological effects of laughter have long been an interest of medicine and psychology. Laughing is often speculated to reduce blood pressure because it induces feelings of relaxation and elation. Participating students watched a series of videos that elicited laughter, and their blood pressure was taken before and after the viewings. An average decrease in blood pressure was observed, though resulting p-values attest that the results were not significant.

This selection contains factual and scientific information, is devoid of any adjectives or flowery descriptions, and is not trying to convince the reader of any particular stance. Though the audience is not directly addressed, the purpose of the passage is to present the results of an experiment to those who would be interested in the biological effects of laughter—most likely a scientific community. Thus, this passage is an example of informative writing.

Below is another passage to help identify examples of the common writing modes, taken from *The Endeavor Journal of Sir Joseph Banks*:

10th May 1769 – THE ENGLISH CREW GET TAHITIAN NAMES

We have now got the Indian name of the Island, Otahite, so therefore for the future I shall call it. As for our own names the Indians find so much dificulty in pronouncing them that we are forcd to indulge them in calling us what they please, or rather what they say when they attempt to pronounce them. I give here the List: Captn Cooke *Toote*, Dr Solander *Torano*, Mr Hicks *Hete*, Mr Gore *Toárro*, Mr Molineux *Boba* from his Christian name Robert, Mr Monkhouse *Mato*, and myself *Tapáne*. In this manner they have names for almost every man in the ship.

This extract contains no elements of an informative or persuasive intent and does not seem to follow any particular line of narrative. The passage gives a list of the different names that the Indians have given the crew members, as well as the name of an island. Although there is no context for the selection, through the descriptions, it is clear that the author and his comrades are on an island trying to communicate with the native inhabitants. Hence, this passage is a journal that reflects the descriptive mode.

These are only a few of the many examples that can be found in the four primary modes of writing.

Determining the Appropriate Mode of Writing

The author's *primary purpose* is defined as the reason an author chooses to write a selection, and it is often dependent on his or her *audience*. A biologist writing a textbook, for example, does so to communicate scientific knowledge to an audience of people who want to study biology. An audience can be as broad as the entire global population or as specific as women fighting for equal rights in the bicycle repair industry. Whatever the audience, it is important that the author considers its demographics—age, gender, culture, language, education level, etc.

If the author's purpose is to persuade or inform, he or she will consider how much the intended audience knows about the subject. For example, if an author is writing on the importance of recycling to anyone who will listen, he or she will use the informative mode—including background information on recycling—and the argumentative mode—evidence for why it works, while also using simple diction so that it is easy for everyone to understand. If, on the other hand, the writer is proposing new methods for recycling using solar energy, the audience is probably already familiar with standard recycling processes and will require less background information, as well as more technical language inherent to the scientific community.

If the author's purpose is to entertain through a story or a poem, he or she will need to consider whom he/she is trying to entertain. If an author is writing a script for a children's cartoon, the plot, language, conflict, characters, and humor would align with the interests of the age demographic of that audience. On the other hand, if an author is trying to entertain adults, he or she may write content not suitable for children. The author's purpose and audience are generally interdependent.

Development

Brainstorming

One of the most important steps in writing an essay is prewriting. Before drafting an essay, it's helpful to think about the topic for a moment or two, in order to gain a more solid understanding of what the task is. Then, spending about five minutes jotting down the immediate ideas that could work for the essay is recommended. It is a way to get some words on the page and offer a reference for ideas for when drafting. Scratch paper is provided for writers to use any prewriting techniques such as webbing, free writing, or listing. The goal is to get ideas out of the mind and onto the page.

Considering Opposing Viewpoints

In the planning stage, it's important to consider all aspects of the topic, including different viewpoints on the subject. There are more than two ways to look at a topic, and a strong argument considers those opposing viewpoints. Considering opposing viewpoints can help writers present a fair, balanced, and informed essay that shows consideration for all readers. This approach can also strengthen an argument by recognizing and potentially refuting the opposing viewpoint(s).

Drawing from personal experience may help to support ideas. For example, if the goal for writing is a personal narrative, then the story should be from the writer's own life. Many writers find it helpful to draw from personal experience, even in an essay that is not strictly narrative. Personal anecdotes or short stories can help to illustrate a point in other types of essays as well.

Moving from Brainstorming to Planning
Once the ideas are on the page, it's time to turn them into a solid plan for the essay. The best ideas from the brainstorming results can then be developed into a more formal outline. An outline typically has one main point (the thesis) and at least three sub-points that support the main point. Here's an example:

Main Idea

- Point #1
- Point #2
- Point #3

Of course, there will be details under each point, but this approach is the best for dealing with timed writing.

Staying on Track
Basing the essay on the outline aids in both organization and coherence. The goal is to ensure that there is enough time to develop each sub-point in the essay, roughly spending an equal amount of time on each idea. Keeping an eye on the time will help. If there are fifteen minutes left to draft the essay, then it makes sense to spend about 5 minutes on each of the ideas. Staying on task is critical to success, and timing out the parts of the essay can help writers avoid feeling overwhelmed.

Parts of the Essay
The *introduction* has to do a few important things:

- Establish the *topic* of the essay in original wording (i.e., not just repeating the prompt)
- Clarify the significance/importance of the topic or purpose for writing (not too many details, a brief overview)
- Offer a *thesis statement* that identifies the writer's own viewpoint on the topic (typically one-two brief sentences as a clear, concise explanation of the main point on the topic)

Body paragraphs reflect the ideas developed in the outline. Three-four points is probably sufficient for a short essay, and they should include the following:

- A *topic sentence* that identifies the sub-point (e.g., a reason why, a way how, a cause or effect)

- A detailed *explanation* of the point, explaining why the writer thinks this point is valid

- Illustrative *examples*, such as personal examples or real-world examples, that support and validate the point (i.e., "prove" the point)

- A *concluding sentence* that connects the examples, reasoning, and analysis to the point being made

The *conclusion*, or final paragraph, should be brief and should reiterate the focus, clarifying why the discussion is significant or important. It is important to avoid adding specific details or new ideas to this paragraph. The purpose of the conclusion is to sum up what has been said to bring the discussion to a close.

Don't Panic!
Writing an essay can be overwhelming, and performance panic is a natural response. The outline serves as a basis for the writing and help writers keep focused. Getting stuck can also happen, and it's helpful to remember that brainstorming can be done at any time during the writing process. Following the steps of the writing process is the best defense against writer's block.

Timed essays can be particularly stressful, but assessors are trained to recognize the necessary planning and thinking for these timed efforts. Using the plan above and sticking to it helps with time management. Timing each part of the process helps writers stay on track. Sometimes writers try to cover too much in their essays. If time seems to be running out, this is an opportunity to determine whether all of the ideas in the outline are necessary. Three body paragraphs is sufficient, and more than that is probably too much to cover in a short essay.

More isn't always *better* in writing. A strong essay will be clear and concise. It will avoid unnecessary or repetitive details. It is better to have a concise, five-paragraph essay that makes a clear point, than a ten-paragraph essay that doesn't. The goal is to write one-two pages of quality writing. Paragraphs should also reflect balance; if the introduction goes to the bottom of the first page, the writing may be going off-track or be repetitive. It's best to fall into the one-two page range, but a complete, well-developed essay is the ultimate goal.

The Final Steps
Leaving a few minutes at the end to revise and proofread offers an opportunity for writers to polish things up. Putting one's self in the reader's shoes and focusing on what the essay actually says helps writers identify problems—it's a movement from the mindset of writer to the mindset of editor. The goal is to have a clean, clear copy of the essay. The following areas should be considered when proofreading:

- Sentence fragments
- Awkward sentence structure
- Run-on sentences
- Incorrect word choice
- Grammatical agreement errors
- Spelling errors
- Punctuation errors
- Capitalization errors

The Short Overview
The essay may seem challenging, but following these steps can help writers focus:

- Take one-two minutes to think about the topic.
- Generate some ideas through brainstorming (three-four minutes).
- Organize ideas into a brief outline, selecting just three-four main points to cover in the essay (eventually the body paragraphs).
- Develop essay in parts:
- Introduction paragraph, with intro to topic and main points
- Viewpoint on the subject at the end of the introduction
- Body paragraphs, based on outline
- Each paragraph: makes a main point, explains the viewpoint, uses examples to support the point
- Brief conclusion highlighting the main points and closing

- Read over the essay (last five minutes).
- Look for any obvious errors, making sure that the writing makes sense.

Organization

Good writing is not merely a random collection of sentences. No matter how well written, sentences must relate and coordinate appropriately with one another. If not, the writing seems random, haphazard, and disorganized. Therefore, good writing must be organized, where each sentence fits a larger context and relates to the sentences around it.

Transition Words

The writer should act as a guide, showing the reader how all the sentences fit together. Consider the seat belt example again:

> Seat belts save more lives than any other automobile safety feature. Many studies show that airbags save lives as well. Not all cars have airbags. Many older cars don't. Air bags aren't entirely reliable. Studies show that in 15% of accidents, airbags don't deploy as designed. Seat belt malfunctions are extremely rare.

There's nothing wrong with any of these sentences individually, but together they're disjointed and difficult to follow. The best way for the writer to communicate information is through the use of transition words. Here are examples of transition words and phrases that tie sentences together, enabling a more natural flow:

- To show causality: as a result, therefore, and consequently
- To compare and contrast: *however, but*, and *on the other hand*
- To introduce examples: *for instance, namely*, and *including*
- To show order of importance: *foremost, primarily, secondly*, and *lastly*

NOTE: This is not a complete list of transitions. There are many more that can be used; however, most fit into these or similar categories. The important point is that the words should clearly show the relationship between sentences, supporting information, and the main idea.

Here is an update to the previous example using transition words. These changes make it easier to read and bring clarity to the writer's points:

> Seat belts save more lives than any other automobile safety feature. Many studies show that airbags save lives as well; however, not all cars have airbags. For instance, some older cars don't. Furthermore, air bags aren't entirely reliable. For example, studies show that in 15% of accidents, airbags don't deploy as designed, but, on the other hand, seat belt malfunctions are extremely rare.

Also, be prepared to analyze whether the writer is using the best transition word or phrase for the situation. Take this sentence for example: "As a result, seat belt malfunctions are extremely rare." This sentence doesn't make sense in the context above because the writer is trying to show the contrast between seat belts and airbags, not the causality.

Logical Sequence

Even if the writer includes plenty of information to support their point, the writing is only coherent when the information is in a logical order. First, the writer should introduce the main idea, whether for a paragraph, a section, or the entire piece. Then they should present evidence to support the main idea by using transitional language. This shows the reader how the information relates to the main idea and to the sentences around it. The writer should then take time to interpret the information, making sure necessary connections are obvious to the reader. Finally, the writer can summarize the information in a closing section.

Though most writing follows this pattern, it isn't a set rule. Sometimes writers change the order for effect. For example, the writer can begin with a surprising piece of supporting information to grab the reader's attention, and then transition to the main idea. Thus, if a passage doesn't follow the logical order, don't immediately assume it's wrong. However, most writing usually settles into a logical sequence after a nontraditional beginning.

Introductions and Conclusions
Examining the writer's strategies for introductions and conclusions puts the reader in the right mindset to interpret the rest of the text. Look for methods the writer might use for introductions such as:

- Stating the main point immediately, followed by outlining how the rest of the piece supports this claim.

- Establishing important, smaller pieces of the main idea first, and then grouping these points into a case for the main idea.

- Opening with a quotation, anecdote, question, seeming paradox, or other piece of interesting information, and then using it to lead to the main point.

Whatever method the writer chooses, the introduction should make their intention clear, establish their voice as a credible one, and encourage a person to continue reading.

Conclusions tend to follow a similar pattern. In them, the writer restates their main idea a final time, often after summarizing the smaller pieces of that idea. If the introduction uses a quote or anecdote to grab the reader's attention, the conclusion often makes reference to it again. Whatever way the writer chooses to arrange the conclusion, the final restatement of the main idea should be clear and simple for the reader to interpret. Finally, conclusions shouldn't introduce any new information.

Effective Language Use
Precision
People often think of precision in terms of math, but precise word choice is another key to successful writing. Since language itself is imprecise, it's important for the writer to find the exact word or words to convey the full, intended meaning of a given situation. For example:

The number of deaths has gone down since seat belt laws started.

There are several problems with this sentence. First, the word *deaths* is too general. From the context, it's assumed that the writer is referring only to deaths caused by car accidents. However, without clarification, the sentence lacks impact and is probably untrue. The phrase "gone down" might be accurate, but a more precise word could provide more information and greater accuracy. Did the numbers show a slow and steady decrease of highway fatalities or a sudden drop? If the latter is true, the writer is missing a chance to make their point more dramatically. Instead of "gone down" they could substitute *plummeted*, *fallen drastically*, or *rapidly diminished* to bring the information to life. Also, the phrase "seat belt laws" is unclear. Does it refer to laws requiring cars to include seat belts or to laws requiring drivers and passengers to use them? Finally, *started* is not a strong verb. Words like *enacted* or *adopted* are more direct and make the content more real. When put together, these changes create a far more powerful sentence:

> The number of highway fatalities has plummeted since laws requiring seat belt usage were enacted.

However, it's important to note that precise word choice can sometimes be taken too far. If the writer of the sentence above takes precision to an extreme, it might result in the following:

The incidence of high-speed, automobile accident related fatalities has decreased 75% and continued to remain at historical lows since the initial set of federal legislations requiring seat belt use were enacted in 1992.

This sentence is extremely precise, but it takes so long to achieve that precision that it suffers from a lack of clarity. Precise writing is about finding the right balance between information and flow. This is also an issue of conciseness (discussed in the next section).

The last thing to consider with precision is a word choice that's not only unclear or uninteresting, but also confusing or misleading. For example:

The number of highway fatalities has become hugely lower since laws requiring seat belt use were enacted.

In this case, the reader might be confused by the word *hugely*. Huge means large, but here the writer uses *hugely* to describe something small. Though most readers can decipher this, doing so disconnects them from the flow of the writing and makes the writer's point less effective.

Conciseness

"Less is more" is a good rule to follow when writing a sentence. Unfortunately, writers often include extra words and phrases that seem necessary at the time, but add nothing to the main idea. This confuses the reader and creates unnecessary repetition. Writing that lacks conciseness is usually guilty of excessive wordiness and redundant phrases. Here's an example containing both of these issues:

> When legislators decided to begin creating legislation making it mandatory for automobile drivers and passengers to make use of seat belts while in cars, a large number of them made those laws for reasons that were political reasons.

There are several empty or "fluff" words here that take up too much space. These can be eliminated while still maintaining the writer's meaning. For example:

- "Decided to begin" could be shortened to "began"
- "Making it mandatory for" could be shortened to "requiring"
- "Make use of" could be shortened to "use"
- "A large number" could be shortened to "many"

In addition, there are several examples of redundancy that can be eliminated:

- "Legislators decided to begin creating legislation" and "made those laws"
- "Automobile drivers and passengers" and "while in cars"
- "Reasons that were political reasons"

These changes are incorporated as follows:

> When legislators began requiring drivers and passengers to use seat belts, many of them did so for political reasons.

There are many general examples of redundant phrases, such as "add an additional," "complete and total," "time schedule," and "transportation vehicle." If asked to identify a redundant phrase on the test, look for words that are close together with the same (or similar) meanings.

Sentence Structure

When examining writing, be mindful of grammar, structure, spelling, and patterns. Sentences can come in varying sizes and shapes, so the point of grammatical correctness is not stamp out creativity or diversity in writing. Rather, grammatical correctness ensures that writing will be enjoyable and clear. One of the most common methods for catching errors is to mouth the words as you read them. Many typos are fixed automatically by our brain, but mouthing the words often circumvents this instinct and helps one read what's actually on the page. Often, grammar errors are caught not by memorization of grammar rules but by the training of one's mind to know whether something *sounds* right or not.

<u>Components of Sentences</u>

Clauses
Clauses contain a subject and a verb. An *independent clause* can function as a complete sentence on its own, but it might also be one component of a longer sentence. *Dependent clauses* cannot stand alone as complete sentences. They rely on independent clauses to complete their meaning. Dependent clauses usually begin with a subordinating conjunction. Independent and dependent clauses are sometimes also referred to as *main clauses* and *subordinate clauses*, respectively. The following structure highlights the differences:

> Apiculturists raise honeybees because they love insects.

Apiculturists raise honeybees is an independent or main clause. The subject is *apiculturists*, and the verb is *raise*. It expresses a complete thought and could be a standalone sentence.

Because they love insects is a dependent or subordinate clause. If it were not attached to the independent clause, it would be a sentence fragment. While it contains a subject and verb—*they love*—this clause is dependent because it begins with the subordinate conjunction *because*. Thus, it does not express a complete thought on its own.

Another type of clause is a *relative clause*, and it is sometimes referred to as an *adjective clause* because it gives further description about the noun. A relative clause begins with a *relative pronoun*: *that, which, who, whom, whichever, whomever*, or *whoever*. It may also begin with a *relative adverb*: *where, why*, or *when.* Here's an example of a relative clause, functioning as an adjective:

> The strawberries that I bought yesterday are already beginning to spoil.

Here, the relative clause is *that I bought yesterday*; the relative pronoun is *that*. The subject is *I*, and the verb is *bought*. The clause modifies the subject *strawberries* by answering the question, "Which strawberries?" Here's an example of a relative clause with an adverb:

> The tutoring center is a place where students can get help with homework.

The relative clause is *where students can get help with homework*, and it gives more information about a place by describing what kind of place it is. It begins with the relative adverb *where* and contains the noun *students* along with its verb phrase *can get*.

Relative clauses may be further divided into two types: essential or nonessential. *Essential clauses* contain identifying information without which the sentence would lose significant meaning or not make sense. These are also sometimes referred to as *restrictive clauses*. The sentence above contains an example of an essential relative clause. Here is what happens when the clause is removed:

> The tutoring center is a place where students can get help with homework.

> The tutoring center is a place.

Without the relative clause, the sentence loses the majority of its meaning; thus, the clause is essential or restrictive.

Nonessential clauses—also referred to as *non-restrictive clauses*—offer additional information about a noun in the sentence, but they do not significantly control the overall meaning of the sentence. The following example indicates a nonessential clause:

> New York City, which is located in the northeastern part of the country, is the most populated city in America.

> New York City is the most populated city in America.

Even without the relative clause, the sentence is still understandable and continues to communicate its central message about New York City. Thus, it is a nonessential clause.

Punctuation differs between essential and nonessential relative clauses, too. Nonessential clauses are set apart from the sentence using commas whereas essential clauses are not separated with commas. Also, the relative pronoun *that* is generally used for essential clauses, while *which* is used for nonessential clauses. The following examples clarify this distinction:

> *Romeo and Juliet* is my favorite play *that Shakespeare wrote*.

The relative clause *that Shakespeare wrote* contains essential, controlling information about the noun *play*, limiting it to those plays by Shakespeare. Without it, it would seem that *Romeo and Juliet* is the speaker's favorite play out of every play ever written, not simply from Shakespeare's repertoire.

> *Romeo and Juliet, which Shakespeare wrote*, is my favorite play.

Here, the nonessential relative clause—"which Shakespeare wrote"—modifies *Romeo and Juliet*. It doesn't provide controlling information about the play, but simply offers further background details. Thus, commas are needed.

Phrases

Phrases are groups of words that do not contain the subject-verb combination required for clauses. Phrases are classified by the part of speech that begins or controls the phrase.

A *noun phrase* consists of a noun and all its modifiers—adjectives, adverbs, and determiners. Noun phrases can serve many functions in a sentence, acting as subjects, objects, and object complements:

> The shallow yellow bowl *sits on the top shelf.*

> Nina just bought *some incredibly fresh organic produce.*

Prepositional phrases are made up of a preposition and its object. The object of a preposition might be a noun, noun phrase, pronoun, or gerund. Prepositional phrases may function as either an adjective or an adverb:

> Jack picked up the book *in front of him.*

The prepositional phrase *in front of him* acts as an adjective indicating which book Jack picked up.

> The dog ran into the back yard.

The phrase *into the backyard* describes where the dog ran, so it acts as an adverb.

Verb phrases include all of the words in a verb group, even if they are not directly adjacent to each other:

> I *should have woken up* earlier this morning.

> The company **is** now *offering* membership discounts for new enrollers.

This sentence's verb phrase is *is offering*. Even though they are separated by the word *now*, they function together as a single verb phrase.

Structures of Sentences

All sentences contain the same basic elements: a subject and a verb. The *subject* is who or what the sentence is about; the *verb* describes the subject's action or condition. However, these elements, subjects and verbs, can be combined in different ways. The following graphic describes the different types of sentence structures.

Sentence Structure	Independent Clauses	Dependent Clauses
Simple	1	0
Compound	2 or more	0
Complex	1	1 or more
Compound-Complex	2 or more	1 or more

A *simple sentence* expresses a complete thought and consists of one subject and verb combination:

> The children ate pizza.

The subject is *children*. The verb is *ate*.

Either the subject or the verb may be *compound*—that is, it could have more than one element:

> *The children and their parents* ate pizza.

> The children *ate pizza and watched a movie.*

All of these are still simple sentences. Despite having either compound subjects or compound verbs, each sentence still has only one subject and verb combination.

Compound sentences combine two or more simple sentences to form one sentence that has multiple subject-verb combinations:

> *The children ate pizza,* and *their parents watched a movie.*

This structure is comprised of two independent clauses: (1) *the children ate pizza* and (2) *their parents watched a movie.* Compound sentences join different subject-verb combinations using a comma and a coordinating conjunction.

> I called my mom**,** *but* she didn't answer the phone.

> The weather was stormy**,** *so* we canceled our trip to the beach.

A *complex sentence* consists of an independent clause and one or more dependent clauses. Dependent clauses join a sentence using *subordinating conjunctions*. Some examples of subordinating conjunctions are *although, unless, as soon as, since, while, when, because, if,* and *before*.

> I missed class yesterday *because* my mother was ill.

> *Before* traveling to a new country, you need to exchange your money to the local currency.

The order of clauses determines their punctuation. If the dependent clause comes first, it should be separated from the independent clause with a comma. However, if the complex sentence consists of an independent clause followed by a dependent clause, then a comma is not always necessary.

A *compound-complex sentence* can be created by joining two or more independent clauses with at least one dependent clause:

> After the earthquake struck, thousands of homes were destroyed, and many families were left without a place to live.

The first independent clause in the compound structure includes a subordinating clause—*after the earthquake struck*. Thus, the structure is both complex and compound.

<u>Types of Sentences</u>
There isn't an overabundance of absolutes in grammar, but here is one: every sentence in the English language falls into one of four categories.

- Declarative: a simple statement that ends with a period

  The price of milk per gallon is the same as the price of gasoline.

- Imperative: a command, instruction, or request that ends with a period

  Buy milk when you stop to fill up your car with gas.

- Interrogative: a question that ends with a question mark

  Will you buy the milk?

- Exclamatory: a statement or command that expresses emotions like anger, urgency, or surprise and ends with an exclamation mark

  Buy the milk now!

Declarative sentences are the most common type, probably because they are comprised of the most general content, without any of the bells and whistles that the other three types contain. They are, simply, declarations or statements of any degree of seriousness, importance, or information.

Imperative sentences often seem to be missing a subject. The subject is there, though; it is just not visible or audible because it is *implied*. Look at the imperative example sentence.

  Buy the milk when you fill up your car with gas.

You is the implied subject, the one to whom the command is issued. This is sometimes called *the understood you* because it is understood that *you* is the subject of the sentence.

Interrogative sentences—those that ask questions—are defined as such from the idea of the word *interrogation*, the action of questions being asked of suspects by investigators. Although that is serious business, interrogative sentences apply to all kinds of questions.

To exclaim is at the root of *exclamatory* sentences. These are made with strong emotions behind them. The only technical difference between a declarative or imperative sentence and an exclamatory one is the exclamation mark at the end. The example declarative and imperative sentences can both become an exclamatory one simply by putting an exclamation mark at the end of the sentences.

  The price of milk per gallon is the same as the price of gasoline!
  Buy milk when you stop to fill up your car with gas!

After all, someone might be really excited by the price of gas or milk, or they could be mad at the person that will be buying the milk! However, as stated before, exclamation marks in abundance defeat their own purpose! After a while, they begin to cause fatigue! When used only for their intended purpose, they can have their expected and desired effect.

Punctuation

<u>Capitalization</u>
Here's a non-exhaustive list of things that should be capitalized.

- The first word of every sentence
- The first word of every line of poetry
- The first letter of proper nouns (World War II)
- Holidays (Valentine's Day)
- The days of the week and months of the year (Tuesday, March)
- The first word, last word, and all major words in the titles of books, movies, songs, and other creative works (In the novel, *To Kill a Mockingbird*, note that *a* is lowercase since it's not a major word, but *to* is capitalized since it's the first word of the title.)
- Titles when preceding a proper noun (President Roberto Gonzales, Aunt Judy)

When simply using a word such as president or secretary, though, the word is not capitalized.

Officers of the new business must include a *president* and *treasurer*.

Seasons—spring, fall, etc.—are not capitalized.

North, *south*, *east*, and *west* are capitalized when referring to regions but are not when being used for directions. In general, if it's preceded by *the* it should be capitalized.

I'm from the South.
I drove south.

<u>Ellipses</u>
An *ellipsis* (. . .) consists of three handy little dots that can speak volumes on behalf of irrelevant material. Writers use them in place of a word(s), line, phrase, list contents, or paragraph that might just as easily have been omitted from a passage of writing. This can be done to save space or to focus only on the specifically relevant material.

Exercise is good for some unexpected reasons. Watkins writes, "Exercise has many benefits such as . . . reducing cancer risk."

In the example above, the ellipsis takes the place of the other benefits of exercise that are more expected.

The ellipsis may also be used to show a pause in sentence flow.

"I'm wondering . . . how this could happen," Dylan said in a soft voice.

<u>Commas</u>
A *comma* (,) is the punctuation mark that signifies a pause—breath—between parts of a sentence. It denotes a break of flow. As with so many aspects of writing structure, authors will benefit by reading their writing aloud or mouthing the words. This can be particularly helpful if one is uncertain about whether the comma is needed.

In a complex sentence—one that contains a subordinate (dependent) clause or clauses—the use of a comma is dictated by where the subordinate clause is located. If the subordinate clause is located before the main clause, a comma is needed between the two clauses.

> I will not pay for the steak, *because I don't have that much money*.

Generally, if the subordinate clause is placed after the main clause, no punctuation is needed. I did well on my exam because I studied two hours the night before. Notice how the last clause is dependent because it requires the earlier independent clauses to make sense.

Use a comma on both sides of an interrupting phrase.

> I will pay for the ice cream, *chocolate and vanilla,* and I will eat it all myself.

The words forming the phrase in italics are nonessential (extra) information. To determine if a phrase is nonessential, try reading the sentence without the phrase and see if it's still coherent.

A comma is not necessary in this next sentence because no interruption—nonessential or extra information—has occurred. Read sentences aloud when uncertain.

I will pay for his chocolate and vanilla ice cream and I will eat it all myself.

If the nonessential phrase comes at the beginning of a sentence, a comma should only go at the end of the phrase. If the phrase comes at the end of a sentence, a comma should only go at the beginning of the phrase.

Other types of interruptions include the following:

- interjections: Oh no, I am not going.
- abbreviations: Barry Potter, M.D., specializes in heart disorders.
- direct addresses: Yes, Claudia, I am tired and going to bed.
- parenthetical phrases: His wife, lovely as she was, was not helpful.
- transitional phrases: Also, it is not possible.

The second comma in the following sentence is called an Oxford comma.

> I will pay for ice cream, syrup, and pop.

It is a comma used after the second-to-last item in a series of three or more items. It comes before the word *or* or *and*. Not everyone uses the Oxford comma; it is optional, but many believe it is needed. The comma functions as a tool to reduce confusion in writing. So, if omitting the Oxford comma would cause confusion, then it's best to include it.

Commas are used in math to mark the place of thousands in numerals, breaking them up so they are easier to read. Other uses for commas are in dates (*March 19, 2016*), letter greetings (*Dear Sally,*), and in between cities and states (*Louisville, KY*).

Semicolons
The *semicolon* (;) might be described as a heavy-handed comma. Take a look at these two examples:

> I will pay for the ice cream and I will pay for the syrup, but I will not pay for the steak.
> I will pay for the ice cream and I will pay for the syrup; I will not pay for the steak.

What's the difference? The first example has a comma and a conjunction separating the two independent clauses. The second example does not have a conjunction, but there are two independent clauses in the sentence. So something more than a comma is required. In this case, a semicolon is used.

Two independent clauses can only be joined in a sentence by either a comma and conjunction or a semicolon. If one of those tools is not used, the sentence will be a run-on. Remember that while the clauses are independent, they need to be closely related in order to be contained in one sentence.

Another use for the semicolon is to separate items in a list when the items themselves require commas.

> The family lived in Phoenix, Arizona; Oklahoma City, Oklahoma; and Raleigh, North Carolina.

Colons

Colons have many miscellaneous functions. Colons can be used to precede further information or a list. In these cases, a colon should only follow an independent clause.

> Humans take in sensory information through five basic senses: sight, hearing, smell, touch, and taste.

> The meal includes the following components:
>
> - Caesar salad
> - spaghetti
> - garlic bread
> - cake

> The family got what they needed: a reliable vehicle.

While a comma is more common, a colon can also precede a formal quotation.

> He said to the crowd: "Let's begin!"

The colon is used after the greeting in a formal letter.

> Dear Sir:
> To Whom It May Concern:

In the writing of time, the colon separates the minutes from the hour (*4:45 p.m.*). The colon can also be used to indicate a ratio between two numbers (*50:1*).

Hyphens

The *hyphen* (-) is a little hash mark that can be used to join words to show that they are linked.

Hyphenate two words that work together as a single adjective (a compound adjective).

> honey-covered biscuits

Some words always require hyphens, even if not serving as an adjective.

> merry-go-round

Hyphens always go after certain prefixes like *anti-* & *all-*.

Hyphens should also be used when the absence of the hyphen would cause a strange vowel combination (*semi-engineer*) or confusion. For example, *re-collect* should be used to describe something being gathered twice rather than being written as *recollect*, which means to remember.

Parentheses and Dashes

Parentheses are half-round brackets that look like this: ( ). They set off a word, phrase, or sentence that is a afterthought, explanation, or side note relevant to the surrounding text but not essential. A pair of commas is often used to set off this sort of information, but parentheses are generally used for information that would not fit well within a sentence or that the writer deems not important enough to be structurally part of the sentence.

> The picture of the heart (see above) shows the major parts you should memorize.
> Mount Everest is one of three mountains in the world that are over 28,000 feet high (K2 and Kanchenjunga are the other two).

See how the sentences above are complete without the parenthetical statements? In the first example, *see above* would not have fit well within the flow of the sentence. The second parenthetical statement could have been a separate sentence, but the writer deemed the information not pertinent to the topic.

The dash (—) is a mark longer than a hyphen used as a punctuation mark in sentences and to set apart a relevant thought. Even after plucking out the line separated by the dash marks, the sentence will be intact and make sense.

> Looking out the airplane window at the landmarks—Lake Clarke, Thompson Community College, and the bridge—she couldn't help but feel excited to be home.

The dashes use is similar to that of parentheses or a pair of commas. So, what's the difference? Many believe that using dashes makes the clause within them stand out while using parentheses is subtler. It's advised to not use dashes when commas could be used instead.

Quotation Marks

Here are some instances where *quotation marks* should be used:

- Dialogue for characters in narratives. When characters speak, the first word should always be capitalized and the punctuation goes inside the quotes. For example:

  > Janie said, "The tree fell on my car during the hurricane."

- Around titles of songs, short stories, essays, and chapter in books
- To emphasize a certain word
- To refer to a word as the word itself

Apostrophes

This punctuation mark, the apostrophe ('), is a versatile little mark. It has a few different functions:

- Quotes: Apostrophes are used when a second quote is needed within a quote.

  > In my letter to my friend, I wrote, "The girl had to get a new purse, and guess what Mary did? She said, 'I'd like to go with you to the store.' I knew Mary would buy it for her."

- Contractions: Another use for an apostrophe in the quote above is a contraction. *I'd* is used for *I would.*

- Possession: An apostrophe followed by the letter *s* shows possession (*Mary's* purse). If the possessive word is plural, the apostrophe generally just follows the word.

    The trees' leaves are all over the ground.

U.S. Government

United States Government and Politics

<u>Constitutional Underpinnings</u>

The role of government is to maintain a society and provide public services through its formal institutions, protect the citizens of the state, and regulate the economic system. To determine how a government should perform these functions and to protect the rights and liberties of the citizens, states enact a *constitution*, a written document that typically establishes the form of government and delegation of powers within the government, delineates limits on government, and defines protected rights, liberties, and privileges.

The many underpinnings, or foundations, upon which the *Constitution* of the United States was founded include:

Articles of Confederation (1781-1789)

The Articles of Confederation established a formal agreement or confederation between the original thirteen states. The Articles of Confederation established a central government composed of a unicameral legislative assembly in which each state was granted a single representative. Passing a bill required votes from nine of the thirteen representatives. Under the Articles of Confederation, the centralized government, the Continental Congress, was granted very limited powers, rendering it largely ineffective. Those powers included:

- Borrowing money from states or foreign government
- Creating post offices
- Appointing military offices
- Declaring war
- Signing treaties with foreign states

The weak central government established under the Articles of Confederation lacked the power to impose taxes, enforce a draft to staff the new army and navy, regulate trade, or enforce the laws enacted in Congress. As such, the sovereignty remained primarily with the states. Under the Articles, the states reserved the powers to impose taxes upon each other and the citizens of their states, regulate trade within their states, coin and print money, and sign treaties with foreign states. The states also often ignored the laws enacted by the Congress because there was no executive branch to enforce the law.

This imbalance of power between the central government and the states led to crisis within the states, resulting in economic difficulties and violence. The lack of common currency and investment in interstate infrastructure greatly hindered economic growth. In the years 1786 and 1787, farmers in several states staged a series of protests over local tax and debt collection imposed on struggling farms, commonly known as Shay's Rebellion.

Constitutional Convention, 1787

The failures of the Articles of Confederation to effectively govern on a national level directly led to the Constitutional Convention, and those experiences influenced the founders' decision to include a more robust federal government in the United States Constitution. The Constitutional Convention faced several challenges, including disputes over representation between large and small states, tension between the southern and northern states over slavery, differing visions of how power would be delegated within the government, and opposition to ceding states' sovereignty to a national federal government.

New Jersey Plan

Led by William Patterson, the New Jersey Plan called for a unicameral legislature that would grant each state a single vote. It proposed a plural executive power selected by the legislature, which would possess no veto power over the legislature, as well as judges appointed by the executive power for the duration of their lives.

The Virginia Plan

Drafted by James Madison, the Virginia Plan featured a bicameral legislature with two houses. The representatives of the lower house were to be selected by the people, and then the lower house would elect the upper house. The number of representatives of each house would be based upon population or the amount of money contributed to the federal government by each state; thus, large states supported the Virginia Plan. In this plan, the legislature could appoint judges and select a single executive with veto power.

Compromises

Connecticut Compromise

This compromise included aspects of both the New Jersey Plan and Virginia Plan in a bicameral legislature. Representation in the House of Representatives was proportional to a state's population, and in the Senate, states enjoyed equal representation with two senators per state.

Slavery Compromises

Several other compromises were made during the Convention, including the *Three-Fifths Compromise,* which, in an effort to appease both the South states who wanted slaves to be counted as part of the population for the purpose of representation but not counted for the purpose of taxes, and the North, who demanded slaves be counted for taxes but not representation, the framers of the Constitution determined that three-fifths of the slave population of each state would be counted for the purpose of both taxes and representation. In an additional compromise called the *Commerce and Slave Trade Compromise,* Congress agreed not to tax exports from states or ban the trading of slaves for twenty years. This eased Southerners' fears that if the Northern states controlled the federal government, then they could enforce antislavery policies.

Constitution vs. Articles of Confederation

The Constitution addressed the weaknesses of the Articles of Confederation in the following ways:

- Unlike the sovereign states under the Articles of Confederation, the people are now the sovereign, and they bestow sovereignty to both the states and federal government, according to principles of Federalism.

- The Constitution creates a robust central government with many specific and implied powers.

- The Constitution empowers the federal government to levy taxes against the states.

- The Constitution establishes an executive branch of the federal government to enforce the laws; it is led by a president who serves as the commander-in-chief.

- The Constitution establishes a federal judiciary branch with a Supreme Court and lower courts to interpret the laws enacted by the legislative branch.

- The Constitution removes the states' power to coin and print money and establishes a national currency; Congress may regulate interstate and international commerce.

- The Constitution specifies representation in Congress based on population and equal representation for each state in the Senate.

- The Constitution requires a simple majority in both houses to enact laws rather than a vote of at least nine out of thirteen, as specified in the Articles of Confederation. In addition, senators vote separately under the Constitution, while states vote as a single bloc in the Constitution.

- The Constitution requires a two-thirds majority vote in the House of Representatives and a two-thirds majority in the Senate to amend the Constitution, while the Articles of Confederation required a unanimous vote.

Federalism

To strengthen the central government, while still appeasing the individual states who preferred to remain sovereign over their territories, the framers of the Constitution based the new government upon the principles of *Federalism*—a compound government system that divides powers between a central government and various regional governments. The Constitution clearly defined the roles of both the state governments and the new federal government, specifying the limited power of the federal government and reserving all other powers not restricted by the Constitution to the states in the Tenth Amendment to the Constitution, commonly referred to as the Reservation Clause.

The Constitution establishes the specific powers granted to the federal and state governments.

- Delegated powers: the specific powers granted to the federal government by the Constitution
- Implied powers: the unstated powers that can be reasonably inferred from the Constitution
- Inherent powers: the reasonable powers required by the government to manage the nation's affairs and maintain sovereignty
- Reserved powers: the unspecified powers belonging to the state that are not expressly granted to the federal government or denied to the state by the Constitution
- Concurrent powers: the powers shared between the federal and state governments

The Constitution would delegate the following expanded powers to the federal government:

- Coin money
- Declare war
- Establish lower federal courts
- Sign foreign treaties
- Expand the territories of the United States, and admit new states into the union
- Regulate immigration
- Regulate interstate commerce

The following powers were reserved for the states:

- Establish local governments
- Hold elections
- Implement welfare and benefit programs
- Create public school systems

- Establish licensing standards and requirements
- Regulate state corporations
- Regulate commerce within the state

The *concurrent* powers granted to both the federal and state governments in the Constitution include:

- The power to levy taxes
- The power to borrow money
- The power to charter incorporations

Ratifying the Constitution

The framers of the Constitution signed the Constitution on September 17, 1787, but the Articles of Confederation required nine of the thirteen states to ratify the document. Conventions were held in all thirteen states and sparked heated debates between those who supported and those who opposed the new system of government. The Federalists supported the expansion of the federal government, and the anti-Federalists feared that a stronger central government would weaken the states. The anti-Federalists also sought additional protection for civil liberties. The debates between these two parties continued for two years and inspired a series of essays known as the *Federalist Papers* and *Anti-Federalist Papers* authored anonymously by leaders of their respective party.

Notable Federalists and authors of the *Federalist Papers* include:

- Alexander Hamilton: founder of the Federalist Party and advocate for a centralized financial system

- George Washington: commander-in-chief of the Continental Army and future first president of the United States

- James Madison: one of the primary drafters of the Constitution and the future fourth president of the United States

- John Jay: president of the Continental Congress and future first chief justice of the United States

- John Adams: future second president of the United States

Notable anti-Federalists and authors of the *Anti-Federalist Papers* include:

- Thomas Jefferson: primary author of the Declaration of Independence and future third president of the United States

- Patrick Henry: governor of Virginia (1776-1779, 1784-1786)

- Samuel Adams: governor of Massachusetts (1794-1797), lieutenant governor of Massachusetts (1789-1794), and president of the Massachusetts Senate (1782-1785, 1787-1788)

- George Mason: one of only three delegates who did not sign the Constitution at the Constitutional Convention and author of Objections to This Constitution of Government (1787) and the Virginia Declaration of Rights of 1776, which served as the basis for the Bill of Rights

The first state to ratify the Constitution was Delaware in a unanimous vote on December 7, 1787. Several other states followed, and eventually, after ten months, New Hampshire became the ninth state to ratify the Constitution in June 1788. However, some states still remained divided between Federalist and anti-Federalist sentiments and had yet to approve the document, including the two most populous states, Virginia and New York. To reconcile their differing views, the Federalists agreed to include a bill of rights if anti-Federalists supported the new Constitution. Federalist sentiment prevailed, and the remaining states approved the document. On May 29, 1790, the last holdout, Rhode Island, ratified the Constitution by two votes. As promised, the Bill of Rights—the first 10 amendments to the Constitution—was added in 1791, providing expanded civil liberty protection and due process of law.

Powers, Structure, and Processes of National Political Institutions

A *political institution* is an organization created by the government to enact and enforce laws, act as a mediator during conflict, create economic policy, establish social systems, and carry out some power. These institutions maintain a rigid structure of internal rules and oversight, especially if the power is delegated, like agencies under the executive branch.

The Constitution established a federal government divided into three branches: legislative, executive, and judicial.

The Three Branches of the U.S. Government

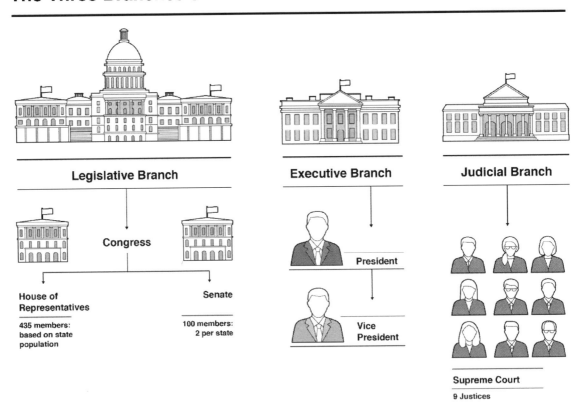

Executive Branch

The executive branch is responsible for enforcing the laws. The executive branch consists of the president, the vice president, the president's cabinet, and federal agencies created by Congress to execute some delegated.

The president of the United States:

- Serves a four-year term and is limited to two terms in office
- Is the chief executive officer of the United States and commander-in-chief of the armed forces
- Is elected by the Electoral College
- Appoints cabinet members, federal judges, and the heads of federal agencies
- Vetoes or signs bills into law
- Handles foreign affairs, including appointing diplomats and negotiating treaties
- Must be thirty-five years old, a natural-born U.S. citizen, and have lived in the United States for at least fourteen years

The vice president:

- Serves four-year terms alongside and at the will of the president
- Acts as president of the Senate
- Assumes the presidency if the president is incapacitated
- Assumes any additional duties assigned by the president

The cabinet members:

- Are appointed by the president
- Act as heads for the fifteen executive departments
- Advise the president in matters relating to their departments and carry out delegated power

Note that the president can only sign and veto laws and cannot initiate them himself. As head of the executive branch, it is the responsibility of the president to execute and enforce the laws passed by the legislative branch.

Although Congress delegates their legislative authority to agencies in an enabling statute, they are located in the executive branch because they are tasked with executing their delegating authority. The president enjoys the power of appointment and removal over all federal agency workers, except those tasked with quasi-legislative or quasi-judicial powers.

Legislative Branch

The legislative branch is responsible for enacting federal laws. This branch possesses the power to declare war, regulate interstate commerce, approve or reject presidential appointments, and investigate the other branches. The legislative branch is *bicameral*, meaning it consists of two houses: the lower house, called the House of Representatives, and the upper house, known as the Senate. Both houses are elected by popular vote.

Members of both houses are intended to represent the interests of the constituents in their home states and to bring their concerns to a national level. Ideas for laws, called bills, are proposed in one chamber and then are voted upon according to the body's rules; should the bill pass the first round of voting, the other legislative chamber must approve it before it can be sent to the president.

The two houses (or chambers) are similar though they differ on some procedures such as how debates on bills take place.

House of Representatives

The House of Representatives is responsible for enacting bills relating to revenue, impeaching federal officers including the president and Supreme Court justices, and electing the president in the case of no candidate reaching a majority in the Electoral College.

In the House of Representatives:

- Each state's representation in the House of Representatives is determined proportionally by population, with the total number of voting seats limited to 435.

- There are six nonvoting members from Washington, D.C., Puerto Rico, American Samoa, Guam, Northern Mariana Islands, and the U.S. Virgin Islands.

- The Speaker of the House is elected by the other representatives and is responsible for presiding over the House. In the event that the president and vice president are unable to fulfill their duties, the Speaker of the House will succeed to the presidency.

- The representatives of the House serve two-year terms.

- The requirements for eligibility in the House include:

    o Must be twenty-five years of age
    o Must have been a U.S. citizen for at least seven years
    o Must be a resident of the state they are representing by the time of the election

Senate

The Senate has the exclusive powers to confirm or reject all presidential appointments, ratify treaties, and try impeachment cases initiated by the House of Representatives.

In the Senate:

- The number of representatives is one hundred, with two representatives from each state.
- The vice president presides over the Senate and breaks the tie, if necessary.
- The representatives serve six-year terms.
- The requirements for eligibility in the Senate include:
    o Must be thirty years of age
    o Must have been a U.S. citizen for the past nine years
    o Must be a resident of the state they are representing at the time of their election

Legislative Process

Although all members of the houses make the final voting, the senators and representatives serve on committees and subcommittees dedicated to specific areas of policy. These committees are responsible for debating the merit of bills, revising bills, and passing or killing bills that are assigned to their committee. If it passes, they then present the bill to the entire Senate or House of Representatives (depending on which they are a part of). In most cases, a bill can be introduced in either the Senate or the House, but a majority vote of both houses is required to approve a new bill before the president may sign the bill into law.

<u>Judicial Branch</u>

The *judicial branch*, though it cannot pass laws itself, is tasked with interpreting the law and ensuring citizens receive due process under the law. The judicial branch consists of the Supreme Court, the highest court in the country, overseeing all federal and state courts. Lower federal courts are the district courts and court of appeals.

The Supreme Court:

- Judges are appointed by the president and confirmed by the Senate.
- Judges serve until retirement, death, or impeachment.
- Judges possess sole power to judge the constitutionality of a law.
- Judges set precedents for lower courts based on their decisions.
- Judges try appeals that have proceeded from the lower district courts.

<u>Checks and Balances</u>

Notice that a system of checks and balances between the branches exists. This is to ensure that no branch oversteps its authority. They include:

- Checks on the Legislative Branch:
    - The president can veto bills passed by Congress.
    - The president can call special sessions of Congress.
    - The judicial branch can rule legislation unconstitutional.
- Checks on the Executive Branch:
    - Congress has the power to override presidential vetoes by a two-thirds majority vote.
    - Congress can impeach or remove a president, and the chief justice of the Supreme Court presides over impeachment proceedings.
    - Congress can refuse to approve presidential appointments or ratify treaties.
- Checks on the Judicial Branch:
    - The president appoints justices to the Supreme Court, as well as district court and court of appeals judges.
    - The president can pardon federal prisoners.
    - The executive branch can refuse to enforce court decisions.
    - Congress can create federal courts below the Supreme Court.
    - Congress can determine the number of Supreme Court justices.
    - Congress can set the salaries of federal judges.
    - Congress can refuse to approve presidential appointments of judges.
    - Congress can impeach and convict federal judges.

The three branches of government operate separately, but they must rely on each other to create, enforce, and interpret the laws of the United States.

Checks and Balances

How Laws are Enacted and Enforced
To enact a new law:

- The bill is introduced to Congress.
- The bill is sent to the appropriate committee for review and revision.
- The approved bill is sent to the Speaker of the House and the majority party leader of the Senate, who places the bill on the calendar for review.
- The houses debate the merits of the bill and recommend amendments.

    - In the House of Representatives, those who wish to debate about a bill are allowed only a few minutes to speak, and amendments to the bill are limited.

    - In the Senate, debates and amendments are unlimited, and those who wish to postpone a vote may do so by filibuster, refusing to stop speaking.

- The approved bill is revised in both houses to ensure identical wording in both bills.
- The revised bill is returned to both houses for final approval.
- The bill is sent to the president, who may

    - Sign the bill into law

    - Veto the bill

    - Take no action, resulting in the bill becoming law if Congress remains in session for ten days or dying if Congress adjourns before ten days have passed

The Role of State Government

While the federal government manages the nation as a whole, state governments address issues pertaining to their specific territory. In the past, states claimed the right, known as nullification, to refuse to enforce federal laws that they considered unconstitutional. However, conflicts between state and federal authority, particularly in the South in regard to first, slavery, and later, discrimination, have led to increased federal power, and states cannot defy federal laws. Even so, the Tenth Amendment limits federal power to those powers specifically granted in the Constitution, and the rest of the powers are retained by the states and citizens. Therefore, individual state governments are left in charge of decisions with immediate effects on their citizens, such as state laws and taxes.

In this way, the powers of government are separated both horizontally between the three branches of government (executive, legislative, and judicial) and vertically between the levels of government (federal, state, and local).

Like the federal government, state governments consist of executive, judicial, and legislative branches, but the exact configuration of those branches varies between states. For example, while most states follow the bicameral structure of Congress, Nebraska has only a single legislative chamber. Additionally, requirements to run for office, length of terms, and other details vary from state to state. State governments have considerable authority within their states, but they cannot impose their power on other states.

Separation of Powers

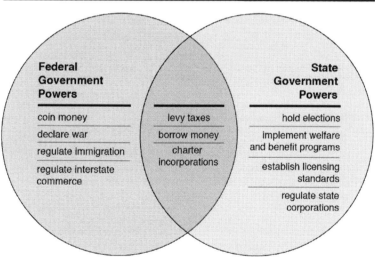

Federal Government Powers		State Government Powers
coin money	levy taxes	hold elections
declare war	borrow money	implement welfare and benefit programs
regulate immigration	charter incorporations	establish licensing standards
regulate interstate commerce		regulate state corporations

The Role of Local Government

Local governments, which include town governments, county boards, library districts, and other agencies, are especially variable in their composition. They often reflect the overall views of their state governments but also have their own values, rules, and structures. Generally, local governments function in a democratic fashion, although the exact form of government depends on its role. Depending on the location within the state, local government may have considerable or minimal authority based on the population and prosperity of the area; some counties may have strong influence in the state, while others may have a limited impact.

<u>Native American Tribes</u>

Native American tribes are treated as dependent nations that answer to the federal government but may be immune to state jurisdiction. As with local governments, the exact form of governance is left up to the tribes, which ranges from small councils to complex systems of government. Other U.S. territories, including the District of Columbia (site of Washington, D.C.) and acquired islands, such as Guam and Puerto Rico, have representation within Congress, but their legislators cannot vote on bills.

<u>Civil Liberties and Civil Rights</u>

The protection of *civil liberties* is one of the most important political values upon which American society is based. Though the terms *civil liberties* and *civil rights* are commonly used interchangeably, they describe two very distinct types of protections. Civil liberties refer to the legal protections afforded to U.S. citizens against government action, while civil rights refer to equal treatment under the law, especially in relation to minority groups, like women, African Americans, and Hispanics.

Civil Liberties

A civil liberty is a protection from legal action by the government. Civil liberties are granted by the Constitution in the first ten amendments, collectively known as the Bill of Rights, which were added to the Constitution in 1791. Civil liberties are conditional and do not afford protection from government action in every scenario. They can be restricted when they infringe on the rights of others; for example, with defamation, child pornography, or "fighting words." They also may be suspended with just cause, such as in the case of limiting the freedom of press to protect national security.

The Bill of Rights

The first ten amendments of the Constitution are called the Bill of Rights. They were passed to win over anti-Federalists during the ratification of the Constitution. Anti-Federalists wanted assurances that the federal government would protect certain fundamental civil liberties. The Bill of Rights includes:

- Amendment I: Establishes freedom of religion, speech, and press; the right to assemble in peaceful protest; and the right to petition the government without fear of reprisal

- Amendment II: Establishes the right to bear arms

- Amendment III: Establishes the right to refuse to quarter, or house, soldiers in time of war

- Amendment IV: Establishes protection against unreasonable search and seizure and requires a warrant based on probable cause supported by specific information

- Amendment V: Protects against self-incrimination in criminal trials, except in cases of military court martial; protects against being tried more than once for the same crime, known as double jeopardy; and protects against seizure of private property for public use without compensation

- Amendment VI: Establishes extensive set of rights to protect defendants in a criminal trial—the right to a speedy and timely trial before a judge and impartial jury of peers, the right to be informed of criminal accusations, the right to present and compel witnesses in defense of the accused, the right to confront witnesses against the accused, and the right to assistance of counsel

- Amendment VII: Protects the right to a trial by jury in civil cases exceeding a dollar amount of $20

- Amendment VIII: Protects against cruel and unusual punishment and excessive fines

- Amendment IX: Establishes the existence of additional fundamental rights unnamed in the Constitution; protects those rights that are not enumerated

- Amendment X: Reserves all powers that are not specified to the federal government or prohibited to the states or the people, establishing the principles of separation of powers and Federalism

Civil Rights

Civil rights concern who is protected, while *civil liberties* concern what is protected. Civil rights refer to protection against unfair treatment based on characteristics such as gender, race, ethnicity, religion, sexual orientation, and disability. The struggle for civil rights has a long history in the United States. Following the Civil War, the ratification of three amendments—Thirteenth, Fourteenth, and Fifteenth, collectively known as the Reconstruction Amendments—expanded the constitutional protection of equal civil rights.

The Thirteenth Amendment abolished slavery and involuntary servitude, except as punishment for a crime. The issue of slavery was no longer in the states' hands. Although the Emancipation Proclamation freed slaves in the Confederacy, the status of former slaves remained uncertain as the war neared its conclusion. Many Northerners did not hold strong views on slavery, but most wanted to punish the South and resolve the primary cause of the bloody Civil War. The Northern states all immediately ratified the amendment, and in December 1865, enough reconstructed Southern states ratified the amendment for it to be adopted into law.

The Fourteenth Amendment prohibited states from depriving life, liberty, or property without due process and from violating equal protection based on race, color, or previous condition of servitude. Now, all persons born or naturalized in the United States were considered legal citizens. Although revolutionary for the theoretical rights of all American citizens, newly freed or otherwise, the Fourteenth Amendment did not provide actual federally enforced equal protection until the Civil Rights Act of 1964.

The Fifteenth Amendment prohibits the government from denying a citizen the right to vote for reasons of race, color, or previous condition of servitude. Adopted in 1870, the last of the Reconstruction Amendments, the Fifteenth Amendment sought to protect newly freed slaves' right to vote. As discussed below, most states interpreted the amendment to only apply to male suffrage. In addition, Southern states passed a series of laws to systematically disenfranchise African Americans, like poll taxes, literacy tests, and residency rules. The use of violence and intimidation for political purpose was also common. Meaningful change did not occur until the Civil Rights Movement, nearly one hundred years later. In 1964, the Twenty-Fourth Amendment prohibited the states and federal government from charging a poll tax or fee to vote. Later, the Voting Rights Act of 1965 empowered the federal government to enforce the Fifteenth Amendment on the states for the first time.

Women's Suffrage

The Fourteenth Amendment specified equal treatment for all citizens; however, it did not establish women's right to vote in elections, known as women's suffrage. Although landowning women were allowed to vote in New Jersey in the late eighteenth century, the right was removed in 1807. The fight for women's suffrage continued in the middle of the nineteenth century. Famous women's rights activists include Susan B. Anthony, Lucy Stone, and Elizabeth Cady Stanton, who authored the

Declaration of Rights and Sentiments, which demanded access to the civil liberties granted to all men. Women gained the right to vote in 1869 in Wyoming and 1870 in Utah.

The women's suffrage movement gained momentum in the early twentieth century after their increased participation in the economy during World War I when much of the workforce went overseas to fight. The National Women's Party picketed outside the White House and led a series of protests in Washington, resulting in the imprisonment of the party's leader, Alice Paul. In 1918, Woodrow Wilson declared his support for women's suffrage despite earlier opposition, and in 1920, Congress passed the Nineteenth Amendment, which made it illegal for states to withhold voting rights based on gender.

Jim Crow Laws
Southern states circumvented the Fourteenth Amendment and imposed what were referred to as Jim Crow laws, which established racial segregation of public facilities. These "separate but equal" facilities included the military, workplaces, public schools, restaurants, restrooms, transportation, and recreational facilities. Despite the label of "separate but equal," most facilities reserved for African Americans were considerably inferior.

In 1896, the Supreme Court handed down a decision in the case of *Plessy vs. Ferguson*, in which Homer Plessy, a Louisiana man of mixed race, attempted to board a railway car reserved for "whites only" and was charged for violating the separate car law. Plessy subsequently filed suit against the state, claiming they violated his Fourteenth Amendment rights. The Supreme Court decided in favor of the state, ruling that the law was not unconstitutional. The Supreme Court upheld separate but equal laws until the 1954 case of *Brown vs. the Board of Education of Topeka* where the Supreme Court ruled that racial segregation of public schools violated the Fourteenth Amendment.

Civil Rights Movement
Brown vs. the Board of Education prohibited segregation in 1954, but the Civil Rights Movement, led by the National Association for the Advancement of Colored People (NAACP) and such famous activists as Martin Luther King Jr. and Malcolm X, did not secure the enforcement of the Fourteenth Amendment until the passage of the Civil Rights Act of 1964, which outlawed discrimination based on gender, race, ethnicity, and religion. African American and Native American women, however, did not gain the right to vote until the Voting Rights Act of 1965, which enforced the voting rights articulated in the Fourteenth Amendment and Fifteenth Amendment. Section 5 of the Voting Rights Act prevented states with a history of discrimination from altering their voting laws without getting approval from the attorney general or a federal district court.

Political Beliefs and Behaviors
Political beliefs are the beliefs held by the citizens of a nation about the government, leaders, policies, and the related political issues of their state. Political beliefs differ among individual citizens, but in America, a strong basis of democracy shapes the political beliefs, behaviors, and attitudes.

Democratic Values
The foundation of democratic values upon which the United States is based include:

- The people are sovereign, and they elect a representative government to exercise that sovereignty.
- The citizens of the nation are equal under the law.
- The peaceful transition of power is valued regardless of election results.

- The private property of individuals cannot be taken by force by the government without due process or fair compensation.
- The civil liberties of the citizens of the state cannot be abridged or violated by the government without due process.
- The government should be accountable to the citizenry.

Political Socialization

American citizens undergo a process of *political socialization* from early childhood to adulthood during which they develop their individual sense of political identity and civic pride. Children learn about politics in the home from an early age, whether from the views, opinions, and facts of family and friends, or through the media to which they are exposed.

In school, they learn about the nation's political history, basic politics, and democratic values, as well as the ideals of patriotism and the processes of government. As they grow older, they join interest groups, labor unions, religious groups, and political organizations that further influence their political beliefs. This socialization shapes not only the political beliefs and values of individual citizens and groups but the political ideals of the nation and public opinion.

Public Opinion

Public opinion is the shared political ideals, opinions, and attitudes of the people of a state regarding the politics, current events, and social issues that influence policy and shape the political atmosphere of a state. Public opinion is the result of political beliefs, socialization, and current events. Political scientists measure public opinion through:

- Distribution of opinion across demographics such as age, race, gender, and religion
- Strength of the opinion
- Stability of the opinion over time

Public opinion refers to the majority opinion in a democratic state. Citizens express public opinion through the interest groups they join, the media they consume and interact with, and the leaders they elect. To measure public opinion, scientists use polls to gather data. Accurate polling requires:

- Random sampling of representative populations
- Unbiased questions
- Clear instructions for how to answer questions
- Controlled procedures such as the use of telephone, mail, Internet, or in-person interviews with an unbiased pollster
- Accurate reporting of the results, including information about methods, inconsistencies, respondents, and possible sources and degree of error

Political Participation

Citizens express their political beliefs and public opinion through participation in politics. The conventional ways citizens can participate in politics in a democratic state include:

- Obeying laws
- Voting in elections

- Running for public office
- Staying interested and informed of current events
- Learning U.S. history
- Attending public hearings to be informed and to express their opinions on issues, especially on the local level
- Forming interest groups to promote their common goals
- Forming political action committees (PACs) that raise money to influence policy decisions
- Petitioning government to create awareness of issues
- Campaigning for a candidate
- Contributing to campaigns
- Using mass media to express political ideas, opinions, and grievances

Voting

In a democratic state, the most common way to participate in politics is by voting for candidates in an election. Voting allows the citizens of a state to influence policy by selecting the candidates who share their views and make policy decisions that best suit their interests, or candidates who they believe are most capable of leading the country. In the United States, all citizens—regardless of gender, race, or religion—are allowed to vote unless they have lost their right to vote through due process, such as felons.

Since the Progressive movement and the increased social activism of the 1890s to the 1920s that sought to eliminate corruption in government, direct participation in politics through voting has increased. Citizens can participate by voting in the following types of elections:

- Direct primaries: Citizens can nominate candidates for public office.

- National, state, and municipal elections: Citizens elect their representatives in government.

- Recall elections: Citizens can petition the government to vote an official out of office before their term ends.

- Referendums: Citizens can vote directly on proposed laws or amendments to the state constitution.

- Voter initiatives: Citizens can petition their local or state government to propose laws that will be approved or rejected by voters.

Electoral Process, Political Parties, and Interest Groups

As members of a Constitutional Republic with certain aspects of a *democracy*, U.S. citizens are empowered to elect most government leaders, but the process varies between branch and level of government. Presidential elections at the national level use the *Electoral College* system. Rather than electing the president directly, citizens cast their ballots to select *electors* that represent each state in the college.

Legislative branches at the federal and state level are also determined by elections. In some areas, judges are elected, but in other states judges are appointed by elected officials. The U.S. has a *two-party system*, meaning that most government control is under two major parties: the Republican Party and the Democratic Party. It should be noted that the two-party system was not designed by the Constitution but gradually emerged over time.

Electoral Process

During the *electoral process*, the citizens of a state decide who will represent them at the local, state, and federal level. Different political officials that citizens elect through popular vote include but are not limited to:

- City mayor
- City council members
- State representative
- State governor
- State senator
- House member
- U.S. Senator
- President

The Constitution grants the states the power to hold their own elections, and the voting process often varies from city to city and state to state.

While a popular vote decides nearly all local and state elections, the president of the United States is elected by the *Electoral College*, rather than by popular vote. Presidential elections occur every four years on the first Tuesday after the first Monday in November.

The electoral process for the president of the United States includes:

Primary Elections and Caucuses

In a presidential election, *nominees* from the two major parties, as well as some third parties, run against each other. To determine who will win the nomination from each party, the states hold *primary elections* or *caucuses*.

During the primary elections, the states vote for who they want to win their party's nomination. In some states, primary elections are closed, meaning voters may only vote for candidates from their registered party, but other states hold *open primaries* in which voters may vote in either party's primary.

Some states hold *caucuses* in which the members of a political party meet in small groups, and the decisions of those groups determine the party's candidate.

Each state holds a number of delegates proportional to its population, and the candidate with the most delegate votes receives the domination. Some states give all of their delegates (*winner-take-all*) to the primary or caucus winner, while some others split the votes more proportionally.

Conventions

The two major parties hold national conventions to determine who will be the nominee to run for president from each party. The *delegates* each candidate won in the primary elections or caucuses are the voters who represent their states at the national conventions. The candidate who wins the most delegate votes is given the nomination. Political parties establish their own internal requirements and procedures for how a nominee is nominated.

Conventions are typically spread across several days, and leaders of the party give speeches, culminating with the candidate accepting the nomination at the end.

Campaigning

Once the nominees are selected from each party, they continue campaigning into the national election. Prior to the mid-1800s, candidates did not actively campaign for themselves, considering it dishonorable to the office, but campaigning is now rampant. Modern campaigning includes, but is not limited to:

- Raising money
- Meeting with citizens and public officials around the country
- Giving speeches
- Issuing policy proposals
- Running internal polls to determine strategy
- Organizing strategic voter outreach in important districts
- Participating in debates organized by a third-party private debate commission
- Advertising on television, through mail, or on the Internet

General Election

On the first Tuesday after the first Monday in November of an election year, every four years, the people cast their votes by secret ballot for president in a *general election*. Voters may vote for any candidate, regardless of their party affiliation. The outcome of the popular vote does not decide the election; instead, the winner is determined by the Electoral College.

Electoral College

When the people cast their votes for president in the general election, they are casting their votes for the *electors* from the *Electoral College* who will elect the president. In order to win the presidential election, a nominee must win 270 of the 538 electoral votes. The number of electors is equal to the total number of senators and representatives from each state plus three electoral votes for Washington D.C. which does not have any voting members in the legislative branch.

The electors typically vote based on the popular vote from their states. Although the Constitution does not require electors to vote for the popular vote winner, no elector voting against the popular vote has ever changed the outcome of an election. Due to the Electoral College, a nominee may win the popular vote and still lose the election.

For example, let's imagine that there only two states, Wyoming and Nebraska, in a presidential election. Wyoming has three electoral votes and awards them all to the winner of the election by majority vote. Nebraska has five electoral votes and also awards them all to the winner of the election by majority vote. If 500,000 people in Wyoming vote and the Republican candidate wins by a vote of 300,000 to 200,000, the Republican candidate will win the three electoral votes for the state. If the same number of people vote in Nebraska, but the Republican candidate loses the state by a vote of 249,000 to 251,000, the Democratic candidate wins the five electoral votes from that state. This means the Republican candidate will have received 549,000 popular votes but only three electoral votes, while the Democratic candidate will have received 451,000 popular votes but will have won five electoral votes. Thus, the

Republican won the popular vote by a considerable margin, but the Democratic candidate will have been awarded more electoral votes, which are the only ones that matter.

	Wyoming	Nebraska	Total # of Votes
Republican Votes	300,000	249,000	**549,000**
Democratic Votes	200,000	251,000	**451,000**
Republican Electoral Votes	3	0	**3**
Democratic Electoral Votes	0	5	**5**

If no one wins the majority of electoral votes in the presidential election, the House of Representatives decides the presidency, as required by the Twelfth Amendment. They may only vote for the top three candidates, and each state delegation votes as a single bloc. Twenty-six votes, a simple majority, are required to elect the president. The House has only elected the president twice, in 1801 and 1825.

Here how many electoral votes each state and the District of Columbia have:

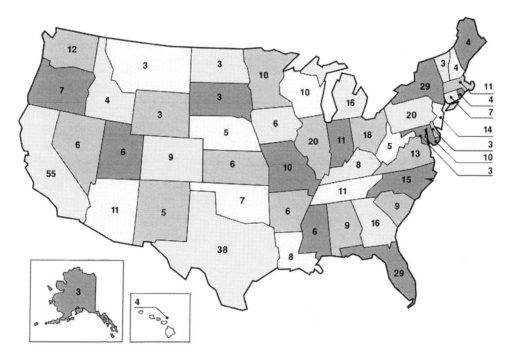

Political Parties

A *political party* is an organized group of voters who share the same political values and support or oppose the same policies. Members of a political party vote for the candidates from their party who they believe share their values and will approve or reject the policies they support or oppose. Political parties often determine the positions party members take on issues of policy, such as the economy, taxation, and social services.

The Founding Fathers of the United States opposed the divisiveness they associated with political parties, and President George Washington railed against the evil of political parties in his Farewell Address. However, the ratification of the Constitution led to the creation of the first two American political parties, the Federalists and the anti-Federalist Democratic-Republican Party. When Andrew Jackson became the fourth president of the United States as a Democrat, his opposition organized under the Whig Party. The Whigs asserted Congress' supremacy over the president and primarily focused on economic concerns, like banking and violations.

Slavery divided the nation and created unrest among the political parties, as members took opposing views and splintered into separate sects of the party or started new parties with members who shared their views. The Whig Party, so divided by the differing views of the members, collapsed. Former Whigs joined or formed the following parties:

- Constitutional Union Party: Devoted itself to a single-issue platform of preserving the Union and recognizing the Constitution as the supreme rule of law. The party did not take a firm issue on slavery, but vigorously opposed secession.

- Democratic Party: Divided into northern and southern factions over slavery, but the Democrats sought to compromise and remain unified.

- Know-Nothing Party: Advocated for an anti-immigration single-party platform, especially immigrants from Catholic countries.

- Republican Party: Formed in response to the Kansas-Nebraska Act, which threatened to extend slavery into new territories, called for the abolition of slavery and argued for a more modernized economy.

Modern Political Parties
The defeat of the South in the Civil War resulted in the Republicans holding power until the 1930s, when Franklin D. Roosevelt, a Democrat, was elected president. Roosevelt instituted the New Deal, which included many social policies that built an expansive social welfare program to provide financial support to citizens during the Great Depression. The Republican Party opposed this interference by the government, and the two parties became more strongly divided. The political landscape again shifted during the Civil Rights Movement, as Southern Democrats fled to the Republican Party over their opposition to enforcing federal civil rights onto states. This strengthened the modern coalition between economic conservatives and social conservatives.

Today, the Democrats and Republicans are still the two major parties, though many third parties have emerged. The Republicans and Democrats hold opposing views on the degree of state intervention into private business, taxation, states' rights, and government assistance.

The ideals of these parties include:

Republican (or the Grand Old Party [GOP])
- Founded by abolitionists
- Support capitalism, free enterprise, and a policy of noninterference by the government
- Support strong national defense
- Support deregulation and restrictions of labor unions
- Advocate for states' rights
- Oppose abortion
- Support traditional values, often based on Judeo-Christian foundations, including considerable opposition to same-sex marriage

Democrat
- Founded by anti-Federalists and rooted in classical Liberalism
- Promote civil rights, equal opportunity and protection under the law, and social justice
- Support government-instituted social programs and safety nets
- Support environmental issues
- Support government intervention and regulation, and advocate for labor unions
- Support universal health care

Some prominent third parties include:

- Reform Party: support political reform of the two-party system
- Green Party: support environmental causes
- Libertarian Party: support a radical policy of nonintervention and small, localized government

Interest Groups

An *interest group* is an organization with members who share similar social concerns or political interests. Members of political interest groups work together to influence policy decisions that benefit a particular segment of society or cause. Interest groups might include:

- Activist groups, like the NAACP, American Civil Liberties Union (ACLU), or People for the Ethical Treatment of Animals (PETA)
- Corporations, like pharmaceutical companies or banks
- Small-business advocates
- Religious groups, like the Concerned Women PAC and the Muslim Public Affairs Council
- Unions, such as the Association of Teacher Educators and International Brotherhood of Electrical Workers

Lobbyists

To promote their causes and influence policy in their favor, many interest groups employ *lobbyists*, paid advocates who work to influence lawmakers. Lobbying is a controversial practice, but it is sanctioned and protected as free speech. Lobbying from interest groups has a powerful impact on many policy decisions made in the United States. Examples of lobbyist groups include American Israel Public Affairs Committee (AIPAC) and Pharmaceutical Research and Manufacturers of America.

Foreign Policy

Foreign policy refers to a state's international policy governing and informing their interactions with other states. A state's foreign policy typically defines the methods they employ to safeguard the state against foreign states, the social and economic goals of the state, and how the state will achieve these goals in the global arena through their relations with foreign states. Foreign policy is typically an executive function, either through the head of state or delegated to the foreign minister.

A state's foreign policy is influenced by several factors, including:

- Public opinion
- Economic and domestic stability
- Current events
- Social and humanitarian interests

The foreign policy of the United States has changed dramatically since the Founding Fathers established a policy of isolationism, which persisted well into the nineteenth century. After World War II, the United States emerged alongside the Soviet Union as the lone remaining global support powers. The United States led Europe and her allies during the Cold War's fight against the spread of Communism. When the Cold War ended after the collapse of the Soviet Union, the United States was left as the only true superpower, enjoying an unrivaled military and one of the world's most productive economies. American foreign policy shifted toward funding sustainable development economic projects in struggling countries and supporting democracy across the globe. The United States remains the leader of the NATO and has entered into several free trade agreements, most notably the North American Free Trade Association between Mexico, America, and Canada.

The president and secretary of state of the United States determine and enforce the U.S. foreign policy. The goals of U.S. foreign policy include:

- Maintain national security
- Promote world peace
- Promote civil rights and democracy
- Ally with other states to solve international problems
- Promote global cooperation and trade

To accomplish these goals, the State Department:

- Employs foreign diplomats to meet and talk with officials from foreign countries
- Maintains U.S. embassies in foreign nations from which to practice diplomacy
- Joins and supports international organizations such as:
    - NATO
    - WTO
    - United Nations

U.S. History, Society, Customs, and Culture

Origins of the American Revolution and Founding of the United States

The French colonies in Canada also threatened the British settlements. France and Britain had been enemies for centuries. Religious differences reinforced their hostility; the British were Protestant and the French were mostly Catholic. Far fewer colonists settled in "New France," but they often clashed with the British, especially over the lucrative fur trade. Both the British and French sought to dominate the trade in beaver pelts, which were used to make hats in Europe. The British and French fought a series of colonial wars between 1689 and 1748 that failed to resolve the struggle for dominance in North America.

Eventually, the contest culminated in the French and Indian War (also known as the Seven Years' War), which ended in 1763. The French initially enjoyed the upper hand because they were able to persuade more Native American tribes to support them. The Native Americans felt the French were less likely to encroach on their territory than the land-hungry British. The Native Americans launched devastating raids along the British colonial frontier. However, the British eventually emerged victorious after they blockaded the French colonies in Canada. This prevented the French from bringing in reinforcements or from resupplying their Native American allies with gunpowder and ammunition. Native American raids subsided and eventually the French surrendered almost all of their colonial possessions in North America. Some historians consider this war the first global conflict because battles were also fought in Europe, Asia, and Africa.

The French defeat radically altered the balance of power in North America. Previously, Native Americans had been able to play the French and British against each other, but now they were without many of their French allies. In addition, the French and Indian War also set the stage for the American Revolution. Although victorious, the British monarchy spent an enormous amount of money and the war doubled the national debt. In order to pay off the debts, King George III began imposing taxes upon the North American colonies, which eventually led to revolution.

Since 1651, the British crown had tried to control trade within its empire, which eventually led to tension and discontent in the North American colonies. That year, the monarchy introduced the Navigation Acts, which prevented the North American colonies from trading directly with other European powers—all goods had to be shipped to Britain first. This was an attempt to keep wealth within the British Empire and to prevent other empires from profiting from their colonies. This was an example of mercantilism—an economic policy that formed the foundation of Britain's empire. Mercantilism called for government regulation in the form of tariffs, a tax on imports from other countries. This raised prices on foreign goods and encouraged British imperial subjects to purchase goods made in Britain or the colonies. This reduced imports and maximized exports, thus enriching the British Empire.

The Molasses Act in 1731 was another outgrowth of mercantilism. This law imposed a higher tax on the molasses that colonists purchased from the Dutch, French, or Spanish colonies. The tax was unpopular with the colonists and British imperial officials eventually decided not to enforce the tax. The Molasses Act had threatened to disrupt the pattern of triangular trade that had emerged in the Atlantic world. First, ships from Britain's North American colonies carried rum to Africa where it was traded for slaves and gold. Then, the ships took the slaves to French and Spanish colonies in the Caribbean and exchanged them for sugar or molasses. In the last part of the triangular trade system, merchants sailed back to North America where the sugar and molasses was used to make rum, and the cycle could start over again.

In addition to economic connections, many other bonds also bridged the Atlantic Ocean. Most colonists shared a common language, common religion, and common culture. However, as the colonies grew in population, they began to develop local institutions and a separate sense of identity. For example, it became common for ministers to receive their education at seminaries in North America rather than Britain. Newspapers also began to focus on printing more local news as well. Perhaps most importantly, the colonies began to exercise more control over their own political affairs. The British government retained control over international issues, such as war and trade, but the colonists controlled their own domestic affairs. Colonies began to form their own political assemblies and elect landowners who represented local districts. In addition, communications between the colonies and Britain were very slow because it took months for a ship to cross the Atlantic and return with a response.

A number of political acts by the British monarchy also led to more discontent among the colonies. After the French and Indian War ended in 1763, the king declared that the colonists could not settle west of the Appalachian Mountains. This was known as the Proclamation of 1763. Many colonists were frustrated because they had expected this territory would be open for expansion after the French had been defeated.

Additionally, taxes were imposed in an effort to help reduce the debt Britain amassed during the French and Indian War. In 1764, Parliament passed the Sugar Act, which reduced the tax on molasses but also provided for greater enforcement powers. Some colonists protested by organizing boycotts on British goods. One year later, in 1765, Parliament passed the Quartering Act, which required colonists to provide housing and food to British troops. This law was also very unpopular and led to protests in the North American colonies.

The Stamp Act of 1765 required the colonists to pay a tax on legal documents, newspapers, magazines and other printed materials. Colonial assemblies protested the tax and petitioned the British government in order to have it repealed. Merchants also organized boycotts and established correspondence committees in order to share information. Eventually, Parliament repealed the Stamp Act but simultaneously reaffirmed the Crown's right to tax the colonies.

In 1767, Parliament introduced the Townshend Acts, which imposed a tax on goods the colonies imported from Britain, such as tea, lead, paint, glass, and paper. The colonies protested again and British imperial officials were assaulted in some cases. The British government sent additional troops to North America to restore order. The arrival of troops in Boston only led to more tension that eventually culminated in the Boston Massacre in 1770, where five colonists were killed and eight were wounded. Except for the duty on tea, most of Townshend Act taxes were repealed after the Boston Massacre.

Parliament passed the Tea Act in 1773 and, although it actually reduced the tax on tea, it was another unpopular piece of legislation. The Tea Act allowed the British East India Company to sell its products directly, effectively cutting out colonial merchants and stirring more Anglo-American anger and resentment. This resulted in the Boston Tea Party in 1773, an incident in which colonial tea merchants disguised themselves as Indians before storming several British ships that were anchored in Boston harbor. Once aboard, the disguised colonists dumped more than 300 chests of tea into the water.

Because the British government was unable to identify the perpetrators, Parliament passed a series of laws that punished the entire colony of Massachusetts. These acts were known as the Coercive or Intolerable Acts. The first law closed the port of Boston until the tea had been paid for (an estimated

$1.7 million in today's currency). The second act curtailed the authority of Massachusetts' colonial government. Instead of being elected by colonists, most government officials were now appointed by the king. In addition, the act restricted town meetings, the basic form of government in Massachusetts, and limited most villages to one meeting per year. This act angered colonists throughout the thirteen colonies because they feared their rights could be stripped away as well. A third act allowed for British soldiers to be tried in Britain if they were accused of a crime. The fourth act once again required colonists to provide food and shelter to British soldiers.

Colonists responded by forming the First Continental Congress in 1774, and all the colonies except for Georgia sent delegates. The delegates sought a compromise with the British government instead of launching an armed revolt. The First Continental Congress sent a petition to King George III affirming their loyalty but demanding the repeal of the Intolerable Acts. The delegates organized a boycott of imports from and exports to Britain until their demands were met.

The colonists began to form militias and gather weapons and ammunition. The first battle of the revolution began at Lexington and Concord in April 1775 when British troops tried to seize a supply of gunpowder and were confronted by about eighty Minutemen. A brief skirmish left eight colonists dead and ten wounded. Colonial reinforcements poured in and harassed the British force as they retreated to Boston. Although the battle did not result in many casualties, it marked the beginning of war.

A month later, the Second Continental Congress convened in Philadelphia. The delegates formed an army and appointed George Washington as commander in chief. Delegates were still reluctant to repudiate their allegiance to King George III and did not do so until they issued the Declaration of Independence on July 4, 1776. The Declaration drew on the ideas of the Enlightenment and declared that the colonists had the right to life, liberty, and the pursuit of happiness. The Declaration stated that the colonists had to break away from Britain because King George III had violated their rights.

After the Battle of Lexington and Concord, British troops retreated to Boston and the colonial militias laid siege to the city. Colonists built fortifications on Bunker Hill outside the city and British troops attacked the position in June 1775. The colonists inflicted heavy casualties on the British and killed a number of officers. However, the defenders ran out of ammunition and British troops captured Bunker Hill on the third assault. Although it was a defeat for the colonists, the Battle of Bunker Hill demonstrated that they could stand and fight against the disciplined and professional British army.

The British army initially had the upper hand and defeated colonial forces in a number of engagements. The Americans did not achieve a victory until the Battle of Trenton in December 1776. Washington famously crossed the Delaware River on Christmas Day and launched a surprise attack against Hessian mercenaries. They captured more than 1,000 soldiers and suffered very minimal casualties. The victory at Trenton bolstered American morale and showed that they could defeat professional European soldiers.

The Battle of Saratoga in New York in the fall of 1777 was an important turning point in the American War for Independence. American troops surrounded and captured more than 6,000 British soldiers. This victory convinced the French king to support the revolutionaries by sending troops, money, weapons, and ships to the American continent. French officers who fought alongside the Patriots brought back many ideas with them that eventually sparked a revolution in France in 1789.

French support was very important in the last major battle of the revolution at Yorktown, Virginia, in 1781. American troops laid siege to General Cornwallis's British forces at Yorktown. The French fleet defeated a British naval squadron sent to relieve Cornwallis. French and American troops began attacking the British fortifications in Yorktown; a sustained artillery bombardment by American guns eventually forced Cornwallis to surrender. This ended the Revolutionary War, and in 1783 the British signed the Treaty of Paris. Britain recognized the United States as an independent country and set the Mississippi River as the nation's western border. However, British troops continued to occupy several forts in the Great Lakes region.

In addition, tens of thousands of colonists who remained loyal to the British Empire fled the United States after the war. They were known as loyalists and many thousands had joined militias and fought against the patriots. Some loyalists fled to Canada or Britain but many remained in the United States. Many Native American tribes had sided with the British as well in an attempt to curb western expansion. No Native American leaders signed the Treaty of Paris and they refused to give up their territories, which led to further conflict as the new American nation began to expand westward.

Adoption of the Constitution and Bill of Rights and Their Impact on the Political Development of the Early United States

America's first system of government was actually laid out in the Articles of Confederation, and not the Constitution. The Articles of Confederation were ratified during the Revolutionary War and went into effect in 1781. The Articles of Confederation created a relatively weak central government and allowed individual states to retain most of the power. Under this system, the national government did not have a president or judiciary. Each state had only one vote in the Confederation Congress and most major decisions required unanimous approval by all thirteen states. Despite this requirement, the Confederation Congress did pass some important legislation, including the Northwest Ordinance, which organized the land west of Appalachian Mountains. The territories eventually became the states of Ohio, Indiana, Michigan, Illinois, Wisconsin, and Minnesota. However, Congress did not have the power to tax and could only request money from the states without any way to enforce its demands. A Revolutionary War veteran named Daniel Shays led an armed insurrection in western Massachusetts in 1787. Although Shay's Rebellion was defeated, it drew attention to the weaknesses of the Articles of Confederation.

The Constitutional Convention met in Philadelphia a few months after the rebellion in order to create a stronger federal government. However, delegates disagreed over how to structure the new system. The Virginia Plan was one proposal that included a bicameral legislature where states were awarded representation based on their population size. This would benefit more populous states at the expense of smaller states. The other main proposal was the New Jersey Plan, which retained many elements of the Articles of Confederation, including a unicameral legislature with one vote per state. This plan would put states on an equal footing regardless of population.

Eventually, delegates agreed to support the Connecticut Compromise (also known as the Great Compromise), which incorporated elements from both the Virginia and New Jersey Plans. Under the new Constitution, Congress would be a bicameral body. In the House of Representatives, states would be allocated seats based on population, but in the Senate each state would have two votes. The Constitution also included a president and judiciary that would each serve to check the power of other branches of government. In addition, Congress had the power to tax and had more enforcement powers.

Slavery was another contentious issue during the Constitutional Convention. Slavery was more common in the Southern states and less common in the North. The Southern states wanted slaves to be counted when calculating representation in Congress but not when it came to assessing taxes. Northern states wanted the opposite and eventually the two sides agreed to the Three-Fifths Compromise where slaves were counted as three-fifths of a person for the purposes of both taxation and representation. The Constitution also included a provision that allowed slave owners to recover slaves who had escaped and permitted the international slave trade to continue until 1808.

Once the Constitution had been drafted, nine of the thirteen states had to ratify it. Vigorous debate erupted over whether or not the Constitution should be approved. Two different political factions emerged. The Federalists supported the Constitution because they felt a stronger central government was necessary in order to promote economic growth and improve national security. Several leading federalists, including Alexander Hamilton, John Jay, and James Madison, published a series of articles urging voters to support the Constitution. However, the Anti-Federalists, including Thomas Jefferson and Patrick Henry, felt that the Constitution took too much power away from the states and gave it to the national government. They also thought there weren't enough protections for individual rights and lobbied for the addition of a Bill of Rights that guaranteed basic liberties. Ultimately, the Constitution was ratified in 1788 and the Bill of Rights was approved a year later.

The Electoral College unanimously elected George Washington as the nation's first president in 1789. Despite this appearance of unity, deep political divisions led to the formation of the nation's first party system. Washington supported the Federalist ideology and appointed several Federalists to his cabinet, including Alexander Hamilton as secretary of the treasury. The Anti-Federalist faction evolved into the Democratic-Republican Party and favored stronger state governments instead of a powerful federal government. As settlers moved into the new Northwest Territories, Washington helped pacify Indians who opposed further expansion. He also successfully put down a rebellion in western Pennsylvania by farmers opposed to a federal tax on whiskey.

A number of different issues divided the Federalists and the Democratic-Republicans, including the French Revolution, which began in 1789. Initially, many Americans supported the French effort to replace their monarchy and create a republican government. However, the French Revolution quickly became more violent, as thousands of suspected opponents of the revolution were executed during the Reign of Terror. The Federalists, including Washington, were horrified by the violence, while Jefferson and the Democratic-Republicans thought the United States should help its former ally. Washington ensured that the country remain officially neutral.

Washington declined to seek a third term and another Federalist, John Adams, became our second president. Adams signed the Alien and Sedition Acts, which made it a criminal offense to criticize the government, and allowed the president to deport aliens suspected of treason. Adams and the Federalists argued that the laws were necessary in order to improve security as Europe became embroiled in a war against the new French republic. Jefferson and the Democratic-Republicans said the laws restricted free speech. Jefferson made the acts an important topic in 1800 when he successfully ran for president.

Jefferson's victory marked a turning point in the political system because the Democratic-Republicans gained more power while the Federalists went into decline. He repealed the Alien and Sedition Acts when he was elected. The Federalists were further weakened when Hamilton was killed in a duel in 1804.

Jefferson accomplished several significant achievements during his presidency, and one of the most important was the Louisiana Purchase in 1803. For $15 million, Jefferson bought French territory west of the Mississippi River that doubled the size of the United States. He then appointed Meriwether Lewis and William Clark to lead an expedition to explore the vast new territory and study its geography, vegetation, and plant life. Clark also brought his African-American slave, York, on the journey. York helped hunt and even saved Clark's life during a flood. The expedition was also aided by Sacagawea, a Shoshone woman, who acted as a guide and interpreter. The explorers also established relations with Native American tribes and set the stage for further western expansion in the 1800s.

Several key Supreme Court decisions were also issued during this time. The case of *Marbury vs. Madison* established the policy of judicial review, which declared that the Supreme Court could rule whether or not an act of Congress was constitutional. The case of *McCullough vs. Maryland* affirmed that Congress had the power to pass laws that were "necessary and proper" in order to carry out its other duties. The case also upheld the supremacy of federal laws over state laws when they came into conflict.

War between the United States and Britain broke out in 1812 because the United States was drawn into a conflict between Britain and France. Britain refused to stop interfering with American ships bound for France and had begun forcibly recruiting American citizens into the British navy. Furthermore, the British still occupied several forts near the Great Lakes and continued to encourage Indians to attack American settlements in the Northwest Territories.

This led to war in 1812, and many Native American leaders allied themselves with the British, including the Shawnee warrior Tecumseh. Tecumseh temporarily united several tribes but his confederacy fell apart when he was killed in battle. This further weakened Native American resistance and facilitated American settlement in the Northwest Territory after the war.

The United States also achieved a victory at the Battle of Lake Erie where several American ships routed a British squadron. However, an American attempt to invade Canada failed, and the British humiliated the nation by invading Washington D.C. and burning down several public buildings, including the White House. The United States did achieve another victory after hostilities had ceased when future president Andrew Jackson repulsed a British attack at New Orleans. The war did not result in any major territorial gains or losses, but it did reaffirm American independence and gave America its national anthem, the "Star Spangled Banner." It also led to the collapse of the Federalist Party, which had opposed the war. The Democratic-Republicans dominated politics for the next decade, which was known as the "Era of Good Feelings," thus marking the end of the first party system.

Causes and Consequences of Territorial Expansion

Constant immigration meant that land prices in the eastern United States rose, and people sought new economic opportunities on the frontier where land was cheaper. The United States government tried purchasing land from Native Americans, but most refused to relinquish their territories. Native Americans continued to defend their land until Tecumseh was defeated in the War of 1812. This defeat helped secure the Northwest Territory, and more settlers began pouring in. After the Louisiana Purchase, Lewis and Clark paved the way for expansion into the Great Plains and further west.

The Cherokee, Chickasaw, Choctaw, Creek, and Seminole tribes of the Southeastern United States were known as the "Five Civilized Tribes" because they had developed a written language and many members had become Christians. Nevertheless, Andrew Jackson signed the Indian Removal Act of 1830, which gave him the power to continue buying land from various tribes. The Cherokee filed a lawsuit to protect their territory and won their arguments before the Supreme Court. However, President Andrew Jackson ignored the ruling and eventually used troops to force many tribes off their land and sent them west to Oklahoma during the 1830s. This was known as the "Trail of Tears" because thousands of Native Americans died from starvation, exposure, and disease along the way.

Furthermore, the concept of Manifest Density emerged during the 1800s and introduced the idea that God wanted Americans to civilize and control the entire continent. This led to conflict when the province of Texas declared its independence from Mexico and asked to be annexed by the United States. President James K. Polk tried to buy Texas, but when Mexico refused, he sent troops into the disputed territory. Mexican troops responding by attacking an American unit, which led to war in 1846.

In the Mexican-American War, American troops won several battles although the Mexican army usually outnumbered them. The Mexican troops were poorly armed and trained, but, on the other hand, the Americans made use of their highly skilled artillery force. They eventually captured Mexico City and forced the Mexican government to sign the Treaty of Guadalupe-Hidalgo in 1848. The treaty recognized American control over Texas and also ceded California, Utah, Colorado, Arizona, New Mexico, and Nevada in exchange for $15 million. Tens of thousands of prospectors flooded into California when gold was discovered there in 1849. The prospectors often encroached on Native American lands, which led to further conflict. In 1854, the United States also acquired additional territories as part of the Gadsden Purchase. The acquisition of so much new territory sparked a debate over whether the land would be open or closed to slavery.

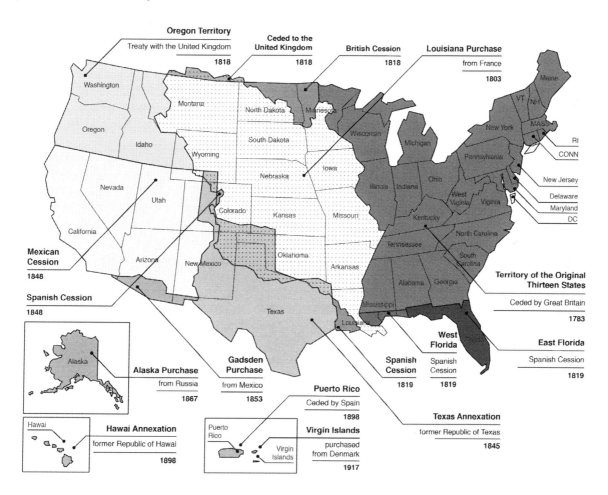

Manifest Destiny also sparked a desire to expand American influence into Central and South America. Adventurers launched several unsuccessful attempts to invade Nicaragua and Cuba.

Several important laws also stimulated western expansion during the second half of the 19th century. Congress passed the Homestead Act in 1862, which allowed citizens to claim 160 acres for only $1.25

per acre. The settler also had to live on the land for five years and make improvements. That same year, Congress also passed the Pacific Railroad Act, which supported the construction of a transcontinental railroad. The United States government provided land and financial support to railroad companies and the first transcontinental link was established in 1869. This facilitated trade and communication between the eastern and western United States.

As Americans poured westward, conflict again broke out between settlers and Native Americans. The discovery of gold in the Black Hills of South Dakota caused prospectors to flood into the area although the U.S. government had recognized the territory belonged to the Sioux. General George Armstrong Custer brought in troops to try and take possession of the Black Hills. This led to disaster when Custer and more than 250 soldiers died at the Battle of Little Big Horn in 1876.

The U.S. government continued its efforts to control Native American tribes. The Dawes Act of 1887 encouraged Native Americans to settle on reservations and become farmers in exchange for U.S. citizenship. Chief Joseph was a leader of the Nez Perce tribe who refused to live on a reservation and tried to flee to Canada. However, the U.S. captured Chief Joseph and his tribe and forced them onto a reservation. Reformers also required Native Americans to send their children to boarding schools where they had to speak English and dress like Caucasians instead of maintaining their traditional culture. The schools were often crowded, and students were also subjected to physical and sexual abuse.

In 1890, the Lakota Indians tried to preserve their traditional beliefs by performing a special ceremony called a Ghost Dance. U.S. government officials felt threatened and sent soldiers to try and disarm the Lakota. This led to the Massacre at Wounded Knee in 1890 where at least 150 Lakota, including many women and children, were slaughtered. It was the last major conflict between Native Americans and U.S. forces.

The United States purchased Alaska from Russia in 1867 for $7.2 million. At the time, the purchase was unpopular with the public, but seal hunting became very profitable and gold was discovered in 1896. Alaska became a state in 1959.

In 1893, American businessmen launched an armed coup, overthrew the queen of Hawaii, and asked Congress to annex Hawaii. The businessmen owned sugar plantations and feared the queen's attempts to enact reform would threaten their political influence. Hawaii became a U.S. territory in 1898 and a state in 1959.

The last phase of American territorial expansion occurred as a result of the Spanish-American War in 1898. New ideas arose in the late 19th century that helped justify further expansion. Some intellectuals applied Charles Darwin's ideas of "survival of the fittest" to the human race and called this new concept Social Darwinism. They used this idea to justify why stronger groups of people colonized and exploited weaker groups. In addition, imperialists also used the idea of the White Man's Burden to justify further expansion. They claimed that Caucasians were obligated to civilize and govern groups thought to be less advanced.

These ideas were used to justify America's new status as a colonial power as a result of the Spanish-American War. Although Spain had once been a powerful empire, it had been in decline. The United States went to war against Spain in 1898 when the American battleship USS Maine exploded in Havana Harbor and killed more than 250 sailors. The U.S. Navy defeated the Spanish fleet in several engagements and then the Army followed up with a victory at San Juan Hill, which included the famous charge by Teddy Roosevelt and the Rough Riders.

The war lasted less than four months and made the United States a world power. The U.S. also acquired several Spanish colonies, including Puerto Rico, Guam, and the Philippines. Guam became an important refueling station for American naval forces in the Pacific and remains a U.S. territory today, along with Puerto Rico. When the United States occupied the Philippines, the Filipino people launched a rebellion in order to obtain their independence. The U.S. Army put down the insurrection, but in doing so, they committed many atrocities against the Filipino people. The Philippines would remain an American territory until 1946.

Causes and Consequences of 19th-Century Sectionalism, the Civil War, and Reconstruction

In the early 1800s, political and economic differences between the North and South became more apparent. Politically, a small but vocal group of abolitionists emerged in the North who demanded a complete end to slavery throughout the United States. William Lloyd Garrison edited the abolitionist newspaper *The Liberator* and vehemently denounced the brutality of slavery. His criticism was so vicious that the legislature of Georgia offered a $5,000 bounty to anyone who could capture Garrison and deliver him to state authorities. Other activists participated in the Underground Railroad—a network that helped fugitive slaves escape to the Northern United States or Canada.

Economic differences emerged as the North began to industrialize, especially in the textile industry where factories increased productivity. However, the Southern economy remained largely agricultural and focused on labor-intensive crops such as tobacco and cotton. This meant that slavery remained an essential part of the Southern economy. In addition, the North built more roads, railroads, and canals, while the Southern transportation system lagged behind. The Northern economy was also based on cash, while many Southerners still bartered for goods and services. This led to growing sectional tension between the North and South as their economies began to diverge further apart.

These economic differences led to political tension as well, especially over the debate about the expansion of slavery. This debate became more important as the United States expanded westward into the Louisiana Purchase and acquired more land after the Mexican-American War. Most Northerners were not abolitionists. However, many opposed the expansion of slavery into the western territories because it would limit their economic opportunities. If a territory was open to slavery, it would be more attractive to wealthy slave owners who could afford to buy up the best land. In addition, the presence of slave labor would make it hard for independent farmers, artisans, and craftsman to make a living, because they would have to compete against slaves who did not earn any wages. For their part, Southerners felt it was essential to continue expanding in order to strengthen the southern economy and ensure that the Southern way of life survived. As intensive farming depleted the soil of nutrients, Southern slave owners sought more fertile land in the west.

Both the North and South also feared losing political power as more states were admitted to the nation. For example, neither side wanted to lose influence in the United States senate if the careful balance of free and slave state representation was disrupted. Several compromises were negotiated in Congress, but they only temporarily quieted debate. The first such effort, called the Missouri Compromise, was passed in 1820, and it maintained political parity in the U.S. Senate by admitting Missouri as a slave state and Maine as a free state. The Missouri Compromise banned slavery in the portion of the Louisiana Purchase that was north of the 36°30' parallel and permitted slavery in the portion south of that line as well as Missouri.

However, the slavery debate erupted again after the acquisition of new territory during the Mexican-American War. The Compromise of 1850 admitted California as a free state and ended the slave trade, but not slavery itself, in Washington D.C., in order to please Northern politicians. In return, Southern politicians were able to pass a stronger fugitive slave law and demanded that New Mexico and Utah be allowed to vote on whether or not slavery would be permitted in their state constitutions. This introduced the idea of popular sovereignty where the residents of each new territory, and not the federal government, could decide whether or not they would become a slave state or a free state. This essentially negated the Missouri Compromise of 1820. The enhanced fugitive slave law also angered many Northerners, because it empowered federal marshals to deputize anyone, even residents of a free state, and force them to help recapture escaped slaves. Anyone who refused would be subject to a $1,000 fine (equivalent to more than $28,000 in 2015).

The debate over slavery erupted again only a few years later when the territories of Kansas and Nebraska were created in 1854. The application of popular sovereignty meant that pro- and anti-slavery settlers flooded into these two territories to ensure that their faction would have a majority when it came time to vote on the state constitution. Tension between pro- and anti-slavery forces in Kansas led to an armed conflict known as "Bleeding Kansas."

John Brown was a militant abolitionist who fought in "Bleeding Kansas" and murdered five pro-slavery settlers there in 1856. He returned to the eastern United States and attacked the federal arsenal at Harper's Ferry, Virginia, in 1859. He hoped to seize the weapons there and launch a slave rebellion, but federal troops killed or captured most of Brown's accomplices and Brown was executed. The attack terrified Southerners and reflected the increasing hostility between North and South.

The sectional differences that emerged in the last several decades culminated in the presidential election of 1860. Abraham Lincoln led the new Republican Party, which opposed slavery on moral and economic grounds. The question of how best to expand slavery into new territories split the Democratic Party into two different factions that each nominated a presidential candidate. A fourth candidate also ran on a platform of preserving the union by trying to ignore the slavery controversy.

Lincoln found little support outside of the North but managed to win the White House since the Democratic Party was divided. Southern states felt threatened by Lincoln's anti-slavery stance and feared he would abolish slavery throughout the country. South Carolina was the first Southern state to secede from the Union and ten more eventually followed. Lincoln declared that the Union could not be dissolved and swore to defend federal installations. The Civil War began when Confederate troops fired on Fort Sumter in Charleston in 1861.

The Civil War

The First Battle of Bull Run (also known as the First Battle of Manassas) in 1861 was the first major infantry engagement of the Civil War. Both the Northern and Southern troops were inexperienced and although they had equal numbers, the Confederates emerged victorious. Many had thought the war would be short, but it continued for another four years.

The Union navy imposed a blockade on the Confederacy and captured the port of New Orleans in 1862. The Union navy was much stronger than the Confederate fleet and prevented the Southern states from selling cotton to foreign countries or buying weapons.

In 1862, Union forces thwarted a Confederate invasion of Maryland at the Battle of Antietam. This engagement was the single bloodiest day of the war and more than 23,000 men on both sides were killed or wounded. Union troops forced the Confederates to retreat, and that gave Lincoln the political capital he needed to issue the Emancipation Proclamation in 1863. This declaration did not abolish slavery, but it did free slaves in Southern territory. It also allowed African Americans to join the Union navy and about 200,000 did so. The 54th Massachusetts Infantry was a famous unit of African American soldiers who led an assault on Fort Wagner in South Carolina in 1863. Although the attack failed, the 54th Massachusetts witnessed African American troops fighting bravely under fire.

The Siege of Vicksburg in 1863 was a major Union victory because they gained control of the Mississippi River and cut the Confederacy in half. This made it difficult the Confederacy to move troops around and communicate with their forces. Grant commanded the Northern forces in the siege and eventually became the Union army's top general.

The Battle of Gettysburg in 1863 marked the turning point of the Civil War. Robert E. Lee led Confederate troops into Pennsylvania, but in three days of heavy fighting, the Union army forced them to retreat. The victory bolstered Northern morale and weakened Southern resolve. Never again would Confederate forces threaten Northern territory.

In 1864, Union general William T. Sherman captured Atlanta and then marched more than 200 miles to Savannah. Along the way, he destroyed anything that could support the Southern war effort, such as railroads and cotton mills. At this point, the Southern economy was beginning to collapse. The North had more manpower than the South and could afford to sustain more casualties. The North also had more industrial capacity to produce weapons and supplies and more railroads to transport men and equipment.

Eventually, Robert E. Lee surrendered to Ulysses S. Grant at Appomattox, Virginia, on April 9, 1865. Five days later, John Wilkes Booth assassinated Lincoln in Washington D.C. Vice President Andrew Johnson, a Democrat, succeeded him and soon came into conflict with Republicans in Congress about how to reintegrate Southern states into the nation. This process was known as Reconstruction and lasted from 1865 to 1877.

Reconstruction

Johnson opposed equal rights for African Americans and pardoned many Confederate leaders. However, many Congressional Republicans wanted to harshly punish Southerners for their attempts to secede from the Union. They were known as Radical Republicans because they also wanted to give former slaves equal rights.

Johnson vetoed bills that were designed to protect the rights of freed slaves, but Congress overrode his vetoes. This led to increasing conflict between Johnson and Congress, which eventually caused Radical Republicans to impeach him. Although Johnson was acquitted in 1868, he had very little power, and Radical Republicans took control of the Reconstruction process.

Republicans passed three important constitutional amendments as part of the Reconstruction process. The 13th amendment was ratified in 1865, and it abolished slavery throughout the country. The 14th Amendment was ratified in 1868 and gave equal rights to all citizens. The 15th Amendment was ratified in 1870 and specifically granted all men the right to vote regardless of race.

Southerners resisted these demands and passed laws that prohibited freed slaves from owning weapons or testifying against whites. They also formed militias and vigilante groups, such as the Ku Klux Klan, in order to intimidate African Americans who tried to vote. Congress sent federal troops into Southern states in order to enforce the law and prevent vigilante violence.

After the much-disputed election of 1876, the Democrats offered to let the Republicans have the White House if they agreed to end Reconstruction. After the Republicans agreed, federal troops were withdrawn and African Americans in the South were subjected to discrimination until the Civil Rights movement of the 1960s. Scholars often consider the Reconstruction era the beginning of Jim Crow and a transition into a new form of "institutionalized racism" that still pervades much of modern U.S. society.

Relationships Among Industrialization, Urbanization, and Immigration in the Late 19th and Early 20th Centuries

After the end of the Civil War, America experienced a period of intense industrialization, immigration, and urbanization, and all three trends were interrelated. The process of industrialization had begun before the Civil War but expanded into more sectors of the economy in the later part of the century. This era is often called the Second Industrial Revolution and included growth in the chemical, petroleum, iron, steel, and telecommunications industries. For example, the Bessemer process made it much easier to produce high quality steel by removing impurities during the smelting process.

The writer Mark Twain called the late 19th century the Gilded Age because the era was also one of extreme social inequality. Some corporations expanded and began to control entire industries. For example, by 1890, the Standard Oil Company produced 88 percent of all the refined oil in the nation. This made a few individuals, such as John D. Rockefeller who owned Standard Oil, extremely wealthy. On the other hand, many workers earned low wages and began to form labor unions, such as the American Federation of Labor in 1886, in order to demand better working conditions and higher pay. Strikes were one of the most common ways workers could express their dissatisfaction, and the Pullman Strike of 1894 was one of the largest such incidents in the 19th century. Workers went on strike after the Pullman Company, which manufactured railroad cars, cut wages by about 25 percent. More than 125,000 workers around the country walked off the job and attacked workers hired to replace them. Federal troops were sent in to end the strike, and more than eighty workers were killed or wounded during confrontations. The strike was unsuccessful, but Congress passed a law making Labor Day a federal holiday in order to placate union members.

Immigration also played an important part in the economic and social changes that occurred during the late 19th century. Immigration patterns changed during this time and immigrants from Southern and Eastern Europe, such as Italy and Poland, began to surpass the number of arrivals from Northern and Western Europe. The immigrants sought economic opportunity in the United States because wages for unskilled workers were higher than in their home countries. Some Americans resented the influx of immigrants because they spoke different languages and practiced Catholicism. In 1924, Congress passed a law that restricted immigration from Southern and Eastern Europe.

Increased urbanization was the last factor that contributed to the rapid changes of the Gilded Age. Factories were located near cities in order to draw upon a large pool of potential employees. Immigrants flooded into cities in search of work, and new arrivals often settled in the same neighborhoods where their compatriots lived. Between 1860 and 1890, the urbanization rate increased from about 20 percent to 35 percent. Cities struggled to keep up with growing populations, and services such as sanitation and water often lagged behind demand. Immigrants often lived in crowded living conditions that facilitated the spread of diseases.

Political, Economic, Social, and Cultural Developments from the Progressive Era Through the New Deal

The social inequalities and economic abuses of the Gilded Age did not go unnoticed, and in the 1890s many reformers began to demand change. This period was called the Progressive Era and included activists in both the Democratic and Republican parties. The Progressives wanted to use scientific methods and government regulation to improve society. For example, they advocated the use of initiative, referendum, and recall to make government more responsive to its citizens. Progressives also argued that it was necessary to breakup large monopolies (known as trust busting) in order to promote equal economic competition. In 1911, Rockefeller's Standard Oil was split up into thirty-four different companies in order to promote competition, and the Federal Trade Commission was established in 1914 in order to prevent other monopolies from forming. Many Progressives also supported several constitutional amendments that were ratified in early 20th century, including the 17th amendment, which established the direct election of U.S. Senators in 1913 (previously state legislatures had elected senators). They also favored the Prohibition of alcohol that went into effect with the 18th Amendment in 1919. Progressives also advocated for women's rights and backed the 19th Amendment, which gave women the right to vote in 1920.

Many journalists who supported the reform movement of the Progressives were known as Muckrakers because they helped expose political corruption and social inequality. Upton Sinclair wrote a novel in 1906 called "The Jungle," which exposed poor working conditions and health violations in the Chicago meatpacking industry. His exposé led to the passages of the Pure Food and Drug Act in 1906, which authorized the federal government to inspect the purity of foodstuffs and medicines. Jacob Riis was a photographer who documented the crowded and unhealthy living conditions that many immigrants and poor workers endured.

World War I, from 1914 to 1918, led to a communist revolution in Russia in 1917. Many Americans wanted to prevent political radicals from gaining influence in the United States. A number of strikes and bombings around the country led the federal government to crack down on anarchists, socialists, and communists in an event known as the First Red Scare. In 1919, U.S. Attorney General A. Mitchell Palmer launched a series of raids and arrested resident aliens suspected of belonging to radical groups. About 500 resident aliens were eventually deported.

In 1933, President Franklin D. Roosevelt introduced the New Deal, which was a series of executive orders and laws passed by Congress in response to the Great Depression. The programs focused on relief, recovery, and reform, and were enacted until 1938. The second New Deal from 1935-1938 promoted the Social Security Act, labor unions, and aided tenant farmers and migrant workers who were struggling from the economic devastation of the Great Depression.

Social Developments
With the ratification of the 19th Amendment in 1920, women obtained the right to vote. This achievement was partly due to women's contributions on the home front during World War I. Women served as Army nurses and worked in factories to help produce weapons, ammunition, and equipment. As more women entered the workforce, they became more financially independent and began to socialize without being supervised by a chaperone, as was the norm during the 19th century. Overall, women during this period, known as "New Women," took on a more active role in public life, pursued higher education in greater numbers, and sought more sexual freedom. During the 1920s, women, known as "flappers," began to flaunt social conventions by wearing short skirts, bobbing hair, smoking cigarettes, and driving automobiles. Nevertheless, a "glass ceiling" still remains in place decades after women's suffrage in regards to a gender wage gap.

Millions of African Americans also moved north during and after World War I in search of work in a phenomenon known as the Great Migration. This led to increased racial tension as whites and blacks competed for jobs and housing. This culminated in a wave of race riots that swept across the country in the summer of 1919. In Chicago, conflict broke out between whites and blacks at a segregated beach, which led to five days of violence during which thirty-eight people were killed and more than 500 injured. The impact of the Great Migration can still be seen in contemporary, heavily segregated Rust Belt cities such as Gary, IN and Milwaukee, WI.

The invention of the automobile also contributed to social change. Henry Ford applied the method of assembly line construction and scientific management to the automobile manufacturing industry. This made it much cheaper to manufacture cars and allowed more people to purchase them. Automobiles allowed young men and women to socialize and date without adult supervision. Automobiles also improved transportation, increased mobility, and spawned the first suburbs.

Cultural Developments

Motion picture cameras were invented in the late 19th century, and the film industry experienced significant growth in the early 20th century. Because the first movies were silent, dialogue was displayed on intertitles and a live orchestra usually performed during a screening. "Birth of a Nation," by D.W. Griffith, was one of the first major cinema blockbusters, and it portrayed the Ku Klux Klan in a heroic light. Millions of Americans saw the film, which helped the Klan spread throughout the Northern and Western United States.

The Great Migration also led to cultural changes during the 1920s known as the Harlem Renaissance. The movement was based in the neighborhood of Harlem and led to a rebirth of black literature, art, music, and fashion. Jazz was an important feature of the Harlem Renaissance and challenged musical conventions by emphasizing improvisation and spontaneity. Jazz became very popular with both whites and blacks during the 1920s. Langston Hughes was a poet of the Harlem Renaissance who encouraged his readers to take pride in their black identity.

Economic Developments

The Panic of 1893 was a worldwide economic depression that devastated the American economy. Businesses went bankrupt, banks collapsed, and unemployment rose to approximately 17 percent. The economy began to recover by 1897, and the beginning of World War I boosted the U.S. economy as European nations bought American goods.

In 1918, the United States emerged from World War I as a major economic power because it had helped finance the Allied war effort and produced large amounts of weapons and equipment. The American agricultural sector also prospered because European farms had been devastated by the war. This sent crop prices up, and farmers used the money to buy more land and equipment. Although the 1920s is usually depicted as an era of economic prosperity, agricultural prices fell after World War I, and farmers were unable to pay back their debts.

Stock market speculation increased during the 1920s, and investors borrowed money in order to purchase shares. This did not cause any concern as long as the stock market went up, but it led to disaster when stock prices fell sharply in October 1929 and investors were unable to repay their loans. The stock market crash may have triggered the Great Depression, but it did not cause it. The Great Depression spread around the globe as nations stopped trading with each other. In the United States, families lost their savings when banks failed because there was no federal insurance. The economy went into a downward spiral because as more people lost their jobs, they had little money to spend, which led to further layoffs and more economic contraction.

Unemployment peaked at 25 percent between 1932 and 1933.

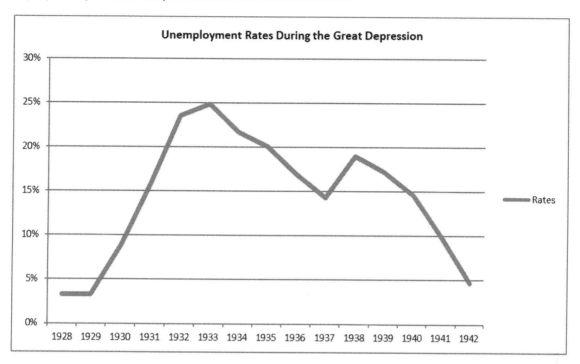

Democratic candidate Franklin D. Roosevelt was elected president in 1932 on his promise to help the economy recover by increasing government spending. After taking office in 1933, Roosevelt introduced a barrage of proposals, called the New Deal, that he hoped would boost employment, stimulate demand, and increase government regulation. Some elements of the New Deal were temporary, such as the Civilian Conservation Corps, which put young men to work improving parks between 1933 and 1942. Other New Deal programs endure to this day, such as the Social Security Administration, which has provided pensions to retirees, temporary payments to unemployed workers, and benefits to handicapped individuals since 1935. In addition, the Securities and Exchange Commission was created in 1934 and continues to regulate stock markets and investment companies. The Wagner Act of 1935 was also an important part of the New Deal because it guaranteed the right of workers to unionize and go on strike. The 21st Amendment was ratified in 1933 and repealed Prohibition, which had been hard to enforce and was unpopular. Roosevelt also hoped it would create jobs and stimulate spending. The New Deal helped reduce unemployment, but the economy did not completely recover until America entered World War II and production increased in order to support the war efforts.

Causes and Consequences of American Participation in World War I & II

World War I began in 1914 with the assassination of Franz Ferdinand, the apparent heir of the Austro-Hungarian Empire. A network of secret alliances meant that most European nations were quickly drawn into the conflict, although President Woodrow Wilson initially tried to keep the United States neutral. The war involved two major European alliances: the Triple Entente of Britain, France, and Russia, and the Central Powers, which included Germany and Austria-Hungary. The British implemented a naval blockade that was very successful, and the Germans retaliated by launching submarine attacks. German submarines attacked any ship carrying supplies to the Triple Entente, including the passenger ship RMS Lusitania in 1915. About 1,200 people died, including more than 100 Americans. The Germans temporarily halted their unrestricted submarine campaign, but eventually resumed the attacks in 1917. In addition, in 1917, Germany asked Mexico to attack the United States in a communiqué known as the

Zimmerman telegram. These events led the United States to join the Triple Entente in 1917, although significant numbers of American troops did not arrive in Europe until 1918. American reinforcement helped the British and French, who had been fighting continuously since 1914, launch a final offensive that defeated Germany in 1918. American forces suffered about 320,000 casualties. As previously noted, World War I also led to significant changes on the home front as women took on new responsibilities, and thousands of African Americans migrated north in search of work. World War I also led to a communist revolution that transformed Russia into the USSR in 1922.

After Germany was defeated in 1918, Wilson made a proposal known as the Fourteen Points and argued that the best way to resolve the conflict was by promoting free trade and democracy. For instance, Wilson wanted nations to respect the right to navigate in international waters and create a League of Nations that would resolve future disputes. Some of his suggestions, such as the League of Nations, were adopted, but many were not. In 1919, Germany was forced to sign the Treaty of Versailles, which imposed harsh economic penalties and restricted the German military. Ultimately, the Treaty of Versailles created resentment in Germany that lead to World War II. America emerged as an important player in world affairs after World War I because the American economy had supplied the Triple Entente with arms and equipment and American soldiers helped to achieve victory.

In the period between the world wars, fascism became popular in many European countries that were ravaged by the Great Depression. Fascism is a political ideology that advocates for a dictatorship in order to provide stability and unity. Adolf Hitler emerged as a prominent fascist leader in Germany and eventually brought the Nazi party to power in 1933. Germany, Italy, and Japan formed an alliance called the Axis and began to threaten other countries. The League of Nations could not diffuse the conflict. World War II broke out when Germany invaded Poland in 1939. Hitler quickly conquered most of Europe, except for Britain, and attacked the USSR in 1941. The United States sent military equipment and weapons to Britain and the USSR, but did not formally join the war until the Japanese attacked Pearl Harbor on December 7, 1941. Again, women played an important role on the home front by working in factories to build guns, tanks, planes, and ships. African Americans, Native Americans, and Japanese Americans also contributed by fighting on the front lines.

American forces first landed in North Africa where they, along with British and French troops, defeated German and Italian forces in 1942. In 1943, Allied forces invaded Italy, and Soviet troops began to push the German army back out of the USSR. Allied troops landed in France in 1944 and the Soviets began to advance on Germany as well. By May 1945, Hitler had committed suicide and Germany had been defeated.

This also brought about an end to the Holocaust. The Holocaust was a genocide committed by Hitler's Nazi Germany and collaborators that resulted in the deaths of more than 6 million Jews and 5 million Romans, gypsies, Afro-Europeans, disabled citizens, and homosexuals. A network of facilities in Germany and its territories were used to house victims for slave labor and mass murder, among other heinous crimes. The Nuremberg trials were part of the aftermath of the Holocaust, which served to prosecute important members of Nazi Germany leadership.

In the Pacific theater, American naval forces defeated the Japanese fleet in several key engagements, including the battle of Midway in 1942. American troops began recapturing territory in the Pacific as well and eventually pushed the Japanese back to their home islands in 1945. The Japanese refused to surrender until American planes dropped atomic bombs on the cities of Nagasaki and Hiroshima in August 1945.

Because World War II devastated most of Europe, the United States and the USSR emerged as the only superpowers when it ended. However, the erstwhile allies were suspicious of each other, which led to the Cold War.

Origins, Developments, and Consequences of the Cold War

Although the United States and the USSR worked together to defeat the Axis powers during World War II, the alliance quickly fell apart. As previously discussed, Americans had been afraid of communist influence since the Russian revolution in 1917. The USSR viewed the United States as a capitalist and imperialist power that threatened Soviet security. The USSR and United States divided Europe into spheres of influence, and this mutual hostility led to the Cold War. For example, the Soviets built a wall around the portion of Berlin, Germany that they occupied. The United States formed a military alliance, called the North Atlantic Treaty Organization, with its allies in Western Europe. The Soviets responded with their own defensive alliance in Eastern Europe, known as the Warsaw Pact. President Harry Truman announced that the United States would try to contain communist influence and would assist countries threatened by communist aggression. The domino theory predicted that once one country succumbed to communism, neighboring nations would also be at risk (thus following like a stack of dominoes). A resurgence of anti-communist sentiment occurred in the early 1950s when Senator Joseph McCarthy pledged to root out spies within the federal government. Known as the Second Red Scare in American history, McCarthy's communist "witch hunts" produced little evidence of his allegations and was censored in 1954 when he refused to reign in his attacks.

The resistance to communism led to a number of indirect conflicts around the globe between the United States and the USSR and China, which had become a communist regime in 1949. For example, Korea was divided into two portions after World War II (at the 38th parallel). When the communist regime in North Korea invaded South Korea in 1950, the United States sent troops to defend South Korea. The USSR and China sent troops, weapons, and equipment to support North Korea. The war ended in a stalemate in 1953, and Korea remains divided to this day. Today, it is divided at a unique demarcation line close to the original 38th parallel separation.

Vietnam was also partitioned into northern and southern regions after World War II. The United States supported South Vietnam and sent troops in ever-increasing numbers. The conflict intensified when North Vietnamese gunboats allegedly attacked a U.S. navy ship in 1964. However, U.S. forces were unable to defeat the Vietnamese communists, who preferred to use guerrilla troops and ambush tactics. The support for the war evaporated in United States as casualties mounted and the draft was unpopular as well. American troops also killed at least 300 civilians in the Vietnamese village of My Lai in 1968. National Guardsmen shot and killed four students and wounded nine others during an anti-war protest at Kent State University in 1970. These scandals made the war extremely unpopular. American troops withdrew in 1973, and South Vietnam was defeated in 1975.

The U.S. and USSR also vied for influence in South America and Africa as well. Some nations refused to pick sides and instead formed the Non-Aligned Movement.

The nuclear arms race and the space race were also important arenas in the Cold War. The Soviets took an early lead in the space race and successfully launched the first satellite into orbit in 1957. The Soviets also put the first man, cosmonaut Yuri Gagarin, into space in 1961. However, the United States surpassed the Soviet Union by landing the first man, Neil Armstrong, on the Moon in 1969.

The United States was the only nuclear power for a brief period after World War II, but the Soviets quickly caught up and detonated their own nuclear bomb in 1949. Both sides developed nuclear missiles during the 1950s. This became a very dramatic issue during the Cuban Missile Crisis. In 1962, President John F. Kennedy learned that the Soviets were installing nuclear missiles in Cuba, which had become a communist regime. The U.S. navy imposed a blockade, and tensions rose as the Soviets refused to back down. Eventually, negotiations ended the crisis and the Soviets agreed to withdraw the missiles in Cuba if the U.S. agreed to withdraw missiles from Turkey that threatened the USSR. Although tensions remained, the nuclear arms race slowed during the 1970s when the U.S. and USSR entered into negotiations. Both the U.S. and USSR promised to reduce nuclear weapons tests and limit their nuclear arsenals. Throughout the Cold War, a concept known as "Mutually Assured Destruction" (MAD) helped prevent nuclear war. Both the United States and the USSR each had thousands of warheads and MAD predicted that no matter who struck first, the other side would have enough surviving firepower to destroy the aggressor.

During the Cold War, a number of protests and demonstrations occurred in the Soviet satellites in Eastern Europe, including Hungary in 1956 and in Czechoslovakia in 1968. The uprisings were suppressed, but demands for reform continued and, in 1985, Mikhail Gorbachev became the leader of the USSR. He promised to make political and economic reforms, but protestors wanted change to occur more rapidly. Revolutions swept through Eastern Europe in 1989, and the communist regimes in Poland, Romania, and elsewhere crumbled. The Berlin Wall fell in 1989, and the Cold War ended when the USSR collapsed in 1991. This left the United States as the sole superpower, although other countries, such as India and China, have become more powerful. Recent scholars, however, are questioning whether the Cold War is once again beginning to heat up with the most recent tensions between Russia and the United States in the early 2000s.

Social, Economic, and Technological Changes Between 1950 and 2000

The post-World War II era led to a number of social, economic, and technological changes in the United States. The counter-culture phenomenon was one of the most powerful social movements in the latter half of the twentieth century in the U.S. The counter-culture movement challenged social norms and rejected traditional authority figures. The movement began in the 1950s with the beatniks, a group of non-conformist writers and artists who were dissatisfied with society. The beatniks sought inspiration in African and Asian cultures and many eschewed materialism.

The counter-culture movement became more popular during the 1960s as millions of children from the Baby Boomers generation entered into adulthood. Veterans came home after World War II and started families, and, by the 1960s, many of these young adults also felt disaffected and rebellious. Their parents criticized them because they began to wear colorful clothing and the boys let their hair grow out. Many members of the counter-culture movement, now called hippies, inherited the beatnik's interest in African and Asian cultures. Writer Ken Kesey traveled around the country on a bus encouraging people to experiment with psychedelic drugs, such as LSD. The counter-culture movement influenced musicians and avant-garde artists.

The counter-culture movement was also closely connected to other protest movements during the 1960s, including the Civil Rights movement, which will be discussed later. Many members of the counter-culture movement during the 1960s also opposed the war in Vietnam. The Baby Boomers could be conscripted to fight in Vietnam whether they wanted to or not. In 1965, young men began burning their draft cards, which was a criminal offense, in protest. Massive demonstrations against the war occurred around the country, especially on college campuses, but many other people also refused to support the war effort, including clergymen and even some veterans who had fought in Vietnam. The counter-culture movement disappeared during the 1970s but had a lasting impact on the social and cultural history of the United States.

Economic Changes

America emerged as one of the most powerful economies in the world after 1945. The US economy, especially manufacturing, was very prosperous during the 1950s and 1960s. The economy successfully switched from wartime production, and consumer demand was very high. During the Great Depression, few families had disposable income. Although most workers earned good wages during World War II, they had little to spend it on because most goods were rationed. Once production of consumer goods resumed, families used their savings to buy cars, household appliances, and televisions. This was good for the economy, and unemployment remained below 5 percent for most of the 1950s and 1960s. However, during the latter part of the 20th century, the manufacturing base in the North and Midwest began to crumble and the area became known as the Rust Belt. Manufacturing jobs began to move from the North and Midwest to states in the South and West, known as the Sun Belt, where land was cheap and wages were low.

The world economy also became increasingly interconnected during the post-World War II era. This accelerated the process of globalization, which is the integration of ideas and products from different cultures. This benefitted the United States economically because businesses, such as McDonald's and Coca-Cola, found many consumers around the world who were eager to consume American goods. However, the process works both ways, and many aspects of foreign culture, such as Japanese cartoons and animation, have become very popular in the United States. Many critics also point out that globalization has hurt the American economy in recent decades because manufacturing jobs have gone overseas to countries in South America and Asia where wages are low.

Technological Changes

Several technological changes have had a significant impact on the U.S. economy as well. The Cold War led to advances in nuclear power and aerospace engineering. The development of computers, in particular, has helped accelerate the transition to a post-industrial economy where information technology and other services have replaced traditional manufacturing jobs. The first computers were used to break coded messages during World War II and had very limited computing power. The invention of transistor technology in 1947 made computers cheaper, smaller, and more reliable. The invention of integrated circuits in the 1960s and 1970s increased computing power and gave birth to the first personal computers. The Internet was created in 1969, but widespread use in business and academia did not begin until the 1980s. These developments have made it much easier to share information and have increased economic opportunities. But, the increasing use of robots, especially in the manufacturing industry, have also made the economy more efficient while also causing layoffs.

Political Realignments from the New Deal and Great Society Through the Rise of Conservatism

President Franklin D. Roosevelt created the New Deal in order to stimulate the economy and improve government regulation. The New Deal also marked an important shift in American politics because the Democratic Party began to favor government intervention while Republicans opposed it. This was a reversal of the parties' previous platforms. The Democratic Party relied on a coalition of labor unions, Catholics, African Americans, and other minorities. The Republican Party included conservatives, evangelicals, and business leaders.

The Great Society was another major government program that the Democratic Party supported. President Lyndon B. Johnson sought to end poverty and improve education. For example, he raised the minimum wage and created programs to provide poor Americans with job training. The Great Society also implemented a number of Civil Rights laws that will be discussed in greater detail later.

The presidential election of 1980 was another watershed moment. Republican nominee Ronald Reagan carried forty-three states, and the Republicans won a majority in the U.S. Senate after twenty-eight years of Democratic control. Reagan presented an optimistic message and broadcasted a television advertisement that proclaimed "It's morning again in America." He promised to restore America's military power, cut government regulations, and reduce taxes. Reagan enjoyed the support of resurgent conservative Christian evangelicals, who wanted to restore morality to American society. They were particularly concerned about issues such as abortion. The Moral Majority, founded by Baptist minister Jerry Falwell in 1979, was one key group that helped Reagan win the election. This coalition helped realign party loyalties, as more liberal Republicans and conservative Democrats shifted their allegiance.

Impact of Race, Gender, and Ethnicity Throughout American History

Race, gender, and ethnicity have been important themes in American history from the colonial era to the present. Individuals from different races, ethnicities, and genders have had very different experiences throughout the same historical events or eras. It is important to distinguish between race and ethnicity: race refers to a group of people with common ancestry, while ethnicity refers to cultural background, such as language and tradition.

Race played an important part in colonial America because both Caucasians and Africans occupied positions of servitude. White immigrants who could not purchase passage to the New World sometimes agreed to become indentured servants. Their employers paid for their passage across the Atlantic, and in exchange, the indentured servant agreed to work without wages for at least five years. However, African slaves were rarely able to free themselves. The strong connection between slavery and race meant that all blacks, whether free or enslaved, were viewed as inferior. After the American Revolution, most free blacks, even those living in northern states, were denied the right to vote. Although the Civil Rights Movement in the 1960s made great gains, many activists claim more must be done in order to overcome the legacy of racial inequality in America.

Chinese and Japanese have also been the victims of discrimination throughout American history as well. For example, in 1882 Congress prohibited Chinese immigration in an act known as the Chinese Exclusion Act. This was the first law to ever prevent an entire ethnic group from immigrating to the United States. Japanese Americans also experienced discrimination during and after World War II, specifically with the implementation of Japanese internment camps in America. This forced 110,000 to 120,000 Japanese Americans into camps, 62 percent of which were United States citizens.

Discrimination against certain ethnicities is also prominent throughout American history as well. For example, many Americans resented the arrival of German and Irish immigrants during the 1800s because they spoke a different language or practiced different religions. Hispanics were also subject to discrimination, and in 1943, a number of Hispanic youths were attacked during the Zoot Suit Riots.

Gender differences in the United States have also been impossible to ignore. For example, until the 1840s, most married women in the United States were unable to enter into contracts, own property, or retain their own wages. As previously discussed, women were unable to vote until the 19th Amendment was ratified in 1920. The Women's Rights Movement in the U.S. ranged from 1848 to 1920. This movement called for a woman's right to vote, the right to bodily autonomy, freedom from sexual violence, the right to hold public office, the right to work, the right to fair wages and equal pay, and the right to own property and obtain an education. Women continue to demand change during the 21st century for reasons such as the gender wage gap, better resources for women's health, female reproductive rights, and for protection of basic human rights, such as bringing greater awareness to rape culture, violence against women, and protection against female sex trafficking.

How Participants in the Political Process Engage in Politics and Shape Policy

The Constitution provides for a series of checks and balances between the legislative, executive, and judicial branches of the federal government. Members of Congress debate and vote on legislation, although the president may request that legislators consider a certain proposal. The president may veto legislation that he or she disagrees with, but Congress can override the veto with a two-thirds majority in both chambers. The Supreme Court may review legislation and declare it unconstitutional. The president selects nominees to the Supreme Court but the Senate must confirm them.

Branch	Role	Checks & Balances on Other Branches	
Executive	Carries out the laws	Legislative Branch • Proposes laws • Vetoes laws • Calls special sessions of Congress • Makes appointments • Negotiates foreign treaties	Judicial Branch • Appoints federal judges • Grants pardons to federal offenders
Legislative	Makes the laws	Executive Branch • Has the ability to override a President's veto • Confirms executive appointments • Ratifies treaties • Has the ability to declare war • Appropriates money • Has the ability to impeach and remove President	Judicial Branch • Creates lower federal courts • Has the ability to impeach and remove judges • Has the ability to propose amendments to overrule judicial decisions • Approves appointments of federal judges
Judicial	Interprets the laws	Executive Branch • Has the ability to declare executive actions unconstitutional	Legislative Branch • Has the ability to declare acts of Congress unconstitutional

Constituents, businesses, professional associations, civic organizations, and other interest groups may lobby members of Congress and ask them to propose legislation or support a certain proposal. Interest groups may also lobby the president and other executive branch officials in order to try and influence policies. The president appoints fifteen men and women to head a variety of executive departments, including defense, transportation, education, and many others. These officials are known as the president's cabinet, and they advise the president on various matters. These discussions are used to help formulate policies, and the cabinet members are responsible for putting the decisions into action. The president may also issue executive orders that instruct federal employees how to enforce certain policies. For example, in 1948, President Harry S. Truman issued an executive order that established racial integration within the armed forces.

Elections are an essential part of our democracy. Although members of Congress are prohibited from accepting gifts, individuals and interest groups can make campaign contributions during elections, which occur every two years in the House, four years for the White House, and six years in the Senate. Individuals can give a maximum of $2,700 per year to individual candidates. Since 2010, individuals, corporations, labor unions, and other contributors can give an unlimited amount to organizations known as super PACs (Political Action Committees). Super PACs may not give money to candidates or parties but can air commercials that support a specific issue.

Although President George Washington warned against creating political parties in his farewell address in 1796, they have been a part of American politics since the founding of our country. The Republicans and Democrats hold conventions to nominate candidates for state and national elections. The parties also create a platform, which is a set of goals and principles, at each convention in order to set priorities and inform members about issues. During elections, parties also organize rallies and urge voters to support their candidates and issues. Some Americans belong to either the Republican or Democratic Party, but voters who belong to neither party are known as independents.

Emergence of the United States as a World Power and the Evolving Role of United States in the World

The United States gained prestige and international status after the Spanish-American War of 1898, because the United States defeated Spain and acquired several colonies. American participation in World War I made the United States an economic and financial leader as well. The United States loaned money to Britain and France and supplied weapons and equipment that helped the Triple Entente achieve victory. The United States and USSR emerged from World War II as the only surviving superpowers because so much of the rest of the world had been devastated. This system was described as bipolar because there were two centers of power.

The United States was the leader of the free world during the Cold War and formed military and economic alliances with other nations. With the collapse of the USSR in 1991, the United States was the only surviving world power. This era was a unipolar system because there were no other major powers that could rival the United States.

Although the U.S. was still considered a world power, September 11, 2001 demonstrated that America was nevertheless vulnerable to attacks. The attacks on 9/11 killed more than 3,000 civilians and first-responders. Although American troops have been stationed in Iraq and Afghanistan for more than a decade, both nations are still unstable, and the lack of progress has damaged American prestige. Furthermore, new economic and military powers have risen to challenge American dominance in world affairs. The Chinese economy has grown significantly, and the Chinese government has expanded and improved its armed forces. India has also boosted its manufacturing industry and has purchased new fighter jets and an aircraft carrier. The European Union, Russia, and Brazil have also emerged as potential rivals that might create a multipolar environment. However, the United States is still the world's largest economy and remains a cultural leader.

The Influence of Religion Throughout American History

Religion has also been an important, albeit divisive, theme in American history since the colonial period. The British colonies in North America attracted settlers from many different religions, including Catholics in Maryland, Quakers in Pennsylvania, Puritans in New England, and Anglicans in Virginia. This led to conflict and tension. For example, Puritans in New England expelled dissenters and even executed four Quakers between 1659 and 1661.

In the 1730s and 1740s, a religious revival known as the First Great Awakening swept through the British colonies in North America. This movement emphasized a more personal connection to Christ, and some Protestant preachers, such as Jonathan Edwards, began to present their sermons in a more passionate and emotional style. This "fire and brimstone" form of religious dissemination became the cornerstone of the First Great Awakening. These passionate sermons—and the emotions that they stirred—caused divisions within Protestant congregations. Those who supported the Great Awakening were known as New Lights while those who opposed it were called Old Lights. The Baptists and Methodists became more popular during the revival because they embraced this new style of preaching.

The Second Great Awakening occurred in the early 1800s and urged Protestants to work not only for their own salvation but for the salvation of others as well. This helped fuel a social reform movement that promoted the abolition of slavery, temperance, and prison reform. The question of slavery caused schisms in the Baptist and Methodist churches during the 1840s. The Second Great Awakening, much like the First Great Awakening, inaugurated the creation of several New Religious Movements (NRMs) in the United States, especially in the southern states.

A third revival occurred in the late 1800s that emphasized temperance. As previously discussed, the religious right emerged after World War II and began to play an important part in American politics, especially during the election of President Ronald Reagan in 1980.

Although Catholics were a minority during the colonial period of American history, Catholicism has become the largest religious denomination in the United States. Many colonial governments actually banned Catholicism, but the American Revolution brought more toleration. However, anti-Catholic sentiment renewed in the 1800s as immigrants from Ireland and Germany, many of whom were Catholic, arrived in ever-increasing numbers. The arrival of Italian immigrants in the late 1800s and early 1900s also increased Protestant-Catholic tension in America. Many Americans feared that Catholic immigrants would be more loyal to Pope than they would be to the Constitution. This led to the creation of the Know-Nothings who sought to limit immigration and physically attacked Catholics. Anti-Catholic sentiment remained an issue even until the presidential election of 1960 when John F. Kennedy, a Catholic, won the Democratic nomination. Kennedy helped allay fears by promising to respect the separation of church and state. Since then, anti-Catholicism has largely disappeared.

Small numbers of Jews immigrated to the U.S. during the colonial period, but large numbers of Jews from Eastern Europe began to arrive in the late 19th and early 20th centuries. Jews contributed to the American economy in many different ways but drew criticism from anti-Semites because of their prominence in the financial industry. The Anti-Defamation League was founded in 1913 to combat anti-Semitic sentiments. In the 1920s, the resurgent Ku Klux Klan revived anti-Semitism. The Anti-Defamation League sponsored events after World War II to commemorate the Holocaust and repudiate Holocaust deniers. Anti-Semitism has declined, but the Anti-Defamation League reported that more than 900 anti-Semitic incidents occurred across the country in 2014.

Muslim immigration in the 1800s remained modest. The first mosque was not constructed in the United States until the 20th century. In the latter part of the 20th century, more Muslims, especially from Pakistan, began arriving in the United States. In the wake of the 9/11 attacks, Islamophobic incidents increased, and Muslims were victims of harassment, intimidation, and assaults. The United States' current battle with ISIS in the Middle East, North Africa, and Europe has also increased Islamophobia, paving the way to an anti-refugee right-wing faction in the current Republican Party. The religious morality of the nation has once again become a hot-button topic in the wake of the recent Clinton-Trump debates for the U.S. Presidency.

Major Economic Transformations in the United States

The American economy has changed dramatically since the 1700s, a century where agriculture was the main economic activity. The First Industrial Revolution began in the early 1800s when steam-powered machines were used to increase productivity, especially in the textile industry. The invention of steamboats and railroads made it much cheaper and faster to ship goods across the country in the mid-1800s as well. After the Civil War, the Second Industrial Revolution led to increased productivity and efficiency in the many industries, including metallurgy, chemicals, telecommunications, and energy. This led to significant social changes as immigration and urbanization increased. Workers began to form labor unions in order to demand better wages and working conditions, which led to strikes and conflict with law enforcement officials.

In the early 20th century, Henry Ford introduced the moving assembly line to the automobile manufacturing industry, which made it easier for middle- and working-class families to buy cars. Other industries adopted Ford's methods, which led to lower prices for many consumer goods. The stock market crash in 1929 helped trigger the Great Depression, which resulted in a vicious downward economic spiral. Franklin D. Roosevelt introduced the New Deal to try and boost the economy, but only the outbreak of World War II led to full employment. The United States emerged from World War II as the world's largest economy and pent-up consumer demand fueled prosperity during the post-war era.

The development of computers in the latter part of the 20th century improved communications and led to greater economic efficiency. However, it also marked the beginning of the post-industrial economy in the United States. Traditional manufacturing jobs began to disappear as robots replaced unskilled workers. On the other hand, careers in the information technology sector grew and became a key component of the new high-tech economy. Many unskilled manufacturing jobs also went overseas to countries in Asia and South America as the global economy became more interconnected.

The Causes and Consequences of Changing Immigration Patterns to the United States

Immigration has always played an important role in American history, although patterns have changed over time. Most immigrants came to the United States in search of better economic opportunities, although some have sought religious and political freedom as well. During the colonial period, most immigrants came from Britain, but during the mid-1800s that began to change. In the 1840s, a fungus destroyed the potato crop in Ireland, which led to widespread famine. Many Irish starved, but millions also emigrated, with many heading to the United States. A wave of revolutions also swept across Europe in 1848 and many participants, especially Germans, fled to the United States when the movements failed. This shift led to tension and conflict between immigrants and those born in America. Native-born Americans resented the immigrants' cultural differences and the increased competition for jobs. In the late 1800s, immigration patterns changed again and arrivals from Southern and Eastern Europe began to increase. In 1924, Congress passed an act that limited immigration from these areas.

In 1965, immigration patterns changed again when Congress passed the Immigration and Nationality Act of 1965 act that changed the way immigration quotas were calculated. Immigrants from Central and South America, as well as Asia, became very numerous. Like their predecessors, most came in search of jobs. Recently, many refugees are fleeing violence that erupted from the U.S. invasion of Iraq in 2003 and the revolutions that swept through the Middle East between 2010 and 2012. Cultural differences and economic competition between immigrants and native-born American citizens continue, especially against Mexicans. Vigilante groups have formed in order to prevent illegal immigrants from crossing the U.S.-Mexico border.

Internal Migration

Migration within the United States has also been an important theme since the colonial period. During the 18th and 19th centuries, the focus was on westward expansion because settlers sought cheap land. This often led to violence between settlers and Native Americans who refused to relinquish their territory.

The 19th century also saw an increase in migration from rural areas to cities as individuals sought employment in factories. This trend continued until the late 20th century and more than 80 percent of Americans now live in cities. World War I led to the Great Migration of African Americans from the South to the North. This influx also created more competition for jobs and housing and resulted in a wave of race riots in 1919.

The Struggles and Achievements of Individuals and Groups for Greater Political and Civil Rights Throughout American History

Although the Declaration of Independence declared "all men are created equal," blacks, women, and other minorities struggled for more than a century to make this dream a reality. The U.S. Constitution legalized slavery, and it was not abolished until the 13th Amendment was ratified in 1865. The 14th Amendment, ratified in 1868, granted African Americans citizenship, and the 15th Amendment, ratified in 1870, explicitly granted them the right to vote. However, white Southerners passed laws, known as the Jim Crow system, that prevented blacks from exercising their rights and, when that failed, they relied on violence and intimidation to oppress African Americans. For example, many Southern states required voters to pass literacy tests and used them to prevent blacks from casting a ballot. Whites were either exempt from the test or were held to much lower standards. Blacks who protested their oppression could be assaulted and even killed with impunity. In the 1896 decision *Plessy vs. Ferguson*, the U.S. Supreme Court ruled that "separate but equal" schools for white and black students were permissible. In reality, black schools were almost always inferior to white schools.

The emergence of the Civil Rights Movement after World War II finally destroyed the Jim Crow system. In the 1954 decision *Brown vs. Board of Education*, the Supreme Court reversed the "separate but equal" doctrine and declared that separate schools were inherently unequal because they stigmatized African American students. In 1957, President Dwight D. Eisenhower used federal troops to force the high school in Little Rock, Arkansas, to integrate and accept nine black students. This encouraged civil rights activists to demand additional reforms. In 1955, Rosa Parks refused to give up her seat on a bus in Montgomery, Alabama, which led to a boycott. Martin Luther King Jr. led the bus boycott and became a national leader in the Civil Rights Movement. In 1960, four students in Greensboro, North Carolina, launched a peaceful sit-in at a segregated lunch counter, which sparked similar protests around the country. White activists from the North went south to help blacks register to vote, and in 1964 three activists were murdered in Mississippi. That same year, King led 250,000 protesters in a march on Washington D.C. where he delivered his famous "I Have a Dream Speech."

Although King advocated for peaceful protests, many other civil rights activists disagreed with him. For example, Malcolm X believed that blacks should use violence to defend themselves. Furthermore, King worked with white activists while Malcom X rejected any cooperation. Malcolm X was assassinated in 1965, and, despite his reputation as a non-violent leader, King was also gunned down in 1968.

Under mounting pressure, Congress passed several important pieces of legislation. The 1964 Civil Rights Act banned discrimination based on race, color, religion, sex, or national origin. The Voting Rights Act of 1965 prohibited the use of poll taxes or literacy tests to prohibit voting. The Civil Rights Act of 1968 banned housing discrimination. In 1967, Carl Stokes became the first black mayor of a major American city, Cleveland. That same year, Thurgood Marshall became the first African American to serve on the Supreme Court. President Gerald Ford declared February to be black history month. In 1989, Colin Powell became the first black chairman of the Joint Chiefs of Staff. Despite these reforms, activists claim institutional racism is still a problem in the 21st century. The Civil Rights movement inspired women, Latinos, and other groups to make similar demands for equal rights.

Women

In 1776, Abigail Adams urged her husband, founding father John Adams, to advocate for women's rights, but it would take more than a century before women could vote. In 1848, activists organized a convention in Seneca Falls, New York, to organize the women's suffrage movement, and their efforts slowly gained momentum. The ratification of the 19th Amendment in 1920 finally gave women the right to vote.

Although women had achieved political equality, they continued to demand reform throughout the 20th century. In the early 1900s, Margaret Sanger provided women with information about birth control, which was illegal at the time. Women entered the industrial workforce in large numbers during World War II, but when the war ended, they were fired so that veterans would have jobs when they came home. Many women were frustrated when told they had to return to their domestic lives. Simone de Beauvoir, a French writer, published her book "The Second Sex" after World War II, and an English translation was published in 1953. It highlighted the unequal treatment of women throughout history and sparked a feminist movement in the United States. In 1963, Betty Friedan published a book, called "The Feminine Mystique," that revealed how frustrated many suburban wives were with the social norms that kept them at home. During the 1960s, women participated in the sexual revolution and exerted more control over their own sexuality. In 1972, Congress passed Title IX, which prohibited sexual discrimination in education and expanded women's sports programs. In the 1970s, women's rights activists also pushed for greater access to birth control, and in 1973 the Supreme Court issued the landmark decision *Roe vs. Wade* which removed many barriers to abortion services. Women also demanded greater protection from domestic abuse and greater access to divorce.

During the 20th century, many American women made notable achievements, including Amelia Earhart, who was the first woman to cross the Atlantic in an airplane in 1928. In 1981, Sandra Day O'Connor became the first woman to serve on the Supreme Court. In 1983, Sally Ride became the first female astronaut. In 1984, Geraldine Ferraro became the first woman to run for vice-president, although she was unsuccessful. However, many activists continue to demand reform in the 21st century. For example, women only account for 20 percent of the U.S. Senate and House of Representatives. Furthermore, women only earn 79 percent of what men in similar jobs are paid. In 1980, President Jimmy Carter declared March to be women's history month.

Hispanics

After World War II, many Hispanics also began to demand greater equality. In 1949, veterans protested a refusal by a Texas town to bury a Mexican American soldier, who died during World War II, in the local cemetery, because only whites could be buried there. Activists called themselves Chicanos, a term that previously was used as a pejorative to describe Mexican Americans. Cesar Chavez was a labor union activist who organized transient Hispanic agricultural workers in an effort to obtain better working conditions in the 1960s and 1970s. Activists encouraged a sense of pride in Chicano identity, especially in arts and literature. In 1968, President Lyndon B. Johnson declared National Hispanic Heritage Month would run from mid-September to mid-October.

In 1959, biochemist Severo Ochoa became the first Hispanic to win a Nobel Prize. Franklin Chang-Diaz became the first Hispanic astronaut in 1986, and he flew a total of seven space shuttle missions. In 1990, Oscar Hijuelos became the first Hispanic American to win the Pulitzer Prize. Sonja Sotomayor became the first Hispanic to serve on the Supreme Court in 2009.

Native Americans

Native Americans suffered centuries of oppression at the hands of European colonists, and later American settlers as they pushed further west. Native Americans resisted attempts to encroach on their lands but were pushed onto smaller and smaller reservations. The Massacre at Wounded Knee in 1890 was the last major conflict between Native Americans and U.S. forces. However, American officials continued to try and force Native Americans to assimilate into white culture.

In 1968, a group of Native Americans formed the American Indian Movement in order to combat racism and demand greater independence. Between 1969 and 1971, a group of Native American activists occupied the federal prison on Alcatraz Island near San Francisco, although it had been closed since 1963. The activists offered to buy back the island for $9.40 in order to draw attention to how the federal government had forced tribes to sell their lands at low prices. Other activists disrupted Thanksgiving Day ceremonies aboard a replica of the Mayflower in Boston in 1970. In 1971, Native American activists also occupied Mount Rushmore, which is located on ground the Native Americans consider sacred. Violence broke out between activists and law enforcement officials in 1973 when Native Americans occupied the town of Wounded Knee, sight of the famous massacre.

In 1970, President Richard Nixon granted Native American tribes more autonomy. In 1978, Congress passed the American Indian Religious Freedom Act, which guaranteed Native Americans' rights to practice their religious ceremonies and visit sacred sites. In 1990, President George H.W. Bush declared November Native American History Month. In 1969, Navarre Scott Momaday became the first Native American to win a Pulitzer Prize for his book "House Made of Dawn." In 2014, Diane Humetewa, a member of the Hopi tribe, became the first Native American woman to serve as a federal judge. However, many Native American communities still suffer from high rates of unemployment, alcoholism, and domestic abuse.

Asian Americans

Asian Americans also faced discrimination throughout American history and in 1882, Congress passed a law banning all Chinese immigrants. During World War II, more than 100,000 Japanese Americans were interned in concentration camps. In 1982, two American autoworkers beat Vincent Chin to death with a baseball bat because his assailants blamed him for the loss of jobs in the automotive manufacturing industry.

In the 1960s, activists demanded that the term "Asian American" replace the word "oriental," because it carried a stigma. Asian Americans also promoted a sense of pride in their cultural identity and successfully pushed for the creation of ethnic studies programs. Ellison Onizuka became the first Asian American astronaut in 1985, although he perished in the space shuttle Challenger disaster. In 1990, President George H.W. Bush declared May Asian Pacific American Heritage Month and Sheryl WuDunn became the first Asian American to win a Pulitzer Prize that same year.

World History

The Major Causes and Consequences of Revolutions, Nationalism, and Imperialism in the Period 1750 CE to 1914 CE

While the colonies were increasing in population and production over their first 150 years, British oversight was loose, and the colonies enjoyed extensive self-government. However, in the mid-1700s, England, in need of revenue, began to enforce laws and create new ones that restricted the freedoms in trade the colonies enjoyed. Starting in 1764, the prime minister of England, Lord George Grenville, began to impose acts that the American colonies resented and protested, including the Sugar Act, the Quartering Act, and the Stamp Act. Groups were formed in protest, such as the Sons of Liberty, and even the colonial governments threatened to refuse to obey the acts. A spirit of nationalism swept through the colonies, who began to view themselves as a collective entity.

In 1765, believing that the colonies had the only right to tax colonists, nine colonies banded together to form the Stamp Act Congress, also known as the *First Congress of the American Colonies*. The Stamp Act Congress sent their grievances to King George III of England. Though the Stamp Act was repealed, Parliament issued a law making it clear that the colonies were under the British government's rule. More laws were enacted to tax the colonies, further stirring discontent in the British colonies. In an attempt to punish and subdue the American colonies, Parliament issued further acts called the *Coercive Acts,* or the *Intolerable Acts,* as they were known in America. These acts only served to unify the colonies and, as a result, the First Continental Congress in 1774 issued another formal complaint. The response from King George III and Parliament was to increase troops in the colonies. In the Second Continental Congress, the colonies again petitioned the king, sending the Olive Branch Petition to King George III. On July 4, 1776, after the failed diplomatic attempts, the Declaration of Independence was adopted, and after the war, it would herald a radical form of self-government never before seen in world history.

Unlike the United States' revolution against a ruler across the ocean, the French Revolution was an internal fight. In 1789, tension between the lower class (peasants) and middle class (bourgeois) and the extravagant wealthy upper class of France came to a head. The Old Regime, headed by the monarchy, was overthrown, and the Third Estate, made up of the bourgeois class, seized power. The American Revolution, overtaxation, years of bad harvests, drastic income inequality, and the Enlightenment influenced the French Revolution. In August 1789, the National Constituent Assembly, a democratic assembly formed during the French Revolution, passed the Declaration of the Rights of Man and of the Citizen, which defined the natural right of men to be free and equal under the law.

France radically changed the government from a monarchy to a democracy with provisions for civil rights, religious freedoms, and decriminalization of various morality crimes, like same-sex relationships. Two political powers emerged: liberal republicans called *Girondists* and radical revolutionaries, known as *Jacobins*. Conflict between the parties resulted in the Reign of Terror—a period of mass executions— and eventually the rise of Napoleon who set up a nationalist military dictatorship. During the revolution, Napoleon Bonaparte consolidated power after becoming famous for his heroism during the revolutionary wars against Britain, Austria, and other monarchies that sought to retain their right of royal rule. However, by 1804, Napoleon declared himself emperor and remilitarized France, and he conquered most of Europe in a series of global conflicts collectively known as the *Napoleonic Wars,* starting in 1803 and continuing until Napoleon's defeat at the Battle of Waterloo in 1815.

After the chaos sparked by the French Revolution that fanned across Europe during the revolutionary wars, European powers met at the Congress of Vienna in November 1814 to June 1815 to rebalance power and restore old boundaries. The Congress of Vienna carved out new territories, changing the map of Europe. France lost all of its conquered territories, while Prussia, Austria, and Russia expanded their own. With the restoration of a balance of power, Europe enjoyed nearly fifty years of peace.

Fueled by the successful American Revolution, Napoleon's rise to power, and the writings of the Enlightenment, a spirit of revolution swept across the Americas. The French colony in Haiti was the first major revolution occurring in 1791. The Haitian Revolution was the largest slave uprising since the Roman Empire, and it holds a unique place in history because it is the only slave uprising to establish a slave-free nation ruled by nonwhites and former slaves. In 1804, the Haitians achieved independence and became the first independent nation in Latin America. When Napoleon conquered Spain in 1808, Latin American colonies refused to recognize his elder brother, Joseph Bonaparte, as the new Spanish monarch and advocated for their own independence. Known as the *Latin American Wars of Independence,* Venezuela, Colombia, Ecuador, Argentina, Uruguay, Paraguay, Chile, Peru, and Bolivia all achieved independence between 1810 and 1830. In 1824, Mexico declared itself a republic when, after several attempts by the lower classes of Mexico to revolt, the wealthier classes joined and launched a final and successful revolt. When Napoleon overtook Portugal, King John VI fled to Brazil and set up court. Later he left his son Pedro behind to rule. Pedro launched a revolution that saw him crowned emperor.

By the mid-1800s, the revolutions of Latin America ceased, and only a few areas remained under European rule. The U.S. president James Monroe issued the Monroe Doctrine, which stated that the Americas could no longer be colonized. It was an attempt to stop European nations, especially Spain, from colonizing areas or attempting to recapture areas. England's navy contributed to the success of the doctrine, as they were eager to increase trade with the Americas and establish an alliance with the United States.

Industrial Revolution
While Europe was in the midst of colonization and revolutions, they experienced an industrial revolution that would impact the social and economic fabric of life. Starting in the 1760s, with humble origins in England's textile economy, it lasted until the 1820s and changed the way people worked and lived. The revolution brought new scientific developments and improvements to agriculture and textile manufacturing. It was also a time of great invention in steam- and water-powered engines, machines, tools, chemicals, transportation, factories, lighting, glass, cement, medicines, and many more. Additional information concerning the Industrial Revolution and the Second Industrial Revolution are included in the section called "The Major Economic Transformations that Have Affected World Societies."

In some ways, it improved people's standard of living, but in many ways, it made life harder. Falling prices on goods made nutrition levels improve and allowed people more buying power. Medicines and better transportation also improved the quality of life for many. However, crowded living quarters in the booming urban centers were often appalling, as were the diseases brought on by working in factory conditions. The use of child labor eventually brought about reform, and labor unions had an effect on working conditions, but it took many years for either of these problems to be properly addressed.

Nationalism and Imperialism
With most revolutions, nationalism, or the devotion to one's country, plays a central role. The American and French revolutions, along with the revolutions of Latin America, were fought with the desire to improve the prosperity and position of its civilians. After the Napoleonic Wars and the Congress of

Vienna, the years of undisturbed peace resulted in a buildup of nationalism. Countries like Italy and Poland resented Austrian and Russian rule as much as they had disliked French occupation. A rise in nationalism in Germany was a constant threat to Austria, as it tried to govern multiple cultures and languages across a wide geographic area. The precarious situation would remain hostile to some degree until the outbreak of World War I. The Industrial Revolution had made the lower and middle classes restless for change and improvements. By 1848, uprisings began to spring up all over Europe, beginning with France. Many who had nationalistic leanings toward a country that was either no longer in existence or had been forced into another country were able to separate from other nations. The Hungarians broke with Vienna, though they were forced back soon after, the Romanians split from papal power, and the Italians threatened rebellion.

The development of imperialism began in the mid-nineteenth century and lasted until the twentieth century, with much of the imperialized world gaining freedom after World Wars I and II. The spread of imperialism that was to follow the revolutions of the eighteenth and nineteenth centuries can be traced, in part, to the idea of nationalism. Some countries believed they were doing a good, and even a moral, thing by conquering and colonizing new territory to spread their culture, traditions, religion, and government. However, a darker side of nationalism—the feeling of superiority and right—caused the takeover of areas and the enforcement of foreign rules and laws.

The British Empire stretched across the world, and at one point had over 450 million people under its rule. With the loss of its American colonies, England began to focus on other areas of the world. In the mid-1700s, India was the first target of British imperialism. Opposition to the ruling Mughal Empire allowed the British army an inroad at the Battle of Plassey in 1757, where General Robert Clive and his army overtook Bengal in northeast India. Next, the British forced the Mughal emperor to give all tax-collecting rights to England. In 1784, Parliament passed the East India Company Act, also known as *Pitt's India Act,* which brought the East India Company's rule in India under control of the British government. Railway systems to expedite the shipment of goods to Great Britain were built, and a new government called the *British Raj* was established. Indians were educated to work in the government and, at first, used their education to promote reform in India. Many of these civil service workers would take on the mantle of nationalism and advocate for India's independence. Great Britain further expanded its empire into areas of Africa and solidified its rule in Australia, capitalizing on exports from Australia and Canada. It also had what is seen as an informal empire in China and other nations due to its ability to dominate trade and influence economic policy.

Imperialism was also seen in Japan, a country that moved from a primitive and feudal system to a strong empire quickly and overtook Taiwan, Korea, many islands in the Pacific Ocean, and parts of China. It was not until the end of World War II that Japan was forced to surrender control of its accumulated empire. Germany, Russia, and the Ottoman Empire also gained land through imperialism during the years before World War I, most of which was lost by the end of the Great War. The United States was initially against imperialism after having been a colony itself and even solidified these ideas in the Monroe Doctrine; however, by the late nineteenth and early twentieth centuries, the United States defeated Spain in the Spanish-American War and annexed Hawaii, Guam, and the Philippines.

The Major Ideological, Economic, and Political Causes and Consequences of the First and Second World Wars and the Cold War

First World War

The onset of World War I began with the precarious balance of power and the geographic divisions written by the Napoleonic Wars' Vienna Congress.

Austria-Hungary's large empire was diverse in culture and included various peoples of several races, languages, and beliefs. However, minorities in their lands in the Balkans grew tired of foreign control. This was especially true in Bosnia, which was all but under control by the nationalistic secret military society, the Black Hand. This nationalistic sentiment grew until, in 1914, Gavrilo Princip, a Serb patriot and member of the Black Hand, assassinated Archduke Franz Ferdinand, heir presumptive to the throne of Austria-Hungary. In response, Emperor Franz Joseph I of Austria-Hungary declared war on the kingdom of Serbia, officially launching the First World War.

Europe had tied itself into a tangled web of alliances and mutual protection pacts. Germany and Austria-Hungary were allies. Russia promised protection to France and Serbia, and England maintained a tacit support to its past allies throughout the mainland. Each of the Allies soon mobilized to support each other. Germany had already planned for declarations of war, however, and was nervous about fighting a two-border war against both France and Russia, so it developed the Schlieffen Plan—a strategy to quickly demolish French resistance before turning around to fight Russia on the Eastern Front. However, this plan relied on the neutrality of England; after Germany invaded Belgium to attack France, England's declaration of war ensured that a long war would be inevitable.

The Great War lasted from 1914 to 1918 and was the deadliest war in European history until World War II, with approximately 16 million combatants and civilians dying in the conflict. The carnage was largely a result of technological innovation outpacing military tactics. World War I was the first military conflict to deploy millions of soldiers and the first war to involve telephones, tanks, aircrafts, chemical weapons, and heavy artillery. These twentieth-century technological innovations were deployed alongside outdated military tactics, particularly trench warfare. As a result, hundreds of thousands of troops would die during battles without achieving any meaningful strategic gains. Countries were devastated by the loss of the male population and struggled to cope with a depleted workforce, and widows and orphans struggled to regain any degree of normalcy.

Due to the high death tolls, the Allies' need of the financial support, and the anger associated with the war, the Treaty of Versailles harshly punished Germany, who the Allies blamed for the war. The Allies coerced Germany into signing the treaty that was a death sentence to their country's economy. It contained a "guilt clause," which, unlike the Congress of Vienna's terms for the similarly belligerent France, made oppressive demands on Germany. The treaty took German lands, enforced a heavy reparations debt that was impossible to pay, and stripped Germany of its colonies. After suffering enormous losses during the war itself, the Treaty of Versailles ensured that no national recovery would be possible.

In the aftermath, Russia, Italy, and Germany turned to totalitarian governments, and colonies of Europe started to have nationalistic, anticolonial movements. The Russian Revolution of 1917 led to a civil war in which the Bolsheviks, or Communists, took control under the guidance of Communist revolutionary Vladimir Lenin and established the Soviet Union. The Communist government turned into a dictatorship when Stalin emerged as leader in 1924. Stalin ruled with an iron fist and executed all of his political opponents, including the Bolsheviks. Dissatisfaction with the treaty in Italy led to the rise of fascist leader Benito Mussolini. Germany suffered through several small revolutions, splintering political parties, and class division; this, combined with wartime debt and hyperinflation—a result of the Treaty of Versailles—caused many to become desperate, especially during the throes of the Great Depression. Adolf Hitler, a popular leader in the National Socialist German Workers' Party (Nazi Party), organized street violence against Communists. In the 1932 parliamentary elections, the Nazis emerged as the largest party in the *Reichstag* (German Parliament), but the Nazis did not have enough votes to name Hitler as chancellor. The street violence against Communists and Jews continued unabated, and on

January 30, 1933, political pressure led to President von Hindenburg naming Adolf Hitler the chancellor of Germany. Hitler immediately expelled Communists, the second most popular political party, from the *Reichstag*, and coerced the *Reichstag* to pass the Enabling Act of 1933, effectively creating a dictatorship.

The start of decolonization in India occurred after World War I, with the Government of India Act of 1919. While the war was raging, Britain promised India more self-rule if they supported the war effort. However, the act did not grant freedom in taxation, foreign policy, or justice and only went as far as allowing local matters to be addressed by native-born citizens. For the Indian National Congress, India's largest political party, this fell short of what they had expected. In the 1920s, Mahatma Gandhi, leader of the Indian National Congress, protested using civil disobedience. In August 1947, England granted independence to India and split the British Indian Empire into India and Pakistan.

Second World War
Nazi Germany had risen to power through the 1920s and 1930s, with Hitler's belief that Germany would only recover its honor if it had a resounding military victory over Europe. Nazi ideology adhered to an extreme nationalism advocating for the superiority of the German people and the necessity of expanding their lands into an empire. Jews, Communists, and other nonconformists were banned from political and social participation.

In 1936, German troops violated the Treaty of Versailles by moving outside Germany's borders, with a remilitarization of the Rhineland. The Rome-Berlin Axis, an alliance between Germany and Italy, was forged in the same year. Germany was the only European power to support Italy's invasion and annexation of Ethiopia, and in exchange, Italy supported Germany's annexation of Austria. In 1936, a civil war broke out in Spain between Spanish nationalist rebels and the government of the Spanish Republic. Mussolini and Hitler supported the Spanish nationalist general Francisco Franco and used the Spanish Civil War as a testing ground for their new alliance. The Allies did not respond to these actions, and when Germany demanded the return of the Sudetenland, a territory in Czechoslovakia, France and Great Britain agreed in hopes of an appeasement despite the protests of the Czech government. Hitler then moved into more areas farther afield, which prompted the Soviet Union to sign a nonaggression pact with Germany. On September 1, 1939, Germany invaded Poland, and on September 3, 1939, France and Great Britain declared war on Germany, jumpstarting the deadliest conflict in world history.

Aside from the incredible casualties resulting from intense fighting and bombings of cities, World War II is marked by the worst war crimes in human history. Germany conducted a systematic genocide of six million Jewish people during the Holocaust, sending two-thirds of Europe's Jewish population to be executed in death camps. Millions of non-Jews were also exterminated during the Holocaust, including Slavs, Poles, Romani, people of color, Communists, homosexuals, and disabled people, among others. It is estimated that anywhere between six and eleven million people were executed in the Holocaust. Although less discussed than the Holocaust, the Japanese military committed similar war crimes across Asia, executing between three and ten million Chinese and Koreans, among others, between 1937 and 1945. In one event, the Rape of Nanking, Japanese soldiers captured Nanking and brutally murdered 300,000 civilians. An additional twenty thousand women, children, and elderly were raped during the massacre. Japanese newspapers closely covered a contest between two Japanese officers to see who could kill more people with a sword during the Rape of Nanking. Stalin also committed heinous war crimes during World War II, with estimates ranging from four to ten million deaths as a result of executions and sentences to the Gulag. The United States has also faced criticism for its decision to drop two nuclear bombs on the Japanese cities of Hiroshima and Nagasaki, killing more than 129,000 civilians, leveling both cities, and ending the war. The American government justified the use of nuclear weapons as the only way to avoid a ground invasion of Japan that would have cost more Japanese and American lives than the bombs.

Towns and cities had been leveled, civilian and soldier death tolls were crippling to economies, and countries struggled well into the 1950s to recover economically. It became a breeding ground for Communism, and in China, the end of the war meant a reprisal of the civil war between Mao Zedong's Communists and nationalists that had been interrupted by world war. Another result of the war was a changed map of the world, as countries were divided or newly formed, and the end of most of Britain's colonialism occurred as a result of the empire's economic and military losses. Following the war, Great Britain, France, Portugal, Belgium, Italy, the Netherlands, and Japan had either granted freedom to colonies or lost areas during the war. Many African and Middle Eastern countries would be granted their independence; however, the newly formed countries' borders were drawn according to those of the former colonies, creating ethnic and religious tensions that still exist today.

In an effort to stop a world war from occurring again, the Allies created the United Nations to be a safeguard and upholder of peace. This proved especially important, yet difficult, as the world was divided between a capitalist Western bloc and a Communist Eastern bloc. Germany was divided between the United States and Soviet Union to maintain peace and to better control the reconstruction of Germany; occupation zones were established, with East Germany occupied by the Soviet Union and West Germany occupied by Great Britain, France, and the United States.

Cold War
Within two years of World War II, the world was involved in a different kind of war—a Cold War—that pitted capitalism and Communism against each other. World War II left Europe on the brink of collapse, leaving the United States and Soviet Union as the world's undisputed remaining superpowers. The United States and its Allies embarked on a campaign of containment in an attempt to keep Communism from spreading to other countries. After World War II, the United States offered European countries the Marshall Plan—a grant of American subsidies to help Europe and Japan recover economically. The largest recipients were England, France, and West Germany. Aside from sincere humanitarian desires, the Marshall Plan also served the interests of the United States by ensuring that Europe's citizens did not resort to Communism out of desperation. In turn, the Soviet Union developed their own plan, the Molotov Plan, to help their Communist Allies' recovery.

In the 1940s, U.S. president Harry S. Truman, in an effort to contain Communism, offered U.S. military and economic protection to any nation threatened by Communist takeover. By 1949, the United States, Canada, and ten European nations agreed to the same idea in an alliance known as the *North Atlantic Treaty Organization (NATO)*. When West Germany was invited into NATO in 1955, the Soviet Union responded with a similar alliance known as the *Warsaw Pact*. The Warsaw Pact and NATO were vehicles for the United States and Soviet Union to flex their military might. In addition to conventional arms, the two superpowers competed in a nuclear arms race throughout the Cold War. The nuclear arms race created a situation where each country could destroy the world many times over at the push of a button. There were several close calls during the conflict due to mixed signals, misunderstandings, or provocation—the most notorious being the Cuban Missile Crisis when the Soviet Union placed nuclear missiles in Cuba, ninety miles away from Florida.

In China, Mao Zedong, the chairman of the Communist Party and leader of the People's Republic of China, attempted to quickly transform China into a Communist state through an ineffective and devastating economic program known as the *Great Leap Forward,* which abolished private ownership of property and featured collective communes. The Great Leap Forward caused a humanitarian disaster, resulting in tens of millions of deaths, due to inefficient economic planning under a poorly devised Communist system.

The United States fought a series of proxy wars against the Soviet Union to prevent the spread of Communism. The Korean War, 1950-1953, was an attempt to keep Communism from spreading into Korea. China and the Soviet Union joined together to fight the United States and Allies until an armistice was signed that divided Korea into a Communist North and a democratic South along the thirty-eighth parallel. The thirty-eighth parallel was an important demarcation during the war itself, as America was cautious to pursue the North Koreans back across the parallel or else risk escalating the proxy war into a conventional one against the Soviets. The Vietnam Conflict, 1955-1975, was another proxy war pitting the United States against Communism. China and the Soviet Union provided extensive aid to the Communist Viet Cong guerilla fighters and the more conventional North Vietnamese army. Although the United States was the superior conventional military force, the American military struggled mightily against the guerillas using the dense jungle as cover. As intense opposition to the war mounted in the United States, the United States withdrew after the North Vietnamese captured Saigon in April 1975. The Soviet Union similarly struggled against guerilla forces backed by the United States during the Soviet-Afghan War, which lasted between 1979 and 1989. The United States provided military and financial support to the Afghans during the conflict, many of who would later found al-Qaeda or join the Taliban to fight the United States, including Osama bin Laden.

Protests and new leaders gave some economic freedom and recovery to these European nations after WWII, but East Germany was excluded. In 1961, a wall was built to separate East and West Germany in an attempt to keep people from fleeing the Soviet-controlled East. However, in 1985, Mikhail Gorbachev became the Soviet leader and began to change politics in the Soviet Union, with *glasnost*—a policy of government transparency and openness—and *perestroika,* a government reform. He allowed the Eastern European satellite countries more economic freedom and limited self-government. The Soviet economy could not keep up with the United States, especially when President Reagan increased American military spending. Pushed to the brink of economic collapse, the Soviet Union could no longer maintain control over their satellites and Allies, who were increasingly agitated for complete autonomy. On November 9, 1989, the Soviet Union ordered the Berlin Wall to be knocked down, an important step toward thawing the Cold War. On December 26, 1991, the Soviet Union officially collapsed and broke up into fifteen distinct countries.

The Major Developments of the Post-Cold War

The collapse of the Soviet Union left the United States as the sole world superpower. In addition, Communism no longer represented a viable political ideology, cementing the market economy as the leading economic system, which is later discussed in greater detail in the section "The Major Economic Transformations that Have Affected World Societies." In the mid-1990s, the Internet emerged as a driving force in globalization, connecting people across the world and providing instantaneous access to vast stores of information. Globalization further presented itself in the form of supranational governance. In 1992, the European Union was established for the purpose of creating a common market for goods and capital. Other supranational political entities would lead the way toward the creation of a globalized economy.

Founded in 1995, the World Trade Organization is a supranational organization composed of 164 member states, and it establishes regulations, norms, and dispute resolution to govern trade agreements between countries. Trade agreements between two entities are referred to as *bilateral agreements,* and any larger type of agreement is classified as *multilateral.* The entity entering into the trade agreement can be either a single nation-state or a trade bloc—an informal group of countries who negotiate as a single entity. The most common type of trade agreement is free trade, which offers preferential treatment through the elimination of trade restrictions, like tariffs and quotas. Trade agreements force countries to rely on the economic health of their trade partners, which naturally leads to interdependence. Examples of trade agreements include the North America Free Trade Agreement and Association of Southeast Asian Nations.

Trade agreements form the basis of a globalized economy as countries seek to maximize the economic principle of economies of scale, which defines how countries can function most efficiently within markets and vis-à-vis competitors. It encourages countries to specialize in what they do best and devote the bulk of their resources to maximizing that specialty. In theory, increasing production will make the output more efficient and cost effective. Incentivizing countries to boost their production and pursue their competitive advantage inherently leads to greater economic interdependence and globalization; trading countries are necessarily dependent on their partners to meet some need. For example, in the North America Free Trade Agreement, the United States provides technology and white-collar skills, while Mexico primarily focuses on manufacturing.

Despite the trend toward supranational political and economic entities, nationalism has reemerged as a powerful force in the post-Cold War Era. Nationalism is best understood as people seeking independence for some collective reason, like geographical proximity or cultural similarities. In addition, nationalism is primarily expressed via its opposition to external influences. Just as nationalism served as a rallying cry for colonial people fighting to gain their independence, nationalism has come back into vogue as the means for people to advocate for greater local control.

The Yugoslav Wars of 1991 to 2001 and eventual collapse of Yugoslavia illustrate how ethnic nationalism exists as a powerful countervailing force to globalization trends. The former Socialist Federal Republic of Yugoslavia contained several republics that consisted of distinct ethnic groups, including Bosnia and Herzegovina, Croatia, Macedonia, Serbia, and Slovenia. Additionally, Serbia was further divided between Kosovo and Vojvodina. After the death of Yugoslavia's founding authoritarian ruler, Josip Broz Tito, the country eventually collapsed under separatist nationalist movements. Following a series of bloody wars and war crimes, collectively known as the Yugoslav Wars, seven newly independent states emerged out of Yugoslavia—Bosnia and Herzegovina, Croatia, Kosovo, Macedonia, Montenegro, Serbia, and Slovenia.

Nationalism is also on the rise in Western democracies as people grapple with the consequences of a globalized economy and greater involvement of supranational political entities beyond their control. In June 2016, the United Kingdom held a referendum on the country's membership in the European Union, and British citizens voted to withdraw, which is commonly referred to as the "Brexit" (British exit). Nationalism greatly influenced British citizens' reluctance to cede any degree of sovereignty, pay taxes, or follow regulations from the European Union. In particular, British citizens resented the quotas of Syrian refugees that the European Union required England to accommodate. A similar spirit of nationalism also carried Donald Trump to the Republican nomination in the United States during the 2016 election. Millions of Americans rejected the global economy and free trade agreement, demanding that America should come first.

Similar to nationalism, religious fundamentalism has increased dramatically in the post-Cold War Era. Specifically, the globalized economy has directly resulted in cultural clashes between the West and Islam. Islamic fundamentalism often resorts to terrorism to fight against their conventionally more powerful enemies. The most infamous modern terrorist attack occurred on September 11, 2001, when terrorists associated with al-Qaeda hijacked four commercial airliners and flew the planes into the

World Trade Center and Pentagon. The 9/11 attack initially led to the United States' invasion of Afghanistan and later contributed to the decision to invade Iraq. These wars heightened the interaction between the Western and Arab worlds, and fundamentalism has increased ever since. Jihadists and religious extremists have flooded the region to defend Islam against what they perceive as the invading West. Additionally, the Arab Spring created a spirit of unrest in many Middle Eastern countries with a history of authoritarian rule. Following the Americans' withdrawal from Iraq and uprisings in neighboring Syria, the religious extremists declared an Islamic State in the region, known as the *Islamic State of Iraq and Levant,* ensuring the proliferation of Islamic fundamentalism and terrorism for the foreseeable future.

Geography

Locating and Using Sources of Geographic Data

Geographic data is essential to fully understanding both the spatial and human realms of geography. In reference to the human population, different factors affect the quality of life one experiences during their lifetime. Geographers attempt to understand why those differences exist through data utilization and comparative analysis. For example, as has been previously mentioned, population density, infant mortality rates, and literacy rates are all useful tools in analyzing human characteristics of a place; however, those are not the only tools geographers utilize. In fact, organizations such as the *Population Reference Bureau* and the *Central Intelligence Agency* both provide an incredible amount of *demographic* data useful to researchers, students, or really anyone curious about the world in which they live.

The *CIA World Factbook* is an indispensable resource for anyone interested in the field of human or physical geography. Providing information such as land area, literacy rates, birth rate, and economic data, this resource is one of the most comprehensive on the Internet. In addition to the CIA World Factbook, the *Population Reference Bureau* (*PRB*) also provides students of geography with an abundant supply of information. In contrast to the CIA source, the *PRB* provides a treasure trove of analyses related to human populations including HIV rates, immigration rates, poverty rates, etc.

In addition to the aforementioned sources, the *United States Census Bureau* provides similar information about the dynamics of the American population. Not only does this source focus on the data geographers need to understand the world, but it also provides information about upcoming classes, online workshops, and even includes an online library of resources for both students and teachers.

Websites for each source can be found below:

- Population Reference Bureau: www.prb.org http://www.prb.org/
- United States Census Bureau: www.census.gov http://www.census.gov/
- CIA World Factbook: https://www.cia.gov/library/publications/the-world-factbook/ https://www.cia.gov/library/publications/the-world-factbook/

Spatial Concepts

Location is the central theme in understanding spatial concepts. In geography, there are two primary types of locations that people utilize on a daily basis. The first type, *relative location*, is used frequently and involves locating objects by notating their proximity to another, better known object. For example, directions from person to person may relate directly to massive shopping centers, major highways, or well-known intersections. Although relative location is important, in the modern world, it's common to use digital satellite-based technologies, which rely on *GPS* (*Global Positioning System*). To determine *Absolute Location*, or the exact latitudinal and longitudinal position on the globe, GPS uses sensors that interact with satellites orbiting the Earth. *Coordinates* correspond with the positions on a manmade grid system using imaginary lines known as *latitude* (also known as *parallels*) and *longitude* (also known as *meridians*).

In order to understand latitude and longitude, one should think of a simple X and Y-axis. The *equator* serves as the X-axis at zero degrees, and measures distance from north to south. The Y-axis is at zero degrees and is represented by the *Prime Meridian*.

In addition to anchoring the grid system to create the basis for absolute location, these major lines of latitude and longitude also divide the Earth into *hemispheres*. The Equator divides the Earth into the northern and southern hemispheres, while the Prime Meridian establishes the eastern and western hemispheres. Coordinates are always expressed in the following format:

Degrees north or south, degrees east or west, or 40°N, 50°E. Since lines of latitude and longitude are great distance from one another, absolute locations are often found in between two lines. In those cases, degrees are broken down into *minutes* and *seconds*, which are expressed in this manner: (40° 53' 44" N, 50° 22' 65" E).

In addition to the Equator and the Prime Meridian, other major lines of latitude and longitude exist to divide the world into regions relative to the direct rays of the sun. These lines correspond with the Earth's *tilt*, and are responsible for the seasons. For example, the northern hemisphere is tilted directly toward the sun from June 22 to September 23, which creates the summer season in that part of the world. Conversely, the southern hemisphere is tilted away from the direct rays of the sun and experiences winter during those same months.

The transitions from season to season involve two factors: the 23 ½ degree tilt of the Earth and the movement of the direct rays of the sun relative to the Earth's revolution. To clarify, the area between the *Tropic of Cancer* (23 ½ degrees north) and the *Tropic of Capricorn* (23 ½ degrees south) can be envisioned as the playing field for the direct rays of the sun. These rays never leave the playing field, and, as a result, the area between those two lines of latitude—the *tropics*—tends to be warmer and experience fewer variations in seasonal temperatures. In contrast, the area between the Tropic of Cancer and the *Arctic Circle* (66 ½ degrees north) is in the *middle latitudes*—the region where most of the Earth's population resides. In the Southern Hemisphere, the middle latitudes exist between the Tropic of Capricorn and the *Antarctic Circle* (66 ½ degrees south). In both of these places, indirect rays of the sun strike the Earth, so seasons are more pronounced and milder temperatures generally prevail. The final region, known as the *high latitudes*, is found north of the Arctic Circle and south of the Antarctic Circle. These regions generally tend to be cold all year, and experience nearly twenty-four hours of sunlight during their respective *summer solstice* and twenty-four hours of darkness during the *winter solstice*.

Regarding the seasons, it is important to understand that those in the Southern Hemispheres are opposite of those in the Northern Hemisphere, due to the position of the direct rays of the sun. When the sun's direct rays are over the Equator, it is known as an *equinox*, and day and night are almost of equal length throughout the world. Equinoxes occur twice a year; the fall, or autumnal equinox, occurs on September 22nd, while the spring equinox occurs on March 20th. Obviously, if seasons are opposite of one another depending on the hemisphere, the corresponding names flip-flop depending on one's location (i.e. when the Northern Hemisphere is experiencing summer, it is winter in the Southern Hemisphere).

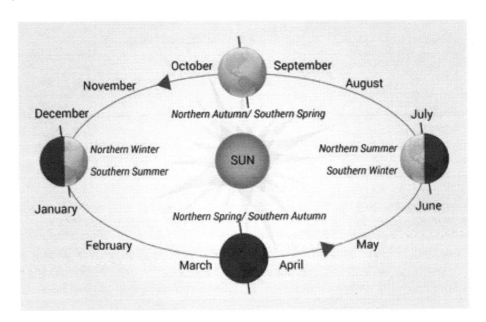

Place
Both absolute and relative location help humans understand their sense of place. Place is a simple concept that helps to define the characteristics of the world around us. For example, people may create *toponyms* to further define and orient themselves with their sense of place. Toponyms are simply names given to locations to help develop familiarity within a certain location. Although not always the case, toponyms generally utilize geographical features, important people in an area, or even wildlife commonly found in a general location. For example, many cities in the state of Texas are named in honor of military leaders who fought in the Texas Revolution of 1836 (such as Houston and Austin), while other places, such as Mississippi and Alabama, utilize Native American toponyms to define their sense of place.

Regions
In addition to location and place, geographers also divide the world into regions in order to more fully understand differences inherent with the world, its people, and its environment. As mentioned previously, lines of latitude such as the Equator, the Tropics, and the Arctic and Antarctic Circles already divide the Earth into solar regions relative to the amount of either direct or indirect sunlight that they receive. Although not the same throughout, the middle latitudes generally have a milder climate than areas found within the tropics. Furthermore, tropical locations are usually warmer than places in the middle latitudes, but that is not always the case. For example, the lowest place in the United States—

Death Valley, California—is also home to the nation's highest-ever recorded temperature. Likewise, the Andes Mountains in Peru and Ecuador, although found near the Equator, are also home to heavy snow, low temperatures, and dry conditions, due to their elevation.

Formal regions are spatially defined areas that have overarching similarities or some level of *homogeneity* or *uniformity*. Although not exactly alike, a formal region generally has at least one characteristic that is consistent throughout the entire area. For example, the United States could be broken down into one massive formal region due to the fact that in all fifty states, English is the primary language. Of course, English isn't the only language spoken in the United States, but throughout that nation, English is heavily used. As a result, geographers are able to classify the United States as a formal region; but, more specifically, the United States is a *linguistic region*—a place where everyone generally speaks the same language.

Functional regions are similar to formal regions in that they have similar characteristics, but they do not have clear boundaries. The best way to understand these sorts of regions is to consider large cities. Each large city encompasses a large *market area*, whereby people in its vicinity generally travel there to conduct business, go out to eat, or watch a professional sporting event. However, once anyone travels farther away from that *primate city*, they transition to a different, more accessible city for their needs. The functional region, or *area of influence*, for that city, town, or sports team transitions, depending upon the availability of other primate cities. For example, New York City has two primary professional baseball, basketball, and football teams. As a result, its citizens may have affinities for different teams even though they live in the same city. Conversely, a citizen in rural Idaho may cheer for the Seattle Seahawks, even though they live over 500 miles from Seattle, due to the lack of a closer primate city.

Effects of Physical Processes, Climate Patterns, and Natural Hazards on Human Societies

The Earth's surface, like many other things in the broader universe, does not remain the same for long; in fact, it changes from day to day. The Earth's surface is subject to a variety of physical processes that continue to shape its appearance. In each process, water, wind, temperature, or sunlight play a role in continually altering the Earth's surface.

Erosion can be caused by a variety of different stimuli including ice, snow, water, wind, and ocean waves. *Wind erosion* is a specific phenomenon that occurs in generally flat, dry areas with loose topsoil. Over time, the persistent winds can dislodge significant amounts of soil into the air, reshaping the land and reeking havoc on those who depend on agriculture for their livelihoods. Erosion can also be caused by water and is responsible for changing landscapes as well. For example, the Grand Canyon was carved over thousands of years by the constant movement of the Colorado River. Over time, the river moved millions of tons of soil, cutting a huge gorge in the Earth along the way. In all cases, erosion involves the movement of soil from one place to another. In water erosion, material carried by the water is referred to as *sediment*. With time, some sediment can collect at the mouths of rivers, forming *deltas*, which become small islands of fertile soil. This process of detaching loose soils and transporting them to a different location where they remain for an extended period of time is referred to as *deposition*, and is the end result of the erosion process.

In contrast to erosion, *weathering* does not involve the movement of any outside stimuli. In this physical process, the surface of the Earth is either broken down physically or chemically. *Physical weathering* involves the effects of atmospheric conditions such as water, ice, heat, or pressure. Through the process of weathering over the course of centuries, large rocks can be broken down with the effects of icy conditions. *Chemical weathering* generally occurs in warmer climates and involves organic material that breaks down rocks, minerals, or soil. This process is what scientists believe led to the creation of fossil fuels such as oil, coal, and natural gas.

Climate Patterns
Weather is defined as the condition of the Earth's atmosphere at a particular time. *Climate* is different; instead of focusing on one particular day, climate is the relative pattern of weather in a place for an extended period of time. For example, the city of Atlanta is in the American South and generally has a humid subtropical climate; however, Atlanta also occasionally experiences snowstorms in the winter months. Despite the occasional snow and sleet storm, over time, geographers, meteorologists, and other Earth scientists have determined the patterns that are indicative to north Georgia, where Atlanta is located. Almost all parts of the world have predictable climate patterns, which are influenced by the surrounding geography.

The Central Coast of California is an example of a place with a predictable climate pattern. Santa Barbara, California, one of the region's larger cities, has almost the same temperature for most of the summer, spring, and fall, with only minimal fluctuation during the winter months. The temperatures there, which average between 75 and 65 degrees Fahrenheit daily regardless as to the time of year, are influenced by a variety of different climatological factors including elevation, location relative to the mountains and ocean, and ocean currents. In the case of Santa Barbara, the city's location on the Pacific Coast and its position near mountains heavily influences its climate. The cold California current, which sweeps down the west coast of the United States, causes the air near the city to be temperate, while the mountains trap cool air over the city and the surrounding area. This pattern, known as the *orographic effect*, or *rain shadow*, also affects temperatures on the leeward side of the mountains by blocking most of the cool air and causing dry conditions to dominate. Temperatures can fluctuate by more than 20 degrees Fahrenheit on opposite sides of the mountain.

Other factors affecting climate include elevation, prevailing winds, vegetation, and latitudinal position on the globe.

Like climate, *natural hazards* also affect human societies. In tropical and subtropical climates, hurricanes and typhoons form over warm water and can have devastating effects. Additionally, tornadoes, which are powerful cyclonic windstorms, also are responsible for widespread destruction in many parts of the United States and in other parts of the world. Like storms, earthquakes, usually caused by shifting plates along faults deep below the Earth's surface, also cause widespread devastation, particularly in nations with a poor or crumbling infrastructure. For example, San Francisco, which experiences earthquakes regularly due to its position near the San Andreas Fault, saw relatively little destruction and deaths (67 total) as a result of the last major earthquake to strike there. However, in 2010, an earthquake of similar magnitude reportedly killed over 200,000 people in the western hemisphere's poorest nation, Haiti. Although a variety of factors may be responsible for the disparity, modern engineering methods and better building materials most likely helped to minimize destruction in San Francisco. Other natural hazards, such as tsunamis, mudslides, avalanches, forest fires, dust storms, flooding, volcanic eruptions, and blizzards, also affect human societies throughout the world.

Characteristics and Spatial Distribution of Earth's Ecosystems

Earth is an incredibly large place filled with a variety of different land and water *ecosystems*. *Marine ecosystems* cover over 75 percent of the Earth's surface and contain over 95 percent of the Earth's water. Marine ecosystems can be broken down into two primary subgroups: *freshwater ecosystems*, which only encompass around 2 percent of the earth's surface; and *ocean ecosystems,* which make up over 70 percent. On land, *terrestrial ecosystems* vary depending on a variety of factors, including latitudinal distance from the equator, elevation, and proximity to mountains or bodies of water. For example, in the high latitudinal regions north of the Arctic Circle and south of the Antarctic Circle, frozen *tundra* dominates. Tundra, which is characterized by low temperatures, short growing seasons, and minimal vegetation, is only found in regions that are far away from the direct rays of the sun.

In contrast, *deserts* can be found throughout the globe and are created by different ecological factors. For example, the world's largest desert, the Sahara, is almost entirely within the tropics; however, other deserts like the Gobi in China, the Mojave in the United States, and the Atacama in Chile, are the result of the orographic effect and their close proximity to high mountain ranges such as the Himalayas, the Sierra Nevada, and the Andes, respectively. In the Middle Latitudes, greater varieties of climatological zones are more common due to fluctuations in temperatures relative to the sun's rays, coupled with the particular local topography. In the Continental United States, *temperate deciduous forest* dominates the southeastern portion of the country. However, the Midwestern states such as Nebraska, Kansas, and the Dakotas, are primarily *grasslands*. Additionally, the states of the Rocky Mountains can have decidedly different climates relative to elevation. In Colorado, Denver, also known as the "Mile High City," will often see snowfalls well into late April or early May due to colder temperatures, whereas towns and cities in the eastern part of the state, with much lower elevations, may see their last significant snowfall in March.

In the tropics, which are situated between the Tropics of Cancer and Capricorn, temperatures are generally warmer, due to the direct rays of the sun's persistence. However, like most of the world, the tropics also experience a variety of climatological regions. In Brazil, Southeast Asia, Central America, and even Northern Australia, tropical rainforests are common. These forests, which are known for abundant vegetation, daily rainfall, and a wide variety of animal life, are absolutely essential to the health of the world's ecosystems. For example, the *Amazon Rain Forest* is also referred to as "the lungs of the world," as its billions of trees produce substantial amounts of oxygen and absorb an equivalent amount of carbon dioxide—the substance that many climatologists assert is causing climate change or *global warming*. Unlike temperate deciduous forests whose trees lose their leaves during the fall and winter months, *tropical rain forests* are always lush, green, and warm. In fact, some rainforests are so dense with vegetation that a few indigenous tribes have managed to exist within them without being influenced by any sort of modern technology, virtually maintaining their ancient way of life in the modern era.

The world's largest ecosystem, the *taiga,* is found primarily in high latitudinal areas, which receive very little of the sun's indirect rays. These forests are generally made up of *coniferous* trees, which do not lose their leaves at any point during the year as *deciduous* trees do. Taigas are cold-climate regions that make up almost 30 percent of the world's land area. These forests dominate the northern regions of Canada, Scandinavia, and Russia, and provide the vast majority of the world's lumber.

Overall, it is important to remember that climates are influenced by five major factors: elevation, latitude, proximity to mountains, ocean currents, and wind patterns. For example, the cold currents off the coast of California provide the West Coast of the United States with pleasant year-round temperatures. Conversely, Western Europe, which is at the nearly the same latitude as most of Canada, is influenced by the warm waters of the *Gulf Stream*, an ocean current that acts as a conveyor belt, moving warm tropical waters to the icy north. In fact, the Gulf Stream's influence is so profound that it even keeps Iceland—an island nation in the far North Atlantic—relatively warm.

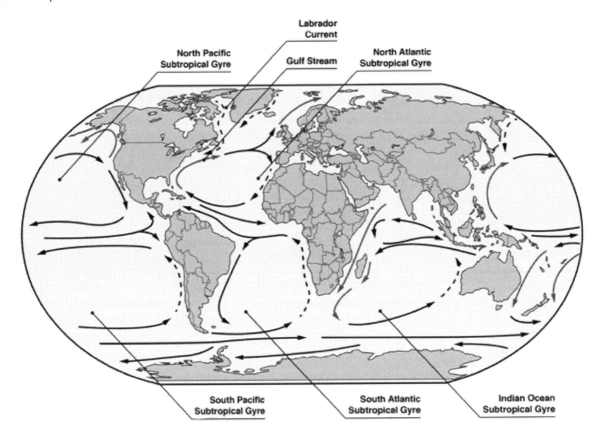

Interrelationships Between Humans and Their Environment

Like any other animal, humans adapt to their environment; but, unlike other animals, humans also adapt their environment to suit their needs. For example, human social systems are created around the goal of providing people with access to what they need to live more productive, fulfilling, and meaningful lives. Sometimes, humans create systems that are destructive, but generally speaking, humans tend to use their environment to make their lives easier. For example, in warmer climates, people tend to wear more comfortable clothing such as shorts, linen shirts, and hats. Additionally, in the excessively sun-drenched nations of the Middle East, both men and women wear flowing white clothing complete with both a head and neck covering, in order to prevent the blistering effects of sun exposure to the skin. Likewise, the native Inuit peoples of northern Canada and Alaska use the thick furs from the animals they kill to insulate their bodies against the bitter cold.

Humans also adapt to their environment to ensure that they have access to enough food and water for survival. Irrigation, or the process of moving water from its natural location to where it's needed, is an example of how humans change their environment in order to survive. For example, the city of Los Angeles, America's second most populous city, did not have adequate freshwater resources to sustain its population. However, city and state officials realized that abundant water resources existed approximately three hundred miles to the east. Rather than relocating some of its population to areas with more abundant water resources, the State of California undertook one of the largest construction projects in the history of the world, the Los Angeles Aqueduct, which is a massive concrete irrigation ditch connecting water-rich areas with the thirsty citizens of Los Angeles.

The Los Angeles Aqueduct is just one example of a human-environment interaction. In other cases, humans utilize what nature provides in close proximity. For example, the very first permanent British Colony in North America, Jamestown, VA, was heavily influenced by its environment. In contrast to the Pilgrims who settled in Plymouth, Massachusetts, Jamestown settlers found themselves in a hot, humid climate with fertile soil. Consequently, its inhabitants engaged in agriculture for both food and profit. Twelve years after Jamestown's foundation in 1607, it was producing millions of dollars of tobacco each year. In order to sustain this booming industry, over time, millions of African slaves and indentured servants from Europe were imported to provide labor. Conversely, the poor soils around Plymouth did not allow for widespread cash crop production, and the settlers in New England generally only grew enough food for themselves on small subsistence farms. Furthermore, slavery failed to take a strong foothold in the New England states, thus creating significantly different cultures within the same country, all due in part to human interaction with the environment.

Renewable and Nonrenewable Resources

When gas prices are high, prices on virtually everything increase. After all, there are very few products that humans can buy that are not transported by either a gasoline- or diesel-powered engine. As a result, an increase in fuel prices leads to an increase in the price of food, goods, or other cargo. Recently, there has been considerable debate regarding the reliance on *nonrenewable resources* like oil, natural gas, and coal. These resources, which are also known as *fossil fuels*, are quite common throughout the world and are generally abundant, and cheaper to use than *renewable resources* like solar, wind, and geothermal energy. While solar energy is everywhere, the actual means to convert the sun's rays into energy is not. Conversely, coal-fired power plants and gasoline-powered engines, which are older technologies in use during the industrial revolution, remain quite common throughout the world. In fact, reliance on non-renewable resources continues to grow, due to the availability coupled with the existing infrastructure. However, use of renewable energy is increasing, as it becomes more economically competitive with nonrenewable resources.

In addition to sources of energy, nonrenewable resources also include anything that can be exhausted. These can include precious metals like gold, silver, and platinum, freshwater underground aquifers, and precious stones such as diamonds, emeralds, and opals. Although abundant, most nonrenewable sources of energy are not sustainable because their creation takes millions of years and can therefore not be reproduced. Renewable resources are sustainable, but must be properly overseen so that they remain renewable. For example, the beautiful African island of Madagascar is home to some of the most amazing rainforest trees in the world. As a result, logging companies cut, milled, and sold thousands of them in order to make quick profits without planning how to ensure the continued health of the forests. As a result of severe deforestation on the island, mudslides became more and more common as the forests gradually shrank from widespread logging. In this case, renewable resources were mismanaged, and thus essentially became nonrenewable, due to the length of time for growth for the replacement of rainforest trees. In the United States, paper companies harvest pine trees to create paper; and because it can take almost twenty years for a pine tree to reach maturity, most of the companies utilize planning techniques to ensure that mature pine trees will always be available. In this manner, these resources remain renewable for human use in a sustainable fashion.

Renewable sources of energy are relatively new in the modern economy. Even though electric cars, wind turbines, and solar panels are becoming more common, they still do not provide enough energy to power the world's economy. As a result, reliance on older, reliable forms of energy continues, which has a devastating effect on the environment. Beijing, China, which has seen a massive boom in industrial jobs, is also one of the most polluted places on Earth. Furthermore, developing nations with very little modern infrastructure also rely heavily on fossil fuels, due to the ease in which they are converted into usable energy. Even the United States, which has one of the most developed infrastructures in the world, still relies almost exclusively on fossil fuels, with only ten percent of the required energy coming from renewable sources.

Spatial Patterns of Cultural and Economic Activities

Spatial patterns refer to where things are in the world. Biomes, regions, and landforms all have spatial patterns regarding where they exist. Additionally, elements of *human geography*—the study of human culture and its effect on the world—also have certain patterns regarding where they appear on Earth.

<u>Ethnicity</u>
An ethnic group, or ethnicity, is essentially a group of people with a common language, society, culture, or ancestral heritage. Different ethnicities developed over centuries through historical forces, the impact of religious traditions, and other factors. Thousands of years ago, it was more common for ethnic groups to remain in one area with only the occasional interaction with outside groups. In the modern world, different ethnicities interact on a daily, if not hourly, basis, due to better transportation resources and the processes of globalization. For example, in the United States, it is not uncommon for a high school classroom to encompass people of Asian, African, Indian, European, or Native descent. That's not to suggest that all American classrooms have ethnic diversity, but, in general, due to a variety of pull-factors, the United States continues to attract people from all over the world. In less developed parts of the world, travel is limited due to the lack of infrastructure. Consequently, ethnic groups develop in small areas that can differ greatly from other people just a few miles away. For example, on the Balkan Peninsula in southeastern Europe, a variety of different ethnic groups live in close proximity to one another. Croats, Albanians, Serbs, Bosnians, and others all share the same land, but have very different worldviews, traditions, and religious influences. In the case of the Balkan Peninsula, such diversity has not always been a positive characteristic. For example, the First World War began there in 1914 related to a dispute regarding Serbia's national independence. Additionally, Bosnia was the scene of a horrible genocide against Albanians in an "ethnic cleansing" effort that continued throughout the late 20th century.

<u>Linguistics</u>
Linguistics, or the study of language, groups certain languages together according to their commonalities. For example, the Romance Languages—French, Spanish, Italian, Romansh, and Portuguese—all share language traits from Latin, the language of the former Roman Empire. These languages, also known as *vernaculars*, or more commonly spoken *dialects*, evolved over centuries of physical isolation on the European continent. The Spanish form of Latin emerged into today's Spanish language. In other parts of the world, the same pattern is true. The Bantu people of Africa travelled extensively and spread their language, now called *Swahili*, which is the first Pan-African language. When thinking of the world as a whole, it is important to understand that thousands of languages exist; however, to interconnect the world, it is important to have a means of communication with which everyone is at least somewhat familiar. A *lingua franca* is essentially the language of business. In other words, when executives from multinational corporations need to communicate regarding business, they often communicate in English, which is considered to be the world's lingua franca, due to the economic dominance of the United States.

<u>Religion</u>
Religion has played a tremendous role in creating the world's cultures. Devout Christians crossed the Atlantic in hopes of finding religious freedom in New England, Muslim missionaries and traders travelled

to the Spice Islands of the East Indies to teach about the Koran, and Buddhist monks traversed the Himalayan Mountains into Tibet to spread their faith. In some countries, religion helps to shape legal systems. These nations, termed *theocracies*, have no separation of church and state and are more common in Islamic nations such as Saudi Arabia, Iran, and Qatar. In contrast, even though religion has played a tremendous role in the history of the United States, its government remains *secular*, or nonreligious, due to the influence of European Enlightenment philosophy at the time of its inception. Like ethnicity and language, religion is also a primary way that people self-identify. As a result, religious influences can shape a region's laws, architecture, literature, and music. For example, when the Ottoman Turks, who are Muslim, conquered Constantinople, which was once the home of the Eastern Orthodox Christian Church, they replaced Christian places of worship with mosques. Additionally, different forms of Roman architecture were replaced with those influenced by Arabic traditions.

Economics

Economic activity also has a spatial component. For example, nations with few natural resources generally tend to import what they need from nations willing to export raw materials to them. Furthermore, areas that are home to certain raw materials generally tend to alter their environment in order to maintain production of those materials. In the San Joaquin Valley of California, an area known for extreme heat and desert-like conditions, local residents have engineered elaborate drip irrigation systems to adequately water lemon, lime, olive, and orange trees, utilizing the warm temperatures to constantly produce citrus fruits. Additionally, other nations with abundant petroleum reserves build elaborate infrastructures in order to pump, house, refine, and transport their materials to nations who require gasoline, diesel, or natural gas. Essentially, different spatial regions on Earth create jobs, infrastructure, and transportation systems that seek to ensure the continued flow of goods, raw materials, and resources out of their location, so long as financial resources keep flowing into the area.

Patterns of Migration and Settlement

Migration is governed by two primary causes: *push factors*, which are reasons causing someone to leave an area, and *pull factors*, which are factors luring someone to a particular place. These two factors often work in concert with one another. For example, the United States of America has experienced significant *internal migration* from the industrial states in the Northeast (such as New York, New Jersey, Connecticut) to the Southern and Western states. This massive migration, which continues into the present-day, is due to high rents in the northeast, dreadfully cold winters, and lack of adequate retirement housing, all of which are push factors. These push factors lead to migration to the *Sunbelt*, a term geographers use to describe states with warm climates and less intense winters.

In addition to internal migrations within nations or regions, international migration also takes place between countries, continents, and other regions. The United States has long been the world's leading nation in regard to *immigration*, the process of having people come into a nation's boundaries. Conversely, developing nations that suffer from high levels of poverty, pollution, warfare, and other violence all have significant push factors, which cause people to leave and move elsewhere. This process, known as *emigration*, is when people in a particular area leave in order to seek a better life in a different—usually better—location.

The Development and Changing Nature of Agriculture

Agriculture is essential to human existence. The *Neolithic Revolution*, or the use of farming to produce food, had a profound effect on human societies. Rather than foraging and hunting for food, human societies became more stable and were able to grow due to more consistent food supplies. In modern times, farming has changed drastically in order to keep up with the increasing world population.

Until the twentieth century, the vast majority of people on Earth engaged in *subsistence farming*, or the practice of growing only enough food to feed one's self, or one's family. Over time, due to inventions such as the steel plow, the mechanical reaper, and the seed drill, farmers were able to produce more crops on the same amount of land. As food became cheaper and easier to obtain, populations grew, but rather than leading to an increase in farmers, fewer people actually farmed. After the advent of mechanized farming in developed nations, small farms became less common, and many were either abandoned or absorbed by massive commercial farms producing both foodstuffs, staple crops, and cash crops.

In recent years, agricultural practices have undergone further changes in order to keep up with the rapidly growing population. Due in part to the *Green Revolution*, which introduced the widespread use of fertilizers to produce massive amounts of crops, farming techniques and practices continue to evolve. For example, *genetically modified organisms*, or *GMOs*, are plants or animals whose genetic makeup has been modified using different strands of DNA in hopes of producing more resilient strains of staple crops, livestock, and other foodstuffs. This process, which is a form of *biotechnology*, attempts to solve the world's food production problems through the use of genetic engineering. Although these crops are abundant and resistant to pests, drought, or frost, they are also the subject of intense scrutiny. For example, the international food company, Monsanto, has faced an incredible amount of criticism regarding its use of GMOs in its products. Many activists assert that "rewiring" mother nature is inherently problematic and that foods produced through such methods are dangerous to human health. Despite the controversy, GMOs and biotechnologies continue to change the agricultural landscape by changing the world's food supply.

Like Monsanto, other agribusinesses exist throughout the world. Not only do these companies produce food for human consumption, but they also provide farming equipment, fertilizers, agrichemicals, and breeding and slaughtering services for livestock. While these companies are found all over the world, they are generally headquartered near the product they produce. For example, General Mills, a cereal manufacturer, is headquartered in the Midwestern United States, near its supply of wheat and corn—the primary ingredients in its cereals.

Contemporary Patterns and Impacts of Development, Industrialization, and Globalization

As mentioned previously, *developing nations* are nations that are struggling to modernize their economy, infrastructure, and government systems. Many of these nations may struggle to provide basic services to their citizens like clean water, adequate roads, or even police protection. Furthermore, government corruption makes life even more difficult for these countries' citizens. In contrast, *developed nations* are those who have relatively high *Gross Domestic Products (GDP)*, or the total value of all goods and services produced in the nation in a given year. To elucidate, the United States, which is one of the wealthiest nations on Earth when ranked by overall GDP, has nearly a 19 trillion dollar GDP; while Haiti, one of the poorest nations in the Western Hemisphere, has nearly a nine billion dollar GDP. This is a difference of almost seventeen trillion dollars. This is not to disparage Haiti or other developing nations; the comparison is simply used to show that extreme inequities exist in very close proximity to one another, and it may be difficult for developing nations to meet the needs of their citizens and move their economic infrastructure forward toward modernization.

In the modern world, industrialization is the initial key to modernization and development. For developed nations, the process of industrialization took place centuries ago. England, where the *Industrial Revolution* began, actually began to produce products in factories in the early 1700s. Later, the United States and some nations of Western Europe followed suit, using raw materials brought in from their colonies abroad to make finished products. For example, cotton was spun into fabric on elaborate weaving machines that mass-produced textiles. As a result, nations that perfected the textile process were able to sell their products around the world, which produced enormous profits. Over time, those nations were able to accumulate wealth, improve their nation's infrastructure, and provide more services for their citizens. Similar to the events of the eighteenth and nineteenth centuries, nations throughout the world are undergoing the same process in today's world. China exemplifies this concept. In China, agriculture was once the predominant occupation, and although it is true that agriculture is still a dominant sector of the Chinese economy, millions of Chinese citizens are flocking to major cities like Beijing, Shanghai, and Hangzhou, due to the availability of factory jobs that allow its workers a certain element of *social mobility*, or the ability to rise up out of one's socioeconomic situation.

Due to improvements in transportation and communication, the world has become figuratively smaller. For example, university students on the Indian Subcontinent now compete directly with students all over the world to obtain the skills employers desire to move their companies forward. Additionally, many corporations in developed nations have begun to *outsource* labor to nations with high levels of educational achievement but lower wage expectations. The process of opening the marketplace to all nations throughout the world, or *globalization*, has only just started to take hold in the modern economy. As industrial sites shift to the developing world, so does the relative level of opportunity for those nation's citizens. However, due to the massive amounts of pollution produced by factories, the process of globalization also has had significant ecological impacts. The most widely known impact, *climate change*, which most climatologists assert is caused by an increase of carbon dioxide in the atmosphere, remains a serious problem that has posed challenges for developing nations, who need industries in order to raise their standard of living, and developed nations, whose citizens use a tremendous amount of fossil fuels to run their cars, heat their homes, and maintain their ways of life.

Demographic Patterns and Demographic Change

Demography, or the study of human populations, involves a variety of closely related stimuli. First, as has been previously addressed, economic factors play a significant role in the movement of people, as do climate, natural disasters, or internal unrest. For example, in recent years, millions of immigrants from the war-torn country of Syria have moved as far as possible from danger. Although people are constantly moving, some consistencies remain throughout the world. First, people tend to live near reliable sources of food and water, which is why the first human civilizations sprung up in river valleys like the Indus River Valley in India, the Nile River Valley in Egypt, and the Yellow River Valley in Asia. Second, extreme temperatures tend to push people away, which is why the high latitudinal regions near the North and South Poles have such few inhabitants. Third, the vast majority of people tend to live in the Northern Hemisphere, due to the simple fact that more land lies in that part of the Earth. In keeping with these factors, human populations tend to be greater where human necessities are easily accessible, or at least more readily available. In other words, such areas have a greater chance of having a higher population density than places without such characteristics.

Demographic patterns on earth are not always stagnate. In contrast, people move and will continue to move as both push and pull factors fluctuate along with the flow of time. For example, in the 1940s, thousands of Europeans fled their homelands due to the impact of the Second World War. Today, thousands of migrants arrive on European shores each month due to conflicts in the Levant and difficult economic conditions in Northern Africa. Furthermore, as previously discussed, people tend to migrate to places with a greater economic benefit for themselves and their families. As a result, developed nations such as the United States, Germany, Canada, and Australia have a net gain of migrants, while developing nations such as Somalia, Zambia, and Cambodia generally tend to see thousands of their citizens seek better lives elsewhere.

It is important to understand the key variables in changes regarding human population and its composition worldwide. Religion and religious conflict play a role in where people choose to live. For example, the Nation of Israel won its independence in 1948 and has since attracted thousands of people of Jewish descent from all over the world. Additionally, the United States has long attracted people from all over the world, due to its promise of religious freedom inherent within its own Constitution. In contrast, nations like Saudi Arabia and Iran do not typically tolerate different religions, resulting in a decidedly uniform religious—and oftentimes ethnic—composition. Other factors such as economic opportunity, social unrest, and cost of living also play a vital role in demographic composition.

Basic Concepts of Political Geography

Nations, states, and nation-states are all terms with very similar meanings, but knowing the differences aids in a better understanding of geography. A nation is an area with similar cultural, linguistic, and historical experiences. A state is a political unit with sovereignty, or the ability to make its own decision in a particular area; and a nation-state is an entity that combines states into one, singular government system. For example, in the United States, the state of Texas is not an independent nation-state. Instead, it is part of the United States and thus, is subject to its laws. In a similar fashion, the United Kingdom encompasses four member states: England, Wales, Northern Ireland, and Scotland. Although people in those states may consider themselves to be *sovereign*, or self-governing, the reality is that those states cannot make decisions regarding international trade, declarations of war, or other important decisions regarding the rest of the world. Instead, they are *semi-autonomous*, meaning that they can make some decisions regarding how their own state is run, but must yield more major powers to a centralized authority. In the United States, this sort of system is called *Federalism*, or the sharing of power among Local, State, and Federal entities, each of whom is assigned different roles in the overall system of government.

Nation-states, and the boundaries that define where they are, are not always permanent. For example, after the fall of the Soviet Union in 1991, new nations emerged that had once been a part of the larger entity called the Union of Soviet Socialists Republics. These formerly sovereign nations were no longer forced to be a part of a unifying communist government, and as a result, they regained their autonomy and became newly independent nations that were no longer *satellite nations* of the Soviet Union. In a historical sense, the United States can be seen as a prime example of how national boundaries change. After the conclusion of the American Revolution in 1781, the Treaty of Paris defined the United States' western boundary as the Mississippi River; today, after a series of conflicts with Native American groups, the Mexican government, Hawaiian leadership, the Spanish, and the purchase of Alaska from the Russians, the boundaries of the United States have changed drastically. In a similar fashion, nations in Europe, Africa, and Asia have all shifted their boundaries due to warfare, cultural movements, and language barriers.

In the modern world, boundaries continue to change. For example, the Kurds, an ethnic minority in the Middle East, are still fighting for the right to control their people's' right to *self-determination*, but have not yet been successful in establishing a nation for themselves. In contrast, the oil-rich region of South Sudan, which has significant cultural, ethnic, and religious differences from Northern Sudan, successfully won its independence in a bloody civil war, which established the nation's newest independent nation. In recent years, Russia has made the world nervous by aggressively annexing the Crimean Peninsula, an area that has been part of the Ukraine since the end of the Cold War. Even the United Kingdom and Canada have seen their own people nearly vote for their own rights to self-determination. In 1995, the French-speaking Canadian province of Quebec narrowly avoided becoming a sovereign nation through a tightly contested referendum. In a similar fashion, Scotland, which is part of the UK, also voted to remain a part of the Crown, even though many people in that state see themselves as inherently different from those in other regions within the nation.

Political geography is constantly changing. Boundaries on maps from ten years ago are not consistent with those of 2016 and beyond. Simply looking at a map of Africa from 1950 can give one a sense of the level of change that takes place in a lifetime. For example, a map of Africa before 1950 looks completely different than a map of Africa from 2016. There are fewer European nations in the names on the 2016 map. *Decolonization*, or the removal of dependency on colonizers, has altered the political landscape of Africa, allowed more autonomy for the African people, and has forever redefined the boundaries of the entire continent.

Economics

The term *economy* is used to describe and calculate the supply and demand of goods and services. Economics is the study of human behavior in response to the production, consumption, and distribution of assets or wealth. It is a multi-tiered dynamic; people need to make personal choices about their own individual spending, while governments must make judgments that shape a whole society. Economics is divided into two subgroups: microeconomics and macroeconomics.

Microeconomics is the study of individual or small group behaviors and patterns in relationship to such things as earning and spending money. It focuses on particular markets within the economy, and looks at single factors that could potentially affect individuals or small groups. For example, the use of coupons in a grocery store can affect an individual's product choice, quantity purchased, and overall savings that a person may later roll into a different purchase. Microeconomics is the study of scarcity, choice, opportunity costs, economics systems, factors of production, supply and demand, market efficiency, the role of government, distribution of income, and product markets.

Macroeconomics examines a much larger scale of the economy. It focuses on how a society or nation's goods, services, spending habits, and other factors affect the people of that entity. It focuses on aggregate factors such as demand and output. For example, if a national company moves its production overseas to save on costs, how will production, labor, and capital be affected? Macroeconomics analyzes all aggregate indicators and the microeconomic factors that influence the economy. Government and corporations use macroeconomic models to help formulate economic policies and strategies.

Economic activity is cyclical with periods of booms and busts, which are typically prompted by extreme changes in the economy. *Booms* are cycles of increased activity resulting in new businesses, technologies, and jobs. However, these are often followed by periods of economic slowdowns, or *busts*, which can lead to recessions and even depressions. For example, the Wall Street Crash of 1929 triggered the Great Depression of the 1930s. During the Great Depression, New York Stock Market share prices dropped dramatically, causing the world's economic output to decrease by one-third and prompting a spike in unemployment levels of 25 percent or greater among global economies.

Microeconomics

Scarcity

People have different needs and wants, and the question arises, are the resources available to supply those needs and wants? Limited resources and high demand create scarcity. When a product is scarce, there is a short supply of it. For example, when the newest version of a cellphone is released, people line up to buy the phone or put their name on a wait list if the phone is not immediately available. The product, the new cellphone, may become a scarce commodity. In turn, because of the scarcity, companies may raise the cost of the commodity, knowing that if it is immediately available, people may pay more for the instant gratification—and vice versa. If a competing company lowers the cost of the phone but has contingencies, such as extended contracts or hidden fees, the buyer will still have the opportunity to purchase the scarce product. Limited resources and extremely high demand create scarcity and, in turn, cause companies to acquire opportunity costs.

Choice and Opportunity Costs

On a large scale, governments and communities have to assess different opportunity costs when it comes to using taxpayers' money. Should the government or community build a new school, repair roads, or allocate funds to local hospitals are all examples of choices taxpayers may have to review at some point in time. How do they decide which choice is the best, since each one has a trade off? By comparing the opportunity cost of each choice, they may decide what they are willing to live without for the sake of gaining something else.

Economic Systems

Economic systems determine what is being produced, who is producing it, who receives the product, and the money generated by the sale of the product. There are two basic types of economic systems: market economies (including free and competitive markets), and planned or command economies.

- Market Economies are characterized by:

    o Privately owned businesses, groups, or individuals provide goods or services based on demand.

    o The types of goods and services provided (supply) are based on that demand.

    o Two types: competitive market and free market.

Competitive Market	Free Market
Due to the large number of both buyers and sellers, there is no way any one seller or buyer can control the market or price.	Voluntary private trades between buyers and sellers determine markets and prices without government intervention or monopolies.

- Planned or Command Economies:

    o In planned or command economies, the government or central authority determines market prices of goods and services.

    o The government or central authority determines what is being produced as well as the quantity of production.

    o Some advantages to command economies include a large number of shared goods such as public services (transportation, schools, or hospitals).

    o Disadvantages of command economies include wastefulness of resources.

Factors of Production

There are four factors of production:

1. Land: both renewable and nonrenewable resources
2. Labor: effort put forth by people to produce goods and services

3. Capital: the tools used to create goods and services
4. Entrepreneurship: persons who combine land, labor, and capital to create new goods and services

The four factors of production are used to create goods and services to make economic profit. All four factors strongly impact one another.

Supply and Demand

Supply and demand is the most important concept of economics in a market economy. Supply is the amount of a product that a market can offer. Demand is the quantity of a product needed or desired by buyers. The price of a product is directly related to supply and demand. The correlation between the price of a product and the demand necessary to distribute resources to the market go hand in hand in a market economy. For example, when there are a variety of treats at a bakery, certain treats are in higher demand than others. The bakery can raise the cost of the more demanded items as supplies get limited. Conversely, the bakery can sell the less desirable treats by lowering the cost of those items as an incentive for buyers to purchase them.

Market Efficiency and the Role of Government (Taxes, Subsidies, and Price Controls)

Market efficiency is directly affected by supply and demand. The government can help the market stay efficient by either stepping in when the market is inefficient and/or providing the means necessary for markets to run properly. For example, society needs two types of infrastructure: physical (bridges, roads, etc.) and institutional (courts, laws, etc.). The government may impose taxes, subsidies, and price controls to increase revenue, lower prices of goods and services, ensure product availability for the government, and maintain fair prices for goods and services.

The Purpose of Taxes, Subsidies, and Price Controls

Taxes	Subsidies	Price Controls
-Generate government revenue -Discourage purchase or use of "bad" products such as alcohol or cigarettes	-Lower the price of goods and services -Reassure the supply of goods and services -Allow opportunities to compete with overseas vendors	-Act as emergency measures when government intervention is necessary -Set a minimum or maximum price for goods and services

Distribution of Income

Distribution of income refers to how wages are distributed across a society or segments of a society. If everyone made the same amount of money, the distribution of income would be equal. That is not the case in most societies. The wealth of people and companies varies. Income inequality gaps are present in America and many other nations. Taxes provide an option to redistribute income or wealth because they provide revenue to build new infrastructure and provide cash benefits to some of the poorest members in society.

Product Markets

Product markets are marketplaces where goods and services are bought and sold. Product markets provide sellers a place to offer goods and services to consumers, and for consumers to purchase those goods and services. The annual value of goods and services exchanged throughout the year is measured by the Gross Domestic Product (GDP), a monetary measure of goods and services made either quarterly or annually. Department stores, gas stations, grocery stores, and other retail stores are all examples of product markets. However, product markets do not include any raw, scarce, or trade materials.

Theory of the Firm

The behavior of firms is composed of several theories varying between short- and long-term goals. There are four basic firm behaviors: perfect competition, profit maximization, short run, and long run. Each firm follows a pattern, depending on its desired outcome. Theory of the Firm posits that firms, after conducting market research, make decisions that will maximize their profits since they are for-profit entities.

- Perfect competition:
  - In perfect competition, several businesses are selling the same product at the same time.
  - There are so many businesses and consumers that none will directly impact the market.
  - Each business and consumer is aware of the competing businesses and markets.
- Profit maximization:
  - Firms decide the quantity of a product that needs to be produced in order to receive maximum profit gains. Profit is the total amount of revenue made after subtracting costs.
- Short run:
  - A short amount of time where fixed prices cannot be adjusted
  - The quantity of the product depends on the varying amount of labor. Less labor means less product.
- Long run:
  - An amount of time where fixed prices can be adjusted
  - Firms try to maximize production while minimizing labor costs.

Overall, microeconomics operates on a small scale, focusing on how individuals or small groups use and assign resources.

Macroeconomics

Macroeconomics analyzes the economy as a whole. It studies unemployment, interest rates, price levels, and national income, which are all factors that can affect the nation as a whole, and not just individual households. Macroeconomics studies all large factors to determine how, or if, they will affect future trend patterns of production, consumption, and economic growth.

Types of Productive Resources and the Role of Money as a Resource

Productive resources are the means used by a society to succeed and survive. The four types are:

1. Natural resources—the raw materials taken from the land, such as corn, beef, lumber, water, oil, and iron.

2. Human resources—the human labor, both mental and physical, that are required to produce goods.

3. Capital resources—the man-made physical resources used to create products, such as machinery, tools, buildings, and equipment.

4. Entrepreneurship—the capability and motivation to cultivate, organize, and oversee the other three resources into a business venture.

Money functions as a method of exchange to obtain goods or services. It replaced the barter system, which was often considered inefficient and disorganized. Economists referred to the barter system as a double coincidence of wants since trades between parties were not always considered equal. Prices of goods are determined by supply and demand. *Inflation* occurs when people have money to spend, but not enough goods can be produced or imported to meet their demand for a product, which causes prices to rise. The amount of money issued by government-controlled central banks and the prices of leading commodities, such as oil, can also affect inflation. *Deflation* is when people save their money and spend less, leaving stores with surplus goods, which causes prices to drop.

Measures of Economic Performance

It is important to measure economic performance to determine if an economy is growing, stagnant, or deteriorating. To measure the growth and sustainability of an economy, several indicators can be used. Economic indicators provide data that economists can use to determine if there are faulty processes or if some form of intervention is needed.

One of the main indicators to measure economic performance is the growth of the country's Gross Domestic Product (GDP). GDP growth provides important information that can be used to determine fiscal or financial policies. The GDP does not measure income distribution, quality of life, or losses due to natural disasters. For example, if a community lost everything to a hurricane, it would take a long time to rebuild the community and stabilize its economy. That is why there is a need to take into account more balanced performance measures when factoring overall economic performance.

Other indicators used to measure economic performance are unemployment or employment rates, inflation, savings, investments, surpluses and deficits, debt, labor, trade terms, the HDI (Human Development Index), and the HPI (Human Poverty Index).

Unemployment

Unemployment occurs when an individual does not have a job, is actively trying to find employment, and is not getting paid. Official unemployment rates do not factor in the number of people who have stopped looking for work, unlike true unemployment rates that do, causing them to be higher.

There are three types of unemployment: cyclical, frictional, and structural.

Cyclical
The product of a business cycle. This usually occurs during a recession.
Frictional
The difficulty of matching qualified workers for specific jobs. An example would be a person changing careers.
Structural
When a person no longer qualifies for a specific job, or failing out of a retraining course for a job.

Given the nature of a market economy and the fluctuations of the labor market, a 100 percent employment rate is impossible to reach.

Inflation

Inflation is when the cost of goods and services rises over time. Supply, demand, and money reserves all affect inflation. Generally, inflation is measured by the Consumer Price Index (CPI), a tool that tracks price changes of goods and services over time. The CPI measures goods and services such as gasoline, cars, clothing, and food. When the cost of goods and services increase, the quantity of the product may decrease due to lower demand. This decreases the purchasing power of the consumer. Basically, as more money is printed, it holds less and less value in purchasing power. For example, when inflation occurs, consumers in the United States are spending and saving less because the U.S. dollar is worth less, and therefore the consumer cannot buy or save as much money. However, if inflation occurs steadily over time, the people can better plan and prepare for future necessities.

Inflation can vary from year to year, usually never fluctuating more than 2 percent. Central banks try to prevent drastic increases or decreases of inflation to prohibit prices from rising or falling far from the minimum. Inflation can also vary based on different monetary currencies. Although rare, any country's economy may experience hyperinflation (when inflation rates increase to over 50 percent), while other economies may experience deflation (when the cost of goods and services decrease over time). Deflation occurs when the inflation rate drops below zero percent.

Business Cycle

A business cycle is when the Gross Domestic Product (GDP) moves downward and upward over a long-term growth trend. These cycles help determine where the economy currently stands, as well as where the economy could be heading. Business cycles usually occur almost every six years, and have four phases: expansion, peak, contraction, and trough. Here are some characteristics of each phase:

- Expansion:
  - Increased employment rates and economic growth
  - Production and sales increase
  - On a graph, expansion is where the lines climb.
- Peak:
  - Employment rates are at or above full employment and the economy is at maximum productivity.
  - On a graph, the peak is the top of the hill, where expansion has reached its maximum.

- Contraction:
  - When growth starts slowing
  - Unemployment is on the rise.
  - On a graph, contraction is where the graph begins to slide back down or contract.
- Trough:
  - The cycle has hit bottom and is waiting for the next cycle to start again.
  - On a graph, the trough is the bottom of the contraction prior to when it starts to climb back up.

When the economy is expanding or "booming," the business cycle is going from a trough to a peak. When the economy is headed down and toward a recession, the business cycle is going from a peak to a trough.

Four phases of a business cycle:

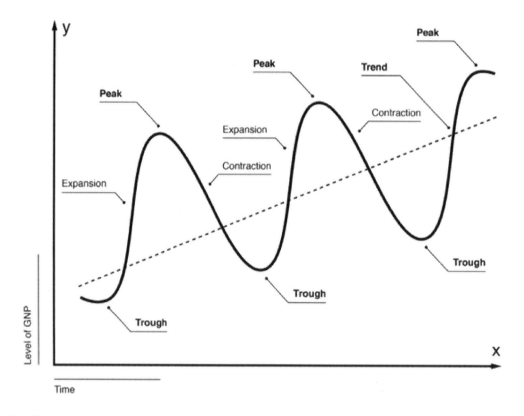

Fiscal Policy

A fiscal policy is when the government is involved in adjusting spending and tax rates to assist the way in which an economy financially functions. Fiscal policies can either increase or decrease tax rates and spending. These policies represent a tricky balancing act, because if the government increases taxes too much, consumer spending and monetary value will decrease. Conversely, if the government lowers taxes, consumers will have more money in their pockets to buy more goods and services, which increases demand and the need for companies to supply those goods and services. Due to the higher demand, suppliers can add jobs to fulfill that demand. While the increase of supply, demand, and jobs are positive for the overall economy, they may result in a devaluation of the dollar and less purchasing power.

Money and Banking

Money is the universal form of currency used throughout goods and services exchanges that holds its value over time. Money provides a convenient way for sellers and consumers to understand the value of their goods and services. As opposed to bartering (when sellers and consumers exchange goods or services as equal trades), money is quick and easy for both buyers and sellers.

There are three main forms of money: commodity, fiat, and bank. Here are characteristics of each form:

- Commodity money: Money as a valuable good, such as precious metals
- Fiat money: The value of the good set by supply and demand rather than the actual value it represents, such as paper money
- Bank money: Money that is credited by a bank to those who deposit it into bank accounts, such as checking and savings accounts or credit

While price levels within the economy set the demand for money, most countries have central banks that supply the actual money. Essentially, banks buy and sell money. Borrowers can take loans and pay back the bank, with interest, providing the bank with extra capital.

A central bank has control over the printing and distribution of money. Central banks serve three main purposes: manage monetary growth to help steer the direction of the economy, be a backup to commercial banks that are suffering, and provide options and alternatives to government taxation.

The Federal Reserve is the central bank of the United States. The Federal Reserve controls banking systems and determines the value of money in the United States. Basically, the Federal Reserve is the bank for banks.

All Western economies have to keep a minimum amount of protected cash called *required reserve*. Once banks meet those minimums, they can then lend or loan the excess to consumers. The required reserves are used within a fractional reserve banking system (fractional because a small portion is kept separate and safe). Not only do banks reserve, manage, and loan money, but they also help form monetary policies.

Monetary Policy

The central bank and other government committees control the amount of money that is made and distributed. The money supply determines monetary policy. Three main features sustain monetary policy:

1. Assuring the minimum amount held within banks (bank reserves). When banks are required to hold more money in reserve funds, banks are less willing to lend money to help control inflation.

2. Adjusting interest rates. For example, if the value of money is low, companies and consumers buy more (products, employees, stocks) because prices are cheap. Just like an investment, it is risky, but can pay off in the long term.

3. The purchase and sales of bonds (otherwise known as open market operations). When buying bonds to increase money and selling bonds to reduce the supply, the central bank helps control the money supply.

In the United States, the Federal Reserve maintains monetary policy. There are two main types of monetary policy: expansionary monetary policy and contractionary monetary policy.

- Expansionary monetary policy:
  - Increases the money supply
  - Lowers unemployment
  - Increases consumer spending
  - Increases private sector borrowing
  - Possibly decreases interest rates to very low levels, even near zero
  - Decreases reserve requirements and federal funds
- Contractionary monetary policy:
  - Decreases the money supply
  - Helps control inflation
  - Possibly increases unemployment due to slowdowns in economic growth
  - Decreases consumer spending
  - Decreases loans and/or borrowing

The Federal Reserve uses monetary policy to try to achieve maximum employment and secure inflation rates. Because the Federal Reserve is the "bank of banks," it truly strives to be the last-resort option for distressed banks. This is because once these kinds of institutions begin to rely on the Federal Reserve for help, all parts of the banking industry—such as those dealing with loans, bonds, interest rates, and mortgages—are affected.

International Trade and Exchange Rates

International trade is when countries import and export goods and services. Countries often want to deal in terms of their own currency. Therefore, when importing or exporting goods or services, consumers and businesses need to enter the market using the same form of currency. For example, if the United States would like to trade with China, the U.S. may have to trade in China's form of currency, the *Yuan*, versus the dollar, depending on the business.

Advantages and Disadvantages of Fixed Versus Floating Exchange Rates			
Fixed Exchange Rate: government intervention to help keep exchange rates stable		Floating or "Flexible" Exchange Rate: Supply and demand determines the exchange rate	
Advantages	*Disadvantages*	*Advantages*	*Disadvantages*
-Stable prices	-Requires a large	-Central bank	-Currency speculation
-Stable foreign	amount of reserve	involvement is not	-Exchange rate risks
exchange rates	funds	needed.	-Inflation increases
-Exports are more	-Possibly mispricing	-Facilitates free trade	
competitive and in turn	currency values		
more profitable	Inflation increases		

The exchange rate is what one country's currency will exchange for another. The government and the market (supply and demand) determine the exchange rate. There are two forms of exchange rates: fixed and floating. Fixed exchange rates involve government interventions (like central banks) to help keep the exchange rates stable. Floating or "flexible" exchange rates constantly change because they rely on supply and demand needs. While each type of exchange rate has advantages and disadvantages, the rate truly depends on the current state of each country's economy. Therefore, each exchange rate may differ from country to country.

While each country may have differing economic statuses and exchange rates, countries rely on one another for goods and services. Prices of imports and exports are affected by the strength of another country's currency. For example, if the United States dollar is at a higher value than another country's currency, imports will be less expensive because the dollar will have more value than that of the country selling its good or service. On the other hand, if the dollar is at a low value compared to the currency of another country, importers will tend to defer away from buying international items from that country. However, U.S. exporters to that country could benefit from the low value of the dollar.

Economic Growth

Economic growth is measured by the increase in the Gross National Product (GNP) or Gross Domestic Product (GDP). The increase of goods and services over time indicates positive movement in economic growth. Keep in mind that the quantity of goods and services produced is not necessarily an indicator of economic growth. The value of the goods and services produced matters more than the quantity.

There are many causes of economic growth, which can be short- or long-term. In the short term, if aggregate demand (the total demand for goods and services produced at a given time) increases, then the overall Gross Domestic Product (GDP) increases as well. Not only will the GDP increase, interest rates may decrease. With reduced interest rates, spending and investing will increase. Consumer and government spending will also increase because there will be more disposable income. Real estate prices will rise, and there will be lower income taxes. All of these short-term factors can stimulate economic growth.

In the long term, if aggregate supply (the total supply of goods or services in a given time period) increases, then there is potential for an increase in capital as well. With more working capital, more infrastructure and jobs can be created. With more jobs, there is an increased employment rate, and education and training for jobs will improve. New technologies will be developed, and new raw materials may be discovered. All of these long-term factors can also stimulate economic growth.

Outside of the short- and long-term causes for economic growth, other factors include low inflation and stability. Lower inflation rates encourage more investing versus higher inflation rates that cause instability in the market. Stability encourages businesses to continue investing. If the market is unstable, investors may question the volatility of the market.

Potential Costs of Economic Growth:

- Inflation: When economic growth occurs, inflation tends to be high. If supply cannot keep up with demand, then the inflation rate may be unmanageable.

- Economic booms and recessions: The economy goes through cycles of booms and recessions. This causes inflation to increase and decrease over time, which puts the economy into a continuous cycle of rising and falling.

- Account inefficiencies: When the economy grows, consumers and businesses increase their import spending. The increase of import spending affects the current account and causes a shortage.

- Environmental costs: When the economy is growing, there is an abundance of output, which may result in more pollutants and a reduction in quality of life.

- Inequalities: Growth occurs differently among members of society. While the wealthy may be getting richer, those living in poverty may just be getting on their feet. So while economic growth is happening, it may happen at two very different rates.

While these potential costs could affect economic growth, if the growth is consistent and stable, then growth can occur without severe inflation swings. Also, as technology improves, new ways of production can reduce negative environmental factors as well.

Major Sectors of the United States Economy and the Interactions Between Businesses and Consumers

Economies consist of the following four business sectors, or parts, that share similar products or services:

- *Primary sector*—gathers natural resources, including industries such as farming, fishing, and oil and gas drilling.

- *Secondary sector*—develops raw materials from the primary sector into finished goods through enhancement, manufacture, or construction, including industries such as car manufacturing, food processing, and steelworks.

- *Tertiary sector*—provides consumer or business services, including industries such as entertainment, travel and tourism, and banking.

- *Quaternary sector*—provides informational and knowledge services, including industries such as universities, consultancies, and research and development companies.

These sectors function like interconnected links in a chain, with each one passing its production along to the next sector. Service industries typically increase as a country develops and constitute the largest sector of both the U.S. and global economies. The U.S. is the leading global economy in terms of size and significance providing twenty percent of the world's total production of goods and services. About eighty percent of this output comes from its innovative, technically advanced services sector, and fifteen percent comes from manufacturing.

Economists often use the circular flow model to describe the movement of supply, demand, and payment between businesses and consumers (also referred to as sectors). Functioning as an interdependent continuous loop, consumers obtain income, goods, and services from business producers. These producers then receive profits and the ability to buy necessary supplies. Money flows one way, and the goods and productive resources flow in the opposite direction. Each sector relies on the other.

Here's an illustration of that:

Circular Flow Model

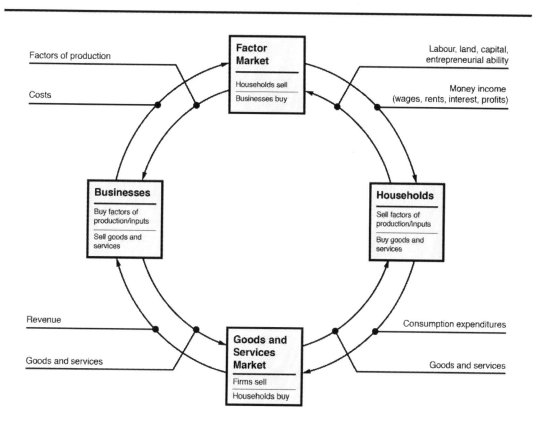

Costs and Benefits of Personal Spending and Savings Choices

Individuals earn an income by trading their labor – both mental and physical – for pay. They then budget their money through spending or saving it. As consumers, every choice has an opportunity cost since they must choose which goods and services they want to buy with a limited income. By purchasing one good or service, they give up the chance to purchase another.

Additionally, consumers have the choice to save money when they don't have enough money to purchase what they want, or when they want to utilize a savings account to use during emergencies or periods of economic difficulty. People also choose to save for *retirement*, a time when they will no longer be working and drawing a salary. Saving money by putting it in a bank is considered low-risk—the bank will pay the saver a low interest rate to keep it safe, but it will not increase much in value. A riskier path is investing money through the purchase of valuable items (or *assets*) in the hopes that they will increase in worth over time and yield returns (or *profits*). *Assets* can include shares in companies, real estate or land investments, or capital such as money, equipment, and structures used to create wealth.

Mathematics and Statistics

Numbers Sense

Place Value of a Given Digit

The number system that is used consists of only ten different digits or characters. However, this system is used to represent an infinite number of values. The place value system makes this infinite number of values possible. The position in which a digit is written corresponds to a given value. Starting from the decimal point (which is implied, if not physically present), each subsequent place value to the left represents a value greater than the one before it. Conversely, starting from the decimal point, each subsequent place value to the right represents a value less than the one before it.

The names for the place values to the left of the decimal point are as follows:

...	Billions	Hundred-Millions	Ten-Millions	Millions	Hundred-Thousands	Ten-Thousands	Thousands	Hundreds	Tens	Ones

*Note that this table can be extended infinitely further to the left.

The names for the place values to the right of the decimal point are as follows:

Decimal Point (.)	Tenths	Hundredths	Thousandths	Ten-Thousandths	...

*Note that this table can be extended infinitely further to the right.

When given a multi-digit number, the value of each digit depends on its place value. Consider the number 682,174.953. Referring to the chart above, it can be determined that the digit 8 is in the ten-thousands place. It is in the fifth place to the left of the decimal point. Its value is 8 ten-thousands or 80,000. The digit 5 is two places to the right of the decimal point. Therefore, the digit 5 is in the hundredths place. Its value is 5 hundredths or $\frac{5}{100}$ (equivalent to .05).

Base-10 System

Value of Digits

In accordance with the base-10 system, the value of a digit increases by a factor of ten each place it moves to the left. For example, consider the number 7. Moving the digit one place to the left (70), increases its value by a factor of 10 ($7 \times 10 = 70$). Moving the digit two places to the left (700) increases its value by a factor of 10 twice ($7 \times 10 \times 10 = 700$). Moving the digit three places to the left (7,000) increases its value by a factor of 10 three times ($7 \times 10 \times 10 \times 10 = 7,000$), and so on.

Conversely, the value of a digit decreases by a factor of ten each place it moves to the right. (Note that multiplying by $\frac{1}{10}$ is equivalent to dividing by 10). For example, consider the number 40. Moving the digit one place to the right (4) decreases its value by a factor of 10 ($40 \div 10 = 4$). Moving the digit two places to the right (0.4), decreases its value by a factor of 10 twice ($40 \div 10 \div 10 = 0.4$) or

$(40 \times \frac{1}{10} \times \frac{1}{10} = 0.4)$. Moving the digit three places to the right (0.04) decreases its value by a factor of 10 three times $(40 \div 10 \div 10 \div 10 = 0.04)$ or $(40 \times \frac{1}{10} \times \frac{1}{10} \times \frac{1}{10} = 0.04)$, and so on.

Exponents to Denote Powers of 10

The value of a given digit of a number in the base-10 system can be expressed utilizing powers of 10. A power of 10 refers to 10 raised to a given exponent such as 10^0, 10^1, 10^2, 10^3, etc. For the number 10^3, 10 is the base and 3 is the exponent. A base raised by an exponent represents how many times the base is multiplied by itself. Therefore, $10^1 = 10$, $10^2 = 10 \times 10 = 100$, $10^3 = 10 \times 10 \times 10 = 1,000$, $10^4 = 10 \times 10 \times 10 \times 10 = 10,000$, etc. Any base with a zero exponent equals one.

Powers of 10 are utilized to decompose a multi-digit number without writing all the zeroes. Consider the number 872,349. This number is decomposed to $800,000 + 70,000 + 2,000 + 300 + 40 + 9$. When utilizing powers of 10, the number 872,349 is decomposed to $(8 \times 10^5) + (7 \times 10^4) + (2 \times 10^3) + (3 \times 10^2) + (4 \times 10^1) + (9 \times 10^0)$. The power of 10 by which the digit is multiplied corresponds to the number of zeroes following the digit when expressing its value in standard form. For example, 7×10^4 is equivalent to 70,000 or 7 followed by four zeros.

Comparing, Classifying, and Ordering Rational Numbers

Rational numbers are any number that can be written as a fraction or ratio. Within the set of rational numbers, several subsets exist that are referenced throughout the mathematics topics. Counting numbers are the first numbers learned as a child. Counting numbers consist of 1,2,3,4, and so on. Whole numbers include all counting numbers and zero (0,1,2,3,4,...). Integers include counting numbers, their opposites, and zero (..., -3, -2, -1, 0, 1, 2, 3, ...). Rational numbers are inclusive of integers, fractions, and decimals that terminate, or end (1.7, 0.04213) or repeat ($0.136\overline{5}$).

When comparing or ordering numbers, the numbers should be written in the same format (decimal or fraction), if possible. For example, $\sqrt{49}$, 7.3, and $\frac{15}{2}$ are easier to order if each one is converted to a decimal, such as 7, 7.3, and 7.5 (converting fractions and decimals is covered in the following section). A number line is used to order and compare the numbers. Any number that is to the right of another number is greater than that number. Conversely, a number positioned to the left of a given number is less than that number.

Structure of the Number System

The mathematical number system is made up of two general types of numbers: real and complex. *Real numbers* are those that are used in normal settings, while *complex numbers* are those composed of both a real number and an imaginary one. Imaginary numbers are the result of taking the square root of -1, and $\sqrt{-1} = i$.

The real number system is often explained using a Venn diagram similar to the one below. After a number has been labeled as a real number, further classification occurs when considering the other groups in this diagram. If a number is a never-ending, non-repeating decimal, it falls in the irrational category. Otherwise, it is rational. More information on these types of numbers is provided in the previous section. Furthermore, if a number does not have a fractional part, it is classified as an integer, such as -2, 75, or 0. Whole numbers are an even smaller group that only includes positive integers and 0. The last group of natural numbers is made up of only positive integers, such as 2, 56, or 12.

Real numbers can be compared and ordered using the number line. If a number falls to the left on the real number line, it is less than a number on the right. For example, $-2 < 5$ because -2 falls to the left of 0, and 5 falls to the right. Numbers to the left of zero are negative while those to the right are positive.

Complex numbers are made up of the sum of a real number and an imaginary number. Some examples of complex numbers include $6 + 2i$, $5 - 7i$, and $-3 + 12i$. Adding and subtracting complex numbers is similar to collecting like terms. The real numbers are added together, and the imaginary numbers are added together. For example, if the problem asks to simplify the expression $6 + 2i - 3 + 7i$, the 6 and -3 are combined to make 3, and the $2i$ and $7i$ combine to make $9i$. Multiplying and dividing complex numbers is similar to working with exponents. One rule to remember when multiplying is that $i * i = -1$. For example, if a problem asks to simplify the expression $4i(3 + 7i)$, the $4i$ should be distributed throughout the 3 and the $7i$. This leaves the final expression $12i - 28$. The 28 is negative because $i * i$ results in a negative number. The last type of operation to consider with complex numbers is the conjugate. The *conjugate* of a complex number is a technique used to change the complex number into a real number. For example, the conjugate of $4 - 3i$ is $4 + 3i$. Multiplying $(4 - 3i)(4 + 3i)$ results in $16 + 12i - 12i + 9$, which has a final answer of $16 + 9 = 25$.

The order of operations—PEMDAS—simplifies longer expressions with real or imaginary numbers. Each operation is listed in the order of how they should be completed in a problem containing more than one operation. Parenthesis can also mean grouping symbols, such as brackets and absolute value. Then, exponents are calculated. Multiplication and division should be completed from left to right, and addition and subtraction should be completed from left to right.

Simplification of another type of expression occurs when radicals are involved. As explained previously, root is another word for radical. For example, the following expression is a radical that can be simplified: $\sqrt{24x^2}$. First, the number must be factored out to the highest perfect square. Any perfect square can be taken out of a radical. Twenty-four can be factored into 4 and 6, and 4 can be taken out of the radical. $\sqrt{4} = 2$ can be taken out, and 6 stays underneath. If $x > 0$, x can be taken out of the radical because it is a perfect square. The simplified radical is $2x\sqrt{6}$. An approximation can be found using a calculator.

There are also properties of numbers that are true for certain operations. The *commutative* property allows the order of the terms in an expression to change while keeping the same final answer. Both addition and multiplication can be completed in any order and still obtain the same result. However, order does matter in subtraction and division. The *associative* property allows any terms to be "associated" by parenthesis and retain the same final answer. For example, $(4 + 3) + 5 = 4 + (3 + 5)$. Both addition and multiplication are associative; however, subtraction and division do not hold this property. The *distributive* property states that $a(b + c) = ab + ac$. It is a property that involves both addition and multiplication, and the *a* is distributed onto each term inside the parentheses.

Integers can be factored into prime numbers. To *factor* is to express as a product. For example, $6 = 3 \cdot 2$, and $6 = 6 \cdot 1$. Both are factorizations, but the expression involving the factors of 3 and 2 is known as a *prime factorization* because it is factored into a product of two *prime numbers*—integers which do not have any factors other than themselves and 1. A *composite number* is a positive integer that can be divided into at least one other integer other than itself and 1, such as 6. Integers that have a factor of 2 are even, and if they are not divisible by 2, they are odd. Finally, a *multiple* of a number is the product of that number and a counting number—also known as a *natural number*. For example, some multiples of 4 are 4, 8, 12, 16, etc.

Properties of Exponents

Exponents are used in mathematics to express a number or variable multiplied by itself a certain number of times. For example, x^3 means x is multiplied by itself three times. In this expression, x is called the *base*, and 3 is the *exponent*. Exponents can be used in more complex problems when they contain fractions and negative numbers.

Fractional exponents can be explained by looking first at the inverse of exponents, which are *roots*. Given the expression x^2, the square root can be taken, $\sqrt{x^2}$, cancelling out the 2 and leaving x by itself, if x is positive. Cancellation occurs because $\sqrt{x}$ can be written with exponents, instead of roots, as $x^{\frac{1}{2}}$. The numerator of 1 is the exponent, and the denominator of 2 is called the root (which is why it's referred to as *square root*). Taking the square root of x^2 is the same as raising it to the $\frac{1}{2}$ power. Written out in mathematical form, it takes the following progression: $\sqrt{x^2} = (x^2)^{\frac{1}{2}} = x$.

From properties of exponents, $2 \cdot \frac{1}{2} = 1$ is the actual exponent of x. Another example can be seen with $x^{\frac{4}{7}}$. The variable x, raised to four-sevenths, is equal to the seventh root of x to the fourth power: $\sqrt[7]{x^4}$. In general, $x^{\frac{1}{n}} = \sqrt[n]{x}$ and $x^{\frac{m}{n}} = \sqrt[n]{x^m}$.

Negative exponents also involve fractions. Whereas y^3 can also be rewritten as $\frac{y^3}{1}$, y^{-3} can be rewritten as $\frac{1}{y^3}$. A negative exponent means the exponential expression must be moved to the opposite spot in a fraction to make the exponent positive. If the negative appears in the numerator, it moves to the denominator. If the negative appears in the denominator, it is moved to the numerator. In general, $a^{-n} = \frac{1}{a^n}$, and a^{-n} and a^n are reciprocals.

Take, for example, the following expression: $\frac{a^{-4}b^2}{c^{-5}}$. Since a is raised to the negative fourth power, it can be moved to the denominator. Since c is raised to the negative fifth power, it can be moved to the numerator. The b variable is raised to the positive second power, so it does not move. The simplified expression is as follows: $\frac{b^2c^5}{a^4}$.

In mathematical expressions containing exponents and other operations, the order of operations must be followed. *PEMDAS* states that exponents are calculated after any parenthesis and grouping symbols, but before any multiplication, division, addition, and subtraction.

Ratios and Proportions

Ratios are used to show the relationship between two quantities. The ratio of oranges to apples in the grocery store may be 3 to 2. That means that for every 3 oranges, there are 2 apples. This comparison can be expanded to represent the actual number of oranges and apples. Another example may be the number of boys to girls in a math class. If the ration of boys to girls is given as 2 to 5, that means there are 2 boys to every 5 girls in the class. Ratios can also be compared if the units in each ratio are the same. The ratio of boys to girls in the math class can be compared to the ratio of boys to girls in a science class by stating which ratio is higher and which is lower.

Rates are used to compare two quantities with different units. *Unit rates* are the simplest form of rate. With unit rates, the denominator in the comparison of two units is one. For example, if someone can type at a rate of 1000 words in 5 minutes, then his or her unit rate for typing is $\frac{1000}{5} = 200$ words in one minute or 200 words per minute. Any rate can be converted into a unit rate by dividing to make the denominator one. 1000 words in 5 minutes has been converted into the unit rate of 200 words per minute.

Ratios and rates can be used together to convert rates into different units. For example, if someone is driving 50 kilometers per hour, that rate can be converted into miles per hour by using a ratio known as the *conversion factor*. Since the given value contains kilometers and the final answer needs to be in miles, the ratio relating miles to kilometers needs to be used. There are 0.62 miles in 1 kilometer. This, written as a ratio and in fraction form, is $\frac{0.62\ miles}{1\ km}$. To convert 50km/hour into miles per hour, the following conversion needs to be set up:

$$\frac{50\ km}{hour} * \frac{0.62\ miles}{1\ km} = 31\ miles\ per\ hour$$

The ratio between two similar geometric figures is called the *scale factor*. For example, a problem may depict two similar triangles, A and B. The scale factor from the smaller triangle A to the larger triangle B is given as 2 because the length of the corresponding side of the larger triangle, 16, is twice the corresponding side on the smaller triangle, 8. This scale factor can also be used to find the value of a missing side, x, in triangle A. Since the scale factor from the smaller triangle (A) to larger one (B) is 2, the larger corresponding side in triangle B (given as 25), can be divided by 2 to find the missing side in A (x= 12.5). The scale factor can also be represented in the equation $2A = B$ because two times the lengths of A gives the corresponding lengths of B. This is the idea behind similar triangles.

Much like a scale factor can be written using an equation like $2A = B$, a *relationship* is represented by the equation $Y = kX$. X and Y are proportional because as values of X increase, the values of Y also increase. A relationship that is inversely proportional can be represented by the equation $Y = \frac{k}{X}$, where the value of Y decreases as the value of x increases and vice versa.

Proportional reasoning can be used to solve problems involving ratios, percentages, and averages. Ratios can be used in setting up proportions and solving them to find unknowns. For example, if a student completes an average of 10 pages of math homework in 3 nights, how long would it take the student to complete 22 pages? Both ratios can be written as fractions. The second ratio would contain the unknown. The following proportion represents this problem, where x is the unknown number of nights:

$$\frac{10\ pages}{3\ nights} = \frac{22\ pages}{x\ nights}$$

Solving this proportion entails cross-multiplying and results in the following equation: $10x = 22 * 3$. Simplifying and solving for x results in the exact solution: $x = 6.6\ nights$. The result would be rounded up to 7 because the homework would actually be completed on the 7th night.

The following problem uses ratios involving percentages:

If 20% of the class is girls and 30 students are in the class, how many girls are in the class?

To set up this problem, it is helpful to use the common proportion: $\frac{\%}{100} = \frac{is}{of}$. Within the proportion, % is the percentage of girls, 100 is the total percentage of the class, *is* is the number of girls, and *of* is the total number of students in the class. Most percentage problems can be written using this language. To solve this problem, the proportion should be set up as $\frac{20}{100} = \frac{x}{30}$, and then solved for x. Cross-multiplying results in the equation $20 * 30 = 100x$, which results in the solution $x = 6$. There are 6 girls in the class.

Problems involving volume, length, and other units can also be solved using ratios. For example, a problem may ask for the volume of a cone to be found that has a radius, $r = 7m$ and a height, $h = 16m$. Referring to the formulas provided on the test, the volume of a cone is given as: $V = \pi r^2 \frac{h}{3}$, where r is the radius, and h is the height. Plugging $r = 7$ and $h = 16$ into the formula, the following is obtained: $V = \pi(7^2)\frac{16}{3}$. Therefore, volume of the cone is found to be approximately $821m^3$. Sometimes, answers in different units are sought. If this problem wanted the answer in liters, $821m^3$ would need to be converted. Using the equivalence statement $1m^3 = 1000L$, the following ratio would be used to solve for liters: $821m^3 * \frac{1000L}{1m^3}$. Cubic meters in the numerator and denominator cancel each other out, and the answer is converted to 821,000 liters, or $8.21 * 10^5$ L.

Other conversions can also be made between different given and final units. If the temperature in a pool is 30ºC, what is the temperature of the pool in degrees Fahrenheit? To convert these units, an equation is used relating Celsius to Fahrenheit. The following equation is used: $T_{\circ F} = 1.8T_{\circ C} + 32$. Plugging in the given temperature and solving the equation for T yields the result: $T_{\circ F} = 1.8(30) + 32 = 86°F$. Both units in the metric system and U.S. customary system are widely used.

Scientific Notation

Scientific Notation is used to represent numbers that are either very small or very large. For example, the distance to the sun is approximately 150,000,000,000 meters. Instead of writing this number with so many zeros, it can be written in scientific notation as $1.5 * 10^{11}$ meters. The same is true for very small numbers, but the exponent becomes negative. If the mass of a human cell is 0.000000000001 kilograms, that measurement can be easily represented by $1.0 * 10^{-12}$ kilograms. In both situations, scientific notation makes the measurement easier to read and understand. Each number is translated to an expression with one digit in the tens place times an expression corresponding to the zeros.

When two measurements are given and both involve scientific notation, it is important to know how these interact with each other:

- In addition and subtraction, the exponent on the ten must be the same before any operations are performed on the numbers. For example, $(1.3 * 10^4) + (3.0 * 10^3)$ cannot be added until one of the exponents on the ten is changed. The $3.0 * 10^3$ can be changed to $0.3 * 10^4$, then the 1.3 and 0.3 can be added. The answer comes out to be $1.6 * 10^4$.

- For multiplication, the first numbers can be multiplied and then the exponents on the tens can be added. Once an answer is formed, it may have to be converted into scientific notation again depending on the change that occurred.

    o The following is an example of multiplication with scientific notation: $(4.5 * 10^3) * (3.0 * 10^{-5}) = 13.5 * 10^{-2}$. Since this answer is not in scientific notation, the decimal is moved over to the left one unit, and 1 is added to the ten's exponent. This results in the final answer: $1.35 * 10^{-1}$.

- For division, the first numbers are divided, and the exponents on the tens are subtracted. Again, the answer may need to be converted into scientific notation form, depending on the type of changes that occurred during the problem.

- *Order of magnitude* relates to scientific notation and is the total count of powers of 10 in a number. For example, there are 6 orders of magnitude in 1,000,000. If a number is raised by an order of magnitude, it is multiplied times 10. Order of magnitude can be helpful in estimating results using very large or small numbers. An answer should make sense in terms of its order of magnitude.

  - For example, if area is calculated using two dimensions with 6 orders of magnitude, because area involves multiplication, the answer should have around 12 orders of magnitude. Also, answers can be estimated by rounding to the largest place value in each number. For example, 5,493,302 * 2,523,100 can be estimated by 5 * 3 = 15 with 6 orders of magnitude.

Basic Concepts of Number Theory

Prime and Composite Numbers
Whole numbers are classified as either prime or composite. A prime number can only be divided evenly by itself and one. For example, the number 11 can only be divided evenly by 11 and one; therefore, 11 is a prime number. A helpful way to visualize a prime number is to use concrete objects and try to divide them into equal piles. If dividing 11 coins, the only way to divide them into equal piles is to create 1 pile of 11 coins or to create 11 piles of 1 coin each. Other examples of prime numbers include 2, 3, 5, 7, 13, 17, and 19.

A composite number is any whole number that is not a prime number. A composite number is a number that can be divided evenly by one or more numbers other than itself and one. For example, the number 6 can be divided evenly by 2 and 3. Therefore, 6 is a composite number. If dividing 6 coins into equal piles, the possibilities are 1 pile of 6 coins, 2 piles of 3 coins, 3 piles of 2 coins, or 6 piles of 1 coin. Other examples of composite numbers include 4, 8, 9, 10, 12, 14, 15, 16, 18, and 20.

To determine if a number is a prime or composite number, the number is divided by every whole number greater than one and less than its own value. If it divides evenly by any of these numbers, then the number is composite. If it does not divide evenly by any of these numbers, then the number is prime. For example, when attempting to divide the number 5 by 2, 3, and 4, none of these numbers divide evenly. Therefore, 5 must be a prime number.

Factors and Multiples of Numbers
The factors of a number are all integers that can be multiplied by another integer to produce the given number. For example, 2 is multiplied by 3 to produce 6. Therefore, 2 and 3 are both factors of 6. Similarly, $1 \times 6 = 6$ and $2 \times 3 = 6$, so 1, 2, 3, and 6 are all factors of 6. Another way to explain a factor is to say that a given number divides evenly by each of its factors to produce an integer. For example, 6 does not divide evenly by 5. Therefore, 5 is not a factor of 6.

Multiples of a given number are found by taking that number and multiplying it by any other whole number. For example, 3 is a factor of 6, 9, and 12. Therefore, 6, 9, and 12 are multiples of 3. The multiples of any number are an infinite list. For example, the multiples of 5 are 5, 10, 15, 20, and so on. This list continues without end. A list of multiples is used in finding the least common multiple, or LCM, for fractions when a common denominator is needed. The denominators are written down and their multiples listed until a common number is found in both lists. This common number is the LCM.

Prime factorization breaks down each factor of a whole number until only prime numbers remain. All composite numbers can be factored into prime numbers. For example, the prime factors of 12 are 2, 2, and 3 ($2 \times 2 \times 3 = 12$). To produce the prime factors of a number, the number is factored and any composite numbers are continuously factored until the result is the product of prime factors only. A factor tree, such as the one below, is helpful when exploring this concept.

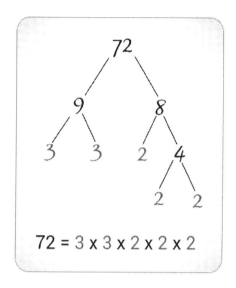

Number Relationships
The set of natural numbers can be separated into a variety of different types such as odds, evens, perfect squares, cubes, primes, composite, Fibonacci, etc. Number theory concepts can be used to prove relationships between these subsets of natural numbers. One of the main goals of number theory is to discover relationships between different subsets and prove that they are true. For example, some number theory proofs involve showing that the sum of two odd numbers is odd and the sum of two even numbers is even.

Order of Operations

When solving equations with multiple operations, special rules apply. These rules are known as the Order of Operations. The order is as follows: Parentheses, Exponents, Multiplication and Division from left to right, and Addition and Subtraction from left to right. A popular pneumonic device to help remember the order is Please Excuse My Dear Aunt Sally (PEMDAS). Evaluate the following two problems to understand the Order of Operations:

1) $4 + (3 \times 2)^2 \div 4$

> First, solve the operation within the parentheses: $4 + 6^2 \div 4$.
> Second, solve the exponent: $4 + 36 \div 4$.
> Third, solve the division operation: $4 + 9$.
> Fourth, finish the operation with addition for the answer, 13.

2) $2 \times (6 + 3) \div (2 + 1)^2$

> $2 \times 9 \div (3)^2$
> $2 \times 9 \div 9$
> $18 \div 9$
> 2

Positive and Negative Numbers

<u>Signs</u>
Aside from 0, numbers can be either positive or negative. The sign for a positive number is the plus sign or the + symbol, while the sign for a negative number is minus sign or the − symbol. If a number has no designation, then it's assumed to be positive.

<u>Absolute Values</u>
Both positive and negative numbers are valued according to their distance from 0. Look at this number line for +3 and -3:

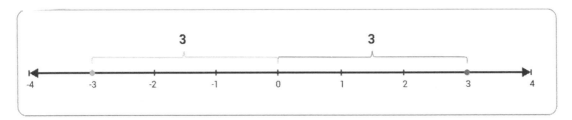

Both 3 and -3 are three spaces from 0. The distance from 0 is called its absolute value. Thus, both -3 and 3 have an absolute value of 3 since they're both three spaces away from 0.

An absolute number is written by placing | | around the number. So, |3| and |−3| both equal 3, as that's their common absolute value.

Implications for Addition and Subtraction

For addition, if all numbers are either positive or negative, simply add them together. For example, 4 + 4 = 8 and -4 + -4 = -8. However, things get tricky when some of the numbers are negative and some are positive.

Take 6 + (-4) as an example. First, take the absolute values of the numbers, which are 6 and 4. Second, subtract the smaller value from the larger. The equation becomes $6 - 4 = 2$. Third, place the sign of the original larger number on the sum. Here, 6 is the larger number, and it's positive, so the sum is 2.

Here's an example where the negative number has a larger absolute value: (-6) + 4. The first two steps are the same as the example above. However, on the third step, the negative sign must be placed on the sum, as the absolute value of (-6) is greater than 4. Thus, -6 + 4 = -2.

The absolute value of numbers implies that subtraction can be thought of as flip the sign of the number following the subtraction sign and simply adding the two numbers. This means that subtracting a negative number will in fact be adding the positive absolute value of the negative number. Here are some examples:

$$-6 - 4 = -6 + -4 = -10$$

$$3 - -6 = 3 + 6 = 9$$

$$-3 - 2 = -3 \pm 2 = -5$$

Implications for Multiplication and Division

For multiplication and division, if both numbers are positive, then the product or quotient is always positive. If both numbers are negative, then the product or quotient is also positive. However, if the numbers have opposite signs, the product or quotient is always negative.

Simply put, the product in multiplication and quotient in division is always positive, unless the numbers have opposing signs, in which case it's negative. Here are some examples:

$$(-6) \times (-5) = 30$$

$$(-50) \div 10 = -5$$

$$8 \times |-7| = 56$$

$$(-48) \div (-6) = 8$$

If there are more than two numbers in a multiplication or division problem, then whether the product or quotient is positive or negative depends on the number of negative numbers in the problem. If there is an odd number of negatives, then the product or quotient is negative. If there is an even number of negative numbers, then the result is positive.

Here are some examples:

$$(-6) \times 5 \times (-2) \times (-4) = -240$$

$$(-6) \times 5 \times 2 \times (-4) = 240$$

Strategies and Algorithms to Perform Operations on Rational Numbers

A rational number is any number that can be written in the form of a ratio or fraction. Integers can be written as fractions with a denominator of 1 ($5 = \frac{5}{1}$; $-342 = \frac{-342}{1}$; etc.). Decimals that terminate and/or repeat can also be written as fractions ($47 = \frac{47}{100}$; $.\overline{33} = \frac{1}{3}$). For more on converting decimals to fractions, see the section *Converting Between Fractions, Decimals,* and *Percent.*

When adding or subtracting fractions, the numbers must have the same denominators. In these cases, numerators are added or subtracted and denominators are kept the same. For example, $\frac{2}{7} + \frac{3}{7} = \frac{5}{7}$ and

$\frac{4}{5} - \frac{3}{5} = \frac{1}{5}$. If the fractions to be added or subtracted do not have the same denominator, a common denominator must be found. This is accomplished by changing one or both fractions to a different but equivalent fraction. Consider the example $\frac{1}{6} + \frac{4}{9}$. First, a common denominator must be found. One method is to find the least common multiple (LCM) of the denominators 6 and 9. This is the lowest number that both 6 and 9 will divide into evenly. In this case the LCM is 18. Both fractions should be changed to equivalent fractions with a denominator of 18. To obtain the numerator of the new fraction, the old numerator is multiplied by the same number by which the old denominator is multiplied. For the fraction $\frac{1}{6}$, 6 multiplied by 3 will produce a denominator of 18. Therefore, the numerator is multiplied by 3 to produce the new numerator $\left(\frac{1 \times 3}{6 \times 3} = \frac{3}{18}\right)$. For the fraction $\frac{4}{9}$, multiplying both the numerator and denominator by 2 produces $\frac{8}{18}$. Since the two new fractions have common denominators, they can be added $\left(\frac{3}{18} + \frac{8}{18} = \frac{11}{18}\right)$.

When multiplying or dividing rational numbers, these numbers may be converted to fractions and multiplied or divided accordingly. When multiplying fractions, all numerators are multiplied by each other and all denominators are multiplied by each other. For example:

$$\frac{1}{3} \times \frac{6}{5} = \frac{1 \times 6}{3 \times 5} = \frac{6}{15}$$

$$\frac{-1}{2} \times \frac{3}{1} \times \frac{11}{100}$$

$$\frac{-1 \times 3 \times 11}{2 \times 1 \times 100} = \frac{-33}{200}$$

When dividing fractions, the problem is converted by multiplying by the reciprocal of the divisor. This is done by changing division to multiplication and "flipping" the second fraction, or divisor. For example, $\frac{1}{2} \div \frac{3}{5} \rightarrow \frac{1}{2} \times \frac{5}{3}$ and $\frac{5}{1} \div \frac{1}{3} \rightarrow \frac{5}{1} \times \frac{3}{1}$. To complete the problem, the rules for multiplying fractions should be followed.

Note that when adding, subtracting, multiplying, and dividing mixed numbers (ex. $4\frac{1}{2}$), it is easiest to convert these to improper fractions (larger numerator than denominator). To do so, the denominator is kept the same. To obtain the numerator, the whole number is multiplied by the denominator and added to the numerator. For example, $4\frac{1}{2} = \frac{9}{2}$ and $7\frac{2}{3} = \frac{23}{3}$. Also, note that answers involving fractions should be converted to the simplest form.

Converting Between Fractions, Decimals, and Percent

To convert a fraction to a decimal, the numerator is divided by the denominator. For example, $\frac{3}{8}$ can be converted to a decimal by dividing 3 by 8 $(\frac{3}{8} = 0.375)$. To convert a decimal to a fraction, the decimal point is dropped and the value is written as the numerator. The denominator is the place value farthest to the right with a digit other than zero. For example, to convert .48 to a fraction, the numerator is 48 and the denominator is 100 (the digit 8 is in the hundredths place). Therefore, $.48 = \frac{48}{100}$. Fractions should be written in the simplest form, or reduced. To reduce a fraction, the numerator and denominator are divided by the largest common factor. In the previous example, 48 and 100 are both divisible by 4. Dividing the numerator and denominator by 4 results in a reduced fraction of $\frac{12}{25}$.

To convert a decimal to a percent, the number is multiplied by 100. To convert .13 to a percent, .13 is multiplied by 100 to get 13 percent. To convert a fraction to a percent, the fraction is converted to a decimal and then multiplied by 100. For example, $\frac{1}{5}$ = .20 and .20 multiplied by 100 produces 20 percent.

To convert a percent to a decimal, the value is divided by 100. For example, 125 percent is equal to 1.25 ($\frac{125}{100}$). To convert a percent to a fraction, the percent sign is dropped and the value is written as the numerator with a denominator of 100. For example, 80% = $\frac{80}{100}$. This fraction can be reduced ($\frac{80}{100} = \frac{4}{5}$).

Representing Rational Numbers and Their Operations

Concrete Models
Concrete objects are used to develop a tangible understanding of operations of rational numbers. Tools such as tiles, blocks, beads, and hundred charts are used to model problems. For example, a hundred chart (10×10) and beads can be used to model multiplication. If multiplying 5 by 4, beads are placed across 5 rows and down 4 columns producing a product of 20. Similarly, tiles can be used to model division by splitting the total into equal groups. If dividing 12 by 4, 12 tiles are placed one at a time into 4 groups. The result is 4 groups of 3. This is also an effective method for visualizing the concept of remainders.

Representations of objects can be used to expand on the concrete models of operations. Pictures, dots, and tallies can help model these concepts. Utilizing concrete models and representations creates a foundation upon which to build an abstract understanding of the operations.

Rational Numbers on a Number Line
A number line typically consists of integers (...3, 2, 1, 0, -1, -2, -3...), and is used to visually represent the value of a rational number. Each rational number has a distinct position on the line determined by comparing its value with the displayed values on the line. For example, if plotting -1.5 on the number line below, it is necessary to recognize that the value of -1.5 is .5 less than -1 and .5 greater than -2. Therefore, -1.5 is plotted halfway between -1 and -2.

Number lines can also be useful for visualizing sums and differences of rational numbers. Adding a value indicates moving to the right (values increase to the right), and subtracting a value indicates moving to the left (numbers decrease to the left). For example, $5 - 7$ is displayed by starting at 5 and moving to the left 7 spaces, if the number line is in increments of 1. This will result in an answer of -2.

Multiplication and Division Problems

Multiplication and division are inverse operations that can be represented by using rectangular arrays, area models, and equations. Rectangular arrays include an arrangement of rows and columns that correspond to the factors and display product totals.

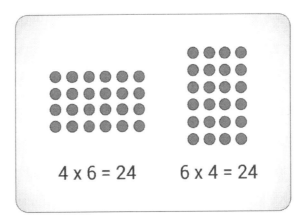

Another method of multiplication can be done with the use of an *area model*. An area model is a rectangle that is divided into rows and columns that match up to the number of place values within each number. For example, $29 \times 65 = 25 + 4$ and $66 = 60 + 5$.The products of those 4 numbers are found within the rectangle and then summed up to get the answer. The entire process is:

$$(60 \times 25) + (5 \times 25) + (60 \times 4) + (5 \times 4)$$

$$1,500 + 240 + 125 + 20$$

$$1,885$$

Here is the actual area model:

	25	**4**
60	60x25 1,500	60x4 240
5	5x25 125	5x4 20

```
  1 , 5 0 0
      2 4 0
      1 2 5
+        2 0
  _____
  1 , 8 8 5
```

Dividing a number by a single digit or two digits can be turned into repeated subtraction problems. An area model can be used throughout the problem that represents multiples of the divisor. For example, the answer to $8580 \div 55$ can be found by subtracting 55 from 8580 one at a time and counting the total number of subtractions necessary.

However, a simpler process involves using larger multiples of 55. First, $100 \times 55 = 5,500$ is subtracted from 8,580, and 3,080 is leftover. Next, $50 \times 55 = 2,750$ is subtracted from 3,080 to obtain 380. $5 \times 55 = 275$ is subtracted from 330 to obtain 55, and finally, $1 \times 55 = 55$ is subtracted from 55 to obtain zero. Therefore, there is no remainder, and the answer is $100 + 50 + 5 + 1 = 156$.

Here is a picture of the area model and the repeated subtraction process:

Determining the Reasonableness of Results

When solving math word problems, the solution obtained should make sense within the given scenario. The step of checking the solution will reduce the possibility of a calculation error or a solution that may be *mathematically* correct but not applicable in the real world. Consider the following scenarios:

A problem states that Lisa got 24 out of 32 questions correct on a test and asks to find the percentage of correct answers. To solve the problem, a student divided 32 by 24 to get 1.33, and then multiplied by 100 to get 133 percent. By examining the solution within the context of the problem, the student should recognize that getting all 32 questions correct will produce a perfect score of 100 percent. Therefore, a score of 133 percent with 8 incorrect answers does not make sense and the calculations should be checked.

A problem states that the maximum weight on a bridge cannot exceed 22,000 pounds. The problem asks to find the maximum number of cars that can be on the bridge at one time if each car weighs 4,000 pounds. To solve this problem, a student divided 22,000 by 4,000 to get an answer of 5.5. By examining the solution within the context of the problem, the student should recognize that although the calculations are mathematically correct, the solution does not make sense. Half of a car on a bridge is not possible, so the student should determine that a maximum of 5 cars can be on the bridge at the same time.

Mental Math Estimation

Once a result is determined to be logical within the context of a given problem, the result should be evaluated by its nearness to the expected answer. This is performed by approximating given values to perform mental math. Numbers should be rounded to the nearest value possible to check the initial results.

Consider the following example: A problem states that a customer is buying a new sound system for their home. The customer purchases a stereo for $435, 2 speakers for $67 each, and the necessary cables for $12. The customer chooses an option that allows him to spread the costs over equal payments for 4 months. How much will the monthly payments be?

After making calculations for the problem, a student determines that the monthly payment will be $145.25. To check the accuracy of the results, the student rounds each cost to the nearest ten (440 + 70 + 70 + 10) and determines that the total is approximately $590. Dividing by 4 months gives an approximate monthly payment of $147.50. Therefore, the student can conclude that the solution of $145.25 is very close to what should be expected.

When rounding, the place-value that is used in rounding can make a difference. Suppose the student had rounded to the nearest hundred for the estimation. The result ($400 + 100 + 100 + 0 = 600; 600 \div 4 = 150$) will show that the answer is reasonable, but not as close to the actual value as rounding to the nearest ten.

Precision and Accuracy

Precision and accuracy are used to describe groups of measurements. *Precision* describes a group of measures that are very close together, regardless of whether the measures are close to the true value. *Accuracy* describes how close the measures are to the true value.

Since accuracy refers to the closeness of a value to the true measurement, the level of accuracy depends on the object measured and the instrument used to measure it. This will vary depending on the situation. If measuring the mass of a set of dictionaries, kilograms may be used as the units. In this case, it is not vitally important to have a high level of accuracy. If the measurement is a few grams away from the true value, the discrepancy might not make a big difference in the problem.

In a different situation, the level of accuracy may be more significant. Pharmacists need to be sure they are very accurate in their measurements of medicines that they give to patients. In this case, the level of accuracy is vitally important and not something to be estimated. In the dictionary situation, the measurements were given as whole numbers in kilograms. In the pharmacist's situation, the measurements for medicine must be taken to the milligram and sometimes further, depending on the type of medicine.

When considering the accuracy of measurements, the error in each measurement can be shown as absolute and relative. *Absolute error* tells the actual difference between the measured value and the true value. The *relative error* tells how large the error is in relation to the true value. There may be two problems where the absolute error of the measurements is 10 grams. For one problem, this may mean the relative error is very small because the measured value is 14,990 grams, and the true value is 15,000 grams. Ten grams in relation to the true value of 15,000 is small: 0.06%. For the other problem, the

142

measured value is 290 grams, and the true value is 300 grams. In this case, the 10-gram absolute error means a high relative error because the true value is smaller. The relative error is 10/300=0.03, or 3%.

Algebra and Functions

Number Patterns

Given a sequence of numbers, a mathematical rule can be defined that represents the numbers if a pattern exists within the set. For example, consider the sequence of numbers 1, 4, 9, 16, 25, etc. This set of numbers represents the positive integers squared, and an explicitly defined sequence that represents this set is $f_n = n^2$. An important mathematical concept is recognizing patterns in sequences and translating the patterns into an explicit formula. Once the pattern is recognized and the formula is defined, the sequence can be extended easily. For example, the next three numbers in the sequence are 36, 49, and 64.

Predicting Values
In a similar sense, patterns can be used to make conjectures, predictions, and generalizations. If a pattern is recognized in a set of numbers, values can be predicted that aren't originally provided. For example, if an experiment results in the sequence of numbers 1, 4, 9, 16, and 25, where 1 represents the first trial, 2 represents the second trial, etc., one expects the tenth trial to result in a value of 100 because that value is equal to the square of the trial number.

Recursively Defined Functions
Similar to recursively defined sequences, recursively defined functions are not explicitly defined in terms of a variable. A recursive function builds on itself and consists of a smaller argument, such as $f(0)$ or $f(1)$ and the actual definition of the function. For example, a recursively defined function is the following:

$$f(0) = 3$$

$$f(n) = f(n-1) + 2n$$

Contrasting an explicitly defined function, a recursively defined function must be evaluated in order. The first five terms of this function are $f(0) = 3, f(1) = 5, f(2) = 9, f(3) = 15,$ and $f(4) = 23$. Some recursively defined functions have an explicit counterpart and, like sequences, they can be used to model real-life applications. The Fibonacci numbers can also be thought of as a recursively defined function if $f(n) = f_n$.

Closed-Form Functions
A *closed-form function* can be evaluated using a finite number of operations such as addition, subtraction, multiplication, and division. An example of a function that's not a closed-form function is one involving an infinite sum. For example, $y = \sum_{n=1}^{\infty} x$ isn't a closed-form function because it consists of a sum of infinitely many terms. Many recursively defined functions can be expressed as a closed-form expression. To convert to a closed-form expression, a formula must be found for the nth term. This means that the recursively defined sequence must be converted to its explicit formula.

Translating Between Verbal and Symbolic Forms

Being able to translate verbal scenarios into symbolic forms is a critical skill in mathematics. This idea is seen mostly when solving word problems. First, the problem needs to be read carefully several times until one can state clearly what is being sought. Then, variables that represent the unknown quantities need to be defined. Equations can be defined using those variables that model the verbal conditions of the given problem. The equations then need to be solved to answer the problem's questions. The problem-solving skills learned in these types of problems is an invaluable skill, and is ultimately more important than finding the answer to each individual problem.

Solving Problems by Quantitative Reasoning

Dimensional analysis is the process of converting between different units using equivalent measurement statements. For instance, running 5 kilometers is approximately the same as running 3.1 miles. This conversion can be found by knowing that 1 kilometer is equal to approximately 0.62 miles.

When setting up the dimensional analysis calculations, the original units need to be opposite one another in each of the two fractions: one in the original amount (essentially in the numerator) and one in the denominator of the conversion factor. This enables them to cancel after multiplying, leaving the converted result.

Calculations involving formulas, such as determining volume and area, are a common situation in which units need to be interpreted and used. However, graphs can also carry meaning through units. The graph below is an example. It represents a graph of the position of an object over time. The y-axis represents the position or the number of meters the object is from the starting point at time s, in seconds. Interpreting this graph, the origin shows that at time zero seconds, the object is zero meters away from the starting point. As the time increases to one second, the position increases to five meters away. This trend continues until 6 seconds, where the object is 30 meters away from the starting position. After this point in time—since the graph remains horizontal from 6 to 10 seconds—the object must have stopped moving.

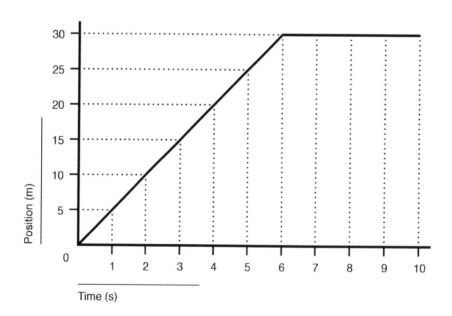

When solving problems with units, it's important to consider the reasonableness of the answer. If conversions are used, it's helpful to have an estimated value to compare the final answer to. This way, if the final answer is too distant from the estimate, it will be obvious that a mistake was made.

Functions

A *function* is defined as a relationship between inputs and outputs where there is only one output value for a given input. As an example, the following function is in function notation: $f(x) = 3x - 4$. The $f(x)$ represents the output value for an input of x. If $x = 2$, the equation becomes $f(2) = 3(2) - 4 = 6 - 4 = 2$. The input of 2 yields an output of 2, forming the ordered pair $(2, 2)$. The following set of ordered pairs corresponds to the given function: $(2, 2), (0, -4), (-2, -10)$. The set of all possible inputs of a function is its *domain*, and all possible outputs is called the *range*. By definition, each member of the domain is paired with only one member of the range.

Functions can also be defined recursively. In this form, they are not defined explicitly in terms of variables. Instead, they are defined using previously-evaluated function outputs, starting with either $f(0)$ or $f(1)$. An example of a recursively-defined function is $f(1) = 2, f(n) = 2f(n - 1) + 2n, n > 1$. The domain of this function is the set of all integers.

Domain and Range

The domain and range of a function can be found visually by its plot on the coordinate plane. In the function $f(x) = x^2 - 3$, for example, the domain is all real numbers because the parabola stretches as far left and as far right as it can go, with no restrictions. This means that any input value from the real number system will yield an answer in the real number system. For the range, the inequality $y \geq -3$ would be used to describe the possible output values because the parabola has a minimum at $y = -3$. This means there will not be any real output values less than -3 because -3 is the lowest value it reaches on the y-axis.

These same answers for domain and range can be found by observing a table. The table below shows that from input values $x = -1$ to $x = 1$, the output results in a minimum of -3. On each side of $x = 0$, the numbers increase, showing that the range is all real numbers greater than or equal to -3.

x (domain/input)	y (range/output)
-2	1
-1	-2
0	-3
-1	-2
2	1

Finding the Zeros of a Function

The zeros of a function are the points where its graph crosses the x-axis. At these points, $y = 0$. One way to find the zeros is to analyze the graph. If given the graph, the x-coordinates can be found where the line crosses the x-axis. Another way to find the zeros is to set $y = 0$ in the equation and solve for x. Depending on the type of equation, this could be done by using opposite operations, by factoring the equation, by completing the square, or by using the quadratic formula. If a graph does not cross the x-axis, then the function may have complex roots.

Rate of Change

Rate of change for any line calculates the steepness of the line over a given interval. Rate of change is also known as the slope or rise/run. The rates of change for nonlinear functions vary depending on the interval being used for the function. The rate of change over one interval may be zero, while the next interval may have a positive rate of change. The equation plotted on the graph below, $y = x^2$, is a quadratic function and non-linear.

The average rate of change from points $(0, 0)$ to $(1, 1)$ is 1 because the vertical change is 1 over the horizontal change of 1. For the next interval, $(1, 1)$ to $(2, 4)$, the average rate of change is 3 because the slope is $\frac{3}{1}$.

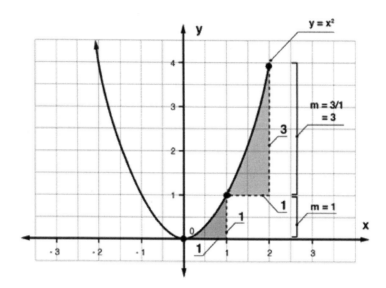

The rate of change for a linear function is constant and can be determined based on a few representations. One method is to place the equation in slope-intercept form: $y = mx + b$. Thus, m is the slope, and b is the y-intercept. In the graph below, the equation is $y = x + 1$, where the slope is 1 and the y-intercept is 1. For every vertical change of 1 unit, there is a horizontal change of 1 unit. The x-intercept is -1, which is the point where the line crosses the x-axis.

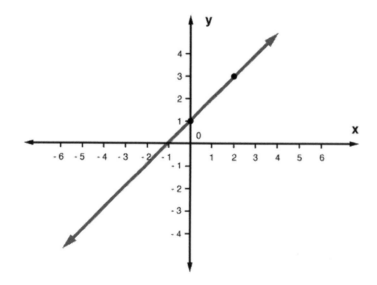

Solving Line Problems

Two lines are parallel if they have the same slope. Two lines are perpendicular if the product of their slope equals -1. Parallel lines never intersect unless they are the same line, and perpendicular lines

146

intersect at a right angle. If two lines aren't parallel, they must intersect at one point. Determining equations of lines based on properties of parallel and perpendicular lines appears in word problems. To find an equation of a line, both the slope and a point the line goes through are necessary. Therefore, if an equation of a line is needed that's parallel to a given line and runs through a specified point, the slope of the given line and the point are plugged into the point-slope form of an equation of a line. Secondly, if an equation of a line is needed that's perpendicular to a given line running through a specified point, the negative reciprocal of the slope of the given line and the point are plugged into the point-slope form. Also, if the point of intersection of two lines is known, that point will be used to solve the set of equations. Therefore, to solve a system of equations, the point of intersection must be found. If a set of two equations with two unknown variables has no solution, the lines are parallel.

Rewriting Expressions

Algebraic expressions are made up of numbers, variables, and combinations of the two, using mathematical operations. Expressions can be rewritten based on their factors. For example, the expression $6x + 4$ can be rewritten as $2(3x + 2)$ because 2 is a factor of both $6x$ and 4. More complex expressions can also be rewritten based on their factors. The expression $x^4 - 16$ can be rewritten as $(x^2 - 4)(x^2 + 4)$. This is a different type of factoring, where a difference of squares is factored into a sum and difference of the same two terms. With some expressions, the factoring process is simple and only leads to a different way to represent the expression. With others, factoring and rewriting the expression leads to more information about the given problem.

In the following quadratic equation, factoring the binomial leads to finding the zeros of the function: $x^2 - 5x + 6 = y$. This equations factors into $(x - 3)(x - 2) = y$, where 2 and 3 are found to be the zeros of the function when y is set equal to zero. The zeros of any function are the x-values where the graph of the function on the coordinate plane crosses the x-axis.

Factoring an equation is a simple way to rewrite the equation and find the zeros, but factoring is not possible for every quadratic. Completing the square is one way to find zeros when factoring is not an option. The following equation cannot be factored: $x^2 + 10x - 9 = 0$. The first step in this method is to move the constant to the right side of the equation, making it $x^2 + 10x = 9$. Then, the coefficient of x is divided it by 2 and squared. This number is then added to both sides of the equation, to make the equation still true. For this example, $\left(\frac{10}{2}\right)^2 = 25$ is added to both sides of the equation to obtain: $x^2 + 10x + 25 = 9 + 25$. This expression simplifies to $x^2 + 10x + 25 = 34$, which can then be factored into $(x + 5)^2 = 34$. Solving for x then involves taking the square root of both sides and subtracting 5. This leads to two zeros of the function: $x = \pm\sqrt{34} - 5$. Depending on the type of answer the question seeks, a calculator may be used to find exact numbers.

Given a quadratic equation in standard form—$ax^2 + bx + c = 0$—the sign of a tells whether the function has a minimum value or a maximum value. If $a > 0$, the graph opens up and has a minimum value. If $a < 0$, the graph opens down and has a maximum value. Depending on the way the quadratic equation is written, multiplication may need to occur before a max/min value is determined.

Exponential expressions can also be rewritten, just as quadratic equations. Properties of exponents must be understood. Multiplying two exponential expressions with the same base involves adding the exponents: $a^m a^n = a^{m+n}$. Dividing two exponential expressions with the same base involves subtracting the exponents: $\frac{a^m}{a^n} = a^{m-n}$. Raising an exponential expression to another exponent includes multiplying the exponents: $(a^m)^n = a^{mn}$. The zero power always gives a value of 1: $a^0 = 1$. Raising either a product or a fraction to a power involves distributing that power:

$$(ab)^m = a^m b^m \text{ and } \left(\frac{a}{b}\right)^m = \frac{a^m}{b^m}$$

Finally, raising a number to a negative exponent is equivalent to the reciprocal including the positive exponent: $a^{-m} = \frac{1}{a^m}$.

Polynomial Identities

Difference of squares refers to a binomial composed of the difference of two squares. For example, $a^2 - b^2$ is a difference of squares. It can be written $(a)^2 - (b)^2$, and it can be factored into $(a - b)(a + b)$. Recognizing the difference of squares allows the expression to be rewritten easily because of the form it takes. For some expressions, factoring consists of more than one step. When factoring, it's important to always check to make sure that the result cannot be factored further. If it can, then the expression should be split further. If it cannot be, the factoring step is complete, and the expression is completely factored.

A sum and difference of cubes is another way to factor a polynomial expression. When the polynomial takes the form of addition or subtraction of two terms that can be written as a cube, a formula is given. The following graphic shows the factorization of a difference of cubes:

This form of factoring can be useful in finding the zeros of a function of degree 3. For example, when solving $x^3 - 27 = 0$, this rule needs to be used. $x^3 - 27$ is first written as the difference two cubes, $(x)^3 - (3)^3$ and then factored into $(x - 3)(x^2 + 3x + 9)$. This expression may not be factored any further. Each factor is then set equal to zero. Therefore, one solution is found to be $x = 3$, and the other two solutions must be found using the quadratic formula. A sum of squares would have a similar process. The formula for factoring a sum of squares is $a^3 + b^3 = (a + b)(a^2 - ab + b^2)$.

The opposite of factoring is multiplying. Multiplying a square of a binomial involves the following rules: $(a + b)^2 = a^2 + 2ab + b^2$ and $(a - b)^2 = a^2 - 2ab + b^2$. The binomial theorem for expansion can be used when the exponent on a binomial is larger than 2, and the multiplication would take a long time. The binomial theorem is given as:

$$(a + b)^n = \sum_{k=0}^{n} \binom{n}{k} a^{n-k} b^k \qquad \binom{n}{k} = \frac{n!}{k!(n-k)!}$$

where

148

The *Remainder Theorem* can be helpful when evaluating polynomial functions $P(x)$ for a given value of x. A polynomial can be divided by $(x - a)$, if there is a remainder of 0. This also means that $P(a) = 0$ and $(x - a)$ is a factor of $P(x)$. In a similar sense, if P is evaluated at any other number b, $P(b)$ is equal to the remainder of dividing $P(x)$ by $(x - b)$.

Zeros of Polynomials

Finding the zeros of polynomial functions is the same process as finding the solutions of polynomial equations. These are the points at which the graph of the function crosses the x-axis. As stated previously, factors can be used to find the zeros of a polynomial function. The degree of the function shows the number of possible zeros. If the highest exponent on the independent variable is 4, then the degree is 4, and the number of possible zeros is 4. If there are complex solutions, the number of roots is less than the degree.

Given the function $y = x^2 + 7x + 6$, y can be set equal to zero, and the polynomial can be factored. The equation turns into $0 = (x + 1)(x + 6)$, where $x = -1$ and $x = -6$ are the zeros. Since this is a quadratic equation, the shape of the graph will be a parabola. Knowing that zeros represent the points where the parabola crosses the x-axis, the maximum or minimum point is the only other piece needed to sketch a rough graph of the function. By looking at the function in standard form, the coefficient of x is positive; therefore, the parabola opens *up*. Using the zeros and the minimum, the following rough sketch of the graph can be constructed:

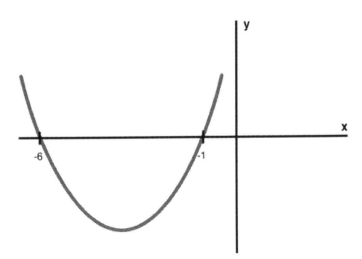

Operations with Polynomials

Addition and subtraction operations can be performed on polynomials with like terms. *Like terms* refer to terms that have the same variable and exponent. The two following polynomials can be added together by collecting like terms: $(x^2 + 3x - 4) + (4x^2 - 7x + 8)$. The x^2 terms can be added as $x^2 + 4x^2 = 5x^2$. The x terms can be added as $3x + -7x = -4x$, and the constants can be added as $-4 + 8 = 4$. The following expression is the result of the addition: $5x^2 - 4x + 4$. When subtracting polynomials, the same steps are followed, only subtracting like terms together.

Multiplication of polynomials can also be performed. Given the two polynomials, $(y^3 - 4)$ and $(x^2 + 8x - 7)$, each term in the first polynomial must be multiplied by each term in the second polynomial. The steps to multiply each term in the given example are as follows:

$$(y^3 * x^2) + (y^3 * 8x) + (y^3 * -7) + (-4 * x^2) + (-4 * 8x) + (-4 * -7)$$

Simplifying each multiplied part, yields $x^2y^3 + 8xy^3 - 7y^3 - 4x^2 - 32x + 28$. None of the terms can be combined because there are no like terms in the final expression. Any polynomials can be multiplied by each other by following the same set of steps, then collecting like terms at the end.

Equations and Inequalities

The sum of a number and 5 is equal to -8 times the number. To find this unknown number, a simple equation can be written to represent the problem. Key words such as *sum*, *equal*, and *times* are used to form the following equation with one variable: $n + 5 = -8n$. When solving for n, opposite operations are used. First, n is subtracted from $-8n$ across the equals sign, resulting in $5 = -9n$. Then, -9 is divided on both sides, leaving $n = -\frac{5}{9}$. This solution can be graphed on the number line with a dot as shown below:

If the problem were changed to say, "The sum of a number and 5 is greater than -8 times the number," then an inequality would be used instead of an equation. Using key words again, *greater than* is represented by the symbol >. The inequality $n + 5 > -8n$ can be solved using the same techniques, resulting in $n < -\frac{5}{9}$. The only time solving an inequality differs from solving an equation is when a negative number is either multiplied times or divided by each side of the inequality. The sign must be switched in this case. For this example, the graph of the solution changes to the following graph because the solution represents all real numbers less than $-\frac{5}{9}$. Not included in this solution is $-\frac{5}{9}$ because it is a *less than* symbol, not *equal to*.

Equations and inequalities in two variables represent a relationship. Jim owns a car wash and charges $40 per car. The rent for the facility is $350 per month. An equation can be written to relate the number of cars Jim cleans to the money he makes per month. Let x represent the number of cars and y represent the profit Jim makes each month from the car wash. The equation $y = 40x - 350$ can be used to show Jim's profit or loss. Since this equation has two variables, the coordinate plane can be used to show the relationship and predict profit or loss for Jim. The following graph shows that Jim must wash at least nine cars to pay the rent, where $x = 9$. Anything nine cars and above yield a profit shown in the value on the y-axis.

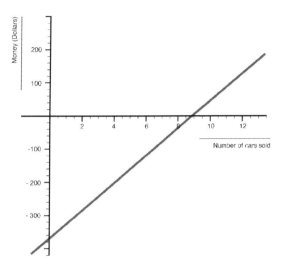

With a single equation in two variables, the solutions are limited only by the situation the equation represents. When two equations or inequalities are used, more constraints are added. For example, in a system of linear equations, there is often—although not always—only one answer. The point of intersection of two lines is the solution. For a system of inequalities, there are infinitely many answers.

The intersection of two solution sets gives the solution set of the system of inequalities. In the following graph, the darker shaded region with the swirls where the shading for the two inequalities overlap. Any set of x and y found in that region satisfies both inequalities. The line with the positive slope is solid, meaning the values on that line are included in the solution. The with the negative line is dotted, so the coordinates on that line are not included.

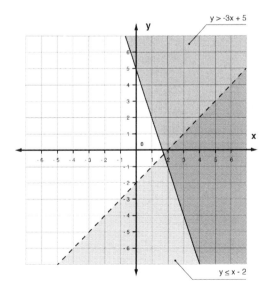

Formulas with two variables are equations used to represent a specific relationship. For example, the formula $d = rt$ represents the relationship between distance, rate, and time. If Bob travels at a rate of 35 miles per hour on his road trip from Westminster to Seneca, the formula $d = 35t$ can be used to represent his distance traveled in a specific length of time. Formulas can also be used to show different roles of the variables, transformed without any given numbers. Solving for r, the formula becomes $\frac{d}{t} = r$. The t is moved over by division so that *rate* is a function of distance and time.

Solving Equations

Solving equations in one variable is the process of isolating that variable on one side of the equation. For example, in $3x - 7 = 20$, the variable x needs to be isolated. Using opposite operations, the -7 is moved to the right side of the equation by adding seven to both sides: $3x - 7 + 7 = 20 + 7$, resulting in $3x = 27$. Dividing by three on each side, $\frac{3x}{3} = \frac{27}{3}$, results in isolation of the variable. It is important to note that if an operation is performed on one side of the equals sign, it has to be performed on the other side to maintain equality. The solution is found to be $x = 9$. This solution can be checked for accuracy by plugging $x=7$ in the original equation. After simplifying the equation, $20 = 20$ is found, which is a true statement.

When solving radical and rational equations, extraneous solutions must be accounted for when finding the answers. For example, the equation $\frac{x}{x-5} = \frac{3x}{x+3}$ has two values that create a 0 denominator: $x \neq 5, -3$. When solving for x, these values must be considered because they cannot be solutions. In the given equation, solving for x can be done using cross-multiplication, yielding the equation $x(x + 3) = 3x(x - 5)$. Distributing results in the quadratic equation yields $x^2 + 3x = 3x^2 - 15x$; therefore, all terms must be moved to one side of the equals sign. This results in $2x^2 - 18x = 0$, which in factored form is $2x(x - 9) = 0$. Setting each factor equal to zero, the apparent solutions are $x = 0$ and $x = 9$. These two solutions are neither 5 nor -3, so they are viable solutions. Neither 0 nor 9 create a 0 denominator in the original equation.

A similar process exists when solving radical equations. One must check to make sure the solutions are defined in the original equations. Solving an equation containing a square root involves isolating the root and then squaring both sides of the equals sign. Solving a cube root equation involves isolating the radical and then cubing both sides. In either case, the variable can then be solved for because there are no longer radicals in the equation.

Methods for Solving Equations

Equations with one variable can be solved using the addition principle and multiplication principle. If $a = b$, then $a + c = b + c$, and $ac = bc$. Given the equation $2x - 3 = 5x + 7$, the first step is to combine the variable terms and the constant terms. Using the principles, expressions can be added and subtracted onto and off both sides of the equals sign, so the equation turns into $-10 = 3x$. Dividing by 3 on both sides through the multiplication principle with $c = \frac{1}{3}$ results in the final answer of $x = \frac{-10}{3}$.

Some equations have a higher degree and are not solved by simply using opposite operations. When an equation has a degree of 2, completing the square is an option. For example, the quadratic equation $x^2 - 6x + 2 = 0$ can be rewritten by completing the square. The goal of completing the square is to get the equation into the form $(x - p)^2 = q$. Using the example, the constant term 2 first needs to be moved over to the opposite side by subtracting. Then, the square can be completed by adding 9 to both sides, which is the square of half of the coefficient of the middle term $-6x$. The current equation is $x^2 - 6x + 9 = 7$. The left side can be factored into a square of a binomial, resulting in $(x - 3)^2 = 7$. To solve for x, the square root of both sides should be taken, resulting in $(x - 3) = \pm\sqrt{7}$, and $x = 3 \pm \sqrt{7}$.

Other ways of solving quadratic equations include graphing, factoring, and using the quadratic formula. The equation $y = x^2 - 4x + 3$ can be graphed on the coordinate plane, and the solutions can be observed where it crosses the x-axis. The graph will be a parabola that opens up with two solutions at 1 and 3.

The equation can also be factored to find the solutions. The original equation, $y = x^2 - 4x + 3$ can be factored into $y = (x - 1)(x - 3)$. Setting this equal to zero, the x-values are found to be 1 and 3, just as on the graph. Solving by factoring and graphing are not always possible. The quadratic formula is a method of solving quadratic equations that always results in exact solutions. The formula is $x = \frac{-b \pm \sqrt{b^2 - 4ac}}{2a}$, where $a, b,$ and c are the coefficients in the original equation in standard form $y = ax^2 + bx + c$. For this example:

$$x = \frac{4 \pm \sqrt{(-4)^2 - 4(1)(3)}}{2(1)} = \frac{4 \pm \sqrt{16 - 12}}{2} = \frac{4 \pm 2}{2} = 1, 3$$

The expression underneath the radical is called the *discriminant*. Without working out the entire formula, the value of the discriminant can reveal the nature of the solutions. If the value of the discriminant $b^2 - 4ac$ is positive, then there will be two real solutions. If the value is zero, there will be one real solution. If the value is negative, the two solutions will be imaginary or complex. If the solutions are complex, it means that the parabola never touches the x-axis. An example of a complex solution can be found by solving the following quadratic: $y = x^2 - 4x + 8$.

By using the quadratic formula, the solutions are found to be:

$$x = \frac{4 \pm \sqrt{(-4)^2 - 4(1)(8)}}{2(1)} = \frac{4 \pm \sqrt{16 - 32}}{2} = \frac{4 \pm \sqrt{-16}}{2} = 2 \pm 2i$$

The solutions both have a real part, 2, and an imaginary part, $2i$.

Measurement and Geometry

Points, Lines, Planes, and Angles

A point is a place, not a thing, and therefore has no dimensions or size. A set of points that lies on the same line is called collinear. A set of points that lies on the same plane is called coplanar.

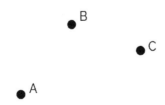

The image above displays point *A*, point *B*, and point *C*.

A line is as series of points that extends in both directions without ending. It consists of an infinite number of points and is drawn with arrows on both ends to indicate it extends infinitely. Lines can be named by two points on the line or with a single, cursive, lower case letter. The lines below are named: line AB or line BA or $\overleftrightarrow{AB}$ or $\overleftrightarrow{BA}$; and line m.

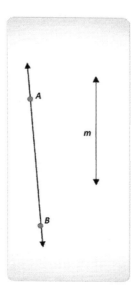

Two lines are considered parallel to each other if, while extending infinitely, they will never intersect (or meet). Parallel lines point in the same direction and are always the same distance apart. Two lines are considered perpendicular if they intersect to form right angles. Right angles are 90°. Typically, a small box is drawn at the intersection point to indicate the right angle.

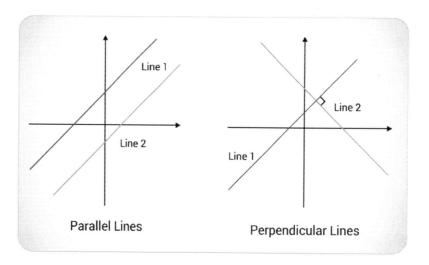

Line 1 is parallel to line 2 in the left image and is written as line 1 || line 2. Line 1 is perpendicular to line 2 in the right image and is written as line 1 ⊥ line 2.

A ray has a specific starting point and extends in one direction without ending. The endpoint of a ray is its starting point. Rays are named using the endpoint first, and any other point on the ray. The following ray can be named ray AB and written $\overrightarrow{AB}$.

A line segment has specific starting and ending points. A line segment consists of two endpoints and all the points in between. Line segments are named by the two endpoints. The example below is named segment *GH* or segment *HG*, written $\overline{GH}$ or $\overline{HG}$.

Two- and Three-Dimensional Shapes

A polygon is a closed geometric figure in a plane (flat surface) consisting of at least 3 sides formed by line segments. These are often defined as two-dimensional shapes. Common two-dimensional shapes include circles, triangles, squares, rectangles, pentagons, and hexagons. Note that a circle is a two-dimensional shape without sides.

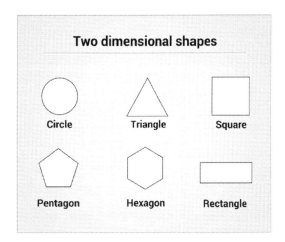

A solid figure, or simply solid, is a figure that encloses a part of space. Some solids consist of flat surfaces only while others include curved surfaces. Solid figures are often defined as three-dimensional shapes. Common three-dimensional shapes include spheres, prisms, cubes, pyramids, cylinders, and cones.

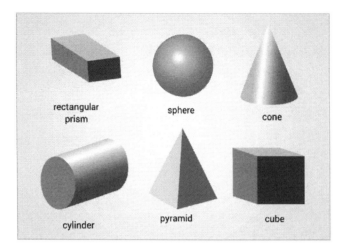

Composing two- or three-dimensional shapes involves putting together two or more shapes to create a new larger figure. For example, a semi-circle (half circle), rectangle, and two triangles can be used to compose the figure of the sailboat shown below.

Similarly, solid figures can be placed together to compose an endless number of three-dimensional objects.

Decomposing two- and three-dimensional figures involves breaking the shapes apart into smaller, simpler shapes. Consider the following two-dimensional representations of a house:

This complex figure can be decomposed into the following basic two-dimensional shapes: large rectangle (body of house); large triangle (roof); small rectangle and small triangle (chimney). Decomposing figures is often done more than one way. To illustrate, the figure of the house could also be decomposed into: two large triangles (body); two medium triangles (roof); two smaller triangles of unequal size (chimney).

Polygons and Solids

A polygon is a closed two-dimensional figure consisting of three or more sides. Polygons can be either convex or concave. A polygon that has interior angles all measuring less than 180° is convex. A concave polygon has one or more interior angles measuring greater than 180°. Examples are shown below.

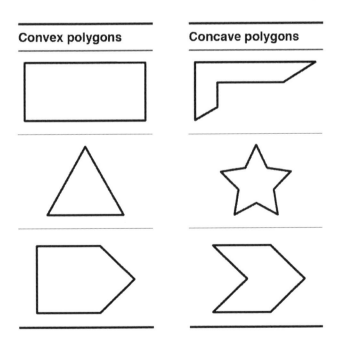

Polygons can be classified by the number of sides (also equal to the number of angles) they have. The following are the names of polygons with a given number of sides or angles:

# of sides	3	4	5	6	7	8	9	10
Name of polygon	Triangle	Quadrilateral	Pentagon	Hexagon	Septagon (or heptagon)	Octagon	Nonagon	Decagon

Equiangular polygons are polygons in which the measure of every interior angle is the same. The sides of equilateral polygons are always the same length. If a polygon is both equiangular and equilateral, the polygon is defined as a regular polygon. Examples are shown below.

Triangles can be further classified by their sides and angles. A triangle with its largest angle measuring 90° is a right triangle. A triangle with the largest angle less than 90° is an acute triangle. A triangle with the largest angle greater than 90° is an obtuse triangle.

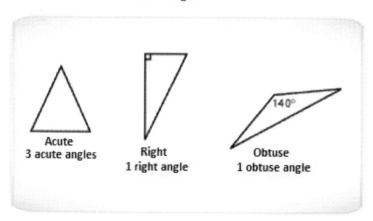

A triangle consisting of two equal sides and two equal angles is an isosceles triangle. A triangle with three equal sides and three equal angles is an equilateral triangle. A triangle with no equal sides or angles is a scalene triangle.

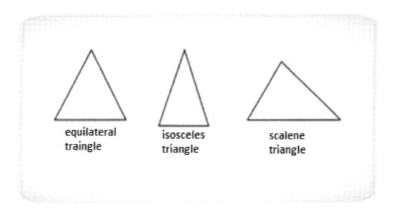

equilateral triangle   isosceles triangle   scalene triangle

Quadrilaterals can be further classified according to their sides and angles. A quadrilateral with exactly one pair of parallel sides is called a trapezoid. A quadrilateral that shows both pairs of opposite sides parallel is a parallelogram. Parallelograms include rhombuses, rectangles, and squares. A rhombus has four equal sides. A rectangle has four equal angles (90° each). A square has four 90° angles and four equal sides. Therefore, a square is both a rhombus and a rectangle.

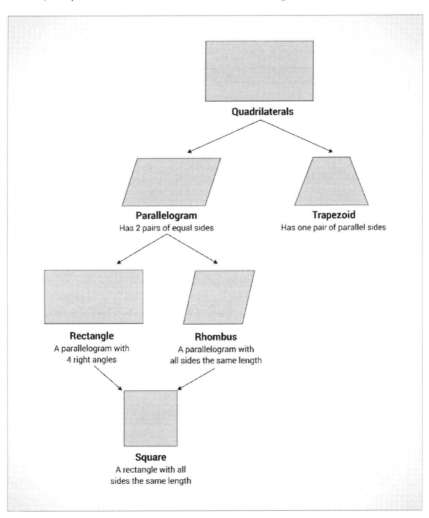

A solid is a three-dimensional figure that encloses a part of space. Solids consisting of all flat surfaces that are polygons are called polyhedrons. The two-dimensional surfaces that make up a polyhedron are

called faces. Types of polyhedrons include prisms and pyramids. A prism consists of two parallel faces that are congruent (or the same shape and same size), and lateral faces going around (which are parallelograms). A prism is further classified by the shape of its base, as shown below:

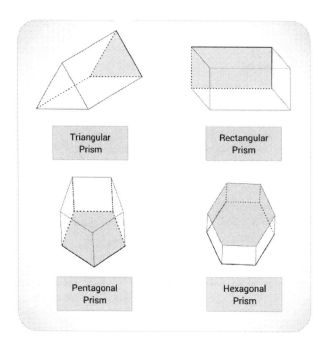

A pyramid consists of lateral faces (triangles) that meet at a common point called the vertex and one other face that is a polygon, called the base. A pyramid can be further classified by the shape of its base, as shown below.

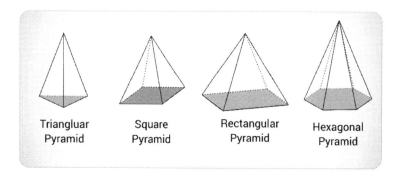

A tetrahedron is another name for a triangular pyramid. All the faces of a tetrahedron are triangles.

Solids that are not polyhedrons include spheres, cylinders, and cones. A sphere is the set of all points a given distance from a given center point. A sphere is commonly thought of as a three-dimensional circle. A cylinder consists of two parallel, congruent (same size) circles and a lateral curved surface. A cone consists of a circle as its base and a lateral curved surface that narrows to a point called the vertex.

Similar polygons are the same shape but different sizes. More specifically, their corresponding angle measures are congruent (or equal) and the length of their sides is proportional. For example, all sides of one polygon may be double the length of the sides of another. Likewise, similar solids are the same shape but different sizes. Any corresponding faces or bases of similar solids are the same polygons that are proportional by a consistent value.

Properties of certain polygons allow that the perimeter may be obtained by using formulas. A rectangle consists of two sides called the length (*l*), which have equal measures, and two sides called the width (*w*), which have equal measures. Therefore, the perimeter (*P*) of a rectangle can be expressed as P = *l* + *l* + *w* + *w*. This can be simplified to produce the following formula to find the perimeter of a rectangle: P = 2*l* + 2*w* or P = 2(*l* + *w*).

A regular polygon is one in which all sides have equal length and all interior angles have equal measures, such as a square and an equilateral triangle. To find the perimeter of a regular polygon, the length of one side is multiplied by the number of sides. For example, to find the perimeter of an equilateral triangle with a side of length of 4 feet, 4 feet is multiplied by 3 (number of sides of a triangle). The perimeter of a regular octagon (8 sides) with a side of length of $\frac{1}{2}$cm is $\frac{1}{2}cm \times 8 = 4cm$.

Classification of Angles

An angle consists of two rays that have a common endpoint. This common endpoint is called the vertex of the angle. The two rays can be called sides of the angle. The angle below has a vertex at point *B* and the sides consist of ray *BA* and ray *BC*. An angle can be named in three ways:

      1. Using the vertex and a point from each side, with the vertex letter in the middle.
      2. Using only the vertex. This can only be used if it is the only angle with that vertex.
      3. Using a number that is written inside the angle.

The angle below can be written ∠*ABC* (read angle *ABC*), ∠*CBA*, ∠*B*, or ∠1.

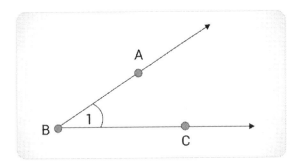

An angle divides a plane, or flat surface, into three parts: the angle itself, the interior (inside) of the angle, and the exterior (outside) of the angle. The figure below shows point *M* on the interior of the angle and point *N* on the exterior of the angle.

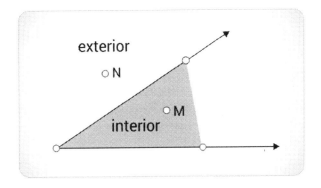

Angles can be measured in units called degrees, with the symbol °. The degree measure of an angle is between 0° and 180° and can be obtained by using a protractor.

A straight angle (or simply a line) measures exactly 180°. A right angle's sides meet at the vertex to create a square corner. A right-angle measures exactly 90° and is typically indicated by a box drawn in the interior of the angle. An acute angle has an interior that is narrower than a right angle. The measure of an acute angle is any value less than 90° and greater than 0°. For example, 89.9°, 47°, 12°, and 1°. An obtuse angle has an interior that is wider than a right angle. The measure of an obtuse angle is any value greater than 90° but less than 180°. For example, 90.1°, 110°, 150°, and 179.9°.

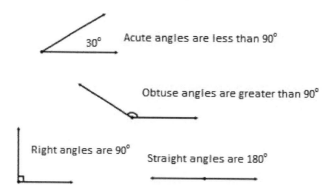

Solving Line Problems

Two lines are parallel if they have the same slope. Two lines are perpendicular if the product of their slope equals -1. Parallel lines never intersect unless they are the same line, and perpendicular lines intersect at a right angle. If two lines aren't parallel, they must intersect at one point. Determining equations of lines based on properties of parallel and perpendicular lines appears in word problems. To find an equation of a line, both the slope and a point the line goes through are necessary. Therefore, if an equation of a line is needed that's parallel to a given line and runs through a specified point, the slope of the given line and the point are plugged into the point-slope form of an equation of a line. Secondly, if an equation of a line is needed that's perpendicular to a given line running through a specified point, the negative reciprocal of the slope of the given line and the point are plugged into the point-slope form. Also, if the point of intersection of two lines is known, that point will be used to solve the set of equations. Therefore, to solve a system of equations, the point of intersection must be found. If a set of two equations with two unknown variables has no solution, the lines are parallel.

Solving Problems with Parallel and Perpendicular Lines

Two lines can be parallel, perpendicular, or neither. If two lines are parallel, they have the same slope. This is proven using the idea of similar triangles. Consider the following diagram with two parallel lines, L1 and L2:

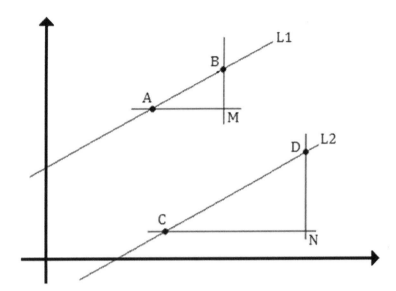

A and B are points on L1, and C and D are points on L2. Right triangles are formed with vertex M and N where lines BM and DN are parallel to the y-axis and AM and CN are parallel to the x-axis. Because all three sets of lines are parallel, the triangles are similar. Therefore, $\frac{BM}{DN} = \frac{MA}{NC}$. This shows that the rise/run is equal for lines L1 and L2. Hence, their slopes are equal.

Secondly, if two lines are perpendicular, the product of their slopes equals -1. This means that their slopes are negative reciprocals of each other. Consider two perpendicular lines, *l* and *n*:

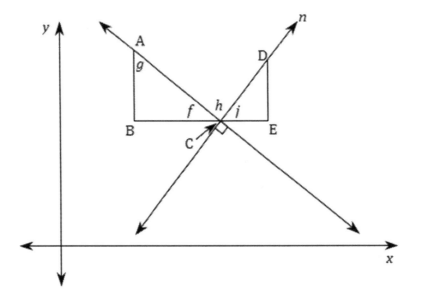

Right triangles ABC and CDE are formed so that lines BC and CE are parallel to the x-axis, and AB and DE are parallel to the y-axis. Because line BE is a straight line, angles $f + h + i = 180 \ degrees$. However, angle h is a right angle, so $f + j = 90 \ degrees$. By construction, $f + g = 90$, which means that $g = j$. Therefore, because angles $B = E$ and $g = j$, the triangles are similar and $\frac{AB}{BC} = \frac{CE}{DE}$. Because slope is equal to rise/run, the slope of line *l* is $-\frac{AB}{BC}$ and the slope of line *n* is $\frac{DE}{CE}$. Multiplying the slopes together gives $-\frac{AB}{BC} \cdot \frac{DE}{CE} = -\frac{CE}{DE} \cdot \frac{DE}{CE} = -1$. This proves that the product of the slopes of two perpendicular lines equals -1. Both parallel and perpendicular lines can be integral in many geometric proofs, so knowing and understanding their properties is crucial for problem-solving.

Effects of Changes to Dimensions on Area and Volume

Similar polygons are figures that are the same shape but different sizes. Likewise, similar solids are different sizes but are the same shape. In both cases, corresponding angles in the same positions for both figures are congruent (equal), and corresponding sides are proportional in length. For example, the triangles below are similar. The following pairs of corresponding angles are congruent: $\angle A$ and $\angle D$; $\angle B$

and ∠E; ∠C and ∠F. The corresponding sides are proportional: $\frac{AB}{DE} = \frac{6}{3} = 2, \frac{BC}{EF} = \frac{9}{4.5} = 2, \frac{CA}{FD} = \frac{10}{5} = 2$. In other words, triangle *ABC* is the same shape but twice as large as triangle *DEF*.

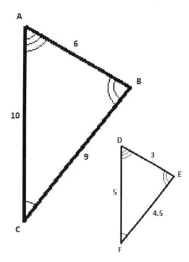

An example of similar triangular pyramids is shown below.

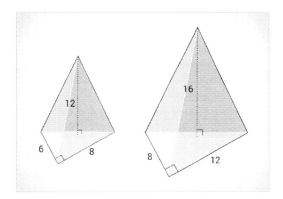

Given the nature of two- and three-dimensional measurements, changing dimensions by a given scale (multiplier) does not change the area of volume by the same scale. Consider a rectangle with a length of 5 centimeters and a width of 4 centimeters. The area of the rectangle is $20cm^2$. Doubling the dimensions of the rectangle (multiplying by a scale factor of 2) to 10 centimeters and 8 centimeters *does not* double the area to $40cm^2$. Area is a two-dimensional measurement (measured in square units). Therefore, the dimensions are multiplied by a scale that is squared (raised to the second power) to determine the scale of the corresponding areas. For the previous example, the length and width are multiplied by 2. Therefore, the area is multiplied by 2^2, or 4. The area of a 5cm × 4cm rectangle is $20cm^2$. The area of a 10cm × 8cm rectangle is $80cm^2$.

Volume is a three-dimensional measurement, which is measured in cubic units. Therefore, the scale between dimensions of similar solids is cubed (raised to the third power) to determine the scale between their volumes. Consider similar right rectangular prisms: one with a length of 8 inches, a width of 24 inches, and a height of 16 inches; the second with a length of 4 inches, a width of 12 inches, and a height of 8 inches. The first prism, multiplied by a scalar of $\frac{1}{2}$, produces the measurement of the second prism. The volume of the first prism, multiplied by $(\frac{1}{2})^3$, which equals $\frac{1}{8}$, produces the volume of the second prism. The volume of the first prism is 8in × 24in × 16in which equals $3{,}072in^3$. The volume of the second prism is 4in × 12in × 8in which equals $384in^3$ ($3{,}072in^3 \times \frac{1}{8} = 384in^3$).

The rules for squaring the scalar for area and cubing the scalar for volume only hold true for similar figures. In other words, if only one dimension is changed (changing the width of a rectangle but not the length) or dimensions are changed at different rates (the length of a prism is doubled and its height is tripled) the figures are not similar (same shape). Therefore, the rules above do not apply.

Trigonometric Ratios in Right Triangles

Trigonometric Functions
Within similar triangles, corresponding sides are proportional, and angles are congruent. In addition, within similar triangles, the ratio of the side lengths is the same. This property is true even if side lengths are different. Within right triangles, trigonometric ratios can be defined for the acute angle within the triangle. The functions are defined through ratios in a right triangle. Sine of acute angle, A, is opposite over hypotenuse, cosine is adjacent over hypotenuse, and tangent is opposite over adjacent. Note that expanding or shrinking the triangle won't change the ratios. However, changing the angle measurements will alter the calculations.

Complementary Angles
Angles that add up to 90 degrees are *complementary*. Within a right triangle, two complementary angles exist because the third angle is always 90 degrees. In this scenario, the *sine* of one of the complementary angles is equal to the *cosine* of the other angle. The opposite is also true. This relationship exists because sine and cosine will be calculated as the ratios of the same side lengths.

The Pythagorean Theorem
The *Pythagorean theorem* is an important relationship between the three sides of a right triangle. It states that the square of the side opposite the right triangle, known as the *hypotenuse* (denoted as c^2), is equal to the sum of the squares of the other two sides ($a^2 + b^2$). Thus, $a^2 + b^2 = c^2$.

Both the trigonometric functions and the Pythagorean theorem can be used in problems that involve finding either a missing side or a missing angle of a right triangle. To do so, one must look to see what sides and angles are given and select the correct relationship that will help find the missing value. These relationships can also be used to solve application problems involving right triangles. Often, it's helpful to draw a figure to represent the problem to see what's missing.

Congruence and Similarity in Terms of Transformations

Rigid Motion
A *rigid motion* is a transformation that preserves distance and length. Every line segment in the resulting image is congruent to the corresponding line segment in the pre-image. Congruence between two figures means a series of transformations (or a rigid motion) can be defined that maps one of the figures onto the other. Basically, two figures are congruent if they have the same shape and size.

Dilation

A shape is dilated, or a *dilation* occurs, when each side of the original image is multiplied by a given scale factor. If the scale factor is less than 1 and greater than 0, the dilation contracts the shape, and the resulting shape is smaller. If the scale factor equals 1, the resulting shape is the same size, and the dilation is a rigid motion. Finally, if the scale factor is greater than 1, the resulting shape is larger and the dilation expands the shape. The *center of dilation* is the point where the distance from it to any point on the new shape equals the scale factor times the distance from the center to the corresponding point in the pre-image. Dilation isn't an isometric transformation because distance isn't preserved. However, angle measure, parallel lines, and points on a line all remain unchanged. The following figure is an example of translation, rotation, dilation, and reflection:

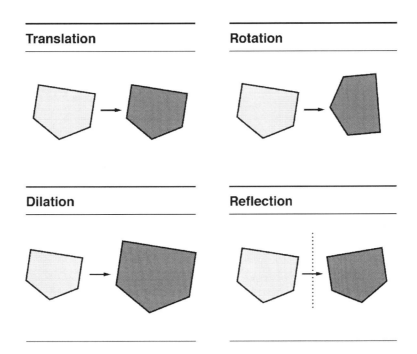

Determining Congruence

Two figures are congruent if there is a rigid motion that can map one figure onto the other. Therefore, all pairs of sides and angles within the image and pre-image must be congruent. For example, in triangles, each pair of the three sides and three angles must be congruent. Similarly, in two four-sided figures, each pair of the four sides and four angles must be congruent.

Similarity

Two figures are *similar* if there is a combination of translations, reflections, rotations, and dilations, which maps one figure onto the other. The difference between congruence and similarity is that dilation can be used in similarity. Therefore, side lengths between each shape can differ. However, angle measure must be preserved within this definition. If two polygons differ in size so that the lengths of corresponding line segments differ by the same factor, but corresponding angles have the same measurement, they are similar.

Triangle Congruence

There are five theorems to show that triangles are congruent when it's unknown whether each pair of angles and sides are congruent. Each theorem is a shortcut that involves different combinations of sides and angles that must be true for the two triangles to be congruent. For example, *side-side-side (SSS)* states that if all sides are equal, the triangles are congruent. *Side-angle-side (SAS)* states that if two pairs of sides are equal and the included angles are congruent, then the triangles are congruent. Similarly, *angle-side-angle (ASA)* states that if two pairs of angles are congruent and the included side lengths are equal, the triangles are similar. *Angle-angle-side (AAS)* states that two triangles are congruent if they have two pairs of congruent angles and a pair of corresponding equal side lengths that aren't included. Finally, *hypotenuse-leg (HL)* states that if two right triangles have equal hypotenuses and an equal pair of shorter sides, then the triangles are congruent. An important item to note is that angle-angle-angle *(AAA)* is not enough information to have congruence. It's important to understand why these rules work by using rigid motions to show congruence between the triangles with the given properties. For example, three reflections are needed to show why *SAS* follows from the definition of congruence.

Similarity for Two Triangles
If two angles of one triangle are congruent with two angles of a second triangle, the triangles are similar. This is because, within any triangle, the sum of the angle measurements is 180 degrees. Therefore, if two are congruent, the third angle must also be congruent because their measurements are equal. Three congruent pairs of angles mean that the triangles are similar.

Proving Congruence and Similarity
The criteria needed to prove triangles are congruent involves both angle and side congruence. Both pairs of related angles and sides need to be of the same measurement to use congruence in a proof. The criteria to prove similarity in triangles involves proportionality of side lengths. Angles must be congruent in similar triangles; however, corresponding side lengths only need to be a constant multiple of each other. Once similarity is established, it can be used in proofs as well. Relationships in geometric figures other than triangles can be proven using triangle congruence and similarity. If a similar or congruent triangle can be found within another type of geometric figure, their criteria can be used to prove a relationship about a given formula. For instance, a rectangle can be broken up into two congruent triangles.

Relationships between Angles
Supplementary angles add up to 180 degrees. *Vertical angles* are two nonadjacent angles formed by two intersecting lines. *Corresponding angles* are two angles in the same position whenever a straight line (known as a *transversal*) crosses two others. If the two lines are parallel, the corresponding angles are equal. *Alternate interior angles* are also a pair of angles formed when two lines are crossed by a transversal. They are opposite angles that exist inside of the two lines. In the corresponding angles diagram above, angles 2 and 7 are alternate interior angles, as well as angles 6 and 3. *Alternate exterior angles* are opposite angles formed by a transversal but, in contrast to interior angles, exterior angles exist outside the two original lines. Therefore, angles 1 and 8 are alternate exterior angles and so are angles 5 and 4. Finally, *consecutive interior angles* are pairs of angles formed by a transversal. These angles are located on the same side of the transversal and inside the two original lines. Therefore, angles 2 and 3 are a pair of consecutive interior angles, and so are angles 6 and 7. These definitions are instrumental in solving many problems that involve determining relationships between angles.

Medians, Midpoints, and Altitudes
A *median* of a triangle is the line drawn from a vertex to the midpoint on the opposite side. A triangle has three medians, and their point of intersection is known as the *centroid*. An *altitude* is a line drawn from a vertex perpendicular to the opposite side. A triangle has three altitudes, and their point of intersection is known as the *orthocenter*. An altitude can actually exist outside, inside, or on the triangle depending on the placement of the vertex. Many problems involve these definitions. For example, given

one endpoint of a line segment and the midpoint, the other endpoint can be determined by using the midpoint formula. In addition, area problems heavily depend on these definitions. For example, it can be proven that the median of a triangle divides it into two regions of equal areas. The actual formula for the area of a triangle depends on its altitude.

Special Triangles

An *isosceles triangle* contains at least two equal sides. Therefore, it must also contain two equal angles and, subsequently, contain two medians of the same length. An isosceles triangle can also be labelled as an *equilateral triangle* (which contains three equal sides and three equal angles) when it meets these conditions. In an equilateral triangle, the measure of each angle is always 60 degrees. Also within an equilateral triangle, the medians are of the same length. A *scalene triangle* can never be an equilateral or an isosceles triangle because it contains no equal sides and no equal angles. Also, medians in a scalene triangle can't have the same length. However, a *right triangle*, which is a triangle containing a 90-degree angle, can be a scalene triangle. There are two types of special right triangles. The *30-60-90 right triangle* has angle measurements of 30 degrees, 60 degrees, and 90 degrees. Because of the nature of this triangle, and through the use of the Pythagorean theorem, the side lengths have a special relationship. If x is the length opposite the 30-degree angle, the length opposite the 60-degree angle is $\sqrt{3}x$, and the hypotenuse has length $2x$. The *45-45-90 right triangle* is also special as it contains two angle measurements of 45 degrees. It can be proven that, if x is the length of the two equal sides, the hypotenuse is $x\sqrt{2}$. The properties of all of these special triangles are extremely useful in determining both side lengths and angle measurements in problems where some of these quantities are given and some are not.

Special Quadrilaterals

A special quadrilateral is one in which both pairs of opposite sides are parallel. This type of quadrilateral is known as a *parallelogram*. A parallelogram has six important properties:

- Opposite sides are congruent.
- Opposite angles are congruent.
- Within a parallelogram, consecutive angles are supplementary, so their measurements total 180 degrees.
- If one angle is a right angle, all of them have to be right angles.
- The diagonals of the angles bisect each other.
- These diagonals form two congruent triangles.

A parallelogram with four congruent sides is a *rhombus*. A quadrilateral containing only one set of parallel sides is known as a *trapezoid*. The parallel sides are known as bases, and the other two sides are known as legs. If the legs are congruent, the trapezoid can be labelled an *isosceles trapezoid*. An important property of a trapezoid is that their diagonals are congruent. Also, the median of a trapezoid is parallel to the bases, and its length is equal to half of the sum of the base lengths.

Quadrilateral Relationships

Rectangles, squares, and rhombuses are *polygons* with four sides. By definition, all rectangles are parallelograms, but only some rectangles are squares. However, some parallelograms are rectangles. Also, it's true that all squares are rectangles, and some rhombuses are squares. There are no rectangles, squares, or rhombuses that are trapezoids though, because they have more than one set of parallel sides.

Diagonals and Angles

Diagonals are lines (excluding sides) that connect two vertices within a polygon. *Mutually bisecting diagonals* intersect at their midpoints. Parallelograms, rectangles, squares, and rhombuses have mutually bisecting diagonals. However, trapezoids don't have such lines. *Perpendicular diagonals* occur when they form four right triangles at their point of intersection. Squares and rhombuses have perpendicular diagonals, but trapezoids, rectangles, and parallelograms do not. Finally, *perpendicular bisecting* diagonals (also known as *perpendicular bisectors*) form four right triangles at their point of intersection, but this intersection is also the midpoint of the two lines. Both rhombuses and squares have perpendicular bisecting angles, but trapezoids, rectangles, and parallelograms do not. Knowing these definitions can help tremendously in problems that involve both angles and diagonals.

Polygons with More Than Four Sides

A *pentagon* is a five-sided figure. A six-sided shape is a *hexagon*. A seven-sided figure is classified as a *heptagon*, and an eight-sided figure is called an *octagon*. An important characteristic is whether a polygon is regular or irregular. If it's *regular*, the side lengths and angle measurements are all equal. An *irregular* polygon has unequal side lengths and angle measurements. Mathematical problems involving polygons with more than four sides usually involve side length and angle measurements. The sum of all internal angles in a polygon equals $180(n - 2)$ degrees, where n is the number of sides. Therefore, the total of all internal angles in a pentagon is 540 degrees because there are five sides so $180(5 - 2)$= 540 degrees. Unfortunately, area formulas don't exist for polygons with more than four sides. However, their shapes can be split up into triangles, and the formula for area of a triangle can be applied and totaled to obtain the area for the entire figure.

Congruency

Two figures are congruent if they have the same shape and same size. The two figures could have been rotated, reflected, or translated. Two figures are similar if they have been rotated, reflected, translated, and resized. Angle measure is preserved in similar figures. Both angle and side length are preserved in congruent figures.

Perimeter and Area

Perimeter is the measurement of a distance around something. Think of perimeter as the length of the boundary, like a fence. In contrast, area is the space occupied by a defined enclosure, like a field enclosed by a fence.

The perimeter of a polygon is the distance around the outside of the two-dimensional figure. Perimeter is a one-dimensional measurement and is therefore expressed in linear units such as centimeters (*cm*), feet (*ft.*), and miles (*mi*). The perimeter (*P*) of the figure below is calculated by: *P* = 9m + 5m + 4m + 6m + 8m → *P* = 32 m.

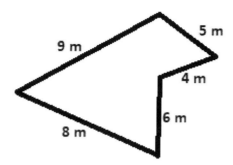

The perimeter of a square is measured by adding together all of the sides. Since a square has four equal sides, its perimeter can be calculated by multiplying the length of one side by 4. Thus, the formula is $P = 4 \times s$, where s equals one side. The area of a square is calculated by squaring the length of one side, which is expressed as the formula $A = s^2$.

Like a square, a rectangle's perimeter is measured by adding together all of the sides. But as the sides are unequal, the formula is different. A rectangle has equal values for its lengths (long sides) and equal values for its widths (short sides), so the perimeter formula for a rectangle is $P = l + l + w + w = 2l + 2w$, where l equals length and w equals width. The area is found by multiplying the length by the width, so the formula is $A = l \times w$.

A triangle's perimeter is measured by adding together the three sides, so the formula is $P = a + b + c$, where $a, b,$ and c are the values of the three sides. The area is calculated by multiplying the length of the base times the height times ½, so the formula is $A = \frac{1}{2} \times b \times h = \frac{bh}{2}$. The base is the bottom of the triangle, and the height is the distance from the base to the peak. If a problem asks to calculate the area of a triangle, it will provide the base and height.

A circle's perimeter—also known as its circumference—is measured by multiplying the diameter (the straight line measured from one end to the direct opposite end of the circle) by π, so the formula is $\pi \times d$. This is sometimes expressed by the formula $C = 2 \times \pi \times r$, where r is the radius of the circle. These formulas are equivalent, as the radius equals half of the diameter. The area of a circle is calculated through the formula $A = \pi \times r^2$. The test will indicate either to leave the answer with π attached or to calculate to the nearest decimal place, which means multiplying by 3.14 for π.

The perimeter of a parallelogram is measured by adding the lengths and widths together. Thus, the formula is the same as for a rectangle, $P = l + l + w + w = 2l + 2w$. However, the area formula differs from the rectangle. For a parallelogram, the area is calculated by multiplying the length by the height: $A = h \times l$

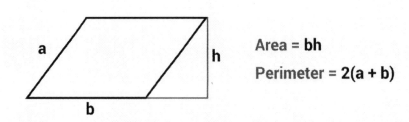

Area = bh

Perimeter = 2(a + b)

The perimeter of a trapezoid is calculated by adding the two unequal bases and two equal sides, so the formula is $P = a + b_1 + c + b_2$. Although unlikely to be a test question, the formula for the area of a trapezoid is $A = \frac{b_1 + b_2}{2} \times h$, where h equals height, and b_1 and b_2 equal the bases.

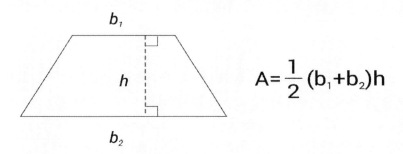

$$A = \frac{1}{2}(b_1 + b_2)h$$

Irregular Shapes

The perimeter of an irregular polygon is found by adding the lengths of all of the sides. In cases where all of the sides are given, this will be very straightforward, as it will simply involve finding the sum of the provided lengths. Other times, a side length may be missing and must be determined before the perimeter can be calculated. Consider the example below:

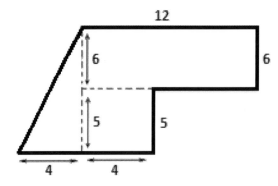

All of the side lengths are provided except for the angled side on the left. Test takers should notice that this is the hypotenuse of a right triangle. The other two sides of the triangle are provided (the base is 4

and the height is 6 + 5 = 11). The Pythagorean Theorem can be used to find the length of the hypotenuse, remembering that a² + b² = c².

Substituting the side values provided yields (4)² + (11)² = c².

Therefore, c = $\sqrt{16 + 121}$ = 11.7

Finally, the perimeter can be found by adding this new side length with the other provided lengths to get the total length around the figure: 4+4+5+8+6+12+11.7=50.7. Although units are not provided in this figure, remember that reporting units with a measurement is important.

The area of an irregular polygon is found by decomposing, or breaking apart, the figure into smaller shapes. When the area of the smaller shapes is determined, these areas are added together to produce the total area of the area of the original figure. Consider the same example provided before:

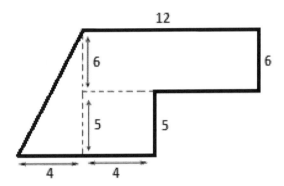

The irregular polygon is decomposed into two rectangles and a triangle. The area of the large rectangles ($A = l \times w \rightarrow A = 12 \times 6$) is 72 square units. The area of the small rectangle is 20 square units ($A = 4 \times 5$). The area of the triangle ($A = \frac{1}{2} \times b \times h \rightarrow A = \frac{1}{2} \times 4 \times 11$) is 22 square units. The sum of the areas of these figures produces the total area of the original polygon: $A = 72 + 20 + 22 \rightarrow A = 114$ square units.

Surface Area of Three-Dimensional Figures

The area of a two-dimensional figure refers to the number of square units needed to cover the interior region of the figure. This concept is similar to wallpaper covering the flat surface of a wall. For example, if a rectangle has an area of 21 square centimeters (written $21cm^2$), it will take 21 squares, each with sides one centimeter in length, to cover the interior region of the rectangle. Note that area is measured in square units such as: square feet or ft^2; square yards or yd^2; square miles or mi^2.

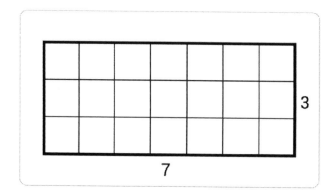

The surface area of a three-dimensional figure refers to the number of square units needed to cover the entire surface of the figure. This concept is similar to using wrapping paper to completely cover the outside of a box. For example, if a triangular pyramid has a surface area of 17 square inches (written $17in^2$), it will take 17 squares, each with sides one inch in length, to cover the entire surface of the pyramid. Surface area is also measured in square units.

Many three-dimensional figures (solid figures) can be represented by nets consisting of rectangles and triangles. The surface area of such solids can be determined by adding the areas of each of its faces and bases. Finding the surface area using this method requires calculating the areas of rectangles and triangles. To find the area (A) of a rectangle, the length (l) is multiplied by the width (w) $\rightarrow A = l \times w$. The area of a rectangle with a length of 8cm and a width of 4cm is calculated: $A = (8cm) \times (4cm) \rightarrow A = 32cm^2$.

To calculate the area (A) of a triangle, the product of $\frac{1}{2}$, the base (b), and the height (h) is found $\rightarrow A = \frac{1}{2} \times b \times h$. Note that the height of a triangle is measured from the base to the vertex opposite of it forming a right angle with the base. The area of a triangle with a base of 11cm and a height of 6cm is calculated: $A = \frac{1}{2} \times (11cm) \times (6cm) \rightarrow A = 33cm^2$.

Consider the following triangular prism, which is represented by a net consisting of two triangles and three rectangles.

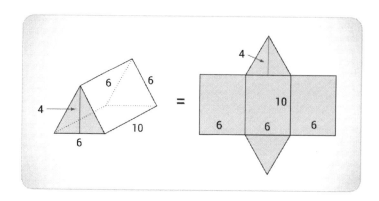

The surface area of the prism can be determined by adding the areas of each of its faces and bases. The surface area (*SA*) = area of triangle + area of triangle + area of rectangle + area of rectangle + area of rectangle.

$$SA = \left(\frac{1}{2} \times b \times h\right) + \left(\frac{1}{2} \times b \times h\right) + (l \times w) + (l \times w) + (l \times w)$$

$$SA = \left(\frac{1}{2} \times 6 \times 4\right) + \left(\frac{1}{2} \times 6 \times 4\right) + (6 \times 10) + (6 \times 10) + (6 \times 10)$$

$$SA = (12) + (12) + (60) + (60) + (60)$$

$$SA = 204 \; square \; units$$

Circles

Circle Angles

The *radius* of a circle is the distance from the center of the circle to any point on the circle. A *chord* of a circle is a straight line formed when its endpoints are allowed to be any two points on the circle. Many angles exist within a circle. A *central angle* is formed by using two radii as its rays and the center of the circle as its vertex. An *inscribed angle* is formed by using two chords as its rays and its vertex is a point on the circle itself. Finally, a *circumscribed angle* has a vertex that is a point outside the circle and rays that intersect with the circle. Some relationships exist between these types of angles, and, in order to define these relationships, arc measure must be understood. An *arc* of a circle is a portion of the circumference. Finding the *arc measure* is the same as finding the degree measure of the central angle that intersects the circle to form the arc. The measure of an inscribed angle is half the measure of its intercepted arc. It's also true that the measure of a circumscribed angle is equal to 180 degrees minus the measure of the central angle that forms the arc in the angle.

Quadrilateral Angles

If a quadrilateral is inscribed in a circle, the sum of its opposite angles is 180 degrees. Consider the quadrilateral ABCD centered at the point O:

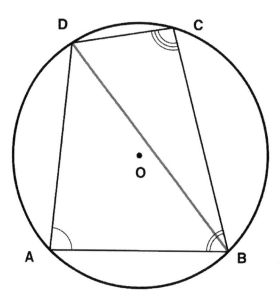

Each of the four line segments within the quadrilateral is a chord of the circle. Consider the diagonal DB. Angle DAB is an inscribed angle leaning on the arc DCB. Therefore, angle DAB is half the measure of the arc DCB. Conversely, angle DCB is an inscribed angle leaning on the arc DAB. Therefore, angle DCB is half the measure of the arc DAB. The sum of arcs DCB and DAB is 360 degrees because they make up the entire circle. Therefore, the sum of angles DAB and DCB equals half of 360 degrees, which is 180 degrees.

Circle Lines

A *tangent line* is a line that touches a curve at a single point without going through it. A *compass* and a *straightedge* are the tools necessary to construct a tangent line from a point P outside the circle to the circle. A tangent line is constructed by drawing a line segment from the center of the circle O to the point P, and then finding its midpoint M by bisecting the line segment. By using M as the center, a compass is used to draw a circle through points O and P. N is defined as the intersection of the two circles. Finally, a line segment is drawn through P and N. This is the tangent line. Each point on a circle has only one tangent line, which is perpendicular to the radius at that point. A line similar to a tangent line is a *secant line*. Instead of intersecting the circle at one point, a secant line intersects the circle at two points. A *chord* is a smaller portion of a secant line.

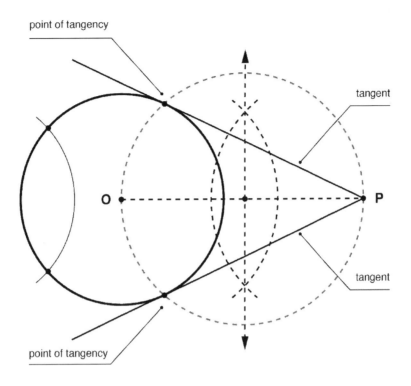

Applying Geometric Concepts to Real-World Situations

Real-World Geometry
Many real-world objects can be compared to geometric shapes. Describing certain objects using the measurements and properties of two- and three-dimensional shapes is an important part of geometry. For example, basic ideas such as angles and line segments can be seen in real-world objects. The corner of any room is an angle, and the intersection of a wall with the floor is like a line segment. Building upon this idea, entire objects can be related to both two- and three-dimensional shapes. An entire room can be thought of as square, rectangle, or a sum of a few three-dimensional shapes. Knowing what properties and measures are needed to make decisions in real life is why geometry is such a useful branch of mathematics. One obvious relationship between a real-life situation and geometry exists in construction. For example, to build an addition onto a house, several geometric measurements will be used.

Density
The *density* of a substance is the ratio of mass to area or volume. It's a relationship between the mass and how much space the object actually takes up. Knowing which units to use in each situation is crucial. Population density is an example of a real-life situation that's modeled by using density concepts. It involves calculating the ratio of the number of people to the number of square miles. The amount of material needed per a specific unit of area or volume is another application. For example, estimating the number of BTUs per cubic foot of a home is a measurement that relates to heating or cooling the house based on the desired temperature and the house's size.

Solving Design Problem

Design problems are an important application of geometry (e.g., building structures that satisfy physical constraints and/or minimize costs). These problems involve optimizing a situation based on what's given and required. For example, determining what size barn to build, given certain dimensions and a specific budget, uses both geometric properties and other mathematical concepts. Equations are formed using geometric definitions and the given constraints. In the end, such problems involve solving a system of equations and rely heavily on a strong background in algebra. *Typographic grid systems* also help with such design problems. A grid made up of intersecting straight or curved lines can be used as a visual representation of the structure being designed. This concept is seen in the blueprints used throughout the graphic design process.

Converting Within and Between Standard and Metric Systems

American Measuring System

The measuring system used today in the United States developed from the British units of measurement during colonial times. The most typically used units in this customary system are those used to measure weight, liquid volume, and length, whose common units are found below. In the customary system, the basic unit for measuring weight is the ounce (oz); there are 16 ounces (oz) in 1 pound (lb) and 2000 pounds in 1 ton. The basic unit for measuring liquid volume is the ounce (oz); 1 ounce is equal to 2 tablespoons (tbsp) or 6 teaspoons (tsp), and there are 8 ounces in 1 cup, 2 cups in 1 pint (pt), 2 pints in 1 quart (qt), and 4 quarts in 1 gallon (gal). For measurements of length, the inch (in) is the base unit; 12 inches make up 1 foot (ft), 3 feet make up 1 yard (yd), and 5280 feet make up 1 mile (mi). However, as there are only a set amount of units in the customary system, with extremely large or extremely small amounts of material, the numbers can become awkward and difficult to compare.

Common Customary Measurements		
Length	**Weight**	**Capacity**
1 foot = 12 inches	1 pound = 16 ounces	1 cup = 8 fluid ounces
1 yard = 3 feet	1 ton = 2,000 pounds	1 pint = 2 cups
1 yard = 36 inches		1 quart = 2 pints
1 mile = 1,760 yards		1 quart = 4 cups
1 mile = 5,280 feet		1 gallon = 4 quarts
		1 gallon = 16 cups

Metric System

Aside from the United States, most countries in the world have adopted the metric system embodied in the International System of Units (SI). The three main SI base units used in the metric system are the meter (m), the kilogram (kg), and the liter (L); meters measure length, kilograms measure mass, and liters measure volume.

These three units can use different prefixes, which indicate larger or smaller versions of the unit by powers of ten. This can be thought of as making a new unit which is sized by multiplying the original unit in size by a factor.

These prefixes and associated factors are:

Metric Prefixes			
Prefix	Symbol	Multiplier	Exponential
kilo	k	1,000	10^3
hecto	h	100	10^2
deca	da	10	10^1
no prefix		1	10^0
deci	d	0.1	10^{-1}
centi	c	0.01	10^{-2}
milli	m	0.001	10^{-3}

The correct prefix is then attached to the base. Some examples:

1 milliliter equals .001 liters.

1 kilogram equals 1,000 grams.

Choosing the Appropriate Measuring Unit
Some units of measure are represented as square or cubic units depending on the solution. For example, perimeter is measured in units, area is measured in square units, and volume is measured in cubic units.

Also be sure to use the most appropriate unit for the thing being measured. A building's height might be measured in feet or meters while the length of a nail might be measured in inches or centimeters. Additionally, for SI units, the prefix should be chosen to provide the most succinct available value. For example, the mass of a bag of fruit would likely be measured in kilograms rather than grams or milligrams, and the length of a bacteria cell would likely be measured in micrometers rather than centimeters or kilometers.

Conversion
Converting measurements in different units between the two systems can be difficult because they follow different rules. The best method is to look up an English to Metric system conversion factor and then use a series of equivalent fractions to set up an equation to convert the units of one of the

measurements into those of the other. The table below lists some common conversion values that are useful for problems involving measurements with units in both systems:

English System	Metric System
1 inch	2.54 cm
1 foot	0.3048 m
1 yard	0.914 m
1 mile	1.609 km
1 ounce	28.35 g
1 pound	0.454 kg
1 fluid ounce	29.574 mL
1 quart	0.946 L
1 gallon	3.785 L

Consider the example where a scientist wants to convert 6.8 inches to centimeters. The table above is used to find that there are 2.54 centimeters in every inch, so the following equation should be set up and solved: $6.8 \ in \ \times \ \frac{2.54 \ cm}{1 \ in} = 17.272 \ cm$. Notice how the inches in the numerator of the initial figure and the denominator of the conversion factor cancel out. (This equation could have been written simply as $6.8 \ in \ \times \ 2.54 \ cm = 17.272 \ cm$, but it was shown in detail to illustrate the steps). The goal in any conversion equation is to set up the fractions so that the units you are trying to convert from cancel out and the units you desire remain.

For a more complicated example, consider converting 2.15 kilograms into ounces. The first step is to convert kilograms into grams and then grams into ounces:

$$2.15 \ kg \ \times \frac{1000 g}{kg} = 2150 \ g$$

Then, use the conversion factor from the table to convert grams to ounces:

$$2150 g \ \times \frac{1 \ oz}{28.35 g} = 75.8 \ oz$$

Statistics and Data Analysis

Interpreting Displays of Data

A set of data can be visually displayed in various forms allowing for quick identification of characteristics of the set. Histograms, such as the one shown below, display the number of data points (vertical axis) that fall into given intervals (horizontal axis) across the range of the set. Suppose the histogram below displays IQ scores of students. Each rectangle represents the number of students with scores between a given ten-point span. For example, the furthest bar to the right indicates that five students scored between 130 and 140.

Histograms can describe the center, spread, shape, and any unusual characteristics of a data set.

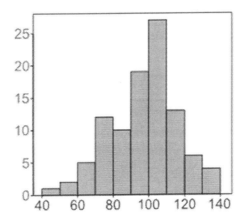

A box plot, also called a box-and-whisker plot, divides the data points into four groups and displays the five-number summary for the set, as well as any outliers. The five-number summary consists of:

- The lower extreme: the lowest value that is not an outlier
- The higher extreme: the highest value that is not an outlier
- The median of the set: also referred to as the second quartile or Q_2
- The first quartile or Q_1: the median of values below Q_2
- The third quartile or Q_3: the median of values above Q_2

To construct a box (or box-and-whisker) plot, the five-number summary for the data set is calculated as follows: the second quartile (Q_2) is the median of the set. The first quartile (Q_1) is the median of the values below Q_2. The third quartile (Q_3) is the median of the values above Q_2. The upper extreme is the highest value in the data set if it is not an outlier (greater than 1.5 times the interquartile range Q_3- Q_1). The lower extreme is the least value in the data set if it is not an outlier (more than 1.5 times lower than the interquartile range). To construct the box-and-whisker plot, each value is plotted on a number line, along with any outliers. The box consists of Q_1 and Q_3 as its top and bottom and Q_2 as the dividing line inside the box. The whiskers extend from the lower extreme to Q_1 and from Q_3 to the upper extreme.

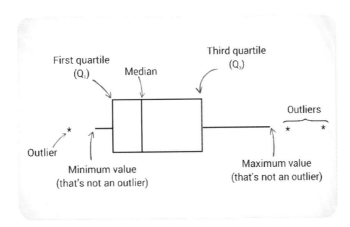

Suppose the box plot displays IQ scores for 12th grade students at a given school. The five-number summary of the data consists of: lower extreme (67); upper extreme (127); Q_2 or median (100); Q_1 (91); Q_3 (108); and outliers (135 and 140). Although all data points are not known from the plot, the points

181

are divided into four quartiles each, including 25% of the data points. Therefore, 25% of students scored between 67 and 91, 25% scored between 91 and 100, 25% scored between 100 and 108, and 25% scored between 108 and 127. These percentages include the normal values for the set and exclude the outliers. This information is useful when comparing a given score with the rest of the scores in the set.

A scatter plot is a mathematical diagram that visually displays the relationship or connection between two variables. The independent variable is placed on the x-axis, or horizontal axis, and the dependent variable is placed on the y-axis, or vertical axis. When visually examining the points on the graph, if the points model a linear relationship, or a line of best-fit can be drawn through the points with the points relatively close on either side, then a correlation exists. If the line of best-fit has a positive slope (rises from left to right), then the variables have a positive correlation. If the line of best-fit has a negative slope (falls from left to right), then the variables have a negative correlation. If a line of best-fit cannot be drawn, then no correlation exists. A positive or negative correlation can be categorized as strong or weak, depending on how closely the points are graphed around the line of best-fit.

Graphical Representation of Data

Like a scatter plot, a line graph compares variables that change continuously, typically over time. Paired data values (ordered pair) are plotted on a coordinate grid with the x- and y-axis representing the variables. A line is drawn from each point to the next, going from left to right. The line graph below displays cell phone use for given years (two variables) for men, women, and both sexes (three data sets).

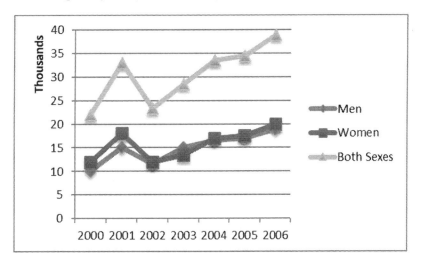

A line plot, also called dot plot, displays the frequency of data (numerical values) on a number line. To construct a line plot, a number line is used that includes all unique data values. It is marked with x's or dots above the value the number of times that the value occurs in the data set.

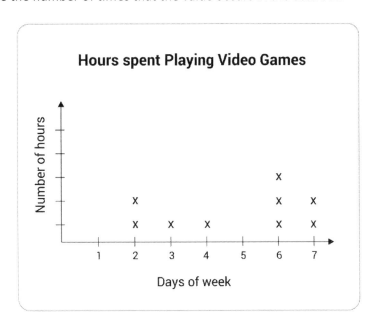

A *bar graph* is a diagram in which the quantity of items within a specific classification is represented by the height of a rectangle. Each type of classification is represented by a rectangle of equal width. Here is an example of a bar graph:

A circle graph, also called a pie chart, shows categorical data with each category representing a percentage of the whole data set. To make a circle graph, the percent of the data set for each category must be determined. To do so, the frequency of the category is divided by the total number of data points and converted to a percent. For example, if 80 people were asked what their favorite sport is and 20 responded basketball, basketball makes up 25% of the data ($\frac{20}{80}$ =.25=25%). Each category in a data set is represented by a *slice* of the circle proportionate to its percentage of the whole.

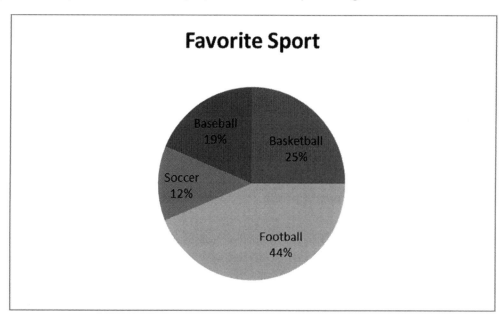

Choice of Graphs to Display Data

Choosing the appropriate graph to display a data set depends on what type of data is included in the set and what information must be displayed. Histograms and box plots can be used for data sets consisting of individual values across a wide range. Examples include test scores and incomes. Histograms and box plots will indicate the center, spread, range, and outliers of a data set. A histogram will show the shape of the data set, while a box plot will divide the set into quartiles (25% increments), allowing for comparison between a given value and the entire set.

Scatter plots and line graphs can be used to display data consisting of two variables. Examples include height and weight, or distance and time. A correlation between the variables is determined by examining the points on the graph. Line graphs are used if each value for one variable pairs with a distinct value for the other variable. Line graphs show relationships between variables.

Line plots, bar graphs, and circle graphs are all used to display categorical data, such as surveys. Line plots and bar graphs both indicate the frequency of each category within the data set. A line plot is used when the categories consist of numerical values. For example, the number of hours of TV watched by individuals is displayed on a line plot. A bar graph is used when the categories consists of words. For example, the favorite ice cream of individuals is displayed with a bar graph. A circle graph can be used to display either type of categorical data. However, unlike line plots and bar graphs, a circle graph does not indicate the frequency of each category. Instead, the circle graph represents each category as its percentage of the whole data set.

Describing a Set of Data

A set of data can be described in terms of its center, spread, shape and any unusual features. The center of a data set can be measured by its mean, median, or mode. The spread of a data set refers to how far the data points are from the center (mean or median). The spread can be measured by the range or the quartiles and interquartile range. A data set with data points clustered around the center will have a small spread. A data set covering a wide range will have a large spread.

When a data set is displayed as a histogram or frequency distribution plot, the shape indicates if a sample is normally distributed, symmetrical, or has measures of skewness or kurtosis. When graphed, a data set with a normal distribution will resemble a bell curve.

If the data set is symmetrical, each half of the graph when divided at the center is a mirror image of the other. If the graph has fewer data points to the right, the data is skewed right. If it has fewer data points to the left, the data is skewed left.

Right-Skewed   Symmetric   Left-Skewed

Kurtosis is a measure of whether the data is heavy-tailed with a high number of outliers, or light-tailed with a low number of outliers.

A description of a data set should include any unusual features such as gaps or outliers. A gap is a span within the range of the data set containing no data points. An outlier is a data point with a value either extremely large or extremely small when compared to the other values in the set.

Normal Distribution

A *normal distribution* of data follows the shape of a bell curve. In a normal distribution, the data set's median, mean, and mode are equal. Therefore, 50 percent of its values are less than the mean and 50 percent are greater than the mean. Data sets that follow this shape can be generalized using normal distributions. Normal distributions are described as *frequency distributions* in which the data set is plotted as percentages rather than true data points. A *relative frequency distribution* is one where the y-axis is between 0 and 1, which is the same as 0% to 100%. Within a standard deviation, 68 percent of the values are within 1 standard deviation of the mean, 95 percent of the values are within 2 standard deviations of the mean, and 99.7 percent of the values are within 3 standard deviations of the mean. The number of standard deviations that a data point falls from the mean is called the *z-score*. The formula for the z-score is $Z = \frac{x-\mu}{\sigma}$, where μ is the mean, σ is the standard deviation, and x is the data point. This formula is used to fit any data set that resembles a normal distribution to a standard normal distribution, in a process known as *standardizing*. Here is a normal distribution with labelled z-scores:

Normal Distribution with Labelled Z-Scores

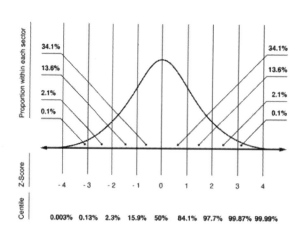

186

Population percentages can be estimated using normal distributions. For example, the probability that a data point will be less than the mean, or that the z-score will be less than 0, is 50%. Similarly, the probability that a data point will be within 1 standard deviation of the mean, or that the z-score will be between -1 and 1, is about 68.2%. When using a table, the left column states how many standard deviations (to one decimal place) away from the mean the point is, and the row heading states the second decimal place. The entries in the table corresponding to each column and row give the probability, which is equal to the area.

Measures of Center and Range

The center of a set of data (statistical values) can be represented by its mean, median, or mode. These are sometimes referred to as measures of central tendency. The mean is the average of the data set. The mean can be calculated by adding the data values and dividing by the sample size (the number of data points). Suppose a student has test scores of 93, 84, 88, 72, 91, and 77. To find the mean, or average, the scores are added and the sum is divided by 6 because there are 6 test scores:

$$\frac{93 + 84 + 88 + 72 + 91 + 77}{6} = \frac{505}{6} = 84.17$$

Given the mean of a data set and the sum of the data points, the sample size can be determined by dividing the sum by the mean. Suppose you are told that Kate averaged 12 points per game and scored a total of 156 points for the season. The number of games that she played (the sample size or the number of data points) can be determined by dividing the total points (sum of data points) by her average (mean of data points): $\frac{156}{12} = 13$. Therefore, Kate played in 13 games this season.

If given the mean of a data set and the sample size, the sum of the data points can be determined by multiplying the mean and sample size. Suppose you are told that Tom worked 6 days last week for an average of 5.5 hours per day. The total number of hours worked for the week (sum of data points) can be determined by multiplying his daily average (mean of data points) by the number of days worked (sample size): $5.5 \times 6 = 33$. Therefore, Tom worked a total of 33 hours last week.

The median of a data set is the value of the data point in the middle when the sample is arranged in numerical order. To find the median of a data set, the values are written in order from least to greatest. The lowest and highest values are simultaneously eliminated, repeating until the value in the middle remains. Suppose the salaries of math teachers are: $35,000; $38,500; $41,000; $42,000; $42,000; $44,500; $49,000. The values are listed from least to greatest to find the median. The lowest and highest values are eliminated until only the middle value remains. Repeating this step three times reveals a median salary of $42,000. If the sample set has an even number of data points, two values will remain after all others are eliminated. In this case, the mean of the two middle values is the median. Consider the following data set: 7, 9, 10, 13, 14, 14. Eliminating the lowest and highest values twice leaves two values, 10 and 13, in the middle. The mean of these values $\left(\frac{10+13}{2}\right)$ is the median. Therefore, the set has a median of 11.5.

The mode of a data set is the value that appears most often. A data set may have a single mode, multiple modes, or no mode. If different values repeat equally as often, multiple modes exist. If no value repeats, no mode exists. Consider the following data sets:

- A: 7, 9, 10, 13, 14, 14
- B: 37, 44, 33, 37, 49, 44, 51, 34, 37, 33, 44
- C: 173, 154, 151, 168, 155

Set A has a mode of 14. Set B has modes of 37 and 44. Set C has no mode.

The range of a data set is the difference between the highest and the lowest values in the set. The range can be considered the span of the data set. To determine the range, the smallest value in the set is subtracted from the largest value. The ranges for the data sets A, B, and C above are calculated as follows: A: $14 - 7 = 7$; B: $51 - 33 = 18$; C: $173 - 151 = 22$.

Best Description of a Set of Data

Measures of central tendency, namely mean, median, and mode, describe characteristics of a set of data. Specifically, they are intended to represent a *typical* value in the set by identifying a central position of the set. Depending on the characteristics of a specific set of data, different measures of central tendency are more indicative of a typical value in the set.

When a data set is grouped closely together with a relatively small range and the data is spread out somewhat evenly, the mean is an effective indicator of a typical value in the set. Consider the following data set representing the height of sixth grade boys in inches: 61 inches, 54 inches, 58 inches, 63 inches, 58 inches. The mean of the set is 58.8 inches. The data set is grouped closely (the range is only 9 inches) and the values are spread relatively evenly (three values below the mean and two values above the mean). Therefore, the mean value of 58.8 inches is an effective measure of central tendency in this case.

When a data set contains a small number of values either extremely large or extremely small when compared to the other values, the mean is not an effective measure of central tendency. Consider the following data set representing annual incomes of homeowners on a given street: $71,000; $74,000; $75,000; $77,000; $340,000. The mean of this set is $127,400. This figure does not indicate a typical value in the set, which contains four out of five values between $71,000 and $77,000. The median is a much more effective measure of central tendency for data sets such as these. Finding the middle value diminishes the influence of outliers, or numbers that may appear out of place, like the $340,000 annual income. The median for this set is $75,000 which is much more typical of a value in the set.

The mode of a data set is a useful measure of central tendency for categorical data when each piece of data is an option from a category. Consider a survey of 31 commuters asking how they get to work with results summarized below.

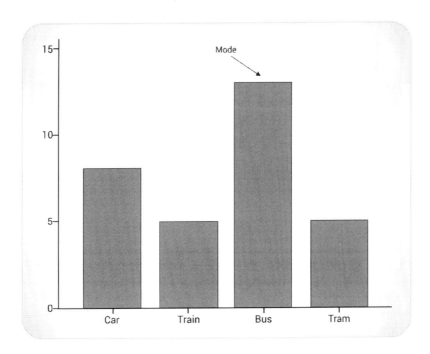

The mode for this set represents the value, or option, of the data that repeats most often. This indicates that the bus is the most popular method of transportation for the commuters.

Effects of Changes in Data
Changing all values of a data set in a consistent way produces predictable changes in the measures of the center and range of the set. A linear transformation changes the original value into the new value by either adding a given number to each value, multiplying each value by a given number, or both. Adding (or subtracting) a given value to each data point will increase (or decrease) the mean, median, and any modes by the same value. However, the range will remain the same due to the way that range is calculated. Multiplying (or dividing) a given value by each data point will increase (or decrease) the mean, median, and any modes, and the range by the same factor.

Consider the following data set, call it set P, representing the price of different cases of soda at a grocery store: $4.25, $4.40, $4.75, $4.95, $4.95, $5.15. The mean of set P is $4.74. The median is $4.85. The mode of the set is $4.95. The range is $0.90. Suppose the state passes a new tax of $0.25 on every case of soda sold. The new data set, set T, is calculated by adding $0.25 to each data point from set P. Therefore, set T consists of the following values: $4.50, $4.65, $5.00, $5.20, $5.20, $5.40. The mean of set T is $4.99. The median is $5.10. The mode of the set is $5.20. The range is $.90. The mean, median and mode of set T is equal to $0.25 added to the mean, median, and mode of set P. The range stays the same.

Now suppose, due to inflation, the store raises the cost of every item by 10 percent. Raising costs by 10 percent is calculated by multiplying each value by 1.1. The new data set, set I, is calculated by multiplying each data point from set T by 1.1. Therefore, set I consists of the following values: $4.95, $5.12, $5.50, $5.72, $5.72, $5.94. The mean of set I is $5.49. The median is $5.61. The mode of the set is

189

$5.72. The range is $0.99. The mean, median, mode, and range of set *I* is equal to 1.1 multiplied by the mean, median, mode, and range of set *T* because each increased by a factor of 10 percent.

Comparing Data

Data sets can be compared by looking at the center and spread of each set. Measures of central tendency involve median, mean, midrange, and mode. The *mode* of a data set is the data value or values that appears the most frequently. The *midrange* is equal to the maximum value plus the minimum value divided by two. The *median* is the value that is halfway into each data set; it splits the data into two intervals. The *mean* is the sum of all data values divided by the number of data points. Two completely different sets of data can have the same mean. For example, a data set having values ranging from 0 to 100 and a data set having values ranging from 44 to 46 could both have means equal to 50. The first data set would have a much wider range, which is known as the *spread* of the data. It measures how varied the data is within each set. Spread can be defined further as either interquartile range or standard deviation. The *interquartile range (IQR)* is the range of the middle fifty percent of the data set. The *standard deviation, s,* quantifies the amount of variation with respect to the mean. A lower standard deviation shows that the data set does not differ much from the mean. A larger standard deviation shows that the data set is spread out farther away from the mean. The formula for standard deviation is $s = \sqrt{\frac{\Sigma(x-\bar{x})^2}{n-1}}$, where *x* is each value in the data set, $\bar{x}$ is the mean, and *n* is the total number of data points in the sample set. The square of the standard deviation is known as the *variance* of the data set. A data set can have outliers, and measures of central tendency that are not affected by outliers are the mode and median. Those measures are labeled as resistant measures of center.

Making Inferences and Justifying Conclusions from Samples, Experiments, and Observational Studies

Data Gathering Techniques

Statistics involves making decisions and predictions about larger sets of data based on smaller data sets. The information from a small subset can help predict what happens in the entire set. The smaller data set is called a *sample* and the larger data set for which the decision is being made is called a *population.* The three most common types of data gathering techniques are sample surveys, experiments, and observational studies. *Sample surveys* involve collecting data from a random sample of people from a desired population. The measurement of the variable is only performed on this set of people. To have accurate data, the sampling must be unbiased and random. For example, surveying students in an advanced calculus class on how much they enjoy math classes is not a useful sample if the population should be all college students based on the research question. There are many methods to form a random sample, and all adhere to the fact that every sample that could be chosen has a predetermined probability of being chosen. Once the sample is chosen, statistical experiments can then be carried out to investigate real-world problems.

An *experiment* is the method in which a hypothesis is tested using a trial-and-error process. A cause and the effect of that cause are measured, and the hypothesis is accepted or rejected. Experiments are usually completed in a controlled environment where the results of a control population are compared to the results of a test population. The groups are selected using a randomization process in which each group has a representative mix of the population being tested. Finally, an *observational study* is similar to an experiment. However, this design is used when there cannot be a designed control and test population because of circumstances (e.g., lack of funding or unrealistic expectations). Instead, existing control and test populations must be used, so this method has a lack of randomization.

Interpreting Statistical Information

To make decisions concerning populations, data must be collected from a sample. The sample must be large enough to be able to make conclusions. A common way to collect data is via surveys and polls. Every survey and poll must be designed so that there is no bias. An example of a biased survey is one with loaded questions, which are either intentionally worded or ordered to obtain a desired response. Once the data is obtained, conclusions should not be made that are not justified by statistical analysis. One must make sure the difference between correlation and causation is understood. Correlation implies there is an association between two variables, and correlation does not imply causation.

Population Mean and Proportion

Both the population mean and proportion can be calculated using data from a sample. The *population mean (μ)* is the average value of the parameter for the entire population. Due to size constraints, finding the exact value of μ is impossible, so the mean of the sample population is used as an estimate instead. The larger the sample size, the closer the sample mean gets to the population mean. An alternative to finding μ is to find the *proportion* of the population, which is the part of the population with the given characteristic. The proportion can be expressed as a decimal, a fraction, or a percentage, and can be given as a single value or a range of values. Because the population mean and proportion are both estimates, there's a *margin of error*, which is the difference between the actual value and the expected value.

T-Tests

A *randomized experiment* is used to compare two treatments by using statistics involving a *t-test*, which tests whether two data sets are significantly different from one another. To use a t-test, the test statistic must follow a normal distribution. The first step of the test involves calculating the *t* value, which is given as $t = \frac{\bar{x}_1 - \bar{x}_2}{s_{\bar{x}_1 - \bar{x}_2}}$, where $\bar{x}_1$ and $\bar{x}_2$ are the averages of the two samples. Also, $s_{\bar{x}_1 - \bar{x}_2} = \sqrt{\frac{s_1^2}{n_1} + \frac{s_2^2}{n_2}}$, where s_1 and s_2 are the standard deviations of each sample and n_1 and n_2 are their respective sample sizes. The *degrees of freedom* for two samples are calculated as $df = \frac{(n_1 - 1) + (n_2 - 1)}{2}$ rounded to the lowest whole number. Also, a significance level α must be chosen, where a typical value is $\alpha = 0.05$. Once everything is compiled, the decision is made to use either a *one-tailed test* or a *two-tailed test*. If there's an assumed difference between the two treatments, a one-tailed test is used. If no difference is assumed, a two-tailed test is used.

Analyzing Test Results

Once the type of test is determined, the t-value, significance level, and degrees of freedom are applied to the published table showing the *t* distribution. The row is associated with degrees of freedom and each column corresponds to the probability. The t-value can be exactly equal to one entry or lie between two entries in a row. For example, consider a t-value of 1.7 with degrees of freedom equal to 30. This *test statistic* falls between the *p* values of 0.05 and 0.025. For a one-tailed test, the corresponding *p* value lies between 0.05 and 0.025. For a two-tailed test, the *p* values need to be doubled so the corresponding *p* value falls between 0.1 and 0.05. Once the probability is known, this range is compared to α. If $p < \alpha$, the hypothesis is rejected. If $p > \alpha$, the hypothesis isn't rejected. In a two-tailed test, this scenario means the hypothesis is accepted that there's no difference in the two treatments. In a one-tailed test, the hypothesis is accepted, indicating that there's a difference in the two treatments.

Evaluating Completed Tests

In addition to applying statistical techniques to actual testing, evaluating completed tests is another important aspect of statistics. Reports can be read that already have conclusions, and the process can be evaluated using learned concepts. For example, deciding if a sample being used is appropriate. Other things that can be evaluated include determining if the samples are randomized or the results are significant. Once statistical concepts are understood, the knowledge can be applied to many applications.

Sample Statistics

A *point estimate* is a single value used to approximate a population parameter. The sample proportion is the best point estimate of the population proportion. It is used because it is an *unbiased estimator,* meaning that it is a statistic that targets the value of the population parameter by assuming the mean of the sampling distribution is equal to the mean of the population distribution. Other unbiased estimators include the mean and variance. *Biased estimators* do not target the value of the population parameter, and such values include median, range, and standard deviation. A *confidence interval* consists of a range of values that is utilized to approximate the true value of a population parameter. The *confidence level* is the probability that the confidence interval does contain the population parameter, assuming the estimation process is repeated many times.

Population Inferences Using Distributions

Samples are used to make inferences about a population. The sampling distribution of a sample mean is a distribution of all sample means for a fixed sample size, *n*, which is part of a population. Depending on different criteria, either a binomial, normal, or geometric distribution can be used to determine probabilities. A normal distribution uses a continuous random variable, and is bell-shaped and symmetric. A binomial distribution uses a discrete random variable, has a finite number of trials, and only has two possible outcomes: a success and a failure. A geometric distribution is very similar to a binomial distribution; however, the number of trials does not have to be finite.

Creating and Interpreting Linear Regression Models

Linear Regression

Regression lines are a way to calculate a relationship between the independent variable and the dependent variable. A straight line means that there's a linear trend in the data. The average daily temperature example above is one in which a straight line represented the data because the shape of the scatterplot resembles a straight line. Technology can be used to find the equation of this line (e.g., a graphing calculator or Microsoft Excel®). In either case, all of the data points are entered, and a line is "fit" that best represents the shape of the data. Other functions used to model data sets include quadratic and exponential models.

Estimating Data Points

Regression lines can be used to estimate data points not already given. For example, if an equation of a line is found that fit the temperature and beach visitor data set, its input is the average daily temperature and its output is the projected number of visitors. Thus, the number of beach visitors on a 100-degree day can be estimated. The output is a data point on the regression line, and the number of daily visitors is expected to be greater than on a 96-degree day because the regression line has a positive slope.

Plotting and Analyzing Residuals

Once the function is found that fits the data, its accuracy can be calculated. Therefore, how well the line fits the data can be determined. The difference between the actual dependent variable from the data set and the estimated value located on the regression line is known as a *residual*. Therefore, the residual is known as the predicted value $\hat{y}$ minus the actual value y. A residual is calculated for each data point and can be plotted on the scatterplot. If all the residuals appear to be approximately the same distance from the regression line, the line is a good fit. If the residuals seem to differ greatly across the board, the line isn't a good fit.

Interpreting the Regression Line

The formula for a regression line is $y = mx + b$, where m is the slope and b is the y-intercept. Both the slope and y-intercept are found in the *Method of Least Squares*, which is the process of finding the equation of the line through minimizing residuals. The slope represents the rate of change in y as x gets larger. Therefore, because y is the dependent variable, the slope actually provides the predicted values given the independent variable. The y-intercept is the predicted value for when the independent variable equals 0. In the temperature example, the y-intercept is the expected number of beach visitors for a very cold average daily temperature of 0 degrees.

Correlation Coefficient

The *correlation coefficient (r)* measures the association between two variables. Its value is between -1 and 1, where -1 represents a perfect negative linear relationship, 0 represents no relationship, and 1 represents a perfect positive linear relationship. A *negative linear relationship* means that as x values increase, y values decrease. A *positive linear relationship* means that as x values increase, y values increase. The formula for computing the correlation coefficient is:

$$r = \frac{n(\sum xy) - (\sum x)(\sum y)}{\sqrt{n(\sum x^2) - (\sum x)^2}\sqrt{n(\sum y^2) - (\Sigma y)^2}}$$

n is the number of data points

Both Microsoft Excel® and a graphing calculator can evaluate this easily once the data points are entered. A correlation greater than 0.8 or less than -0.8 is classified as "strong" while a correlation between -0.5 and 0.5 is classified as "weak."

Correlation Versus Causation

Correlation and causation have two different meanings. If two values are correlated, there is an association between them. However, correlation doesn't necessarily mean that one variable causes the other. *Causation* (or "cause and effect") occurs when one variable causes the other. Average daily temperature and number of beachgoers are correlated and have causation. If the temperature increases, the change in weather causes more people to go to the beach. However, alcoholism and smoking are correlated but don't have causation. The more someone drinks the more likely they are to smoke but drinking alcohol doesn't cause someone to smoke.

Regression Models

Regression lines are straight lines that calculate a relationship between nonlinear data involving an independent variable and a dependent variable. A regression line is of the form $y = mx + b$, where m is the slope and b is the y-intercept. Both the slope and y-intercept are found using the *Method of Least Squares*, which involves minimizing residuals – the difference between the dependent variable from the data set and the estimated value located on the regression line. The slope represents the rate of change in y as x increases. The y-intercept is the predicted value when the independent variable is equal to 0. Technology, such as a graphing calculator or Microsoft Excel®, can also be utilized to find the equation of this line. In either case, the data points are entered, and a line is "fit" that best represents the shape of the data.

Here is an example of a data set and its regression line:

The Regression Line is the Line of Best Fit

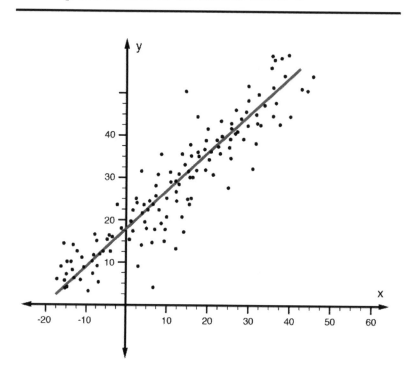

Regression models are highly used for forecasting, and linear regression techniques are the simplest models. If the nonlinear data follows the shape of exponential, logarithmic, or power functions, those types of functions can be used to more accurately model the data rather than lines.

Here is an example of both an exponential regression and a logarithmic regression model:

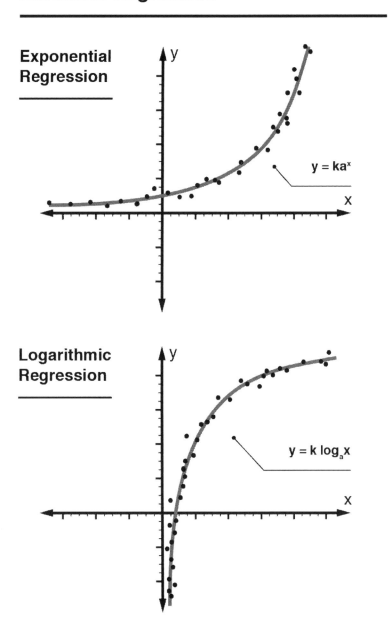

Nonlinear Regression

Exponential Regression

$y = ka^x$

Logarithmic Regression

$y = k \log_a x$

The Law of Large Numbers and the Central Limit Theorem

The *Law of Large Numbers* states that as the number of experiments increase, the actual ratio of outcomes will approach the theoretical probability. The *Central Limit Theorem* states that through using a sufficiently large sample size N, meaning over 30, the sampling distribution of the mean approaches a normal distribution with a mean of μ and variance of σ^2/N. The variance of the actual population is σ^2 and its mean is μ. In other words, as the sample size increases, the distribution will behave normally.

Estimating Parameters

A point estimate of a population parameter is a single statistic. For example, the sample mean is a point estimate of the population mean. Once all calculations are made, a confidence interval is used to express the accuracy of the sampling method used. The confidence interval consists of a confidence level, the statistic, and a margin of error. A 95% confidence level indicates that 95% of all confidence intervals will contain the population parameter. Also, the margin of error gives a range of values above and below the sample statistic, which helps to form a confidence interval.

The Principles of Hypotheses Testing

The P-value approach to hypothesis testing involves assuming a null hypothesis is true and then determining the probability of a test statistic in the direction of the alternative hypothesis. The test statistic is defined as the t-statistic $t^* = \frac{\bar{x}-\mu}{s/\sqrt{n}}$, which follows a t-distribution with n-1 degrees of freedom. The P-value is then calculated as the probability that if the null hypothesis is true, a more extreme test statistic in the direction of the alternative hypothesis would be observed. A significance level, α, is set (usually at 0.05 or 0.001) and the P-value is compared to α. If $P \leq \alpha$, one rejects the null hypothesis and accepts the alternative hypothesis. If $P > \alpha$, one accepts the null hypothesis.

Measuring Probabilities with Two-Way Frequency Tables

When measuring event probabilities, two-way frequency tables can be used to report the raw data and then used to calculate probabilities. If the frequency tables are translated into relative frequency tables, the probabilities presented in the table can be plugged directly into the formulas for conditional probabilities. By plugging in the correct frequencies, the data from the table can be used to determine if events are independent or dependent.

Differing Probabilities

The probability that event A occurs differs from the probability that event A occurs given B. When working within a given model, it's important to note the difference. $P(A|B)$ is determined using the formula $P(A|B) = \frac{P\ (A \text{ and } B)}{P(B)}$ and represents the total number of A's outcomes left that could occur after B occurs. $P(A)$ can be calculated without any regard for B. For example, the probability of a student finding a parking spot on a busy campus is different once class is in session.

Uniform and Non-Uniform Probability Models

A *uniform probability model* is one where each outcome has an equal chance of occurring, such as the probabilities of rolling each side of a die. A *non-uniform probability model* is one where each outcome has an unequal chance of occurring. In a uniform probability model, the conditional probability formulas for $P(B|A)$ and $P(A|B)$ can be multiplied by their respective denominators to obtain two formulas for $P(A \text{ and } B)$. Therefore, the multiplication rule is derived as $P(A \text{ and } B) = P(A)P(B|A) = P(B)P(A|B)$. In a model, if the probability of either individual event is known and the corresponding conditional probability is known, the multiplication rule allows the probability of the joint occurrence of A and B to be calculated.

Binomial Experiments

In statistics, a *binomial experiment* is where each trial can have only two possible outcomes: a success or a failure. An example of a binomial experiment is rolling a die 10 times with the goal of rolling a 5. Rolling a 5 is a success while any other value is a failure. In a binomial experiment, each event is independent of the others, and the probability of success is constant in every event. In this example, each roll of the die has nothing do to with the others and the probability of rolling a 5 is $^1/_6$. In any binomial experiment, x is the number of resulting successes, n is the number of trials, P is the probability of success in each trial, and $Q = 1 - P$ is the probability of failure within each trial. The probability of obtaining x successes within n trials is $\binom{n}{x} P^x (1 - P)^{n-x}$, where $\binom{n}{x} = \frac{n!}{x!(n-x)!}$ is the binomial coefficient. Within its calculation, $n!$ is n factorial that's defined as $n \cdot (n - 1) \cdot (n - 2) \cdots 2 \cdot 1$. Therefore, the probability of obtaining four rolls of a 5 in 10 trials is $\binom{10}{4} \left(\frac{1}{6}\right)^4 \left(\frac{5}{6}\right)^6$.

Statistical Questions

A statistical question is answered by collecting data with variability. Data consists of facts and/or statistics (numbers), and variability refers to a tendency to shift or change. Data is a broad term, inclusive of things like height, favorite color, name, salary, temperature, gas mileage, and language. Questions requiring data as an answer are not necessarily statistical questions. If there is no variability in the data, then the question is not statistical in nature. Consider the following examples: what is Mary's favorite color? How much money does your mother make? What was the highest temperature last week? How many miles did your car get on its last tank of gas? How much taller than Bob is Ed?

None of the above are statistical questions because each case lacks variability in the data needed to answer the question. The questions on favorite color, salary, and gas mileage each require a single piece of data, whether a fact or statistic. Therefore, variability is absent. Although the temperature question requires multiple pieces of data (the high temperature for each day), a single, distinct number is the answer. The height question requires two pieces of data, Bob's height and Ed's height, but no difference in variability exists between those two values. Therefore, this is not a statistical question. Statistical questions typically require calculations with data.

Consider the following statistical questions:

How many miles per gallon of gas does the 2016 Honda Civic get? To answer this question, data must be collected. This data should include miles driven and gallons used. Different cars, different drivers, and different driving conditions will produce different results. Therefore, variability exists in the data. To answer the question, the mean (average) value could be determined.

Are American men taller than Chinese men? To answer this question, data must be collected. This data should include the heights of American men and the heights of Chinese men. All American men are not the same height and all Chinese men are not the same height. Some American men are taller than some Chinese men and some Chinese men are taller than some American men. Therefore, variability exists in the data. To answer the question, the median values for each group could be determined and compared.

The following are more examples of statistical questions: What proportion of 4th graders have a favorite color of blue? How much money do teachers make? Is it colder in Boston or Chicago?

Statistical Processes

Samples and Populations
Statistics involves making decisions and predictions about larger data sets based on smaller data sets. Basically, the information from one part or subset can help predict what happens in the entire data set or population at large. The entire process involves guessing, and the predictions and decisions may not be 100 percent correct all of the time; however, there is some truth to these predictions, and the decisions do have mathematical support. The smaller data set is called a *sample* and the larger data set (in which the decision is being made) is called a *population*. A *random sample* is used as the sample,

which is an unbiased collection of data points that represents the population as well as it can. There are many methods of forming a random sample, and all adhere to the fact that every potential data point has a predetermined probability of being chosen.

Goodness of Fit

Goodness of fit tests show how well a statistical model fits a given data set. They allow the differences between the observed and expected quantities to be summarized to determine if the model is consistent with the results. The *Chi-Squared Goodness of Fit Test* (or *Chi-Squared Test* for short) is used with one categorical variable from one population, and it concludes whether or not the sample data is consistent with a hypothesized distribution. Chi-Squared is evaluated using the following formula: $\chi^2 = \sum \frac{(O-E)^2}{E}$, where O is the observed frequency value and E is the expected frequency value. Also, the *degree of freedom* must be calculated, which is the number of categories in the data set minus one. Then a Chi-Squared table is used to test the data. The *degree of freedom value* and a *significance value,* such as 0.05, are located on the table. The corresponding entry represents a critical value.

If the calculated χ^2 is greater than the critical value, the data set does not work with the statistical model. If the calculated χ^2 is less than the critical value, the statistical model can be used.

Communications

This knowledge area encompasses a general understanding of the principles of effective communication and public-speaking techniques, as well as general knowledge of public media, media relations, and the goals and techniques of public diplomacy and their use to support work functions.

Principles of Effective Communication

Good public speakers all have several characteristics in common. It is not enough to simply write a speech, but it must also be delivered in a manner that is both engaging and succinct. The following qualities are inherent to good public speaking.

Confidence is possibly the most important attribute a speaker can have. It instills trust in the listener that the person knows what he or she is talking about and that he or she is credible and competent. Confidence is displayed by making brief eye contact—about 2-3 seconds—with different members of the audience to demonstrate that the speaker is engaged. It is also displayed in his or her tone of voice—strong, light-hearted, and natural. A nervous speaker can easily be identified by a small, quivering voice. Confidence is also conveyed by the speaker facing the audience; turning one's back may demonstrate insecurity.

Authenticity is another quality of an effective speaker, as it makes a person more relatable and believable to the audience. Speeches that are memorized word-for-word can give the impression of being inauthentic as the monologue does not flow quite naturally, especially if the speaker accidentally fumbles or forgets. Memorizing speeches can also lead to a monotonous tone, which is sure to put the audience to sleep, or worse, a misinterpreted tone, which can cause the audience to stop listening entirely or even become offended. Therefore, speeches should be practiced with a natural intonation and not be memorized mechanically.

Connection with the audience is another important aspect of public speaking. Speakers should engage with their listeners by the use of storytelling and visual or auditory aids, as well as asking questions that the audience can participate in. Visual and auditory aids could range from an interesting PowerPoint presentation to a short video clip to physical objects the audience can pass around to a soundtrack. The use of appropriate humor also allows the audience to connect with the speaker on a more personal level and will make the speech sound more like a conversation than a one-sided lecture. Speakers who are passionate about their subject inspire their listeners to care about what they're saying; they transfer their energy into the audience. This level of connection will encourage their listeners to want to be there.

Succinctness and *purposeful repetition* ensures that the audience's attention remains focused on the message at hand. Repeating the overall point of the speech in different ways helps listeners remember what the speaker is trying to tell them, even when the speech is over. A speech that is longer than necessary will cause listeners to become bored and stop absorbing information. Keeping the speech short and sweet and leaving more time for questions at the end will ensure that the audience stays engaged.

There are many different styles a speaker can utilize, but the most important thing speakers should keep in mind is maintaining a connection with the audience. This will help ensure that the audience will remain open and focused enough to hear and absorb the message.

Public Speaking

All information should be presented with a clear beginning, middle, and end. Distinct organization always makes any work more clear, concise, and logical. For a presentation, this should involve choosing a primary topic and then discussing it in the following format:

- Introducing the speaker and the main topic
- Providing evidence, supporting details, further explanation of the topic in the main body
- Concluding it with a firm resolution and repetition of the main point

The beginning, middle, and end should also be linked with effective transitions that make the presentation flow well. For example, a presentation should always begin with an introduction by the speaker, including what he/she does and what he/she is there to present. Good transitional introductions may begin with statements such as *For those who do not know me, my name is...*, *As many of you know, I am...* or *Good morning everyone, my name is ___, and I am the new project manager*. A good introduction grabs the attention and interest of the audience.

After an introduction has been made, the speaker will then want to state the purpose of the presentation with a natural transition, such as *I am here to discuss the latest editions to our standard of procedure...* or *This afternoon, I would like to present the results of our latest findings*. Once the purpose has been identified, the speaker will want to adhere to the main idea announced. The presenter should be certain to keep the main idea to one sentence as too much information can confuse an audience; an introduction should be succinct and to the point.

Supporting information should always be presented in concise, easy-to-read formats such as bullet points or lists—if visual aids are presented during the presentation. Good transitions such as *Let's begin with...* or *Now to look at...* make the presentation flow smoothly and logically, helping listeners to keep ideas organized as they are presented. Keeping the material concise is extremely important in a presentation, and visual aids should be used only to emphasize points or explain ideas. All the supporting information should relate back to the main idea, avoiding unnecessary tangents.

Finally, a firm conclusion involves repeating the main point of the presentation by either inspiring listeners to act or by reiterating the most important points made in the speech. It should also include an expression of gratitude to the audience as well as transition to opening the floor for questions.

Public Media

Mass media refers to the various methods by which the majority of the general public receives news and information. Mass media includes television, newspapers, radio, magazines, online news outlets, and social media networks. The general public relies on mass media for political knowledge and cultural socialization, as well as the majority of their knowledge of current events, social issues, and political news.

Evolution of Mass Media
- Until the end of the nineteenth century, print media such as newspapers and magazines was the only form of mass communication.

- In the 1890s, after the invention of the radio, broadcast media become a popular form of communication, particularly among illiterate people.

- In the 1940s, television superseded both print and broadcast media as the most popular form of mass media.

- In 1947, President Harry Truman gave the first political speech on television.

- In 1952, Dwight Eisenhower was the first political candidate to air campaign ads on television.

- Today, the Internet is the most widespread mass media technology, and citizens have instant access to news and information, as well as interactive platforms on which they can communicate directly with political leaders or share their views through social media, blogs, and independent news sites.

Influence of Mass Media on Politics

Mass media has a powerful effect on public opinion and politics. Mass media:

- Shapes public interests

- Enables candidates to reach voters wherever they are

- Determines what is and is not considered important in society based on how it prioritizes events and issues

- Provides the context in which to report events

- Is paid for by advertisers who may pressure news outlets to suppress or report information in their own interests

Media Relations

Media relations is the relationship between the media and an organization. Organizations work with the media in order to build credibility with the public and inform the public on certain decisions being made within the organization, from policies to proposals. More specifically, media relations involve the specific relationships between journalists and the organization itself. The risk involved in creating media relations through an organization is that the organization has no control over what the media puts out. Thus, it's important to develop a positive relationship between the media and the organization. Usually, an organization will have one person or a media relations personnel to deal with journalists, editors, and/or reporters regarding what the story or information involves.

Media relations personnel should be knowledgeable of different media outlets, such as blogs, television, and radio, and must be informed of the angle of different news sources, their relationships with the public, and the types of stories they like to produce. Knowledge of this type of information will ensure that the personnel will find the most appropriate media source for their purposes. Personnel must also be aware what audience each media outlet has and thus choose the media with the knowledge of that particular audience in mind.

Purposes for an organization to use media relations may include ways to boost the organization's presence in the public, information that's important to public interest, launch of products or services, engagement in community service or activities, or simply negative publicity that is going to come out anyway.

Again, developing a positive relationship with the media is important for media relations; one of the main goals of using media relations is so that the organization will be viewed in a positive light by the public. Some of the mediums used in relations are named in the following list:

Newspaper: Newspapers are popular for local ads and news. They usually rely on people paying for the newspaper or payment from businesses purchasing ad space. Newspapers are a great way to reach a dedicated local audience.

Internet: The internet is a media source used to reach a global platform. The internet has multiple mediums to reach different kinds of audiences. These include online articles from reputable news companies, video games, blogs, websites, etc. The following is a list of common types of tools used for digital media:

- Smartphones/apps
- Email
- Microsoft Office
- iMovie
- Skype
- Twitter
- Facebook
- Instagram
- Google Drive
- Various blogging websites
- Online bulletin boards
- Wikis
- Podcasts

Broadcasting: Broadcasting is used in film or radio, and it's considered a sequencing of radio or film shows that are put in a particular order for an audience. Through broadcasting, multiple shows can be put out at the same time, or sometimes a broadcasting network will be split or shared between two networks.

Television: Television is another popular form of media communications, as many channels feature news programs on air. Some journalists must work with both television and social media and make sure their message is appropriate for both mediums. The intermingling of social media and television is a new phenomenon that should not be ignored by media relations personnel.

Public Diplomacy

Diplomacy is the act of meeting with officials from foreign states to discuss matters of international interest, foster harmonious relationships, organize international partnerships, broker agreements, and resolve disputes. *Public diplomacy* is different in that it is designed to circulate information to a foreign public in order to advance goals of foreign or national policy. Public diplomacy is done in a transparent way as possible, and is often called "people's diplomacy." Countries will conduct public diplomacy in such a way as to send a positive image of their country to a receiving country's public.

For example, Canada participated in public diplomacy in 2015 when they worked with a certain story within the media to showcase the acceptance of Syrian refugees into their country. Millions of Syrians witnessing a devastating civil war sought refuge in countries elsewhere, only to find themselves and their families turned away from sanctuary. Canada's actions, however, led by Prime Minister Justin Trudeau, welcomed the Syrians into their country, charming many countries in the process.

Public diplomacy uses many different mediums, such as educational exchange programs, language training, visitor programs, broadcasting, and certain cultural exchanges.

Diplomacy
States conduct diplomacy to negotiate compromises between states; accomplish militaristic, economic, environmental, and humanitarian goals; and garner allies in case of future crisis or conflict.

Diplomacy remains front and center to any efforts within a country or between countries to minimize conflict and, in many cases, maximize cooperation. Both cooperation and conflict are necessary in order for diplomacy to truly prosper; if there is no conflict, there is no need for diplomacy, and if there is no cooperation, there can be no common ground for establishing any diplomatic efforts.

Diplomacy is thought of as a management of international relations by way of negotiations, typically carried out by ambassadors or diplomats. It is regarded as a machine for action in times of conflict, and is used as the first line of defense in disagreements. Diplomacy is usually defined in bilateral terms, but given the increase in power of international conferences and organizations, diplomacy measures are characterized by a semblance of plurality, thus becoming multilateral in nature. Concerning the means of diplomacy, there are six main devices:

- Persuasion: This is clearly the first line of defense in that logical cases can be presented without overhead or other bargaining devices

- Rewards: A state can offer another state goods or services in exchange for accepting their policy measures

- Promise of rewards and concessions: Diplomats can offer reassurance that, if their policy measures are accepted, then the country will match their investment

- Threat of use of force: Diplomacy, by its very definition, cannot preclude violence; however, there can be ultimatum, boycotts, walkouts, or even threat of war should the parties continue to disagree

- Non-violent punishment: The opposite of rewarding, punishment can come in the form of non-violence.

- Use of pressure: Diplomatic efforts that fall under the use of pressure include propaganda, exploitation of events, and creation of scenes or situations that seek to change opposing parties' views

Management Principles, Psychology, and Human Behavior

Basic Management and Supervisory Techniques and Methods (PHR)

Generally speaking, there are four basic functions of management: planning, organizing, directing, and controlling. Let's consider all four in greater detail. Before everything, an organization must develop a plan. An organization's plan is its roadmap to success, pinpointing its future goals and recommending the best course of action to reach them. In order to carry out the plan, careful organizing is essential. Organizing involves structuring tasks, locating and acquiring sufficient resources (human resources, financial resources, etc.) to complete tasks, and allocating those resources appropriately. Next is directing, also known as leading or commanding. Directing is people management: giving clear direction, feedback, and motivation to staff so that employees know what is expected of them and can complete their work as effectively as possible. The last function of management is controlling, which is when management evaluates performance by establishing standards, measuring performance based on these standards, and making adjustments as necessary.

Establishing Relationships: Organization and Individuals
In order to best serve its organization, HR must have good relationships with other departments and individuals within the organization. The key to any relationship is communication. HR should maintain open dialogue with other departments and help managers with any employee-related issues. While HR must ensure that departments comply with company policies, it's better to coach and educate managers about following policy rather than complaining about every mistake. When HR is a team player and not just a distant authority figure, it's easier for managers to approach HR and solve problems together.

In this way, HR can also demonstrate its usefulness in aiding organization decisions. Any change in the organization will inevitably affect employees, so HR can help balance the needs of the organization with the needs of workers and advise on decisions that will satisfy everyone. HR also acts as a bridge between executive decisions in the organization and how those decisions will be translated into new policies and procedures.

Managing Organizational Change
In order to remain competitive, adopt industry best practices, and adapt to changing markets, an organization will undergo change at many points. Change might be undertaken to benefit company shareholders and increase the profitability of the company. Change can also occur to reduce costs and increase efficiency. However, especially from an HR perspective, it's important to keep in mind how change affects employees. The truth is that most people don't like change. Also, work force changes in particular (such as outsourcing or downsizing) are certain to be met with employee resistance. Even more minor changes like revised vacation policies may go through an unpopular adjustment period. Change management helps to smooth over these difficulties.

Change Management
Change is inevitable for any organization, especially in fields affected by global markets and technological innovation. Change management seeks to aid organizations through significant transitions in resource allocation, operations, business processes, or any other large-scale changes. Careful change management helps the organization to function effectively even while undergoing a major evolution.

Implementing Change

How should an organization implement change? The classic 1961 text *The Planning of Change* tackles this question. The book outlines three strategies for managing change: the empirical-rational strategy, the normative-reductive strategy, and the power-coercive strategy.

The empirical-rational strategy assumes that people are rational and will naturally follow any course that's in their self-interest. Therefore, they are likelier to accept change when they think it will directly benefit them. To implement change in line with this strategy, an organization must either 1) demonstrate the benefit of the change or 2) demonstrate the harm of the status quo (or both). One way of accomplishing this is to incentivize change. For example, a growing company is gaining new employees, but it doesn't want to expand its available parking. The company decides to limit the number of parking spots and encourage public transportation use. Employees are reluctant to give up the freedom to drive, so the company holds an educational seminar about how to save money by using public transportation and also offers monthly reimbursement for employees who use public transportation.

The next approach proposed in *The Planning of Change* is the normative-reeducative strategy. This strategy assumes that people will closely follow social norms and expectations. In order to implement change, it's necessary to first change people's idea of what is socially acceptable. This is the strategy that harnesses the power of advertising. For example, think of anti-tobacco advertising campaigns over the past few decades. Throughout most of the twentieth century, smoking was socially acceptable just about anywhere. However, especially in the 1990s and 2000s, aggressive anti-smoking advertisements attacked the tobacco industry and started anti-smoking education programs for students. The social norm turned *against* smoking in most public places, and now there are more anti-smoking laws than ever before.

Finally, the power-coercive strategy assumes that people are followers who will listen to authority and do as they are told. This approach to change is basically, "My way or the highway!" Where the empirical-rational strategy seeks to demonstrate how change will benefit employees, the power-coercive strategy says that *not* following change will be *harmful* to employees, who might be punished or even fired for failure to comply. For example, a factory undergoes an intense safety inspection and decides to completely renovate its safety standards. Employees now have new dress code requirements. If they don't follow the dress code, they aren't allowed to work that day; after the third dress code violation, they will be fired.

Deciding which strategy to employ depends on the overall character of the organization (for example, an otherwise friendly and collegial office might respond negatively to usage of the power-coercive strategy) as well as the importance and sensitivity of the change (the power-coercive strategy would be useful for changes with clear legal or financial liabilities, such as when an organization must follow new government regulations).

Reinforcing Value and Expectations

HR is responsible for formulating and enforcing policies about employee behavior. Of course, HR must first educate employees about the organization's expectations. Let's look at some approaches to developing desired behaviors.

Communication

The first step of any business interaction is communication. No matter how carefully an idea is researched and planned, it could all fall apart if it isn't properly communicated to those who must carry it out. For this reason, all HR policies must be clearly communicated to employees, particularly when new policies are enacted or when the same HR issues occur often. Communication can occur in a variety of ways, such as through e-mail, individual interviews, or department meetings.

Modeling

Modeling provides a hands-on approach to teaching new behaviors. Some can learn quickly from reading a book or listening to a presentation. For others, the easiest way to learn is by doing—or by watching other people. Employees can learn new behaviors and skills by watching a manager or trainer perform them first. However, while training situations may involve formal modeling, employees also learn from informal modeling as they observe the behavior of other workers. So it's important to enforce HR policies at all levels of an organization, including upper management. If managers are getting away with unacceptable behaviors like sneaking out of work early or using abusive language in the office, other employees can learn from that modeled undesirable behavior. Both formal and informal modeling should provide positive examples for workers.

Coaching

HR coaching helps employees achieve their potential and continue to develop their skills, matching them with the needs of the organization. Through evaluations and employee self-assessments, HR can nurture strengths while providing training to overcome weaknesses. Coaching can also help employees progress on their career path by identifying areas for advancement within the organization. This gives employees an incentive to stay with the organization and pursue self-improvement goals.

Human Psychology and Behavior

There are many different theoretical perspectives to explain human behavior. The following are some of the most prevalent approaches to understanding human behavior.

The *systems approach* seeks to evaluate and explain human behavior as the individual interacts with the different social systems that they are a part of, including the family, community, and work environment. The systems approach emphasizes the importance of a person's perceived role in society or family, such as father, wife, or student. The Stanford Prison Experiment of 1971 confirmed the importance of social roles, when students—who were given the roles of guards and prisoners in a simulated prison experience—began to dramatically and even dangerously adopt those roles.

Another important theory to explain human behavior is the *conflict theory,* which focuses on division of power, oppression, and conflict between social groups and within social systems, and what happens when groups or people have competing interests. Recently in social work, with an increased emphasis on social justice, the conflict theory has gained more influence as it looks at dominant and privileged groups as contrasted with oppressed and underprivileged populations.

The *rational choice* or *social exchange perspective* explains human behavior in the context of the social give and take of resources. Each person is making rational choices in their interactions with others, primarily motivated by selfish reasons and with the desire to minimize costs to themselves, while maximizing the benefits received.

The *social constructionist perspective* has to do with how people derive meaning from their world and how they analyze and classify society around them. Socially and culturally, shared understandings are developed about people and their places in the world, which leads to an ever-changing social construct.

The *psychodynamic theory*, built on Freud's work, emphasizes the unconscious and internal drives and motives that rule human behavior. Some other important components of the psychodynamic perspective are the significance of childhood experiences and the use of defense mechanisms as a means of protection from unacceptable feelings and impulses.

As previously discussed, the *developmental perspective* looks at how humans grow and change throughout the lifespan and the impact that this has on human behavior. At each stage of life, there are different emotional, physical, and psychological changes that occur, and there are different developmental tasks that must be overcome.

Another way of explaining human behavior is the *social learning perspective*, built on the idea that people learn how to behave as they interact with their environment. This learning may take place through classical conditioning, which is the development of automatic responses to stimuli in the environment, or operant conditioning, in which the behaviors that are rewarded increase, and the behaviors that are punished decrease. The third form of learning is observational learning, which explains how people learn the behaviors that are modeled for them.

Finally, *the humanistic approach* emphasizes the uniqueness, individuality, free will, and value of each human being. Human behavior is viewed as an attempt to reach toward self-actualization and to find a sense of purpose and fulfillment. Abraham Maslow, a renowned humanist psychologist, developed his hierarchy of needs to explain the human progression from having basic needs met to becoming self-transcendent.

Strengths-Based and Resilience Theories
Rather than focusing on problems and pathology, the strengths perspective (or *strengths-based approach*) in social work encourages social workers to focus on a client's strengths or assets and to build upon the client's inherent resiliency and positive characteristics. Outcome studies regarding use of the strengths perspective are limited. However, it is posited that a strength-based approach could help to remove some of the stigma attached to groups or to conditions (e.g., mental illness, poverty).

Defense Mechanisms and Human Behavior
Sigmund Freud's *psychoanalytic theory* focused on the conflicts, drives, and unacceptable desires in the unconscious mind and how they affect a person. One method of dealing with unconscious conflicts is through *defense mechanisms*, which are the mind's way of protecting a person from unacceptable thoughts. Here are some of the most common defense mechanisms:

- *Repression* is when a person suppresses thoughts or memories that are too difficult to handle. They are pushed out of the conscious mind, and a person may experience memory loss or have psychogenic amnesia related to those memories.

- *Displacement* takes place when someone displaces the feelings they have toward one person, such as anger, and puts it on another person who may be less threatening. For example, someone may express anger toward a spouse, even if they are really angry with a boss.

- *Sublimation* is when the socially unacceptable thought is transformed into healthy, acceptable creativity in another direction. Pain may become poetry, for example.

- *Rationalization* is when unacceptable feelings or thoughts are rationally and logically explained and defended.

- *Reaction formation* occurs when the negative feeling is covered up by a false or exaggerated version of its opposite. In such a case, a person may display strong feelings of affection toward someone, though internally and unconsciously hate that person.

- *Denial* is refusing to accept painful facts or situations and instead acting as if they are not true or have not happened.

- *Projection* is putting one's own feelings onto someone else and acting as if they are the one who feels that way instead of oneself.

Group Theories

The following is a list of groups in social work that individuals use for greater social functioning and fellowship in order to learn better coping skills.

The *Mutual Aid Model* is derived from theoretical work by social work pioneer, William Schwartz. This model is also referred to as self-help or support groups. Clients within the group need and help each other as they tackle problems that are common across group members. This model is commonly used with groups focused on substance abuse.

Cognitive-behavioral group work utilizes cognitive-behavioral therapy (CBT) interventions, initially used in individual work and applies those interventions to a group setting. Although mutual aid is not emphasized or a core component, group discussion is valued, and group members do interact with each other. The focus is on learning skills and changing behavior in order for individuals to function more effectively.

Systems-Centered therapy groups are based on the work of Yvonne Agazarian (*Theory of Living Human Systems*). Human systems have energy and use that energy for survival, development, and mastery of the environment. Group members use functional subgrouping to work together, explore similarities and differences, learn perspective taking, and resolve conflicts.

Interpersonal Learning Groups were made well known by Irvin Yalom, a pioneer in group theory and practice. This approach uses group interaction as the mechanism for achieving awareness, insight, and change. The leader of the group must facilitate interpersonal learning.

Systems and Ecological Perspectives

Systems Theory in social work refers to the view that human behavior is explained by the influences of the various systems to which individuals belong. When evaluating and conceptualizing an individual's behavior, that behavior must be considered in the context of the individual's family, society, and other systems.

- All systems are seen as possessing interrelated parts and exerting influence on each other.

- There are many iterations of the premise of the basic systems theory.

- In practice, systems theory allows a social worker to understand the dynamics of a client's systems better, while also creating an appropriate intervention approach.

- The originator of systems theory in social work was Ludwig von Bertalanffy, a biologist, who was influenced by sociologists Max Weber and Emile Durkheim.

Talcott Parsons expanded on earlier work with his framework of *structural functionalism,* which proposes that a system is defined by its function in its social environment.

Four states of social systems:

- Adaptation to the social environment
- Goal attainment
- Integration with other systems
- Latency or homeostasis (social patterns and norms are maintained)

Designations of social systems in social work:

- Microsystems: small systems (e.g., an individual or a couple)
- Mezzosystems: medium-sized systems (e.g., extended families, groups to which the individual belongs)
- Macrosystems: large systems (e.g., organizations, communities)

The *ecological systems perspective* is concerned with the transactions between systems:

- People and families must be considered within cultural and societal contexts, which also necessitates examining the events that have occurred in an individual's life.

- Changes made by the individual that cause the entire system to shift must also be considered.

Common interventions based on systems theory:

- Strengthening a part of the system in order to improve the whole system

- Creating a genogram: a family tree constructed with a client in order to improve understanding of the familial relationships and to identify recurring patterns

- Connecting clients to organizations or individuals who can help them to function better within and between their systems

- Developing an ecomap: an Illustration of client's systems, such as family and community and how it changes over time

Person-in-Environment
Carel Germain described person-in environment interaction, based upon earlier work in systems theory. This perspective takes into consideration an individual's environmental and systemic influences. It is specific to social work, which differentiates it from other like professions.

- Life stress: the normal tension that occurs as the result of both external demands and internal experiences. What is experienced as stressful varies across people and their perceptions. For example, two people placed in the same environment may have completely different experiences due to the ways in which they experience and perceive the situation.

- Adaptation: when the environment and the individual change in response to the interaction with each other

- Coping: individual use of one's own strengths and problem-solving abilities to navigate life stress and develop self-esteem and hope

- Power: a source of stress to the individual and the larger system misused by groups

- Human relatedness: the ability of individuals to cultivate relationships

- Three related concepts are *self-direction*, *competence*, and *self-esteem*. These attributes are interdependent and occur cross-culturally.

Impact of Social Institutions on Society
Social institutions exist to meet the needs of individuals, promote pro-social behavior, define social norms, and create order.

There are five major social institutions:

Family
- Regulates sexual behavior (monogamy)
- Creates and provides for new society members
- Socializes new society members

Religion
- Provides explanations for the unexplainable
- Supports societal norms and values
- Provides a means of coping with life situations

Government
- Institutionalizes norms (by creating laws)
- Enforces laws
- Protects members of society
- Provides a means of resolving conflict

Education
- Prepares society members to contribute to the society in specified roles
- Teaches skills necessary to function within the society

Economics
- Produces and distributes goods needed by society members
- Provides services necessary to the society

Social Change and Community Development Theories
Community development theory focuses on oppressed people who are in the process of overcoming social problems that were imposed upon them by external forces. In the process of community development, members of a community learn how to improve that community and gain control of their local environment. *Community-level change* brings people together and demonstrates the power of solidarity. This theory also acknowledges the reality that many problems are at the social, rather than individual, level. An implication of the theory is that therapy addresses only the symptoms of a problem and not the underlying causes.

<u>The Influence of Social Context on Behavior</u>
There are many ways in which a social context can influence individual behavior, either positively or negatively. Social psychology looks at the person-environment interaction and explores the many ways the social setting influences a person's attitudes and actions.

Attitudes toward, and influenced by, those around play a major role in a person's behaviors. *Attribution theory* has to do with how one views the behavior of others, whether attributing their behaviors to disposition or situation. If one wrongly attributes someone's negative action to their disposition—the *fundamental attribution error*—then one may think more negatively about others than is deserved.

The concept of *conformity*—the tendency for a person to conform personal behaviors to the behaviors of those around them—helps explain everything from style trends to mass genocide. Solomon Asch performed a study that showed that people tend to conform to the people around them, even if it means giving an answer they know is false. The phenomenon of conformity stems from the idea that people act in a way to get approval from others and to avoid disapproval, called *normative social influence*. Another impact of the social sphere that people live in is *deindividuation*, in which a person loses a sense of personal responsibility or individualism. This may happen in crowds at a concert or sports event, or a riot, leading people to behave in ways they would not normally behave if they did not feel anonymous and emotionally charged by the social setting.

People tend to automatically form groups, often developing the in-group and out-group concepts. The *in-group* consists of those who are part of the group, who share its identity and unifying characteristics. The *out-group* consists of those outside the group, particularly those who may be in opposition or share opposite beliefs to those in the in-group. This in-group and out-group concept may lead to patriotism or working together towards a common goal, but it may also lead to prejudice and discrimination. Groups also tend to engage in *group think*, where no one is willing to share an opinion contrary to the group, or *group polarization*, in which people in the group become stronger and stronger in their opinions as they spend time with others who have similar beliefs.

Some other key concepts related to the effects of social context on behavior are social loafing and social facilitation. *Social loafing* happens in a context of shared responsibility for a task. In this case, there is a tendency for some people to abdicate responsibility, assuming that others will fulfill the obligations of the work. *Social facilitation*, on the other hand, is when having an audience inspires people to perform tasks they do well even better. Alternatively, it can also cause them to do worse in tasks they find more difficult or challenging.

Leadership

Quality leadership skills are essential to any organization, and thus, leadership training is typically provided to mid and upper management. Signs of effective leadership skills are strategic thinking, solving problems as they come, and managing time in the most financially responsible manner. While these skills are essential, there are also more human characteristics that must be mentioned. A successful leader must have the ability to: build confidence within his or her team or organization, obtain the trust of others, inspire others, and engender a sense of pride and purpose within his or her company.

<u>Management and Leadership Development</u>
Management and leadership development is a critical component for organizations to invest in. For this practice to be effective, managers must exercise their capacities to establish objectives and means of attainment. Concurrently, management and leadership development is designed to equip the workforce

with the requisite tools and skills to compete in a functional organization. The primary purpose of management and leadership development is to provide a holistic approach for individuals, managers, and leadership. Individuals are able to increase their skills and knowledge working within an organizational apparatus. Managers find more efficient ways to execute predetermined objectives. Leaders improve their ability in a decision-making process that incorporates creative input from the organization's members and accomplishes mutually shared goals.

Motivational Strategies

Foreign Service Officers (FSOs) are motivated individuals driven to serve others. Just like in any other leadership position, FSOs possess the ability to provide emotional support and are aware of strategies dealing with effective communication and supporting team members. The following sections contain ideas on how to motivate others in the workplace.

Empowerment

Empowering others is a valuable tool for the FSO to learn. To empower someone else means having the ability to inspire in the other person a sense of control and efficacy over their own life and work. Empowerment not only means inspiring someone, but also advocating for them, their ideas, and their career. Empowerment is a key tool for an effective leader as well as an effective team.

Empowerment should begin with a trustworthy relationship between a manager and employee or a team member and their peers. To gain trust, an individual must be trustworthy, so it's important for an FSO to apply the principle of honesty in everything they do. Developing trust among team members also means allowing them to have the opportunity to make their own decisions without correcting them or trying to control the process or outcome. Even if mistakes are made, it's important for the other person to make the mistakes themselves (if the mistake is not harmful to others) and to let the process happen organically. Trust will commence out of giving the other person total freedom to do their best work.

Communication

One characteristic of people who succeed in motivating others is effective communication. Effective communication among team members and between a manager and employee must be easy and accessible in order for the job to get done correctly. If coworkers or employees are unclear or confused about their job duties, frustration or errors occur as a result. One helpful tip is that if one is unsure whether someone knows how to do something or not, assume that they don't. Withholding valuable information will hinder growth within employees and the organization.

Setting boundaries is an important part of communication; everyone should be clear on what their own role is in relation to everyone else's, as well as what's expected of them. Effective communication will aid in the organization's health as a whole as well as the health of its employees. Good communication is a necessity for helping with diversity within a workplace as well. It's important for us to learn about cultures other than our own and find out if or how their communication is different from our own. Paying attention to cultural differences is key to effective communication. If our listeners or audience is turned off by the way we are communicating, we must be willing to change our methods.

Rewards Systems

Rewards systems are a way to encourage employees and let them know that they are valued within the company. Rewards can come in the form of external rewards, which are things like bonuses, paid time off, or a raise, while internal rewards are the satisfaction that employees get from doing their jobs. Internal rewards are different from external rewards in that internal rewards can only come from the person experiencing joy in their work and cannot come from external validation.

It's also important to remember what kinds of rewards are appropriate. Rewards should go beyond satisfying the basic needs of employees. It may also help to look to other successful organizations to see what kinds of rewards they offer their employees, and how their employees value these rewards. Rewards should be fair for all employees involved based on their skill and position, and they should also be among a wide range of benefits: money, time, and flexibility are all reward-worthy notions that can be dispersed among employees who have earned them.

Equal Employment Practices

Equal employment practices (EEP) are ways employers and human resource administrators can ensure best practices are put to use when hiring, training, and retaining employees. Equal employment opportunity was first put into place to prevent discrimination against race or color. Furthering equal employment opportunity was the Executive Order 11246 signed by Lyndon B. Johnson in order to prohibit discrimination against race, sex, creed, religion, color, or national origin. More protected classes have been added to the order, including age and Americans with disabilities, among others.

The U.S. government has an Equal Opportunity Commission website with a list on how to prevent discrimination. On the site, it mentions that human resource managers should train employees on EEO laws, encourage an inclusive culture, and foster open communication in order to prevent and manage disputes. They also promote hiring workers from a diverse pool of applicants and that the criteria in selecting an employee should not disproportionately exclude a certain race, unless "the criteria are valid predictors of successful job performance and meet the employer's business needs." All employees should have equal access to workplace networks, and compensation practices should be monitored by the employers to ensure fair ratings.

Computers and the Internet

Word Processing

For companies that work with creating or manipulating documents or any other text, word processing is an essential application to have available. Word processing software provides a medium to write text and format that text with different fonts, colors, sizes, margins, page breaks, section headers, formulas, and more. There are also features like spell-check, which automatically proofs spelling as well as errors at the sentence level. Note that spell check will even pick up awkward syntax. Microsoft Word™ processors often come with built-in thesauruses as well as their own collection of images and shapes for the user to insert into the document if they wish. Among other important features, some word processor applications are able to create tables, charts, and graphs for those who need visual support in their documents. There are many kinds of word processing software. The best-known word processing software is Microsoft Word, but here is a list of some other word processing software:

- Microsoft Word™
- Google Docs™
- Pages (for Mac) ™
- WordPerfect™
- OpenOffice™
- AbiWord™
- WordPad™
- WordStar™
- Apache Open Office™

Databases

A database is a collection of data that is organized inside a computer. A database management system (DBMS) is the system required in order to view and manage data. Databases are used quite frequently in the modern world, and perhaps without us even realizing it. When we go to the doctor, chances are all of our information will be stored in their database system so that they can access information already recorded from us. The same situation happens in banks, pharmacies, or universities—we will find that our information is stored inside a large database for easy access through text or numbers.

Social media also has databases that are for extremely large systems—Facebook™, Twitter™, Google™, and Amazon™ use NOSQL systems, storage systems known as "big data." These large databases are needed in order to hold the capacity of information that is coming through them—posts, pictures, texts, and videos from millions of users are all part of this system. These databases are fairly new technology designed specifically for the mass amounts of data we've begun to accumulate as a technological society. We also, as a society, have the option to participate in various systems of cloud storage, which are database programs designed by companies like Google™ or Apple™ to hold our personal information online. Cloud storage can hold photos, videos, music, and documents, and are usually accessible through applications as long as the user has an internet connection.

Spreadsheets

Spreadsheets are tabular documents that contain columns and rows, which are adjustable to the number of columns and rows suitable for the user's purposes. Spreadsheets contain cells created by the intersections of columns and rows that are capable of holding text or numbers. Some cells, if formatted properly, can even be the result of calculations from cells above or beside it. Spreadsheets are used in producing graphs and charts, making budgets, and for sorting through data. It can also act as an inventory for a small business or to keep track of storage information for other purposes. The most popular spreadsheet currently in use is Microsoft Excel™, followed closely by Open Office™ and Google Documents™.

	A	B	C	D
1				
2				
3				
4				

Email and the Internet

Email
Known as electronic mail, "email" is one of the fastest and most efficient ways to communicate electronically in the twenty-first century. Having sufficient knowledge of email is crucial in today's working atmosphere. It's important for communication, and it's also imperative that an email is written with all the following things kept in mind:

Tone
Every distinct piece of writing has its own tone; whether serious or funny, tragic or happy, the author usually creates a tone for their text with specific word and syntax choices. Within an email, it's important to identify the audience before getting started on any kind of text. Is your audience a busy executive? Are they a government official? A coworker? A friend? Audience is important to know when determining what kind of tone to use for your electronic communication. Let's look at the following emails below written to a government official and gauge which one is the better email to send.

Email 1:

Dear Mr. Badeaux,

Thank you for allowing me to come in tomorrow evening to present my proposal to you about clean water in the Ichetucknee River. This proposal is very important to us over here at Clean Water International, and we hope we are able to answer any questions you may have regarding the subject. Please let us know if you need anything from us before we arrive at your place of operation tomorrow. Looking forward to seeing you then.

Best Regards,

Clean Water International

Email 2:

> Hey Mr. Badeaux,
>
> We're going to come in tomorrow to see y'all over there about the proposal. Don't forget about us. We can't wait to talk to you and hear what you have to say regarding our proposal to you! We're going to need about two hours of your time. Thanks so much.
>
> Clean Water International

Let's look at the two emails closely. All emails should begin with a greeting. The first greeting, "Dear," is more appropriate for the audience, who is probably a busy executive. "Hey" is more of an informal tone used towards a friend or acquaintance. Next, it's always considered good form to start by thanking the recipient for their time, especially since our audience is someone who will be giving their time to Clean Water International by listening to one of their proposals. The first email thanks Mr. Badeaux, but the second email skips this part.

Also, notice that the second email uses "y'all," which is appropriate for an informal conversation, but not for a formal business transaction. Additionally, the first email uses "serving" language, asking what they can do to serve the other person rather than what the other person can do for them. The second email states "We can't wait to hear . . . what you have to say regarding our proposal" and "We're going to need . . ." which is more of a demanding tone rather than an attitude of service. When identifying your audience, tone is one of the most important aspects of written communication to ensure a positive reception from your audience.

Internet

The internet is a system designed to connect computers across an interconnected web of networks. The idea of an internet began in the 1960s, but a modern use of connected networks for commercial purposes did not come into fruition until the 1990s. Today, the internet infiltrates almost every aspect of modern existence. We are connected on a global scale with smart phones, TVs, cable, computers, and cars.

Social media is a modern phenomenon that allows people to stay connected with their family and friends. Through social media sites like Facebook™ and Twitter™, users can follow anyone they choose depending on their personal preference. For example, many people follow political posts on Facebook™ or Twitter™ to get caught up on the latest news. Some people follow their favorite celebrities or sites with funny animal videos that are posted daily. On social media, there is something for everyone. Social media not only allows people to stay connected, but also gives a platform to those who are struggling for independence and have no way else to reach a global audience. This example can be seen in the Arab Spring beginning in 2010, where the revolutionaries used social media to gain awareness, organize groups, and call for protests through Facebook™ and Twitter™.

The internet is also used as hub for research and academia. Sites like Jstor™ and Europeana™, among others, are digital library collections that have stored thousands of books and articles for the purpose of preserving texts digitally. Google Scholar™ is also a useful tool for researchers because it provides a way to search through many library databases at the same time using specific keywords or dates. Other sites list literary or scientific text that is now in the public domain, such as *Public Domain Review* and *Project Gutenberg*. Many libraries are converting to digital databases as a way to preserve digital texts as well as gain easy access to information through key words and phrases.

FSOT Oral Assessment (FSOA)

Depending on the anticipated hiring needs, the Department of State invites a variable number of qualified candidates who have passed the FSOT to take the Oral Assessment (FSOA). This raw number, as well as the percentage, fluctuates over time based on the current and projected open positions and hiring targets at the Department of State. It should be noted that the selection process is highly competitive and even those candidates with excellent qualifications may not receive invitations or may need to repeat the process when more positions become available.

Candidates who receive an Oral Assessment invitation will travel to Washington, DC, or potentially San Francisco to test, depending on the Department of State's budget and schedule for a given year. Oral Assessments occur twice annually. It is recommended that candidates make travel and lodging plans as soon as their FSOA is scheduled and confirmed. Additionally, candidates requiring "Reasonable Accommodations" at the test center for FSOA administration should email ReasonableAccommodations@state.gov as soon as their testing appointment is confirmed to request the appropriate provisions.

The following tips can help when making travel arrangements:

- Plan to arrive at least a day or two early, particularly if traveling across time zones. The FSOA can be stressful and demanding, so being well rested can not only make the experience more manageable for candidates, but also help them feel sharper during test day.

- Schedule travel with a time cushion for unanticipated delays and inevitable travel challenges. Doing so can help prevent a candidate from facing last minute scrambling, or worse, missing the testing appointment. Delayed flights, traffic jams, difficulty navigating public transportation, and other mishaps are frequent issues during any travel. Planning what feels like an excessive amount of time for each step of the travel logistics can ensure these obstacles are navigated without compromising timeliness to the testing appointment.

- The test day often ends as late as 7:00pm local time, so candidates should make return travel arrangements accordingly.

- Pack professional attire. Essentially, the FSOA is a job interview and candidates need to dress as such. Footwear should be neat, but comfortable.

- Arrive to the assessment center early. Candidates are required to arrive by 6:45am on their scheduled test day, but arriving at least 30 minutes prior to that is recommended. Late arrivals are not accepted, and candidates will be turned away. Not all candidates follow the same schedule on test day, which is a tightly organized affair with many moving parts to accommodate all candidates and components of the FSOA. As such, it is imperative that candidates follow their own test day schedule and not rely on fellow test takers for the next set of directions or timetable.

- Get your bearings. The address of the assessment center in Washington, DC is 1800 G Street, NW, which is at the intersection of 18th and G Street. The address of the testing center in San Francisco is revealed to candidates scheduled there approximately 30 days before their scheduled FSOA. It is wise to rehearse commuting to the assessment center the day before test day so that any difficulties finding the site are encountered and eliminated prior to the rushed morning of the test.

- Ensure all of the required documents, which are listed on Department of State's website under downloads, are packed for travel and for test day. To facilitate the process of medical clearance, overseas candidates who are traveling with family members should have an available list of the dates of birth and Social Security numbers of those in their party.

- Pack and bring snacks and drinks for test day. Sandwiches, snacks, and nonalcoholic beverages from outside are permitted and a 45-minute lunch break is built into the test day schedule. Water is available at the test center along with a secure area for coats, bags, and personal belongings. It should be noted that some test takers will have gaps of time between modules of the FSOA, so reading or other quiet activities are usually permitted and can help pass the time.

The Dimensions Measured by the Oral Assessment

The different exercises that comprise the FSOA are designed to measure the candidate's aptitude in the following 13 dimensions:

1. Composure: maintaining self-control and poise during challenging or stressful situations, and being flexible and adaptable to changes and unforeseen circumstances.

2. Cultural Adaptability: respecting and working amicably with those of different races, cultures, beliefs, economic status, value systems, etc.

3. Experience and Motivation: effectively applying previously obtained knowledge and skills and demonstrating unwavering motivation to work in the Foreign Service.

4. Information Integration and Analysis: absorbing and retaining complex information presented in different formats, remembering details unaided by notes, drawing sound conclusions, and critically analyzing and using resources.

5. Initiative and Leadership: identifying and taking responsibility for needed tasks, following through on work until completion, influencing and motivating others positively, etc.

6. Judgment: exercising sound decisions that are appropriate, fair, and reasonable, and prioritizing competing needs and responsibilities in a rational way.

7. Objectivity and Integrity: conducting oneself in an honest, fair, and unbiased manner.

8. Oral Communication: speaking eloquently, precisely, and intelligently using language that is grammatically correct, appropriate for the situation, persuasive, and accurate.

9. Planning and Organizing: effectively prioritizing demands in a way that makes logical sense in terms of urgency, resources, time, and ability, and keeping track of responsibilities, details, data, etc.

10. Quantitative Analysis: efficiently and correctly analyzing and manipulating quantitative data.

11. Resourcefulness: devising innovative solutions and demonstrating flexibility and adaptability when changes occur or crises arise.

12. Working with Others: communicating and collaborating with others in an efficient, productive, and respectful manner using appropriate verbal and nonverbal language.

13. Written Communication: adhering to the conventions of standard English language in writing that is clear, precise, professional, effective, and produced efficiently.

Each candidate's aptitude in these thirteen dimensions are assessed by four Foreign Service Officers drawn from different career tracks, roles, and geographic areas. The assessments and situations that candidates undergo are designed to demonstrate their performance in the various dimensions. The evaluators are specially trained on objectively conducting and scoring performance assessments.

A candidate's performance is evaluated against established standards rather than the other candidates undergoing the same assessments. In this way, the FSOA is not a direct competition between candidates for the "best" performance. The Department of State has an established cutoff or minimum score that candidates must obtain to move forward in the application process. Theoretically, on any given test day, all or none of the candidates might achieve that score and move forward.

There are three distinct activities that comprise the Oral Assessment. Prior to participating in any of the activities, each candidate must sign a Non-Disclosure Agreement.

1. The Group Exercise

There are four phases that together comprise the Group Exercise.

Preparation Phase
In the first exercise encountered on test day, groups of three to six candidates come together to form an Embassy task force. The goal of the task force is to decide how to allocate different resources to competing projects occurring in their assigned host country. Candidates are given 30 minutes to independently read a packet containing information about the task force prior to beginning the exercise. The packet contains common background materials that all members receive, as well five pages detailing candidate-specific information. During this preparation phase, candidates are monitored in their group rooms to ensure that they work alone; communication with others is not permitted. The common materials that all candidates receive include:

- General instructions

- A memo written from the point of view of one of the fictitious countries' senior U.S. Embassy officials that appoints the candidate to a task force charged with evaluating proposals for allocations of scarce resources

- The United States' objectives and plans

- Background information and a map of the host country

- Lists of the important and/or relevant government officials in the U.S. Embassy of the host country

In addition, each candidate receives five pages of candidate-specific information, which details a specific project that he or she will present and advocate for.

Presentation Phase

After the 30-minute preparation phase, four BEX assessors, who still know nothing about the candidates, enter the group room and sit in the corners to observe. The candidates are briefed on the ground rules by the head assessor and then given the go-ahead to begin presenting their individual projects in a group-determined, unassigned order. It is important for candidates to listen carefully to all the instructions. Each candidate must present all of the relevant aspects (such as the necessary resources and U.S. interests) of his or her individual project to the other group members in no more than six minutes. It is wise for candidates to leave time at the end of each presentation for the presenting candidate to solicit questions from the others.

Discussion Phase

Once all members have presented their individual projects, the head assessor signals the start of the discussion phase and provides additional instructions pertinent to the tasks to accomplish. The discussion phases lasts 20-25 minutes, depending on the number of members in the group. During this time, candidates have two goals: to advocate for their assigned project and to help the group reach a consensus on how they recommend the Ambassador allocate the limited resources amongst the various vying projects. Assessors will be observing the manner in which each candidate describes and advocates for his or her projects, works with others, communicates, and helps lead group members to an agreed upon proposal for the Ambassador.

Tips and notable rules for the discussion phase are as follows:

- The limited resource is not necessarily money, so "funding" a project is not always the most appropriate vernacular for candidates to use while advocating for their project or competing ones.

- It is forbidden for candidates to alter the project they were assigned in any way, nor may they make up additional information besides what was given. Likewise, candidates cannot create their own project to use in lieu of the one they were given, even if they dislike their assigned one.

- Candidates are not allowed to strengthen their arguments or provide "evidence" with real life facts or situations.

- After listening to all presentations and considering the positive and negative aspects of each member's project, a candidate may opt to relinquish his or her project in favor of another.

- Candidates may take notes, but they cannot use the notes during the subsequent briefing stage.

The Ambassador's Briefing

After the discussion phase, each candidate must meet privately with two assessors and explain the group's consensus in three to four minutes. The time for candidates to prepare for this is limited, so it is important that candidates hone their briefing skills and fully understand the results of the group's deliberations and rationale. One assessor serves as the Ambassador and asks follow-up questions that the candidate must address after his or her briefing.

The four phases of the group exercise are designed to demonstrate and evaluate the following dimensions: composure, planning and organizing, objectivity and integrity, integration and analysis, working with others, initiative and leadership, oral communication, and judgement. It is critical that candidates are active participants in all phases so that the assessors can have a means on which to evaluate them. The most successful candidates display behaviors, explanations, and motivations that are consistent with the exercise's objective, which is to assist the Ambassador's decision on how to best apportion the U.S. government's limited resources among different deserving projects. They also demonstrate strong leadership skills by inciting motivation in all group members to bring their best ideas, negotiation skills, and diplomacy and helping the group reach a consensus in a timely fashion. Strong candidates remain calm and composed when others disagree with their ideas and help diffuse arguments and reconcile differences in the group, bridging members together rather than allowing factions to form. Effective candidates can advocate for their project, but integrate the needs and merits of the other projects and explain their rationale clearly and logically. They may suggest creative solutions, unique ideas, and demonstrate listening and negotiating skills.

2. The Structured Interview

For the Structured Interview portion of the FSOA, candidates meet individually with two assessors. Unlike in the Group Exercise where assessors have no background information on the candidates they are observing, the assessors review portions of each candidate's application, preferred career track, and Statement of Interest prior to the interview. However, they do not read the personal narratives. Assessors will pose questions to the candidate they are interviewing about his or her experience, background, and interest in becoming a Foreign Service Officer.

The following tips and pointers can assist candidates in having a successful Structured Interview:

- Should it directly apply to an answer solicited by the assessors, candidates can draw upon experiences and motivations cited in their personal narratives since the assessors have not reviewed this material prior to the interview.

- It is important that candidates respond to the specific questions they are asked instead of simply providing a response that better highlights their qualifications or motivations.

- The assessors are trained to conduct the interviews in a completely neutral manner, without providing verbal or non-verbal feedback regarding a candidate's performance. This lack of emotional expression can shake a candidate's confidence should he or she not be prepared for such a stoic interaction. Candidates should not worry that they are underwhelming or disappointing the assessors; assessors intentionally maintain this neutrality throughout all interviews.

- Candidates should expect to be interrupted, cut short, or even seemingly ignored while assessors shuffle papers or otherwise seem unimpressed. Again, these actions do not signal positive or negative reactions, but rather that the assessors likely feel they have acquired all they need about a given subject from the candidate's responses. Because there is limited time for the Structured Interview and three components to get through, it behooves the assessors (and certainly the candidate) to move on as soon as possible to ensure there is sufficient time to get through all of the questions and components.

The Structured Interview lasts about one hour and is comprised of three distinct portions.

1. Experience and Motivation Interview: questions will address a candidate's personality, education and work experience, understanding of the Foreign Service and reasons for applying, specific applicable skills and traits, and responses to previous opportunities and setbacks. The questions are designed to help assessors determine the candidate's potential to be a successful

Foreign Service Officer, particularly in his or her selected career track. The following tips can help candidates in this module of the Structured Interview:

- o Providing persuasive, succinct, and direct answers allows candidates to showcase their qualifications in an efficient manner so that there is ample time for all questions.

- o Candidates should ensure that they are well-versed in general information regarding the Foreign Service, their desired career track, and the attributes and experience that would be helpful for FSOs before participating in the interview.

- o As long as it is appropriate for a given question, it is better for candidates to flesh out their answers with a justification or rationale (the "why" or "how") rather than just give the "what" response. For example, instead of just describing an experience interning at the United Nations Headquarters in New York City, the candidate should comment on what was learned and how the opportunity uniquely prepares themselves or is indicative for success as a Foreign Service Officer.

- o Candidates should expect to be interrupted to move forward, or to provide clarification or details during responses.

- o Candidates should practice and determine stories and scenarios from their past that demonstrates each of the 13 dimensions so that they can easily pull these out during their responses.

2. Hypothetical Scenarios: a series of hypothetical, though realistic, scenarios posed that are intended to assess the candidate's situational judgment as it pertains to commonly encountered situations as a Foreign Service Officer. Assessors provide the candidate with a short reading that gives background information on the hypothetical situation such as the candidate's Embassy role in the country in the scenario and facts about that country. The following tips can help candidates in this module of the Structured Interview:

- o Candidates will not necessarily receive hypothetical situations and questions that pertain to their selected career track. It is primarily the candidate's judgement and sensibility of his or her proposed solutions that are assessed rather than his or her specific knowledge of Embassy operations or specific governmental regulations.

- o The hypothetical scenario module requires candidates to demonstrate their critical thinking skills, creativity and ingenuity, decision-making under time- and pressure-constraints, flexibility and ability in considering alternative approaches, and capacity to explain their thinking effectively and maturely. Candidates should answer the questions associated with the scenarios as thoroughly as possible, addressing both the short- and long-term ramifications of their proposed ideas.

- o Candidates should aim to be clear and complete, by addressing the main points quickly before being cut off by an assessor. They should still be able to verbalize their rationale, assumptions, train of thought and alternatives they considered.

- o When devising a solution, candidates should consider their assigned fictitious position in the Embassy and use this information to inform their actions. For example, they should exercise their level authority to the fullest, and refrain from pawning the task onto someone else, unless it exceeds their "role's" power or expertise.

- o Composure, Cultural Adaptability, Judgement, Information Integration and Analysis, Initiation and Leadership, Objectivity and Integrity, Planning and Organizing, Resourcefulness, and Working with Others are the dimensions scored during this module.

3. Past Behavior Interview: candidates receive a sheet of questions pertaining to the various dimensions this module evaluates. The sheet has two questions per dimension, and candidates have five minutes to review the options, select one question per dimension, and formulate their responses. A research-informed job analysis helped determine the attributes that successful Foreign Service Officers embody. These serve as the dimensions addressed in the questions, for questions designed to elicit examples from the candidates' own experiences in specific areas. The questions for each dimension will focus on specific examples from the candidates' past experiences. The following tips can help candidates in this module of the Structured Interview:

- o Candidates should give concrete examples that directly relate to the intended dimension. Scores for responses that do not explicitly answer the posed question are penalized.

- o Candidates should select examples from their past experiences that best highlight their positive qualities in the attribute and refrain from citing examples that showcase "failures" or weaknesses.

- o This module is not the time to be modest. Even if discussing a group project or achievement, candidates should assert their valuable contributions and instrumental role in facilitating the success of the project.

- o Composure, Cultural Adaptability, Objectivity and Integrity, Oral Communication, Planning and Organizing, Initiative and Leadership, and Working with Others are the dimensions evaluated in this module.

3. Case Management Exercise

The Case Management Exercises last 90 minutes and is designed to assess writing and management skills. Assessors provide the candidate with a memo listing the necessary tasks for the assignment. It also contains a summary of the primary problem and ongoing issues, email correspondences between employees describing their thoughts about the issues, a staff performance review, an organizational chart, and applicable rules and ordinances. Calculations with the data are required and must be completed manually on paper or mentally; calculators are prohibited. Candidates must read and analyze the provided information, and then prepare a written memo in response that takes into account the quantitative and qualitative data provided to offer sound recommendations.

Most candidates consider the Case Management Exercise to be the most difficult portion of the FSOA. It requires quick reading, analytical skills, critical considerations, an understanding of what might be in the best interest for the United States, and persuasive writing all under a time crunch. Candidates often receive a binder chocked full of material to review and they must consider the merit and relevancy of the information provided. The most successful candidates keep the primary goal in mind—providing a wise recommendation that prioritized the United States' best interests. Of the mountain of provided materials, those that are factual should usually take precedence over subjective sources. Candidates should ensure that their written responses justify their decisions, explain their rationale, and end with a strong, persuasive summary.

It is recommended that candidates budget 10-15 minutes for reviewing, revising, and editing their work after writing before the 90 minutes has elapsed. Assessors are expecting candidates to demonstrate skilled data analysis, as well as high-quality writing that adheres to the conventions of the English language, is clear, and is of a certain level of professionalism.

Information Integration and Analysis, Judgement, Objectivity and Integrity, Written Communication and Quantitative Skills, and Working with Others are the dimensions measured in the Case Management exercise.

Final Tips for Overall Success

In addition to the tips and guidance provided in the previous section, the following advice can be applied in general for a successful FSOA administration:

- Spend time reviewing the 13 dimensions. While the terms are commonly used in daily life, the specific meaning and qualities ascribed to the title for each dimension is somewhat unique. Assessors are evaluating candidates on these dimensions, so a fluent and comprehensive understanding, rather than just familiarity, is a crucial strategy for optimizing one's score.

- Review the different career tracks offered in the Foreign Service. Although candidates will select the track that interests them most, for the Hypothetical Situations module, knowledge of the offered tracks and the responsibilities of the roles under those tracks can help candidates speak from a more informed position and thus craft stronger responses.

- Practice speaking and writing. It may seem obvious that practicing speaking for an oral assessment is important, but a surprisingly low percentage of FSOA candidates actually dedicate some of their study and preparation time explicitly to this work. Candidates must be able to converse fluently, confidently, and intelligently under high pressure situations with minimal time to prepare or think. It is critical that they get right to the point by listening carefully to the question posed and responding in a direct and concise manner. Several of the modules require argumentative and persuasive responses, which is a skill that takes practice and time to hone. Additionally, the need to be able to communicate effectively in writing is equally important, especially in the Case Management Exercise. Successful candidates practice their writing, revising, and editing skills and review the important tenants of standard English grammar, spelling, and writing.

- Don't allow other candidates to rattle you. It's human nature to compare oneself to others, especially in situations where they are being evaluated. However, it is important for candidates to remember that the FSOA is not an adversarial process. Each candidate merely needs to achieve the minimum passing score and candidates are not scored relative to one another. It is likely that on any given test day, one or more candidates has previously taken the FSOA and is retesting. He or she may appear more practiced and calm. Other candidates may come across as more experienced either in the testing process itself or in terms of his or her education and background. It behooves the candidates to stay within themselves and refrain from comparisons as this often increases anxiety and feelings of inferiority, shakes confidence, and ultimately negatively impacts the candidate. The Oral Assessment is not a direct competition; candidates should focus on themselves and doing their personal best.

- During the group exercise, offer to go first when sharing individual projects. This demonstrates leadership, courage, and confidence. However, it should be noted that the person who goes first sets the standard for the day. Although candidates are not scored relative to one another, the person who goes first misses out on the opportunity to listen to their colleagues present and consider strengths, weaknesses, the most relevant information, and forgotten omissions of their explanation. These drawbacks of presenting first can be minimized by ample practice.

- Respect and abide by the rules and directions. If the Case Management Exercise states that candidates cannot exceed two pages in their response, do *not* exceed two pages, even by one word, as this can cause even an otherwise outstanding response to earn zero points. Similarly, if instructed to provide a briefing in two to three minutes, talk for at least two, but no more than three, minutes. Part of the assessment process is simply evaluating whether candidates can follow explicit directions.

- Stay informed. Many of the modules and questions (particularly in the Case Management Exercise and Hypothetical Situations) may address current or common Embassy issues. Even though hypothetical, candidates who can speak knowledgeably about these types of current affairs come across as dedicated, smart, and suited for work as a Foreign Service Officer.

- Present yourself warmly and expressively, even though the assessors will be flat. As mentioned, assessors are instructed to remain neutral and expressionless. Particularly during the Structured Interview, this can cause candidates to speak in monotone and wear blank facial expressions as there is no energy return from the other side of the conversation. However, the motivation, passion, commitment, and personality of candidates will fail to be conveyed if they fall prey to this tendency.

- Appear confident even if you are nervous. Sit up straight, smile, make eye contact, give assessors your undivided attention when they are speaking, and otherwise stay as engaged, professional, and poised as possible.

Scoring

While candidates participate in each module of the Oral Assessment, the assessors carefully observe and take copious notes on their performance. Upon completion of each module, the assessors personally enter the score they've assigned to a candidate into the computer. A candidate's overall score is found by taking the average of the individual scores. The overall score ranges from a low of 1 to a high of 7. Each of the three distinct exercises that comprise the Oral Assessment contribute equally to the overall total score. A minimum score of 5.25 is needed for a candidate to move forward in the application process.

Practice Questions

Job Knowledge

1. Which political concept describes a ruling body's ability to influence the actions, behaviors, or attitudes of a person or community?
    a. Authority
    b. Sovereignty
    c. Power
    d. Legitimacy

2. What were the consequences of the Spanish-American War?
    a. The U.S. acquired colonies in the Caribbean and Pacific oceans.
    b. The U.S. acquired large swaths of territory in the Southwestern United States.
    c. It led to the formation of the League of Nations.
    d. It ended the Great Depression.

3. Which political theorist considered violence necessary in order for a ruler to maintain political power and stability?
    a. John Locke
    b. Jean-Jacques Rousseau
    c. Karl Marx
    d. Niccolo Machiavelli

4. What consequences did the Great Migration have?
    a. It led to conflict with Native Americans in the West in the 1800s.
    b. It led to increased racial tension in the North in the early 1900s.
    c. It led to increased conflict with Mexican immigrants in the 1900s.
    d. It led to increased conflict with Irish and German immigrants in the 1800s.

5. Which political orientation emphasizes maintaining traditions and stability over progress and change?
    a. Socialism
    b. Liberalism
    c. Conservatism
    d. Libertarianism

6. All are true of an area with an extremely high population density EXCEPT which of the following?
    a. Competition for resources is intense
    b. Greater strain on public services exists
    c. Most are found in rural areas
    d. Most are found in urban areas

7. Which political orientation emphasizes a strong central government and promotes violence as a means of suppressing dissent?
    a. Communism
    b. Socialism
    c. Nationalism
    d. Fascism

8. What determines the exchange rate in a "floating" or "flexible" exchange?
    a. The government
    b. Taxes
    c. The Federal Reserve
    d. The market

9. Under Federalism, which is considered a concurrent power held by both the states and the federal government?
    a. Hold elections
    b. Regulate immigration
    c. Expand the territories of a state
    d. Pass and enforce laws

10. Two cards are drawn from a shuffled deck of 52 cards. What's the probability that both cards are Kings if the first card isn't replaced after it's drawn and is a King?
    a. $1/169$
    b. $1/221$
    c. $1/13$
    d. $4/13$

11. Which part of the legislative process differs in the House and the Senate?
    a. Who may introduce the bill
    b. How debates about a bill are conducted
    c. Who may veto the bill
    d. What wording the bill contains

12. Which of the following statements best describes the relationship, if any, between the revolutions in America and France?
    a. The French Revolution inspired the American Revolution.
    b. The American Revolution inspired the French Revolution.
    c. They both occurred simultaneously.
    d. There was no connection between the French and American revolutions.

13. Which political party was founded to advocate for the abolition of slavery?
    a. Constitutional Union
    b. Southern Democrat
    c. Republican
    d. Libertarian

14. What advantage(s) did the North have over the South during the Civil War?
    a. The North was defending their homes from damage.
    b. The North had free labor at home.
    c. The North had a larger navy.
    d. The North had more experienced military leaders.

15. Which of the following is NOT a power of the mass media?
    a. Ability to shape public opinion
    b. Ability to regulate communications
    c. Ability to influence the importance of events in society
    d. Ability to determine the context in which to report events

16. Which of the following could be considered a pull factor for a particular area?
    a. High rates of unemployment
    b. Low GDP
    c. Educational opportunity
    d. High population density

17. Which form of government most limits the civil liberties of the people?
    a. Authoritarianism
    b. Communism
    c. Socialism
    d. Federal monarchy

18. Which of the following correctly lists the factors of production?
    a. Land, labor, material, entrepreneurship
    b. Land, labor, capital, equity
    c. Land, a building, capital, labor
    d. Land, labor, capital, entrepreneurship

19. The U.S. foreign policy currently includes all but which of the following goals?
    a. Prevent the spread of Communism
    b. Solve international problems
    c. Promote global cooperation
    d. Maintain national security

20. For a group of 20 men, the median weight is 180 pounds and the range is 30 pounds. If each man gains 10 pounds, which of the following would be true?
    a. The median weight will increase, and the range will remain the same.
    b. The median weight and range will both remain the same.
    c. The median weight will stay the same, and the range will increase.
    d. The median weight and range will both increase.

21. Which practice of international relations most limits the sovereignty of a state?
    a. Diplomacy
    b. Foreign aid
    c. Treaty
    d. Cooperation

22. Which form of economic exchange allowed the Chinese to maintain political control over their empire?
    a. Potlatches
    b. Tribute
    c. Bartering
    d. All of the above

23. Which of the following best describes a principle of Realism in international relations?
    a. It supports international cooperation for mutual benefit.
    b. It seeks to establish international organizations and values the contributions of nongovernmental organizations.
    c. All states are interested in advancing their self-interests by expanding their power.
    d. It seeks to reduce the net conflict in the world.

24. What did Radical Republicans hope to accomplish during Reconstruction?
    a. Equal rights for freed slaves.
    b. Leniency for former Confederates.
    c. Acquittal of President Johnson during impeachment.
    d. Effective segregation laws.

25. Which of the following is the primary problem with map projections?
    a. They are not detailed
    b. They do not include physical features
    c. They distort areas near the poles
    d. They only focus on the Northern Hemisphere

26. Which of the following is the subgroup of economics that studies large-scale economic issues such as unemployment, interest rates, price levels, and national income?
    a. Microeconomics
    b. Macroeconomics
    c. Scarcity
    d. Supply and demand

27. A pair of dice is thrown, and the sum of the two scores is calculated. What's the expected value of the roll?
    a. 5
    b. 6
    c. 7
    d. 8

28. Which of the following civilizations developed the first democratic form of government?
    a. Roman Empire
    b. Ancient Greece
    c. Achaemenid Empire
    d. Zhou dynasty

29. Which of the following documents outlawed slavery throughout the United States?
    a. U.S. Constitution
    b. Compromise of 1850
    c. Emancipation Proclamation
    d. 13th Amendment

30. In which manner is absolute location expressed?
    a. The cardinal directions (north, south, east, and west)
    b. Through latitudinal and longitudinal coordinates
    c. Location nearest to a more well-known location
    d. Hemispherical position on the globe

31. Which kind of market does not involve government interventions or monopolies while trades are made between suppliers and buyers?
    a. Free
    b. Command
    c. Gross
    d. Exchange

32. Which measure for the center of a small sample set is most affected by outliers?
    a. Mean
    b. Median
    c. Mode
    d. None of the above

33. The Silk Roads had which of the following results?
    a. Spread of Buddhism from India to China
    b. Resulted in the devastation of European economies
    c. Introduction of the Bubonic Plague to the New World
    d. Resulted in the Great War

34. Which constitutional amendment gave women the right to vote in the United States?
    a. 15th
    b. 18th
    c. 19th
    d. 20th

35. Literacy rates are more likely to be higher in which area?
    a. Developing nations
    b. Northern Hemispherical Nations
    c. Developed Nations
    d. Near centers of trade

36. In a business cycle, a recession occurs between which cycles?
    a. Expansion, peak
    b. Peak, contraction
    c. Contraction, trough
    d. Trough, expansion

37. What is the probability of randomly picking the winner and runner-up from a race of 4 horses and distinguishing which is the winner?
    a. $\frac{1}{4}$
    b. $\frac{1}{2}$
    c. $\frac{1}{16}$
    d. $\frac{1}{12}$

38. Which of the following statements most accurately describes the Mongol Empire?
    a. The Mongol army was largely a cavalry force.
    b. Mongol rulers did not tolerate other religions.
    c. Mongol rulers neglected foreign trade.
    d. The Mongol Empire is known for its discouragement of literacy and the arts.

39. Which Supreme Court decision struck down the "separate but equal" doctrine?
    a. *Roe vs. Wade*
    b. *Brown vs. Board of Education*
    c. *Plessy vs. Ferguson*
    d. *Marbury vs. Madison*

40. All of the following are negative demographic indicators EXCEPT which of the following?
    a. High Infant Mortality Rates
    b. Low Literacy Rates
    c. High Population Density
    d. Low Life Expectancy

41. Which option does NOT sustain monetary policies?
    a. Closed market operations
    b. Open market operations
    c. Assuring bank reserves
    d. Adjusting interest rates

42. What is the solution to the following system of equations?
$$x^2 - 2x + y = 8$$
$$x - y = -2$$
    a. $(-2, 3)$
    b. There is no solution.
    c. $(-2, 0)\ (1, 3)$
    d. $(-2, 0)\ (3, 5)$

43. Renaissance scholars and artists were inspired by which classical civilization?
    a. Ancient Greece
    b. Ancient Egypt
    c. The Zhou dynasty
    c. The Ottoman Empire

44. Which event(s) contributed to increasing sectional tension before the Civil War?
    a. Malcom X's death
    b. The "Bleeding Kansas" conflict
    c. The 13th Amendment
    d. Shay's Rebellion

45. Which of the following is NOT a factor in a location's climate?
    a. Latitudinal position
    b. Elevation
    c. Longitudinal position
    d. Proximity to mountains

46. Which statement is true about inflation and purchasing power?
    a. As inflation decreases, purchasing power increases.
    b. As inflation increases, purchasing power decreases.
    c. As inflation increases, purchasing power increases.
    d. As inflation decreases, purchasing power decreases.

47. Mom's car drove 72 miles in 90 minutes. How fast did she drive in feet per second?
    a. 0.8 feet per second
    b. 48.9 feet per second
    c. 0.009 feet per second
    d. 70. 4 feet per second

48. Which of the following statements best describes King Louis XIV of France?
    a. He abdicated his throne during the French Revolution.
    b. He supported the American Revolution.
    c. He was the ultimate example of an absolute monarch.
    d. He created the concept of the Mandate of Heaven.

49. What consequences did World War II have?
    a. It led to the creation of the League of Nations.
    b. It led to a communist revolution in Russia.
    c. It made the U.S. the only superpower in the world.
    d. None of the above.

50. Which of the following is true regarding the physical process of weathering?
    a. It is the same as erosion.
    b. It involves wind and rain.
    c. It does not involve moving particles.
    d. It is only a problem in cold climates.

51. Which of the following refers to the value of a good set by supply and demand rather than the actual value it represents?
    a. Commodity money
    b. Fiat money
    c. Bank money
    d. Reserve money

52. The area of a given rectangle is 24 centimeters. If the measure of each side is multiplied by 3, what is the area of the new figure?
    a. 48cm
    b. 72cm
    c. 216cm
    d. 13,824cm

53. Which of the following consequences did NOT result from the discovery of the New World in 1492 CE?
    a. Proof that the world was round instead of flat
    b. The deaths of millions of Native Americans
    c. Biological exchange between Europe and the New World
    d. The creation of new syncretic religions

54. What consequences did the Neolithic Revolution have?
    a. Native Americans domesticated cattle and horses.
    b. Native Americans began to grow crops.
    c. Native Americans developed steel weapons and tools.
    d. Native Americans began to emigrate to Canada.

55. A developing nation is more likely to have which of the following?
    a. Complex highway networks
    b. Higher rates of subsistence farmers
    c. Stable government systems
    d. Little economic instability

56. Which of the following lists all four phases of the business cycle?
    a. Expansion, crest, peak, trough
    b. Expansion, contraction, peak, trench
    c. Peak, trough, contraction, expansion
    d. Peak, rise, trough, decline

57. Which of the following was a consequence of industrialization in Europe during the 1800s?
    a. The birth of the working class
    b. The expansion of European empires in Africa and Asia
    c. Improved transportation and economic efficiency
    d. All of the above

58. What consequences did the New Deal have?
    a. It established a number of federal agencies and programs that continue to function in the 21st century.
    b. It led to a third political party.
    c. It established a two-term limit in the White House.
    d. It led to the Great Depression.

59. Which is NOT true of nonrenewable resources?
    a. They tend to be used more frequently than renewables.
    b. They are thought to be responsible for climate change.
    c. They are relied upon heavily in developing economies.
    d. They have slowed industrial growth.

60. How is economic growth measured?
    a. By the rise in the inflation of a country
    b. By the amount of reserves that a country holds
    c. By the amount of exports that a country has
    d. By the GDP of a country

Situational Judgement

The Situational Judgement Test (SJT) is designed to determine an individual's ability to select the most and least effective way to handle a situation.

Situation 1

You have an innovative plan for your unit that, in your opinion, will improve performance. Not everyone in the unit is of the same opinion, and some downright oppose your plan. Even though the plan has not been put in motion, someone has already written a letter of complaint and sent it to your superior.

What would you do?
- a. Don't worry about anyone else's opinion, and implement the plan.
- b. Ignore the letter of complaint, and push forward with the plan.
- c. Have a meeting with the unit, including the person who wrote the complaint to your superior, and explain to everyone again the chain-of-command and how it is to be used.
- d. Discipline the person who wrote the letter of complaint so that no one else in the unit will break the chain-of-command in the future.
- e. Give up your plan in the wake of opposition, and see what the unit would like to do.

Situation 2

You have had a successful working relationship with an aide assigned to you. On a personal level, you dislike the assignee based on your opinion that they are arrogant and too critical of others. A senior officer is thinking of giving the aide a promotion, which would greatly benefit his/her future and put the aide on a fast track for future promotions.

What would you do?
- a. Attempt to dissuade the senior officer by sharing your personal feelings about the aide.
- b. You want the aide to just go away, so you give a recommendation for promotion.
- c. You do not want the aide to be rewarded, so you recommend that the senior officer give it to someone else.
- d. Other than expressing your opinion of the aide, you do not interfere with the selection process.
- e. List your complaints about the aide in an anonymous letter to the senior officer.

Situation 3

A coworker, who is another officer in your division, has to give an important speech in a few days. The officer has spent a great deal of time and effort on the report, but is still nervous about presenting it. After being asked by the officer to look over the report, you find some items that you feel need to be changed. You discuss these items with the other officer, who disagrees with you. You are positive that the changes you identified need to be made.

What would you do?
  a. Mention the conversation to a senior officer prior to the speech as a way to make yourself look better, since you are right and the other officer wouldn't listen to you.
  b. Do everything you can to convince the officer to review the report and supporting information and make the changes you have recommended.
  c. Avoid going to the speech if at all possible.
  d. Attempt to get a senior officer involved to order that the report be changed.
  e. Do not say or do anything. You are not giving the speech.

Situation 4

You have been teamed up with another FSO on an important one-month assignment to draft a report. Unfortunately, early in the project, your coworker has become ill and is required to be on leave. The illness keeps him/her out of the office much longer than expected. At the one-month mark on the report, your coworker is still ill and remains on leave. There is no way of knowing when your coworker will return to work and his/her expertise is needed to complete the assignment.

What would you do?
  a. Order a subordinate onto the project in an attempt to complete the report.
  b. To the best of your ability, put in as many hours as it takes to finish it yourself.
  c. Don't give any details; just ask for the deadline to be extended.
  d. Relay the situation to your superior and request help to finish the report.
  e. Wait indefinitely for the coworker to return without regard to the timeline for the report.

Situation 5

After a long day at work, you are at home and you realize you forgot to sign documents that need to go on to another unit for completion. The documents cannot move forward without your signature. While the documents are not urgent in nature, your oversight will cause another officer to be delayed and have to stay at work later than usual.

What would you do?
  a. Go back to work and sign the papers.
  b. The documents are not urgent, so you wait until the next day to sign them.
  c. Show up to work early the next day to sign the documents, get them moving first thing in the morning, and hope the other officer won't have to stay late.
  d. Get a subordinate at your office to sign your name on the documents so they can move forward.
  e. Call the officer that this will impact and explain that the documents will be late in arriving.

Situation 6

You are a Consular Officer. A week before you are about to be transferred to a new unit you receive a message from the officer in charge of that unit. The officer explains you are entering the unit at a critical time, as they are leading training exercises for evacuating Americans in the case of a disaster. The message goes on to indicate that you are expected to be a valuable contributor from the moment you arrive, with minimal assistance. However, your experience in this area is minimal.

What would you do?
a. Send a courteous thank you message in return and attempt to study for the new position.
b. Send no response to the email. You should have no problem taking on this new position.
c. Discreetly ask one of the officers in the new unit if he/she will be able to train you upon arrival.
d. You think you should remain with your current unit, so you request that your transfer be cancelled.
e. Respond to the senior officer's message with a request for a meeting, where you can discuss the transition into the new position.

Situation 7

A coworker, who is another officer, has lied about his/her time off. The officer had requested leave for a week to visit an ailing family member. The request for leave was granted. Through social media, you learned the officer was at the beach on vacation, hundreds of miles away from the ailing family member he/she was supposedly visiting.

What would you do?
a. Go see the commanding officer immediately to relay what you just discovered.
b. Anonymously send the social media evidence of the officer's actions to the commanding officer.
c. Since you now have a bargaining chip, you tell the officer you will keep this information to yourself in exchange for him taking on part of your weekly workload.
d. Tell the officer if he/she does anything unethical like that again you will have no choice but to report it.
e. You mind your own business and do nothing.

Situation 8

After being in the same unit and performing the same job for two years, you are beginning to feel burned out. Even though you are successful in your current position, you wonder what other options may be available. You have been asking around to people in other units to gauge their experiences. Within a month the rumors in your unit have started that are you are looking for a transfer.

What would you do?
a. Address the concerns that are brought up and refocus on your current position.
b. Ask for a leave of absence so you can find a way to handle the situation.
c. Send a formal request for transfer to your senior officer, acknowledging the truth of the rumors.
d. Refocus on your position and ignore the rumors, even though they are true.
e. Continue looking for a new unit to transfer to, but deny the rumors that are circulating.

Situation 9

Your current workload has you extremely busy, but you are managing to meet your deadlines and are producing quality work. A senior officer has asked if you would perform an additional assignment in conjunction with the work you are performing. While you would like to impress the senior officer and take on the additional work, you are already pushing yourself with your current workload. If you took on the extra work, the quality of work on both assignments would suffer.

What would you do?

    a. Tell the senior officer that you would be glad to do the work, and then pass it on to a coworker to complete.

    b. Apologize to the senior officer, and say you are too busy and that you cannot do the extra assignment.

    c. Ask for a few days to think about it.

    d. You can't say no so you take the assignment; you will just have to find a way to complete the work as quickly as possible.

    e. Present an offer to pass the assignment to another qualified coworker, but inform the senior officer that unfortunately you are unable to complete the work yourself at this time.

Situation 10

While assigned to a field office, you become aware that a coworker is extremely overworked with assignments being sent from other offices. The coworker's senior officers do not seem to notice that this person is overworked because your coworker does an excellent job, but they need to work extra hours to get the tasks completed.

What would you do?

    a. You do nothing. That situation has nothing to do with you.

    b. Sympathize with the coworker about his/her workload.

    c. Assist the coworker and help with his/her workload as much as possible.

    d. Request a meeting with the coworker's senior officer to inform the officer of the situation.

    e. Task one of your subordinates to assist this person in the workload.

Situation 11

You are in attendance at a meeting where two officers get in a heated dispute over policy changes. It is considered common knowledge around work that these two officers do not like each other on a personal level, but no one is sure why. Unable to come to an agreement on the policy, they ask you to settle the disagreement.

What would you do?

    a. Resolve the dispute on the side of the officer that you favor.

    b. Resolve the dispute on the side of the officer who can benefit your career the most in the future.

    c. Put all personal feelings aside and choose what you believe is the best option.

    d. Point out the officers' blatant issues with each other as the reason they cannot agree, and then remove yourself from the situation.

    e. Disregard the request to settle the dispute on the policy; this is a good time to lecture these two on the importance of teamwork and cooperation when working for the United States Foreign Service.

Situation 12

You are working on reports for your senior officers with a coworker. The reports are used by the officers to track the training and readiness of soldiers for the most hazardous and difficult missions. You noticed your coworker appears to be manipulating these numbers, and they are not being entered correctly. If the soldiers are reported as having a higher amount of training than is required for these missions and then chosen, this could pose a huge risk to the missions and put lives in jeopardy.

What would you do?
  a. Do nothing yet, but monitor the coworker to see what is going on.
  b. Report this issue to your senior officer right away.
  c. Review your coworker's numbers and correct them yourself.
  d. Leave an anonymous note to your coworker to stop changing the numbers in the report and make sure what is turned in is accurate.
  e. Wait for coworker to finish assignment, and then you will have proof of what is going on.

Situation 13

A senior officer asks you in private how you feel about your supervisor. Your supervisor reports to this senior officer. You feel the officer in question overall does a good job, but could do better in a certain aspect of his/her job.

What would you do?
  a. Express just that: They do a good job overall, but could use improvement in this one area.
  b. Refuse to answer the question.
  c. Give the supervisor a glowing review, without mentioning his/her weak area.
  d. Discuss the solutions to improving the area where the officer is weak.
  e. Write a note that explains your thoughts about the officer.

Situation 14

You are serving on a board of three officers interviewing three candidates for promotion. Candidate 1 is a known family friend of your commanding officer, but is the most impressive of the three candidates through the interview process. Candidate 2 seems to be another good choice for the position. Candidate 3 did not do well in the interview process and does not seem like a good choice for promotion at this point. The other two officers on the board have voted, one for each of the first two candidates. You have the deciding vote.

What would you do?
  a. You cast your vote for the second candidate, to avoid the appearance of favoritism.
  b. You remove yourself from the board so that you do not have to vote.
  c. You vote for Candidate 3, so you do not have to decide who gets the promotion.
  d. You vote for Candidate 1, because that candidate is most qualified.
  e. You refrain from the vote and ask for a new group of candidates.

Situation 15

You are given an important assignment that involves working with an officer from a different unit. This officer appears to already have "one foot out the door," as retirement is near. The officer does not put much effort into the assignment, leaving you to do the bulk of the work.

What would you do?
    a. Explain your feelings to your new coworker. Point out that the situation is not fair to you and that the work is very important and should be shared equally.
    b. Put in a request for a new partner on the assignment.
    c. Say nothing and do all the work necessary to successfully complete the assignment.
    d. Just do the best you can with the realization the assignment will likely be unsuccessful due to lack of participation of your coworker.
    e. Inform your senior officer of the situation.

Situation 16

You have had a feeling that one of your subordinates may have an ambitious agenda and be deliberately undermining your work. Other officers have discussed that this subordinate wants to take your job.

What would you do?
    a. Publicly attempt to humiliate the subordinate and reprimand him/her.
    b. Do nothing and the situation may just go away.
    c. Discuss the situation with the subordinate and explain that you expect his/her cooperation and support.
    d. Ask for another officer to step in and discuss the problem with your subordinate.
    e. File a report for insubordination to your senior officer.

Situation 17

Recently it has come to your attention that office supplies are disappearing from the supply closet at a much faster rate than usual. There is no apparent reason that would account for the change in supply usage. Your gut is telling you that the officer that is last to leave the office may be taking items with him/her after everyone else has left. You do not have any evidence of your suspicion, but it does seem like things disappear on the shifts for which this officer is the last to leave.

What would you do?
    a. Report your suspicions to a senior officer.
    b. Secretly set up hidden cameras in an attempt to catch the thief.
    c. Discuss your suspicions with the officer you suspect and ask for an explanation.
    d. Discuss with fellow officers to see what they think is going on.
    e. Don't do anything.

Situation 18

You are a Political Officer. Rumors have been circulating that your office in your host country is going to be shut down due to budgetary restraints. You are in attendance at a meeting between local community leaders and senior officers from your unit. The community leaders are willing to lobby to keep the office open in return for the support from policy makers in Washington, D.C. for the local military leadership in new initiatives, specifically disaster-relief coordination efforts. A community leader asks your opinion on the matter being discussed.

What would you do?
  a. Answer the question honestly to the best of your ability, but explain you are not a senior officer.
  b. Tell the leader you are not a senior officer and cannot give your opinion.
  c. Defer the question to a senior officer without giving your opinion.
  d. Give a thorough answer even though you have little knowledge on this topic.
  e. Answer the question, but keep it positive; do not mention any possible negative result of what is being proposed.

Situation 19

A subordinate in your unit has recently been showing signs of burnout and seems frustrated with his/her current position over the last month. You notice this coincides with a decline in the quality and quantity of his/her work. This negative attitude has been affecting the overall work environment with the fellow officers in the unit.

What would you do?
  a. Report the situation to your senior officer.
  b. Do nothing and hope the situation will improve on its own.
  c. Point out this behavior and bad performance in a meeting with the entire unit.
  d. Meet with the subordinate to discuss these issues, along with the effects on the unit, and present possible solutions.
  e. Reassign the subordinate to alleviate the problem in your unit.

Situation 20

In your current position, one of your many responsibilities is to brief a small team of some activities that are confidential in nature. You have accidentally sent an email containing some of this confidential information to an officer that is not on this team, and who does not have the security clearance to have access to the information you sent.

What would you do?
  a. Immediately email this person and request they destroy the information you just sent. Then, immediately inform your supervisor of your mistake.
  b. Tell your supervisor what happened and let him/her handle it.
  c. Do nothing. Wait and see what happens.
  d. Ask your senior officer if they can request that the individual be cleared for a higher security level since they have been presented with the material.
  e. Send an email to the same person saying your email was hacked and to disregard any previous messages.

Situation 21

You are a Public Diplomacy Officer. Officers in the U.S. Embassy in your host country have been awaiting training to serve as a contact for local reporters seeking accurate and current facts about U.S. policy and culture. A request was made to be in the next training cycle, but officers from the U.S. Embassy in a neighboring country were chosen for the next block of training—even though they had not been waiting as long and the informant position is in your host country, not the neighboring one. You have no evidence, but you have a feeling your unit may not have been given the training block requested due to the training director disliking you on a personal level.

What would you do?

    a. Ask the director if your Public Diplomacy Officers can attend the same training along with the other soldiers selected.

    b. Meet with the training director to determine the reason you Public Diplomacy Officers in the U.S. Embassy in your host country were passed over, and emphasize the importance of this training to your officers.

    c. Do nothing; the decision has been made.

    d. Send a critical letter to the director and your senior officer over this perceived injustice.

    e. Discuss the situation with the other country's U.S. Embassy's senior Public Diplomacy Officer to see if they would give up their training spots so your officers could have them.

Situation 22

You are a Management Officer. When you joined a new unit within the management section of the Embassy a couple of months ago, the leader of the office was very helpful. You were given a great deal of training to carry out the duties and responsibilities of your new position. You are now feeling pretty confident in your abilities, but still have not been given the freedom to work your position independently.

What would you do?

    a. Tell the unit leader's supervisor that they need to back off and give you the leeway to do your job.

    b. Provide evidence and demonstrate your competence so the leader will leave you alone.

    c. Meet with the leader, thank him for all the assistance and guidance, and discuss that you feel ready to work more independently.

    d. Try to avoid the leader as much as possible and maybe the situation will correct itself.

    e. Request another officer be assigned to your unit so that the leader will need to refocus attention on someone else.

Situation 23

Almost two months ago you were assigned to a new unit. In that brief amount of time you have identified numerous deficiencies in existing operations and have developed solutions for these problems. The majority of the people you have discussed these issues with agree with your proposed solutions. However, the senior officer believes the solutions are too risky and may cause more harm than good.

What would you do?
  a. Implement your proposed solutions, believing the senior officer will come around once he/she witnesses their success.
  b. Accept the senior officer's decision and work within the current structure without making your changes.
  c. Using the majority support of the unit, again confront the senior officer with your solutions.
  d. In detail, create a comprehensive report on the benefits of implementing your proposed solutions. Deliver your report and subsequently accept your senior officer's decision either way.
  e. Accept the senior officer's decision, then keep a log of the ways your solutions could have improved performance.

Situation 24

You have always excelled in your work, and you received a promotion six months ago. Recent budget cuts have affected the quality of your work over the last few weeks. The budget cuts prevented you from having what you needed to perform your job efficiently and in the proper way. Your senior officer, however, is unaware of the budget effects and has expressed that you are the problem, your work is not up to par, and the performance drop is a result of poor management on your part.

What would you do?
  a. Ask for advice or ideas from other officers who are dealing with the same issues resulting from budget problems.
  b. Tell your senior officer the problem lies with your subordinates.
  c. Get a list of complaints from your senior officer.
  d. Ask for time off to get some perspective.
  e. Defend your position and remind the senior officer of the budget cuts.

Situation 25

Supply and delivery logistics are maintained in a foreign U.S. Embassy's computer program. While you are coordinating a long line of deliveries, the computer system crashes. You are advised by computer support the problem may take an hour or more to fix. The delivery drivers are already getting impatient. What would you do?
  a. Request guidance from a senior officer.
  b. Ask the drivers if they have any other deliveries they could make in the meantime and return later.
  c. Try to avoid the drivers by going on a break.
  d. Ask for assistance in advising all drivers of the issue and the possible wait time, and accommodate them in whatever way you can.
  e. Receive the deliveries anyway.

English Expression

For the answer choices below in response to the passages, choose the option that is most consistent with standard English in the underlined section. If you think the underlined section sounds best as-is, then choose Choice A.

Read the selection about travelling in an RV and answer Questions 1 – 7.

I have to admit that when my father bought a recreational vehicle (RV), I thought he was making a huge mistake. I didn't really know anything about RVs, but I knew that my dad was as big a "city slicker" as there was. (1) <u>In fact, I even thought he might have gone a little bit crazy.</u> On trips to the beach, he preferred to swim at the pool, and whenever he went hiking, he avoided touching any plants for fear that they might be poison ivy. Why would this man, with an almost irrational fear of the outdoors, want a 40-foot camping behemoth?

(2) <u>The RV</u> was a great purchase for our family and brought us all closer together. Every morning (3) <u>we would wake up, eat breakfast, and broke camp.</u> We laughed at our own comical attempts to back The Beast into spaces that seemed impossibly small. (4) <u>We rejoiced as "hackers."</u> When things inevitably went wrong and we couldn't solve the problems on our own, we discovered the incredible helpfulness and friendliness of the RV community. (5) <u>We even made some new friends in the process.</u>

(6) <u>Above all, it allowed us to share adventures. While travelling across America,</u> which we could not have experienced in cars and hotels. Enjoying a campfire on a chilly summer evening with the mountains of Glacier National Park in the background, or waking up early in the morning to see the sun rising over the distant spires of Arches National Park are memories that will always stay with me and our entire family. (7) <u>Those are also memories that my siblings and me</u> have now shared with our own children.

1. Which of the following would be the best choice for this sentence (reproduced below)?

   In fact, I even thought he might have gone a little bit crazy.

   a. (No change; best as written.)
   b. Move the sentence so that it comes before the preceding sentence.
   c. Move the sentence to the end of the first paragraph.
   d. Omit the sentence.

2. In context, which is the best version of the underlined portion of this sentence (reproduced below)?

   The RV was a great purchase for our family and brought us all closer together.

   a. The RV
   b. Not surprisingly, the RV
   c. Furthermore, the RV
   d. As it turns out, the RV

3. Which is the best version of the underlined portion of this sentence (reproduced below)?

Every morning we would wake up, eat breakfast, and broke camp.

    a. we would wake up, eat breakfast, and broke camp.
    b. we would wake up, eat breakfast, and break camp.
    c. would we wake up, eat breakfast, and break camp?
    d. we are waking up, eating breakfast, and breaking camp.

4. Which is the best version of the underlined portion of this sentence (reproduced below)?

We rejoiced as "hackers."

    a. We rejoiced as "hackers."
    b. To a nagging problem of technology, we rejoiced as "hackers."
    c. We rejoiced when we figured out how to "hack" a solution to a nagging technological problem.
    d. To "hack" our way to a solution, we had to rejoice.

5. Which is the best version of the underlined portion of this sentence (reproduced below)?

We even made some new friends in the process.

    a. We even made some new friends in the process.
    b. In the process was the friends we were making.
    c. We are even making some new friends in the process.
    d. We will make new friends in the process.

6. Which is the best version of the underlined portion of this sentence (reproduced below)?

Above all, it allowed us to share adventures. While travelling across America, which we could not have experienced in cars and hotels.

    a. Above all, it allowed us to share adventures. While travelling across America,
    b. Above all, it allowed us to share adventures while traveling across America,
    c. Above all, it allowed us to share adventures; while traveling across America,
    d. Above all, it allowed us to share adventures—while traveling across America,

7. Which is the best version of the underlined portion of this sentence (reproduced below)?

Those are also memories that my siblings and me have now shared with our own children.

    a. Those are also memories that my siblings and me
    b. Those are also memories that me and my siblings
    c. Those are also memories that my siblings and I
    d. Those are also memories that I and my siblings

Read the following section about Fred Hampton and answer Questions 8 – 20.

Fred Hampton desired to see lasting social change for African American people through nonviolent means and community recognition. (8) <u>In the meantime,</u> he became an African American activist during the American Civil Rights Movement and led the Chicago chapter of the Black Panther Party.

Hampton's Education

Hampton was born and raised (9) <u>in Maywood of Chicago, Illinois in 1948.</u> Gifted academically and a natural athlete, he became a stellar baseball player in high school. (10) <u>After graduating from Proviso East High School in 1966, he later went on to study law at Triton Junior College. While studying at Triton, Hampton joined and became a leader of the National Association for the Advancement of Colored People (NAACP). As a result of his leadership, the NAACP gained more than 500 members.</u> Hampton worked relentlessly to acquire recreational facilities in the neighborhood and improve the educational resources provided to the impoverished black community of Maywood.

The Black Panthers

The Black Panther Party (BPP) (11) <u>was another that </u>formed around the same time as and was similar in function to the NAACP. Hampton was quickly attracted to the (12) <u>Black Panther Party's approach</u> to the fight for equal rights for African Americans. Hampton eventually joined the chapter and relocated to downtown Chicago to be closer to its headquarters.

His charismatic personality, organizational abilities, sheer determination, and rhetorical skills (13) <u>enable him to quickly rise</u> through the chapter's ranks. Hampton soon became the leader of the Chicago chapter of the BPP where he organized rallies, taught political education classes, and established a free medical clinic. (14) <u>He also took part in the community police supervision project. He played an instrumental role</u> in the BPP breakfast program for impoverished African American children.

Hampton's (15) <u>greatest</u> <u>acheivement</u> as the <u>leader</u> of the BPP may be his fight against street gang violence in Chicago. In 1969, (16) <u>Hampton was held by a press conference</u> where he made the gangs agree to a nonaggression pact known as the Rainbow Coalition. As a result of the pact, a multiracial alliance between blacks, Puerto Ricans, and poor youth was developed.

Assassination

(17) <u>As the Black Panther Party's popularity and influence grew, the Federal Bureau of Investigation (FBI) placed the group under constant surveillance.</u> In an attempt to neutralize the party, the FBI launched several harassment campaigns against the BPP, raided its headquarters in Chicago three times, and arrested over one hundred of the group's members. Hampton was shot during such a raid that occurred on the morning of December 4th, 1969.

(18) <u>In 1976; seven years after the event,</u> it was revealed that William O'Neal, Hampton's trusted bodyguard, was an undercover FBI agent. (19) <u>O'Neal will provide</u> the FBI with detailed floor plans of the BPP's headquarters, identifying the exact location of Hampton's bed. It was because of these floor plans that the police were able to target and kill Hampton.

The assassination of Hampton fueled outrage amongst the African American community. It was not until years after the assassination that the police admitted wrongdoing. (20) <u>The Chicago City Council now are commemorating December 4th as Fred Hampton Day.</u>

8. In context, which is the best version of the underlined portion of this sentence (reproduced below)?

<u>In the meantime,</u> he became an African American activist during the American Civil Rights Movement and led the Chicago chapter of the Black Panther Party.

    a. In the meantime,
    b. Unfortunately,
    c. Finally,
    d. As a result,

9. Which is the best version of the underlined portion of this sentence (reproduced below)?

Hampton was born and raised <u>in Maywood of Chicago, Illinois in 1948.</u>

    a. in Maywood of Chicago, Illinois in 1948.
    b. in Maywood, of Chicago, Illinois in 1948.
    c. in Maywood of Chicago, Illinois, in 1948.
    d. in Chicago, Illinois of Maywood in 1948.

10. Which of the following sentences, if any, should begin a new paragraph?

<u>After graduating from Proviso East High School in 1966, he later went on to study law at Triton Junior College. While studying at Triton, Hampton joined and became a leader of the National Association for the Advancement of Colored People (NAACP). As a result of his leadership, the NAACP gained more than 500 members.</u>

    a. (No change; best as written.)
    b. After graduating from Proviso East High School in 1966, he later went on to study law at Triton Junior College.
    c. While studying at Triton, Hampton joined and became a leader of the National Association for the Advancement of Colored People (NAACP).
    d. As a result of his leadership, the NAACP gained more than 500 members.

11. Which of the following facts would be the most relevant to include here?

The Black Panther Party (BPP) <u>was another that</u> formed around the same time as and was similar in function to the NAACP.

    a. was another that
    b. was another activist group that
    c. had a lot of members that
    d. was another school that

12. Which is the best version of the underlined portion of this sentence (reproduced below)?

Hampton was quickly attracted to the Black Panther Party's approach to the fight for equal rights for African Americans.

a. Black Panther Party's approach
b. Black Panther Parties approach
c. Black Panther Partys' approach
d. Black Panther Parties' approach

13. Which is the best version of the underlined portion of this sentence (reproduced below)?

His charismatic personality, organizational abilities, sheer determination, and rhetorical skills enable him to quickly rise through the chapter's ranks.

a. enable him to quickly rise
b. are enabling him to quickly rise
c. enabled him to quickly rise
d. will enable him to quickly rise

14. Which is the best version of the underlined portion of this sentence (reproduced below)?

He also took part in the community police supervision project. He played an instrumental role in the BPP breakfast program for impoverished African American children.

a. He also took part in the community police supervision project. He played an instrumental role
b. He also took part in the community police supervision project but played an instrumental role
c. He also took part in the community police supervision project, he played an instrumental role
d. He also took part in the community police supervision project and played an instrumental role

15. Which of these, if any, is misspelled?

Hampton's (15) greatest acheivement as the leader of the BPP may be his fight against street gang violence in Chicago.

a. (No change; best as written.)
b. greatest
c. acheivement
d. leader

16. Which is the best version of the underlined portion of this sentence (reproduced below)?

In 1969, Hampton was held by a press conference where he made the gangs agree to a nonaggression pact known as the Rainbow Coalition.

a. Hampton was held by a press conference
b. Hampton held a press conference
c. Hampton, holding a press conference
d. Hampton to hold a press conference

17. Which is the best version of the underlined portion of this sentence (reproduced below)?

As the Black Panther Party's popularity and influence grew, the Federal Bureau of Investigation (FBI) placed the group under constant surveillance.

a. (No change; best as written)
b. The Federal Bureau of Investigation (FBI) placed the group under constant surveillance as the Black Panther Party's popularity and influence grew.
c. Placing the group under constant surveillance, the Black Panther Party's popularity and influence grew.
d. As their influence and popularity grew, the FBI placed the group under constant surveillance.

18. Which is the best version of the underlined portion of this sentence (reproduced below)?

In 1976; seven years after the event, it was revealed that William O'Neal, Hampton's trusted bodyguard, was an undercover FBI agent.

a. In 1976; seven years after the event
b. In 1976, seven years after the event,
c. In 1976 seven years after the event,
d. In 1976. Seven years after the event,

19. Which is the best version of the underlined portion of this sentence (reproduced below)?

O'Neal will provide the FBI with detailed floor plans of the BPP's headquarters, *identifying the exact location of Hampton's bed.*

a. O'Neal will provide
b. O'Neal provides
c. O'Neal provided
d. O'Neal, providing

20. Which is the best version of the underlined portion of this sentence (reproduced below)?

The Chicago City Council now are commemorating December 4ᵗʰ as Fred Hampton Day.

a. The Chicago City Council now are commemorating December 4ᵗʰ as Fred Hampton Day.
b. Fred Hampton Day by the Chicago City Council, December 4, is now commemorated.
c. Now commemorated December 4ᵗʰ is Fred Hampton Day.
d. The Chicago City Council now commemorates December 4ᵗʰ as Fred Hampton Day.

Read the essay entitled "Education is Essential to Civilization" and answer Questions 21 – 35.

Early in my career, (21) a master's teacher shared this thought with me "Education is the last bastion of civility." While I did not completely understand the scope of those words at the time, I have since come to realize the depth, breadth, truth, and significance of what he said. (22) Education provides society with a vehicle for (23) raising it's children to be civil, decent, human beings with something valuable to contribute to the world. It is really what makes us human and what (24) distinguishes us as civilised creatures.

248

Being "civilized" humans means being "whole" humans. Education must address the mind, body, and soul of students. (25) It would be detrimental to society, only meeting the needs of the mind, if our schools were myopic in their focus. As humans, we are multi-dimensional, multi-faceted beings who need more than head knowledge to survive. (26) The human heart and psyche have to be fed in order for the mind to develop properly, and the body must be maintained and exercised to help fuel the working of the brain. Education is a basic human right, and it allows us to sustain a democratic society in which participation is fundamental to its success. It should inspire students to seek better solutions to world problems and to dream of a more equitable society. Education should never discriminate on any basis, and it should create individuals who are self-sufficient, patriotic, and tolerant of (27) others' ideas.

(28) All children can learn. Although not all children learn in the same manner. All children learn best, however, when their basic physical needs are met and they feel safe, secure, and loved. Students are much more responsive to a teacher who values them and shows them respect as individual people. Teachers must model at all times the way they expect students to treat them and their peers. If teachers set high expectations for (29) there students, the students will rise to that high level. Teachers must make the well-being of students their primary focus and must not be afraid to let students learn from their own mistakes.

In the modern age of technology, a teacher's focus is no longer the "what" of the content, (30) but more importantly, the 'why.' Students are bombarded with information and have access to ANY information they need right at their fingertips. Teachers have to work harder than ever before to help students identify salient information (31) so to think critically about the information they encounter. Students have to (32) read between the lines, identify bias, and determine who they can trust in the milieu of ads, data, and texts presented to them.

Schools must work in consort with families in this important mission. While children spend most of their time in school, they are dramatically and indelibly shaped (33) with the influences of their family and culture. Teachers must not only respect this fact, (34) but must strive to include parents in the education of their children and must work to keep parents informed of progress and problems. Communication between classroom and home is essential for a child's success.

Humans have always aspired to be more, do more, and to better ourselves and our communities. This is where education lies, right at the heart of humanity's desire to be all that we can be. Education helps us strive for higher goals and better treatment of ourselves and others. I shudder to think what would become of us if education ceased to be the "last bastion of civility." (35) We must be unapologetic about expecting excellence from our students? Our very existence depends upon it.

21. Which is the best version of the underlined portion of this sentence (reproduced below)?

Early in my career, a master's teacher shared this thought with me "Education is the last bastion of civility."

a. a master's teacher shared this thought with me "Education is the last bastion of civility."
b. a master's teacher shared this thought with me: "Education is the last bastion of civility."
c. a master's teacher shared this thought with me: "Education is the last bastion of civility".
d. a master's teacher shared this thought with me. "Education is the last bastion of civility."

22. Which is the best version of the underlined portion of this sentence (reproduced below)?

Education provides society with a vehicle

a. Education provides
b. Education provide
c. Education will provide
d. Education providing

23. Which is the best version of the underlined portion of this sentence (reproduced below)?

for raising it's children to be civil, decent, human beings with something valuable to contribute to the world.

a. raising it's children to be
b. raises its children to be
c. raising its' children to be
d. raising its children to be

24. Which of these, if any, is misspelled?

It is really what makes us human and what distinguishes us as civilised creatures.

a. (No change; best as written.)
b. distinguishes
c. civilised
d. creatures

25. Which is the best version of the underlined portion of this sentence (reproduced below)?

It would be detrimental to society, only meeting the needs of the mind, if our schools were myopic in their focus.

a. (No change; best as is)
b. It would be detrimental to society if our schools were myopic in their focus, only meeting the needs of the mind.
c. Only meeting the needs of our mind, our schools were myopic in their focus, detrimental to society.
d. Myopic is the focus of our schools, being detrimental to society for only meeting the needs of the mind.

26. Which of these sentences, if any, should begin a new paragraph?

The human heart and psyche have to be fed in order for the mind to develop properly, and the body must be maintained and exercised to help fuel the working of the brain. Education is a basic human right, and it allows us to sustain a democratic society in which participation is fundamental to its success. It should inspire students to seek better solutions to world problems and to dream of a more equitable society.

a. (No change; best as written.)
b. The human heart and psyche have to be fed in order for the mind to develop properly, and the body must be maintained and exercised to help fuel the working of the brain.
c. Education is a basic human right, and it allows us to sustain a democratic society in which participation is fundamental to its success.
d. It should inspire students to seek better solutions to world problems and to dream of a more equitable society.

27. Which is the best version of the underlined portion of this sentence (reproduced below)?

Education should never discriminate on any basis, and it should create individuals who are self-sufficient, patriotic, and tolerant of others' ideas.

a. others' ideas.
b. other's ideas
c. others ideas
d. others's ideas

28. Which is the best version of the underlined portion of this sentence (reproduced below)?

All children can learn. Although not all children learn in the same manner.

a. All children can learn. Although not all children learn in the same manner.
b. All children can learn although not all children learn in the same manner.
c. All children can learn although, not all children learn in the same manner.
d. All children can learn, although not all children learn in the same manner.

29. Which is the best version of the underlined portion of this sentence (reproduced below)?

If teachers set high expectations for there students, the students will rise to that high level.

a. there students
b. they're students
c. their students
d. thare students

30. Which is the best version of the underlined portion of this sentence (reproduced below)?

In the modern age of technology, a teacher's focus is no longer the "what" of the content, <u>but more importantly, the 'why.'</u>

a. but more importantly, the 'why.'
b. but more importantly, the "why."
c. but more importantly, the 'why'.
d. but more importantly, the "why".

31. Which is the best version of the underlined portion of this sentence (reproduced below)?

Teachers have to work harder than ever before to help students identify salient information <u>so to think critically</u> about the information they encounter.

a. so to think critically
b. and to think critically
c. but to think critically
d. nor to think critically

32. Which is the best version of the underlined portion of this sentence (reproduced below)?

Students have to <u>read between the lines, identify bias, and determine</u> who they can trust in the milieu of ads, data, and texts presented to them.

a. read between the lines, identify bias, and determine
b. read between the lines, identify bias, and determining
c. read between the lines, identifying bias, and determining
d. reads between the lines, identifies bias, and determines

33. Which is the best version of the underlined portion of this sentence (reproduced below)?

While children spend most of their time in school, they are dramatically and indelibly shaped <u>with the influences</u> of their family and culture.

a. with the influences
b. for the influences
c. to the influences
d. by the influences

34. Which is the best version of the underlined portion of this sentence (reproduced below)?

Teachers must not only respect this fact, <u>but must strive</u> to include parents in the education of their children and must work to keep parents informed of progress and problems.

a. but must strive
b. but to strive
c. but striving
d. but strived

35. Which is the best version of the underlined portion of this sentence (reproduced below)?

We must be unapologetic about expecting excellence from our students? Our very existence depends upon it.

a. We must be unapologetic about expecting excellence from our students? Our very existence depends upon it.
b. We must be unapologetic about expecting excellence from our students, our very existence depends upon it.
c. We must be unapologetic about expecting excellence from our students—our very existence depends upon it.
d. We must be unapologetic about expecting excellence from our students our very existence depends upon it.

Read the following passage and answer Questions 36 – 40.

Although many Missourians know that Harry S. Truman and Walt Disney hailed from their great state, probably far fewer know that it was also home to the remarkable George Washington Carver. (36) As a child, George was driven to learn, and he loved painting. At the end of the Civil War, Moses Carver, the slave owner who owned George's parents, decided to keep George and his brother and raise them on his farm.

He even went on to study art while in college but was encouraged to pursue botany instead. He spent much of his life helping others (37) by showing them better ways to farm, his ideas improved agricultural productivity in many countries. One of his most notable contributions to the newly emerging class of Negro farmers was to teach them the negative effects of agricultural monoculture, i.e. (38) growing the same crops in the same fields year after year, depleting the soil of much needed nutrients and results in a lesser yielding crop.

Carver was an innovator, always thinking of new and better ways to do things, and is most famous for his over three hundred uses for the peanut. Toward the end of his career, (39) Carver returns to his first love of art. Through his artwork, he hoped to inspire people to see the beauty around them and to do great things themselves. (40) Because Carver died, he left his money to help fund ongoing agricultural research. Today, people still visit and study at the George Washington Carver Foundation at Tuskegee Institute.

36. Which of the following would be the best choice for this sentence (reproduced below)?

As a child, George was driven to learn, and he loved painting.

a. (No change; best as is)
b. Move to the end of the first paragraph.
c. Move to the beginning of the first paragraph.
d. Move to the end of the second paragraph.

37. Which is the best version of the underlined portion of this sentence (reproduced below)?

He spent much of his life helping others by showing them better ways to farm, his ideas improved agricultural productivity in many countries.

a. by showing them better ways to farm, his ideas improved agricultural productivity
b. by showing them better ways to farm his ideas improved agricultural productivity
c. by showing them better ways to farm . . . his ideas improved agricultural productivity
d. by showing them better ways to farm; his ideas improved agricultural productivity

38. Which is the best version of the underlined portion of this sentence (reproduced below)?

One of his most notable contributions to the newly emerging class of Negro farmers was to teach them the negative effects of agricultural monoculture, i.e. growing the same crops in the same fields year after year, depleting the soil of much needed nutrients and results in a lesser yielding crop.

a. growing the same crops in the same fields year after year, depleting the soil of much needed nutrients and results in a lesser yielding crop.
b. growing the same crops in the same fields year after year, depleting the soil of much needed nutrients and resulting in a lesser yielding crop.
c. growing the same crops in the same fields year after year, depletes the soil of much needed nutrients and resulting in a lesser yielding crop.
d. grows the same crops in the same fields year after year, depletes the soil of much needed nutrients and resulting in a lesser yielding crop.

39. Which is the best version of the underlined portion of this sentence (reproduced below)?

Toward the end of his career, Carver returns to his first love of art.

a. Carver returns
b. Carver is returning
c. Carver returned
d. Carver was returning

40. Which is the best version of the underlined portion of this sentence (reproduced below)?

Because Carver died, he left his money to help fund ongoing agricultural research.

a. Because Carver died,
b. Although Carver died,
c. When Carver died,
d. Finally Carver died,

Read the following passage and answer Questions 41 – 42.

(41) Christopher Columbus is often credited for discovering America. This is incorrect. First, it is impossible to "discover" something where people already live; however, Christopher Columbus did explore places in the New World that were previously untouched by Europe, (42) so the ships set sail from Palos, Spain. Another correction must be made, as well: Christopher

Columbus was not the first European explorer to reach the present day Americas! Rather, it was Leif Erikson who first came to the New World and contacted the natives, nearly five hundred years before Christopher Columbus.

41. Which is the best version of the underlined portion of this sentence (reproduced below)?

Christopher Columbus is often credited for discovering America. This is incorrect.

a. Christopher Columbus is often credited for discovering America. This is incorrect.
b. Christopher Columbus is often credited for discovering America this is incorrect.
c. Christopher Columbus is often credited for discovering America, this is incorrect.
d. Christopher Columbus is often credited for discovering America: this is incorrect.

42. Which of the following facts would be the most relevant to include here?

however, Christopher Columbus did explore places in the New World that were previously untouched by Europe, so the ships set sail from Palos, Spain.

a. so the ships set sail from Palos, Spain.
b. so Columbus discovered Watling Island in the Bahamas.
c. so the ships were named them the Santa María, the Pinta, and the Niña.
d. so the term "explorer" would be more accurate.

Sentence Selection: Select the one sentence that best meets the requirements of standard written English.

Questions 43 – 47

43.
a. Accompanied by a master's degree in advanced engineering or business administration is a bachelor's degree in aircraft engineering.
b. A bachelor's degree in aircraft engineering is commonly accompanied by a master's degree in advanced engineering or business administration.
c. In advanced engineering or business administration you get a master's degree and in aircraft engineering you get a bachelor's degree and one follows the other.
d. A bachelor's degree in aircraft engineering are commonly accompanied by a master's degree in advanced engineering or business administration.

44.
a. In May 2015, the United States Bureau of Labor Statistics (BLS) reported that the median annual salary of aircraft engineers was $107, 830.
b. In May of 2015, the United States Bureau of Labor Statistics (BLS) reported that the median annual salary of aircraft engineers was $107, 830.
c. In May of 2015 the United States Bureau of Labor Statistics (BLS) reported that the median annual salary of aircraft engineers was $107, 830.
d. In May, 2015, the United States Bureau of Labor Statistics (BLS) reported that the median annual salary of aircraft engineers was $107, 830.

45.
    a. American airports and airspace closed to all national and international flights.
    b. American airports and airspace close to all national and international flights.
    c. American airports and airspaces closed to all national and international flights.
    d. American airspace and airports were closed to all national and international flights.

46.
    a. In 1020, seventeen years later. The legendary Viking died.
    b. In 1020, seventeen years later; the legendary Viking died.
    c. In 1020 seventeen years later the legendary Viking died.
    d. In 1020, seventeen years later, the legendary Viking died.

47.
    a. Clearly, Odysseus isn't making the same mistake twice in trusting people to automatically abide by custom.
    b. Clearly Odysseus isn't making the same mistake twice in trusting people to automatically abide by custom.
    c. Clearly, Odysseus isn't making the same mistake twice; trusting people to automatically abide by custom.
    d. Odysseus isn't making the same mistake twice in trusting people, clearly, to automatically abide by custom.

Sentence Correction: For the next eight questions, select the answer choice that needs to be used in place of the underlined text to make the sentence correct, or indicate that the underlined text is not in error.

Questions 48 – 55

48. They fear that the melting of icebergs will cause the <u>oceans levels</u> to rise and flood coastal regions.
    a. NO ERROR
    b. Ocean levels
    c. Ocean's levels
    d. Levels of the oceans

49. <u>Although often associated with devastation, not all flooding results</u> in adverse circumstances.
    a. NO ERROR
    b. Although often associated with devastation not all flooding results in adverse circumstances.
    c. Although often associated with devastation. Not all flooding results in adverse circumstances.
    d. While often associated with devastation, not all flooding results in adverse circumstances.

50. The flooding of such rivers <u>is caused</u> nutrient-rich silts to be deposited on the floodplains.
    a. NO ERROR
    b. Cause
    c. Causing
    d. Causes

51. Such technologies can also be used <u>to project</u> the severity of an anticipated flood.
    a. NO ERROR
    b. Projecting
    c. Project
    d. Projected

52. He had <u>to conceal</u> himself in order to achieve revenge.
   a. NO ERROR
   b. To be concealed
   c. Concealed
   d. Concealing

53. To conceal <u>ones </u>identity is to withhold trust.

   a. NO ERROR
   b. One's
   c. Someone's
   d. Oneself

54. <u>Other accounts describes</u> clashes where the Skraelings defeated the Viking explorers with long spears, while still others claim the Vikings dominated the natives.
   a. NO ERROR
   b. Other account's describe
   c. Other accounts describe
   d. Others account's describes

55. During their time in present-day Newfoundland, Leif's expedition made contact with the natives whom they referred to as Skraelings <u>(which translates to 'wretched ones' in Norse).</u>
   a. NO ERROR
   b. (which translates to "wretched ones" in Norse.)
   c. (which translates to 'wretched ones' in Norse.)
   d. (which translates to "wretched ones" in Norse).

Paragraph Organization: For each item in this section, select the ordering of sentences that results in the most organized paragraph.

Questions 56 – 60

56. Sentence 1: Many students entering college may shy away from a major because they don't know much about it.

Sentence 2: For example, many students won't opt for a career as an actuary, because they aren't exactly sure what it entails.

Sentence 3: When selecting a career path, it's important to explore the various options available.

Sentence 4: They would be missing out on a career that is very lucrative and in high demand.

   a. 1, 2, 3, 4
   b. 2, 3, 1, 4
   c. 3, 1, 2, 4
   d. 4, 1, 2, 3

57. Sentence 1: One solution is to install a water softener to reduce the mineral content of water, but this can be costly.

Sentence 2: Hard water has a high mineral count, including calcium and magnesium.

Sentence 3: Hard water can stain dishes, ruin clothes, and reduce the life of any appliances it touches, such as hot water heaters, washing machines, and humidifiers.

Sentence 4: The mineral deposits from hard water can stain hard surfaces in bathrooms and kitchens as well as clog pipes.

    a. 2, 4, 3, 1
    b. 1, 2, 4, 3
    c. 4, 3, 2, 1
    d. 3, 2, 1, 4

58. Sentence 1: A famous children's author recently published a historical fiction novel under a pseudonym; however, it did not sell as many copies as her children's books.

Sentence 2: In her earlier years, she had majored in history and earned a graduate degree in Antebellum American History, which is the time frame of her new novel.

Sentence 3: In fact, her new novel was nominated for the prestigious Albert J. Beveridge Award, but still isn't selling like her children's books, which fly off the shelves because of her name alone.

Sentence 4: Critics praised this newest work far more than the children's series that made her famous.

    a. 2, 3, 4, 1
    b. 1, 2, 3, 4
    c. 3, 2, 4, 1
    d. 1, 2, 4, 3

59. Sentence 1: Addiction is defined as a compulsion to seek the substance despite negative consequences.

Sentence 2: However, more than 85 percent of those addicts will not achieve their goal.

Sentence 3: According to the National Institute of Drug Abuse, nearly 35 million smokers expressed a desire to quit smoking in 2015.

Sentence 4: Cigarettes contain a drug called nicotine, one of the most addictive substances known to man.

    a. 1, 2, 4, 3
    b. 4, 1, 3, 2
    c. 2, 1, 3, 4
    d. 1, 2, 3, 4

60. Sentence 1: It has recently been brought to my attention that most people believe that 75% of your body heat is lost through your head.

Sentence 2: I had certainly heard this before, and am not going to attempt to say I didn't believe it when I first heard it.

Sentence 3: It is natural to be gullible to anything said with enough authority.

Sentence 4: But the "fact" that the majority of your body heat is lost through your head is a lie.

    a. 4, 3, 2, 1
    b. 1, 2, 3, 4
    c. 1, 2, 4, 3
    d. 3, 4, 1, 2

Paragraph Revision: This section consists of different paragraphs. Read each paragraph carefully, and then answer the questions that follow it.

Questions 61 – 65

Sentence 1: Thus far the protective work of the Audubon Association has been successful.

Sentence 2: Now there are twenty colonies, which contain all told, about 5,000 egrets and about 120,000 herons and ibises which are guarded by the Audubon wardens.

Sentence 3: Today, the plume hunters <u>who does</u> not dare to raid the guarded rookeries are trying to study out the lines of flight of the birds, to and from their feeding-grounds, and shoot them in transit.

Sentence 4: Their motto is—"Anything to beat the law, and get the plumes." It is there that the state of Florida should take part in the war.

61. The writer discovers the following sentence has been left out of the paragraph: "One of the most important is on Bird Island, a mile out in Orange Lake, central Florida, and it is ably defended by Oscar E. Baynard." Which sentence is this sentence most likely to be placed after?
    a. Sentence 1
    b. Sentence 2
    c. Sentence 3
    d. Sentence 4

62. Choose the best choice for the underlined text in Sentence 4. If you think the text is correct as-is, choose Choice *A*.
    a. who does
    b. whom does
    c. who do
    d. whom do

Sentence 1: <u>Cynthia keeps</u> to a strict vegetarian diet.

Sentence 2: <u>Keeping this diet are part</u> of her religion.

Sentence 3: She cannot have any meat or fish dishes.

Sentence 4: This is more than a preference.

63. The writer discovers the following sentence has been left out of the paragraph: "Her body has never developed the enzymes to process meat or fish, so she becomes violently ill if she accidentally eats any of the offending foods." Which sentence is this sentence most likely to be placed after?
    a. Sentence 1
    b. Sentence 2
    c. Sentence 3
    d. Sentence 4

64. Choose the best choice for the underlined text in Sentence 1. If you think the text is correct as-is, choose Choice A.
    a. Cynthia keeps
    b. Cynthia keeping
    c. Cynthia keep
    d. Cynthia has keeping

65. Choose the best choice for the underlined text in Sentence 2. If you think the text is correct as-is, choose Choice A.
    a. Keeping this diet are part
    b. Keeping this diet is part
    c. Keeping this diets are part
    d. Keeping this diets is part

Written Essay

On the FSOT, you will be presented with multiple essay topics to choose from. The test allows you seven minutes to choose the topic before you get started. If you don't choose a topic before seven minutes, they will choose one for you. Then, you will have twenty-five minutes to develop and write your essay. Reviewers of your essay will look for a clear, organized essay with grammatically correct sentences. You will have 2800 characters, or spaces, to write your essay, then the screen will time out.

The following is an example topic essay:

> Some people feel that sharing their lives on social media sites such as Facebook, Instagram, and Snapchat is fine. They share every aspect of their lives, including pictures of themselves and their families, what they ate for lunch, who they are dating, and when they are going on vacation. They even say that if it's not on social media, it didn't happen. Other people believe that sharing so much personal information is an invasion of privacy and could prove dangerous. They think sharing personal pictures and details invites predators, cyberbullying, and identity theft.

Write an essay to someone who is considering whether to participate in social media. Take a side on the issue and argue whether or not he/she should join a social media network. Use specific examples to support your argument.

Answer Explanations

Job Knowledge

1. C: Power is the ability of a ruling body or political entity to influence the actions, behavior, and attitude of a person or group of people. Authority, Choice *A*, is the right and justification of the government to exercise power as recognized by the citizens or influential elites. Similarly, legitimacy, Choice *D*, is another way of expressing the concept of authority. Sovereignty, Choice *B*, refers to the ability of a state to determine and control their territory without foreign interference.

2. A: The Spanish-American War of 1898 made the U.S. a colonial power because it acquired many former Spanish colonies. The Mexican-American War of 1846-48 led to the acquisition of California, Nevada, Utah, Arizona, and New Mexico, Choice *B*. World War I led to the formation of the League of Nations in 1919, Choice *C*. The Great Depression ended when Americans joined World War II in 1941, Choice *D*.

3. D: In his book, *The Prince*, Niccolo Machiavelli advocated that a ruler should be prepared to do whatever is necessary to remain in power, including using violence and political deception as a means to coerce the people of a state or eliminate political rivals. John Locke, Choice *A*, contributed and advocated liberal principles, most prominently the right to life, liberty, and health. Jean-Jacques Rousseau, Choice *B*, heavily influenced the French Revolution and American Revolution by advocating individual equality, self-rule, and religious freedom. Karl Marx, Choice *C*, wrote that the struggle between the bourgeois (ruling class) and the proletariat (working class) would result in a classless society in which all citizens commonly owned the means of production.

4. B: More than one million African Americans in the South went north in search of jobs during and after World War I. The Great Migration led to increased racial tension as blacks and whites competed for housing and jobs in northern cities. The Great Migration also led to the Harlem Renaissance.

5. C: Conservatism emphasizes maintaining traditions and believes political and social stability is more important than progress and reform. In general, Socialism, Choice *A*, seeks to establish a democratically elected government that owns the means of production, regulates the exchange of commodities, and distributes the wealth equally among citizens. Liberalism, Choice *B*, is based on individualism and equality, supporting the freedoms of speech, press, and religion, while Libertarian ideals, Choice *D*, emphasize individual liberties and freedom from government interference.

6. C: Population density, which is the total number of people divided by the total land area, generally tends to be much higher in urban areas than rural ones. This is true due to high-rise apartment complexes, sewage and freshwater infrastructure, and complex transportation systems, allowing for easy movement of food from nearby farms. Consequently, competition among citizens for resources is certainly higher in high-density areas, as are greater strains on infrastructure within urban centers.

7. D: Fascism considers a strong central government, martial law, and violent coercion as necessary means to maintain political stability and strengthen the state. Neither the politics of Communism, a society in which the people own the means of production, nor Socialism, a society in which the government owns the means of production, promote violence but instead advocate a classless society that eliminates the class struggle. Thus, Choices *A* and *B* are incorrect. Nationalism, Choice *C*, emphasizes preserving a nation's culture, often to the exclusion of other cultures, but violence is not officially promoted as a means for suppressing dissent, as is the case with Fascism.

8. D: The market. The market, through supply and demand, determines the exchange rate with a "flexible" or "floating" exchange rate. The government, Choice *A*, is not the correct answer because it is involved in "fixed" exchange rates to help keep exchange rates stable. Taxes, Choice *B*, is also incorrect because they create government revenue. The Federal Reserve, Choice *C*, is the bank of banks.

9. D: Both the states and the federal government may propose, enact, and enforce laws. States pass legislation that concerns the states in their state legislative houses, while the federal government passes federal laws in Congress. Only states may hold elections and determine voting procedures, even for federal offices such as the president of the United States, and only the federal government may expand any state territory, change state lines, admit new states into the nation, or regulate immigration and pass laws regarding naturalization of citizens.

10. B: For the first card drawn, the probability of a King being pulled is $4/52$. Since this card isn't replaced, if a King is drawn first, the probability of a King being drawn second is $3/51$. The probability of a King being drawn in both the first and second draw is the product of the two probabilities: $4/52$ x $3/51 = 12/2652$ which, divided by 12, equals $1/221$.

11. B: The process by which the House and Senate may debate a bill differs. In the House, how long a speaker may debate a bill is limited, while in the Senate, speakers may debate the bill indefinitely and delay voting on the bill by filibuster—a practice in which a speaker refuses to stop speaking until a majority vote stops the filibuster or the time for the vote passes. In both the House and the Senate, anyone may introduce a bill. Only the president of the United States may veto the bill, so neither the House nor Senate holds that power. Before the bill may be presented to the president to be signed, the wording of the bill must be identical in both houses. Another procedural difference is that the number of amendments is limited in the House but not the Senate; however, this does not appear as an answer choice.

12. B: The American Revolution occurred first in 1775, and a number of European soldiers fought for the patriots. The American Revolution, in part, inspired the French Revolution. The Marquis de Lafayette came to America in 1777 and was wounded during the Battle of Brandywine. He returned to France after the American Revolution and became a leader in the French Revolution in 1789.

13. C: The Republican Party emerged as the abolitionist party during the antebellum period and succeeded in abolishing slavery after the North's victory in the Civil War. The Constitutional Union Party supported slavery but opposed Southern secession, while the Southern Democrats supported slavery and secession. The Whig Party splintered in the 1850s as a result of tension over slavery, leading to the creation of the Republican Party and Constitutional Union Party.

14. C: The North had a population of about 18.5 million while the South had only 5.5 million citizens and 3.5 million slaves. This meant the Union could more easily replace men while the Confederacy could not. The South was defending their homes from damage, since most of the war happened in the South, so Choice *A* is incorrect. Choice *B* is incorrect—the South had free labor at home, so they didn't have to worry about leaving their farms to go to war. Finally, Choice *D* is incorrect; the South had more experienced military leaders due to their participation in the Mexican-American War.

15. B: The mass media does not have the ability to regulate communications. The mass media has the ability to shape public opinion, making Choice *A* incorrect. Mass media selects which events to report on and thereby influences the perceived importance of events in society and determines the context in which to report events, making Choices *C* and *D* incorrect. Only the federal government may regulate communications through agencies such as the Federal Communications Commission (FCC).

16. C: Pull factors are reasons people immigrate to a particular area. Obviously, educational opportunities attract thousands of people on a global level and on a local level. For example, generally areas with strong schools have higher property values, due to the relative demand for housing in those districts. The same is true for nations with better educational opportunities. Unemployment, low GDP, and incredibly high population densities may serve to deter people from moving to a certain place and can be considered push factors.

17. A: An authoritarian government is ruled by a single party that holds complete control over the powerful central government. Authoritarian governments limit political freedom and civil liberties to diminish any opposition. Communism, Choice *B*, is one in which the class struggle between the ruling and working classes is eliminated because the means of production belongs to the people. Similarly, Socialism, Choice *C*, is classless, but in this type of government, the government owns the means of production and is often democratic. Unlike a regular monarchy, a federal monarchy, Choice *D*, is a federal government in which political power is divided between the monarch (head of state) and regional governments, resulting in checks and balances of power.

18. D: The factors of production are land, labor, capital, and entrepreneurship. The other choices all include at least one option that is not a factor of production.

19. A: Since the Cold War ended, the U.S. foreign policy no longer centers on preventing the spread of Communism but instead focuses on promoting the ideals of democracy, promoting global cooperation through diplomacy and international organizations, and solving international problems through those channels. The U.S. foreign policy considers national security as the nation's most important goal.

20. A: If each man gains 10 pounds, every original data point will increase by 10 pounds. Therefore, the man with the original median will still have the median value, but that value will increase by 10. The smallest value and largest value will also increase by 10 and, therefore, the difference between the two won't change. The range does not change in value and, thus, remains the same.

21. C: A treaty is an agreement between states or groups of states that functions like a contract by binding the participants to the agreed-upon terms. Examples of treaties include peace treaties, trade agreements, and military defense pacts. Participating states give up some degree of sovereignty, as they are bound to the terms of the treaty until it's revoked, in exchange for the desired benefit. Cooperation and diplomacy, Choices *A* and *D*, are essential for the formation of treaties, but they do not involve the same degree of limiting the ability to govern within the state. Foreign aid, Choice *B*, is a voluntary transfer of resources between countries. Although the foreign aid might be attached to terms restricting the aid beneficiary's government, treaties always involve exchanging some degree of internal sovereignty for the treaty's intended mutual benefit; thus, treaties is the best answer.

22. B: The Chinese required other countries to pay tribute in order to establish trade relations. Foreign emissaries also had to prostrate themselves before the Chinese emperor. Potlatches, Choice *A*, were a Native American form of gift giving. Bartering, Choice *C*, was a common form of economic exchange, but it had no political significance.

23. C: Realism focuses on how states pursue their self-interest and asserts that the international system inevitably leads to conflict. Realism necessarily assumes that all states are interested in advancing their self-interests by expanding their power. In contrast, Liberalism advocates for equality between states and supports international and nongovernmental organizations' role in international relations. Choices *A* and *B* describe principles of Liberalism. Choice *D* is factually incorrect and more closely associated with Liberalism.

24. A: Radical Republicans wanted to ensure that recently freed slaves had the economic and political rights that would enable them to achieve self-sufficiency in the post-Civil War era. Democrats, such as Andrew Johnson, preferred leniency towards the South while Radical Republicans wanted a harsher punishment, making Choice *B* incorrect. This led to conflict between Johnson and Radical Republicans who almost succeeded in having him impeached in 1868.

25. C: Map projections, such as the Mercator Projection, are useful for finding positions on the globe, but they attempt to represent a spherical object on a flat surface. As a result, they distort areas nearest the poles, which misrepresent the size of Antarctica, Greenland, and other high latitudinal locations. Map projects can include great detail; some illustrate the physical features in an area, and most include both the northern and southern hemispheres.

26. B: Macroeconomics. Macroeconomics studies the economy on a large scale and focuses on issues such as unemployment, interest rates, price levels, and national income. Microeconomics, Choice *A*, studies more individual or small group behaviors such as scarcity or supply and demand. Scarcity, Choice *C*, is not correct because it refers to the availability of goods and services. Supply and demand, Choice *D*, is also incorrect because it refers to the quantity of goods and services that is produced and/or needed.

27. D: The expected value is equal to the total sum of each product of individual score and probability. There are 36 possible rolls. The probability of rolling a 2 is $1/36$. The probability of rolling a 3 is $2/36$. The probability of rolling a 4 is $3/36$. The probability of rolling a 5 is $4/36$. The probability of rolling a 6 is $5/36$. The probability of rolling a 7 is $6/36$. The probability of rolling an 8 is $5/36$. The probability of rolling a 9 is $4/36$. The probability of rolling a 10 is $3/36$. The probability of rolling an 11 is $2/36$. Finally, the probability of rolling a 12 is $1/36$. Therefore, the expected value is the sum of each product of a roll and probability, which equals 7.

28. B: Ancient Greeks created many of the cultural and political institutions that form the basis of modern western civilization. Athens was an important Greek democracy, and all adult men could participate in politics after they had completed their military service. The Roman Empire, Choice *A*, evolved from the Roman Republic, but it was not democratic. The Achaemenid Empire and Zhou Dynasty, Choices *C* and *D*, were imperial monarchies that did not allow citizens to have much, if any, political voice.

29. D: 13th Amendment. The U.S. Constitution, Choice *A*, actually legalized slavery by counting slaves as three-fifths of a person. The Compromise of 1850, Choice *B*, banned the slave trade in Washington D.C. but also created a stronger fugitive slave law. The Emancipation Proclamation, Choice *C*, only banned slavery in the Confederacy. The 13th Amendment finally banned slavery throughout the country.

30. B: Latitudinal and longitudinal coordinates delineate absolute location. In contrast to relative location, which describes a location as compared to another, better-known place, absolute location provides an exact place on the globe through the latitude and longitude system. Choice A, cardinal directions (north, south, east, west) are used in absolute location, but coordinates must be added in order to have an absolute location. Using other, better known locations to find a location, Choice C, is referred to as relative location, and absolute location is far more precise than simply finding hemispherical position on the globe.

31. A: Free. A free market does not involve government interventions or monopolies while trading between buyers and suppliers. However, in a command market, the government determines the price of goods and services. Gross and exchange markets refer to situations where brokers and traders make exchanges in the financial realm.

32. A: An outlier is a data value that is either far above or far below the majority of values in a sample set. The mean is the average of all the values in the set. In a small sample set, a very high or very low number could drastically change the average (or mean) of the data points. Outliers will have no more of an effect on the median (the middle value when arranged from lowest to highest) than any other value above or below the median. If the same outlier does not repeat, outliers will have no effect on the mode (value that repeats most often).

33. A: The Silk Roads were a network of trade routes between Asia and the Mediterranean. Merchants and Pilgrims traveled along the Silk Roads and brought new ideas and technologies, as well as trade goods. For example, Buddhism spread from India to China. Chinese technologies also spread westward, including gunpowder and the printing press. The Silk Roads also spread the Bubonic Plague to Europe, but it did not arrive in the New World until Columbus landed there in 1492.

34. C: The 19th amendment gave women the right to vote. The 15th Amendment, Choice A, gave blacks the right to vote. The 18th Amendment, Choice B, introduced alcohol prohibition. The 20th amendment, Choice D, repealed prohibition.

35. C: Developed Nations have better infrastructural systems, which can include government, transportation, financial, and educational institutions. Consequently, its citizens tend to have higher rates of literacy, due to the sheer availability of educational resources and government sanctioned educational systems. In contrast, developing nations, Choice A, struggle to provide educational resources to their citizens. Nations in the Northern Hemisphere, Choice B, have no greater availability to educational resources than those in the Southern Hemisphere, and centers of trade, Choice D, don't necessarily equate to higher levels of education, as many may exist in poorer nations with fewer resources.

36. C: Contraction and trough. A recession occurs between the contraction and trough phases of the business cycle. Between expansion and peak phases, employment and productivity are on the rise, causing a "boom." Between the peak and contraction, unemployment rates are starting to fall, but have not yet hit an all-time low. Between trough and expansion phases, the economy is getting back on its feet and starting to increase employment again.

37. D: The probability of picking the winner of the race is $\frac{1}{4}$ $\left(\frac{number\ of\ favorable\ outcomes}{number\ of\ total\ outcomes}\right)$. Assuming the winner was picked on the first selection, three horses remain from which to choose the runner-up (these are dependent events). Therefore, the probability of picking the runner-up is $\frac{1}{3}$. To determine the probability of multiple events, the probability of each event is multiplied: $\frac{1}{4} \times \frac{1}{3} = \frac{1}{12}$.

38. A: The Mongol army was largely a cavalry force. The Mongols were a nomadic people who trained as horsemen from a young age. They used their highly mobile army to build a huge empire in Asia, the Middle East, and Eastern Europe. Mongol rulers were relatively tolerant of other religions because they wanted to reduce conflict within their empire, making Choice *B* incorrect. They also encouraged trade because they produced few of their own goods, making Choice *C* incorrect. The Mongol rulers also encouraged literacy and appreciated visual art, making Choice *D* incorrect.

39. B: *Brown vs. Board of Education* ruled that separate schools for blacks and whites were inherently unequal and sparked demands for more civil rights. *Roe v. Wade* in 1973, Choice *A*, increased access to abortion. *Plessy vs. Ferguson*, Choice *C*, established the "separate but equal" doctrine. *Marbury vs. Madison* in 1803, Choice *D*, established the doctrine of judicial review.

40. C: Although it can place a strain on some resources, population density is not a negative demographic indicator. For example, New York City, one of the most densely populated places on Earth, enjoys one of the highest standards of living in the world. Other world cities such as Tokyo, Los Angeles, and Sydney also have tremendously high population densities and high standards of living. High infant mortality rates, low literacy rates, and low life expectancies are all poor demographic indicators that suggest a low quality of life for the citizens living in those areas.

41. A: Closed market operations. Monetary policies are sustained by assuring bank reserves, adjusting interest rates, and open market operations. Closed market operations do NOT uphold monetary policies.

42. D: This system of equations involves one quadratic function and one linear function, as seen from the degree of each equation. One way to solve this is through substitution. Solving for y in the second equation yields $y = x + 2$. Plugging this equation in for the y of the quadratic equation yields $x^2 - 2x + x + 2 = 8$. Simplifying the equation, it becomes $x^2 - x + 2 = 8$. Setting this equal to zero and factoring, it becomes $x^2 - x - 6 = 0 = (x - 3)(x + 2)$. Solving these two factors for x gives the zeros $x = 3, -2$. To find the y-value for the point, each number can be plugged in to either original equation. Solving each one for y yields the points $(3, 5)$ and $(-2, 0)$.

43. A: Renaissance scholars and artists sought to emulate classical Greek and Roman culture. They translated Greek and Roman political philosophers and literature. They also copied classical architecture. Europeans had little direct contact with China until the thirteenth century, which was long after the Zhou Dynasty collapsed, making Choice *C* incorrect.

44. B: The "Bleeding Kansas" conflict contributed to sectional tension before the Civil War. The application of popular sovereignty in Kansas led to conflict as free-soil and pro-slavery forces rushed into the territory. Malcolm X's death, Choice *A*, was in 1965, almost 100 years after the Civil War ended. The 13th Amendment, Choice *C*, was ratified in 1865 and was approved at the very end of the Civil War. Shay's Rebellion, Choice *D*, was an uprising during 1786 and 1787 in Massachusetts.

45. C: Longitudinal position, or a place's location either east or west, has no bearing on the place's climate. In contrast, a place's latitudinal position, or its distance away from the direct rays of the sun in the Tropics, greatly affects its climate. Additionally, proximity to mountains, which can block wind patterns, and elevation, which generally lowers temperature by three degrees for every one thousand feet gained, also impact climate.

46. B: As inflation increases, purchasing power decreases. As more money is printed, the monetary value of the dollar drops and, in turn, decreases the purchasing power of goods and services. So, as inflation increases, consumers are not spending as much and the value of the dollar is low.

47. D: This problem can be solved by using unit conversions. The initial units are miles per minute. The final units need to be feet per second. Converting miles to feet uses the equivalence statement 1 mile=5,280 feet. Converting minutes to seconds uses the equivalence statement 1 minute=60 seconds. Setting up the ratios to convert the units is shown in the following equation: $\frac{72\ miles}{90\ minutes} * \frac{1\ minute}{60\ seconds} * \frac{5280\ feet}{1\ mile} = 70.4$ feet per second. The initial units cancel out, and the new, desired units are left.

48. C: Louis the XIV was an absolute monarch who ruled during the sixteenth century. He concentrated power on the throne by forcing nobles to spend most of their time at the royal court. The French Revolution occurred about two hundred years after he died. Absolute monarchs like Louis the XIV bolstered their prestige by claiming they were appointed by God. The Mandate of Heaven was a similar concept, but it was developed by the Zhou Dynasty in China about two thousand years before Louis XIV was born.

49. D: World War I led to the League of Nations and the communist revolution in Russia, Choices *A* and *B*. The USSR and U.S. both emerged as two rival superpowers after World War II. It was thus a bipolar, rather than unipolar, world. The tension and mistrust between the U.S. and USSR eventually led to the Cold War, which ended in 1991.

50. C: Unlike erosion, which is caused by moving particles from water or wind, weathering occurs due to fluctuations in temperatures, the impact of long-term sun exposure, or exposure to chemicals that break down rocks, trees, or soil. Over time, the effects of freezing temperatures can break down massive rocks or lead to other significant changes in the landscape. Weathering does not involve wind and rain, since those particles are constantly moving to exact change on the earth's surface. Also, weathering takes place in all climates, not just cold ones.

51. B: Fiat money. Commodity money, Choice *B*, refers to a good that has value, such as a precious metal. Bank money, Choice *C*, is money that is credited by a bank to those people who have their money deposited there. The term Reserve money, Choice *D*, does not refer to anything.

52. C: 216cm. Because area is a two-dimensional measurement, the dimensions are multiplied by a scale that is squared to determine the scale of the corresponding areas. The dimensions of the rectangle are multiplied by a scale of 3. Therefore, the area is multiplied by a scale of 3^2 (which is equal to 9):

$$24cm \times 9 = 216cm$$

53. A: Most scholars already knew the world was round by 1492. On the other hand, the arrival of Europeans in North and South America introduced deadly diseases that killed millions of native peoples. Europeans had developed immunity to diseases such as smallpox, while Native Americans had not. In addition, Europeans introduced a number of new plants and animals to the New World, but they also adopted many new foods as well, including potatoes, tomatoes, chocolate, and tobacco. Finally, Europeans tried to convert Native Americans to Christianity, but Indians did not completely give up their traditional beliefs. Instead, they blended Christianity with indigenous and African beliefs to create new syncretic religions.

54. B: Native Americans began to grow crops. During the Neolithic Revolution, Native Americans began to cultivate beans, squash, chilies, and other vegetables. However, they did not domesticate many large animals, Choice *A*—only the dog in North America and the llama in Central America. Horses and cattle only arrived in North America as a result of European exploration. Native Americans also did not develop steel or iron, Choice *C*—Native Americans only obtained these items by trading with Europeans. Despite these limits, Native Americans did develop a semi-sedentary lifestyle, formed social hierarchies, and created new religious beliefs.

55. B: Developing nations tend to have higher levels of impoverished citizens. As a result, many of their citizens must rely on subsistence farming, or producing enough food to feed their families, in order to survive. In contrast, developed nations tend to produce surpluses of food and very few, if any, of its citizens engage in subsistence farming. Developing nations are less likely to have complex highway systems, stable governments, and economic stability due to financial pressures.

56. C: The four phases of the business cycle are peak, trough, expansion, contraction. The other answer choices include at least one wrong phase.

57. D: The Industrial Revolution is probably one of the most important turning points in world history. The United States and Western Europe, especially Britain, were the first areas to industrialize. Steam engines were used to improve economic and transportation efficiency. They also gave western empires a military advantage over less developed countries in Asia and Africa. Finally, industrialization required large amounts of unskilled labor, which created the working class.

58. A: The New Deal introduced a number of programs designed to increase regulation and boost the economy. Many of them remain in effect today, such as the Social Security Administration and the Securities and Exchange Commission. The New Deal also led to the Republican and Democratic parties to reverse their ideological positions on government intervention. It did not lead to a third party, Choice *B*. President Franklin D. Roosevelt was actually elected to four terms in office and the official two-term limit was not established until the 22nd Amendment was ratified in 1951. Until then, the two-term limit had been an informal custom established by President George Washington when he left office in 1797. Thus, Choice *C* is incorrect. Choice *D* is also incorrect. The Great Depression led to the New Deal, and not the other way around.

59. D: Most nonrenewable resources are easier to harness and utilize than renewable sources. That may sound counterintuitive, but the reality is that it is harder to develop solar, wind, and geothermal infrastructure than it is to build a coal-fired power plant for the production of electricity. Consequently, developing nations tend to rely on these reliable sources in order to fuel their equally developing economy.

60. D: The GDP is used to measure an economy's growth. The inflation of a country doesn't tell us anything about their growth. A country may hold a lot of money in reserves but this does not tell us if they are growing or not. The same can be said for having a lot of exports. It does indicate that an economy is necessarily growing.

Situational Judgement

Situation 1:

Most Effective - C: Having an open meeting with everyone would reemphasize the important of the chain-of-command and resolve problems at the lowest possible level.

Least Effective - E: Giving up your position because of opposition would demonstrate weakness as a leader and lead to similar actions in future decisions.

Situation 2:

Most Effective - D: This is a case of "integrity first." It is fine to voice your opinion to the aid, but better to refrain from interfering with the selection process based on personal feelings.

Least Effective - B or E: Giving a recommendation to make the aide go away would not uphold the core value of integrity. An honest opinion should always be given. The same could be said for an anonymous letter. Officers should always be forthright and honest when giving recommendations.

Situation 3:

Most Effective - B: Part of being a good officer is to help peers. Try and point out what you would change in the speech and include why you would do it, and let the senior officer make the decision.

Least Effective - A: Never go to a superior with the intention of trying to make yourself look better by slandering a coworker. This is an integrity violation and will erode your credibility as an officer.

Situation 4:

Most Effective - D: Situations come up in every unit that can impact the mission. In this situation, notify your supervisor immediately so they can get someone to replace the ill coworker and accomplish the mission.

Least Effective - B: Do not try to finish the project by yourself. Notify your supervisor immediately any time a situation arises that may impact completing the mission on time.

Situation 5:

Most Effective - A: Be a professional and return to work. Sign the documents so that you are not causing another officer to work late due to your honest mistake.

Least Effective - D: Having a subordinate forge the documents puts your integrity and that of the subordinate at risk. Do not let a minor mistake like forgetting to sign a piece of paper ruin your credibility.

Situation 6:

Most effective - E: A response to the new commander's email would be the best solution to this scenario. Let him know that you are excited to take the new position and that you would like to set up a date and time to discuss the new role. This will help ensure a smooth transition.

Least Effective - B: Always take the opportunity to respond to an email from your new commander. It is the professional thing to do and will allow time to discuss what is expected of the new position, answer any questions, and learn how to excel.

Situation 7:

Most Effective - D: This is an opportunity to teach, coach, and mentor a fellow officer by discussing the Air Force core values. By talking to the coworker and not telling his/her superior officer, you offer this person a chance to grow from the mistake without hurting his/her career.

Least Effective - C: Resorting to blackmail would make you just as guilty as your peer and would put your integrity on the line.

Situation 8:

Most Effective - C: It is normal to reach a plateau in assignments. Let your senior officer know, and express that you are looking for a more challenging assignment to further your career and benefit the Air Force.

Least Effective - E: Remember, integrity first. Be honest in everything you do and no one can question your integrity.

Situation 9:

Most effective - E: Be honest with the officer and let him/her know that you are already dealing with a maximum workload. In addition, you have offered a solution to the problem by offering to distribute the work to another qualified coworker.

Least Effective - D: Taking on additional work without sufficient time will cause the quality of both projects to diminish.

Situation 10:

Most Effective - D: Inform the senior officer of the situation and see if the projects can be redistributed to help alleviate stress for coworkers that are overwhelmed.

Least Effective - A: You were attentive to notice the situation; this is a good time to put service before self and offer a solution to the problem.

Situation 11:

Most Effective - C: They asked you to resolve the dispute, so be the professional and make a decision.

Least Effective - E: Giving a lecture to both officers that asked you to settle the dispute would probably turn both of them against you. They must value your opinion, or they would not have asked for your assistance.

Situation 12:

Most Effective - B: Safety issues need to be addressed immediately. It is your duty as an officer to notify the senior officer in charge if a coworker is manipulating numbers that could lead to an accident or incident.

Least Effective - A: It is your responsibility to speak up in this scenario. Again, integrity first. Anyone can prevent an accident.

Situation 13:

Most Effective - A: If the senior officer asks the question, they want an answer. Be honest, and offer a candid assessment in the area in which he/she could improve.

Least Effective - B: Again, if a senior officer asks the question, he/she is looking for an answer. Refusing makes you and your supervisor look bad.

Situation 14:

Most Effective - D: Make the correct decision and vote for the most qualified candidate.

Least Effective - C: By voting for Candidate 3, you are not being honest. Remember the honest decision is not always going to be the easiest. If you are always honest, no one will ever question your integrity.

Situation 15:

Most Effective - A: Let your new coworker know that you want to do your best on this project, you value his/her help, and you think the work should be shared equally. In addition, offer congratulations on the coworker's upcoming retirement and encourage him/her to finish strong.

Least Effective - D: Do not have the frame of mind that the project is going to be mediocre or it will. Talk to your new coworker and come up with a plan to share the workload and develop a quality product.

Situation 16:

Most Effective - C: Talk with the subordinate and let him/her know what you have heard and that you need his/her support in accomplishing the unit's mission.

Least Effective - B: Something has to be done in this scenario. If not, the situation is going to get worse.

Situation 17:

Most Effective - C: The best action to take in this scenario would be to question the last officer to leave the supply room. This would allow him/her to explain the situation without directly accusing him/her of stealing, and it would be an initial step in the investigative process.

Least Effective - E: If no action is taken, supplies are going to keep disappearing, and the situation is not going to get any better.

Situation 18:

Most Effective - A: Give an honest opinion on the subject, and explain you are not a subject-matter expert. In addition, refer to media and to the Embassy's public affairs office for further information.

Least Effective - B: Not answering the question could portray a negative opinion of the officer.

Situation 19:

Most Effective - D: Meet with the unit and discuss the issue that has been presented. Offer a solution to the problem, stay positive, and make sure there is an opportunity for subordinates to take a break.

Least Effective - A: Always try and solve the problem before going to senior leadership. This would create distrust among subordinates and show senior officers a lack of leadership and inability to handle simple unit challenges.

Situation 20:

Most Effective - A: Be honest and admit your mistake. The person receiving the email will be more than willing to delete the material. Your supervisor will appreciate the honesty and inform the chain-of-command.

Least Effective - E: Do not lie about the situation. All classified email chains are monitored, and covering up this mistake could lead to revocation of a security clearance.

Situation 21:

Most Effective - B: Meeting with the training director may open up an opportunity for training in the near future. It also shows the commanding officer cares about the mission of the U.S. Embassy in the host country.

Least Effective - D: Sending out letters would be perceived as a false accusation, damage your reputation, and could have an effect on future requests for training.

Situation 22:

Most Effective - C: The leader may not have realized they were creating this environment. Meeting with the superior will clear the air, and it should afford an opportunity to work more independently.

Least Effective - A: Telling the supervisor to back off would create animosity and make the situation worse.

Situation 23:

Most Effective - D: Ultimately, the boss has the final decision. A well thought out plan with actions and contingencies may sway his/her decision.

Least Effective - A: This would be insubordination no matter how the plan worked out. Either way, the boss would feel disrespected.

Situation 24:

Most Effective - A: Budget cuts will affect everyone in the unit. Talking to peers can offer solutions that may not have been previously discovered.

Least Effective - B: Do not blame subordinates. This will erode trust in the unit.

Situation 25:

Most Effective - D: Keeping the drivers informed of the delay will help with them understand the situation. Accommodating them will help build rapport for future deliveries.

Least Effective - C: This would frustrate the drivers even more and may have an effect on future deliveries.

English Expression

1. B: Move the sentence so that it comes before the preceding sentence. For this question, place the underlined sentence in each prospective choice's position. To keep as-is is incorrect because the father "going crazy" doesn't logically follow the fact that he was a "city slicker." Choice C is incorrect because the sentence in question is not a concluding sentence, and does not transition smoothly into the second paragraph. Choice D is incorrect because the sentence doesn't necessarily need to be omitted since it logically follows the very first sentence in the passage.

2. D: Choice *D* is correct because "As it turns out" indicates a contrast from the previous sentiment, that the RV was a great purchase. Choice *A* is incorrect because the sentence needs an effective transition from the paragraph before. Choice *B* is incorrect because the text indicates it *is* surprising that the RV was a great purchase because the author was skeptical beforehand. Choice *C* is incorrect because the transition "Furthermore" does not indicate a contrast.

3. B: This sentence calls for parallel structure. Choice *B* is correct because the verbs "wake," "eat," and "break" are consistent in tense and parts of speech. Choice *A* is incorrect because the words "wake" and "eat" are present tense while the word "broke" is in past tense. Choice *C* is incorrect because this turns the sentence into a question, which doesn't make sense within the context. Choice *D* is incorrect because it breaks tense with the rest of the passage. "Waking," "eating," and "breaking" are all present participles, and the context around the sentence is in past tense.

4. C: Choice *C* is correct because it is clear, concise, and fits within the context of the passage. Choice *A* is incorrect because "We rejoiced as 'hackers'" does not give reason *why* hacking was rejoiced. Choice *B* is incorrect because it does not mention a solution being found and is therefore not specific enough. Choice *D* is incorrect because the meaning is eschewed by the helping verb "had to rejoice," and the sentence does not give enough detail as to what the problem entails.

5. A: The original sentence is correct because the verb tense as well as the order of the sentence makes sense in the given context. Choice *B* is incorrect because the order of the words makes the sentence more confusing than it otherwise would be. Choice *C* is incorrect because "We are even making" is in present tense. Choice *D* is incorrect because "We will make" is future tense. The surrounding text of the sentence is in past tense.

6. B: Choice *B* is correct because there is no punctuation needed if a dependent clause ("while traveling across America") is located behind the independent clause ("it allowed us to share adventures"). Choice *A* is incorrect because there are two dependent clauses connected and no independent clause, and a complete sentence requires at least one independent clause. Choice *C* is incorrect because of the same reason as Choice *A*. Semicolons have the same function as periods: there must be an independent clause on either side of the semicolon. Choice *D* is incorrect because the dash simply interrupts the complete sentence.

7. C: The rules for "me" and "I" is that one should use "I" when it is the subject pronoun of a sentence, and "me" when it is the object pronoun of the sentence. Break the sentence up to see if "I" or "me" should be used. To say "Those are memories that I have now shared" makes more sense than to say "Those are memories that me have now shared." Choice *D* is incorrect because "my siblings" should come before "I."

8. D: Choice *D* is correct because Fred Hampton becoming an activist was a direct result of him wanting to see lasting social change for African American people. Choice *A* doesn't make sense because "In the meantime" denotes something happening at the same time as another thing. Choice *B* is incorrect because the text's tone does not indicate that becoming a civil rights activist is an unfortunate path. Choice *C* is incorrect because "Finally" indicates something that comes last in a series of events, and the word in question is at the beginning of the introductory paragraph.

9. A: Choice *A* is correct because there should be a comma between the city and state. Choice *B* is incorrect because the comma after "Maywood" interrupts the phrase "Maywood of Chicago." Choice *C* is incorrect because a comma after "Illinois" is unnecessary. Finally, Choice *D* is incorrect because the order of the sentence designates that Chicago, Illinois is in Maywood, which is incorrect.

10. C: This is a difficult question. The paragraph is incorrect as-is because it is too long and thus loses the reader halfway through. Choice *C* is correct because if the new paragraph began with "While studying at Triton," we would see a smooth transition from one paragraph to the next. We can also see how the two paragraphs are logically split in two. The first half of the paragraph talks about where he studied. The second half of the paragraph talks about the NAACP and the result of his leadership in the association. If we look at the passage as a whole, we can see that there are two main topics that should be broken in two.

11. B: The BPP is another activist group. We can figure out this answer by looking at context clues. We know that the BPP is "similar in function" to the NAACP. To find out what the NAACP's function is, we must look at the previous sentences. We know from above that the NAACP is an activist group, so we can assume that the BPP is also an activist group.

12. A: Choice *A* is correct because the Black Panther Party is one entity, therefore the possession should show the "Party's approach" with the apostrophe between the "y" and the "s." Choice *B* is incorrect because the word "Parties" should not be plural. Choice *C* is incorrect because the apostrophe indicates that the word "Partys" is plural. The plural of "party" is "parties." Choice *D* is incorrect because, again, the word "parties" should not be plural; instead, it is one unified party.

13. C: Choice *C* is correct because the passage is told in past tense, and "enabled" is a past tense verb. Choice *A*, "enable," is present tense. Choice *B*, "are enabling," is a present participle, which suggests a continuing action. Choice *D*, "will enable," is future tense.

14. D: Choice *D* is correct because the conjunction "and" is the best way to combine the two independent clauses. Choice *A* is incorrect because the word "he" becomes repetitive since the two clauses can be joined together. Choice *B* is incorrect because the conjunction "but" indicates a contrast, and there is no contrast between the two clauses. Choice *C* is incorrect because the introduction of the comma after "project" with no conjunction creates a comma splice.

15. C: The word "acheivement" is misspelled. Remember the rules for "*i* before *e* except after *c*." Choices *B* and *D*, "greatest" and "leader," are both spelled correctly.

16. B: Choice *B* is correct because it provides the correct verb tense and also makes sense within the context of the passage. Choice *A* is incorrect because it doesn't make sense for someone to be "held by a press conference." Choice *C* is incorrect because, with this use of the sentence, it would create a fragment because the verb "holding" has no helping verb in front of it. Choice *D* is incorrect because it adds an infinitive ("to hold") where a past tense form of a verb should be.

17. A: Choice *A* is correct because it provides the most clarity. Choice *B* is incorrect because it doesn't name the group until the end, so the phrase "the group" is vague. Choice *C* is incorrect because it indicates that the BPP's popularity grew as a result of placing the group under constant surveillance, which is incorrect. Choice *D* is incorrect because there is a misplaced modifier; this sentence actually says that the FBI's influence and popularity grew, which is incorrect.

18. B: Choice *B* is correct. Choice *A* is incorrect because there should be an independent clause on either side of a semicolon, and the phrase "In 1976" is not an independent clause. Choice *C* is incorrect because there should be a comma after introductory phrases in general, such as "In 1976," and Choice *C* omits a comma. Choice *D* is incorrect because the sentence "In 1976." is a fragment.

19. C: Choice *C* is correct because the past tense verb "provided" fits in with the rest of the verb tense throughout the passage. Choice *A*, "will provide," is future tense. Choice *B*, "provides," is present tense. Choice *D*, "providing," is a present participle, which means the action is continuous.

20. D: The correct answer is Choice *D* because this statement provides the most clarity. Choice *A* is incorrect because the noun "Chicago City Council" acts as one, so the verb "are" should be singular, not plural. Choice *B* is incorrect because it is perhaps the most confusingly worded out of all the answer choices; the phrase "December 4" interrupts the sentence without any indication of purpose. Choice *C* is incorrect because it is too vague and leaves out *who* does the commemorating.

21. B: Choice *B* is correct. Here, a colon is used to introduce an explanation. Colons either introduce explanations or lists. Additionally, the quote ends with the punctuation inside the quotes, unlike Choice *C*.

22. A: The verb tense in this passage is predominantly in the present tense, so Choice *A* is the correct answer. Choice *B* is incorrect because the subject and verb do not agree. It should be "Education provides," not "Education provide." Choice *C* is incorrect because the passage is in present tense, and "Education will provide" is future tense. Choice *D* doesn't make sense when placed in the sentence.

23. D: The possessive form of the word "it" is "its." The contraction "it's" denotes "it is." Thus, Choice *A* is wrong. The word "raises" in Choice *B* makes the sentence grammatically incorrect. Choice *C* adds an apostrophe at the end of "its." While adding an apostrophe to most words would indicate possession, adding '*s* to the word "it" indicates a contraction.

24. C: The word *civilised* should be spelled *civilized*. The words "distinguishes" and "creatures" are both spelled correctly.

25. B: Choice *B* is correct because it provides clarity by describing what "myopic" means right after the word itself. Choice *A* is incorrect because the explanation of "myopic" comes before the word; thus, the meaning is skewed. It's possible that Choice *C* makes sense within context. However, it's not the *best* way to say this. Choice *D* is confusingly worded. Using "myopic focus" is not detrimental to society; however, the way *D* is worded makes it seem so.

26. C: Again, we see where the second paragraph can be divided into two parts due to separate topics. The first section's main focus is education addressing the mind, body, and soul. The first section, then, could end with the concluding sentence, "The human heart and psyche . . ." The next sentence to start a new paragraph would be "Education is a basic human right." The rest of this paragraph talks about what education is and some of its characteristics.

27. A: Choice *A* is correct because the phrase "others' ideas" is both plural and indicates possession. Choice *B* is incorrect because "other's" indicates only one "other" that's in possession of "ideas," which is incorrect. Choice *C* is incorrect because no possession is indicated. Choice *D* is incorrect because the word "other" does not end in *s*. *Others's* is not a correct form of the word in any situation.

28. D: This sentence must have a comma before "although" because the word "although" is connecting two independent clauses. Thus, Choices *B* and *C* are incorrect. Choice *A* is incorrect because the second sentence in the underlined section is a fragment.

29. C: Choice *C* is the correct choice because the word "their" indicates possession, and the text is talking about "their students," or the students of someone. Choice *A*, "there," means at a certain place and is incorrect. Choice *B*, "they're," is a contraction and means "they are." Choice *D* is not a word.

30. B: Choice *B* uses all punctuation correctly in this sentence. In American English, single quotes should only be used if they are quotes within a quote, making choices *A* and *C* incorrect. Additionally, punctuation here should go inside the quotes, making Choice *D* incorrect.

31. B: Choice *B* is correct because the conjunction "and" is used to connect phrases that are to be used jointly, such as teachers working hard to help students "identify salient information" and to "think critically." The conjunctions *so, but,* and *nor* are incorrect in the context of this sentence.

32. A: Choice *A* has consistent parallel structure with the verbs "read," "identify," and "determine." Choices *B* and *C* have faulty parallel structure with the words "determining" and "identifying." Choice *D* has incorrect subject/verb agreement. The sentence should read, "Students have to read . . . identify . . . and determine."

33. D: The correct choice for this sentence is that "they are . . . shaped by the influences." The prepositions "for," "to," and "with" do not make sense in this context. People are *shaped by*, not *shaped for, shaped to,* or *shaped with.*

34. A: To see which answer is correct, it might help to place the subject, "Teachers," near the verb. Choice *A* is correct: "Teachers . . . must strive" makes grammatical sense here. Choice *B* is incorrect because "Teachers . . . to strive" does not make grammatical sense. Choice *C* is incorrect because "Teachers must not only respect . . . but striving" eschews parallel structure. Choice *D* is incorrect because it is in past tense, and this passage is in present tense.

35. C: Choice *C* is correct because it uses an em-dash. Em-dashes are versatile. They can separate phrases that would otherwise be in parenthesis, or they can stand in for a colon. In this case, a colon would be another decent choice for this punctuation mark because the second sentence expands upon the first sentence. Choice *A* is incorrect because the statement is not a question. Choice *B* is incorrect because adding a comma here would create a comma splice. Choice *D* is incorrect because this creates a run-on sentence since the two sentences are independent clauses.

36. B: The best place for this sentence given all the answer choices is at the end of the first paragraph. Choice *A* is incorrect; the passage is told in chronological order, and leaving the sentence as-is defies that order, since we haven't been introduced to who raised George. Choice *C* is incorrect because this sentence is not an introductory sentence. It does not provide the main topic of the paragraph. Choice *D* is incorrect because again, it defies chronological order. By the end of paragraph two we have already gotten to George as an adult, so this sentence would not make sense here.

37. D: Out of these choices, a semicolon would be the best fit because there is an independent clause on either side of the semicolon, and the two sentences closely relate to each other. Choice *A* is incorrect because putting a comma between two independent clauses (i.e. complete sentences) creates a comma splice. Choice *B* is incorrect; omitting punctuation here creates a run-on sentence. Choice *C* is incorrect because an ellipses (. . .) is used to designate an omission in the text.

38. B: This is another example of parallel structure. Choice *A* is incorrect because the verbs in the original sentence are "growing," "depleting," and "results," the last of which has a different form than the first two. Choices *C* and *D* add "depletes" and "grows," both of which abandon the "-ing" verbs.

39. C: Choice C is correct because it keeps with the verb tense in the rest of the passage: past tense. Choice A is in present tense, which is incorrect. Choice B is present progressive, which means there is a continual action, which is also incorrect. Choice D is incorrect because "was returning" is past progressive tense, which means that something was happening continuously at some point in the past.

40. C: The correct choice is the subordinating conjunction, "When." We should look at the clues around the phrase to see what fits best. Carver left his money "when he died." Choice A, "Because," could perhaps be correct, but "When" is the more appropriate word to use here. Choice B is incorrect; "Although" denotes a contrast, and there is no contrast here. Choice D is incorrect because "Finally" indicates something at the very end of a list or series, and there is no series at this point in the text.

41. A: There should be no change here. Both underlined sentences are complete and do not need changing. Choice B is incorrect because since there is no punctuation between the two independent clauses, it is considered a run-on. Choice C is incorrect because placing a comma between two independent clauses creates a comma splice. Choice D is incorrect. The underlined portion could *possibly* act with a colon. However, it's not the best choice, so omit Choice D.

42. D: Choice D is correct. The text before this underlined phrase talks about the difference between "discovery" and "exploration," so making a decision on what term to label Columbus would be the best choice. The other three choices may be true to the historical narrative of Columbus; however, they do not fit within the surrounding text.

43. B: Choice B is the most clear, straightforward sentence out of all the answer choices. Choice A is inverted and is therefore a bit awkward. Choice C is unorganized and very confusing to follow. It also uses the second person "you," so this is incorrect. Finally, Choice D is incorrect; the sentence incorrectly uses the plural verb "are" rather than "is."

44. A: The comma is properly placed after the introductory phrase "In May of 2015." Choice B is missing the word "in." Choice C does not separate the introductory phrase from the rest of the sentence. Choice D places an extra, and unnecessary, comma prior to 2015.

45. D: Airspace and airports must be closed by people; they don't just close themselves, so it is proper to include an action to indicate that they were sealed off. Choice B is incorrect because the verb *close* is in the incorrect tense. Choice C is also incorrect because *airspace* does not need to become *airspaces* and the issue still remains: while there is action, it is not in the proper form to indicate human action. Choice D is correct because it correctly uses the helping verb "were."

46. D: Choice D is correct because the interrupting phrase, "seventeen years later," is separated by commas. Choice A is incorrect because putting a period between "later" and "The" causes the first sentence to become a fragment. Choice B is incorrect because of the same reason: the semicolon should have an independent clause on either side of it, and the first half of the sentence is not an independent clause. Choice C needs commas to separate the interrupting phrase or else the words become mashed together, causing confusion.

47. A: Reading through the sentence, one can see that it flows and uses proper punctuation and grammar, which means that Choice A is the correct answer. Choice B lacks the necessary comma after "Clearly", making it incorrect. Choice C utilizes an unnecessary semicolon. Choice D makes the sentence awkward by placing *clearly* in the middle of the sentence.

48. B: In this sentence, the word *ocean* does not require an *s* after it to make it plural because "ocean levels" is plural. Therefore, Choices *A* and *C* are incorrect. Because the sentence is referring to multiple – if not all ocean levels – *ocean* does not require an apostrophe (*'s*) because that would indicate that only one ocean is the focus, which is not the case. Choice *D* does not fit well into the sentence and, once again, we see that *ocean* has an *s* after it. This leaves Choice *B*, which correctly completes the sentence and maintains the intended meaning.

49. A: Choice *C* can be eliminated because creating a new sentence with *not* is grammatically incorrect and it throws off the rest of the sentence. Choice *B* is incorrect because a comma is definitely needed after *devastation* in the sentence. Choice *D* is also incorrect because "while" is a poor substitute for "although." *Although* in this context is meant to show contradiction with the idea that floods are associated with devastation. Therefore, none of these choices would be suitable revisions because the original was correct.

50. D: In the sentence, *is caused* is an awkward use of the verb here, so Choice *A* is incorrect. Choice *B* is incorrect because it does not agree with the subject, "flooding." *Causing,* Choice *C,* is a verb and it is in the present continuous tense, which appears to agree with the verb flooding, but it is incorrectly used without a helping verb. This leaves Choice *D*, *causes*, which does fit because it is in the indefinite present tense. Fitting each choice into the sentence and reading it in your mind will also reveal that Choice *D*, *causes*, correctly completes the sentence. Apply this method to all the questions when possible.

51. A: To *project* means to anticipate or forecast. This goes very well with the sentence because it describes how new technology is trying to estimate flood activity in order to prevent damage and save lives. "Project" in this case needs to be assisted by "to" in order to function in the sentence. Therefore, Choice *A* is correct. Choices *B* and *D* are the incorrect tenses. Choice *C* is also incorrect because it lacks *to*.

52. A: Choice *D* is incorrect; *concealing* is the improper tense and it throws off the sentence. Choice *B* is a very good possibility, but the "be" is ultimately unnecessary in the context of the sentence, so it can be eliminated. Choice *C* is also very tempting because "concealed" would fit into the sentence, but it isn't as strong as the original "to conceal." This is because "to conceal" suggests the active use of the word towards an objective. "He had concealed himself" is more passive than "He had to conceal." The latter suggests a more direct action, which is what the author is trying to communicate. This makes Choice *A*, NO ERROR, the best option.

53. B: The issue with this word is that it lacks proper punctuation. "One" is referring to an individual, and it needs to show possession of "identity." Therefore, *ones* must have an apostrophe to show ownership and to be correct. Thus, Choice *B*, *one's*, is the correct answer.

54. C: Choice *C* is correct. The subject and verb agree with each other (accounts describe) and there is no apostrophe because no possession is being shown. Choices *B* and *D* are incorrect because there is no possession—"accounts" is simply plural. Choice *A* is incorrect because the subject and verb do not agree with each other (accounts describes).

55. D: Choice *D* uses the correct punctuation. American English uses double quotes unless placing quotes within a quote (which would then require single quotes). Thus, Choices *A* and *C* are incorrect. Choice *B* is incorrect because the period should go outside of the parenthesis, not inside.

56. C: Choice *C* is the correct answer. The first sentence that stands out as the topic sentence is Sentence 3, because it speaks in general terms about what the following sentences will explain more in detail: "When selecting a career path, it's important to explore the various options available." Then, Sentence 1 is the best choice because because it gives an expanding detail on the topic sentence: "Many students entering college may shy away from a major because they don't know much about it." Then, we get an example for this sentence from Sentence 2: "For example, many students won't opt for a career as an actuary, because they aren't exactly sure what it entails." Finally we end with Sentence 4, which wraps up the previous three sentences: "They would be missing out on a career that is very lucrative and in high demand."

57. A: The correct answer Choice is *A*. Again, the topic sentence tells us in general about the topic: "Hard water has a high mineral count, including calcium and magnesium." Then we are told *about* hard mineral deposits in Sentence 4: "The mineral deposits from hard water can stain hard surfaces in bathrooms and kitchens as well as clog pipes." With Sentence 3 we get more information on staining, including examples: "Hard water can stain dishes, ruin clothes, and reduce the life of any appliances it touches, such as hot water heaters, washing machines, and humidifiers." Finally, we can end with the solution in Sentence 1: "One solution is to install a water softener to reduce the mineral content of water, but this can be costly." This is a classic problem-solution structure.

58. D: Sentences 1 and 2 flow easily right away: Sentence 1 gives a topic sentence—it introduces an author and gives a situation. Sentence 2 tells about the author, her history, and the new novel, which are introduced in Sentence 1. Sentence 4 goes more into detail and tells us about the new novel and how it's praised even more than the children's series. Finally, Sentence 3 gives an example of Sentence 4: "In fact, her new novel was nominated for the prestigious Albert J. Beveridge Award, but still isn't selling like her children's books, which fly off the shelves because of her name alone," which completes the paragraph.

59. B: Sentence 4 is the topic sentence because it describes what the paragraph will be about: cigarettes. We see the word "addictive" in Sentence 4, so Sentence 1 is the next logical sentence because it defines *what addiction is*. Sentence 3 is also a logical next sentence because it should come before Sentence 2, which expands on Sentence 3. Thus we have: "Cigarettes contain a drug called nicotine, one of the most addictive substances known to man. Addiction is defined as a compulsion to seek the substance despite negative consequences. According to the National Institute of Drug Abuse, nearly 35 million smokers expressed a desire to quit smoking in 2015. However, more than 85 percent of those addicts will not achieve their goal."

60. B: This paragraph is in order from Sentence 1 through 4. The topic sentence says "It has recently been brought to my attention that most people believe that 75% of your body heat is lost through your head," outlining the main idea of the paragraph. Sentence 2 depicts what the author thinks about that statement. Sentence 3 expands on Sentence 2, saying: "It is natural to be gullible to anything said with enough authority." Sentence 4 refutes the idea in Sentence 1, "But the "fact" that the majority of your body heat is lost through your head is a lie," effectively concluding the paragraph.

61. B: This sentence is most likely to be placed after Sentence 2. In Sentence 2, we see the author introduce the notion of a "colony," and then in Sentence 3 we see the author give an example of one of those colonies, on Bird Island.

62. C: "the plume hunters <u>who do</u> not dare to raid the guarded rookeries" is the best choice here. Read each choice in the blank and see which one sounds the best. This is the choice that works with the agreement with the plural subject, "plume hunters." We would say "plume hunters" *do*, not *does*. *Whom* is used to refer to the object of a verb or preposition.

63. D: This sentence is most likely to be placed after Sentence 4. Sentence 4 says "This is more than a preference." In order to understand *how* Cynthia's being vegetarian is more than a preference, we would need this new sentence, which explains that "her body has never developed the enzymes to process meat or fish, so she becomes violently ill if she accidentally eats any of the offending foods." This sentence goes best after Sentence 4.

64. A: Choice *A* is the best answer. The sentence is correct as-is. "Cynthia keeps" is appropriate subject-verb agreement and establishes that the tense is in the present. The other choices are incorrect. Say each answer choice aloud in the blank and you will see how awkward Choices *B, C,* and *D* sound.

65. B: "Keeping this diet is part of her religion." Choice *B* is the correct answer. Again, read each answer choice in the blank to see which one sounds the best. Choice *B* has the correct subject/verb agreement and keeps the tense within the paragraph.

Dear FSOT Test Taker,

We would like to start by thanking you for purchasing this study guide for your FSOT exam. We hope that we exceeded your expectations.

Our goal in creating this study guide was to cover all of the topics that you will see on the test. We also strove to make our practice questions as similar as possible to what you will encounter on test day. With that being said, if you found something that you feel was not up to your standards, please send us an email and let us know.

We have study guides in a wide variety of fields. If you're interested in one, try searching for it on Amazon or send us an email.

Thanks Again and Happy Testing!
Product Development Team
info@studyguideteam.com

FREE Test Taking Tips DVD Offer

To help us better serve you, we have developed a Test Taking Tips DVD that we would like to give you for FREE. **This DVD covers world-class test taking tips that you can use to be even more successful when you are taking your test.**

All that we ask is that you email us your feedback about your study guide. Please let us know what you thought about it – whether that is good, bad or indifferent.

To get your **FREE Test Taking Tips DVD**, email freedvd@studyguideteam.com with "FREE DVD" in the subject line and the following information in the body of the email:

    a. The title of your study guide.

    b. Your product rating on a scale of 1-5, with 5 being the highest rating.

    c. Your feedback about the study guide. What did you think of it?

    d. Your full name and shipping address to send your free DVD.

If you have any questions or concerns, please don't hesitate to contact us at freedvd@studyguideteam.com.

Thanks again!

Made in the USA
Middletown, DE
22 August 2018